D0143223

REVISIONING WOMEN, HEALTH, AND HEALING

REVISIONING WOMEN, HEALTH, AND HEALING

Feminist, Cultural, and Technoscience Perspectives

edited by

ADELE E. CLARKE and
VIRGINIA L. OLESEN

Routledge   New York and London

Published in 1999 by
Routledge
29 West 35th Street
New York, NY 10001

Published in Great Britain by
Routledge
11 New Fetter Lane
London EC4P 4EE

Copyright © 1999 by Routledge

Printed in the United States of America on acid-free paper

All rights reserved. No part of this book may be reprinted or reproduced or utilized in any form or by any electronic, mechanical, or other means, now known or hereafter invented, including photocopying and recording or in any information storage or retrieval system, without permission in writing from the publishers.

Copyright acknowledgments
Anne Balsamo, "Public Pregnancies and Cultural Narratives of Surveillance" from her *Technologies of the Gendered Body: Reading Cyborg Women.* Durham, NC: Duke University Press, 1996.
Ruth Behar, "The Girl in the Cast" from *The Vulnerable Observer: Anthropology that Breaks Your Heart.* Boston: Beacon Press, 1996.
Donna Haraway, "The Virtual Speculum in the New World," from her *Modest-Witness@Second-Millennium. FemaleMan©_Meets_OncMouse™: Feminism and Technoscience.* New York and London: Routledge, 1997.
In **Emily Martin**'s chapter "The Woman in the Flexible Body," the following are credited: The cover of *Science* magazine, March 14, 1993, vol. 260, used with permission from PPD Pharmaco, Inc. and Vincent Perez, artist. "Female to Male Ratios in Autoimmune Disease" by Ahmed S. Ansar, W. J. Penhale, and N. Talal, previously published in *American Journal of Pathology* 121(3) (Dec. 1985), pp. 531–51, used with permission from *American Journal of Pathology.* Flexibility ad, used with permission by Hewlett-Packard Company. Nike kids "Agile" ad used with permission by Nike.

Library of Congress Cataloging-in-Publication Data

Revisioning women, health, and healing : feminist, cultural, and technoscience
    perspectives / Adele E. Clarke and Virginia L. Olesen, editors.
        p.   cm.
    Includes index.
        ISBN (invalid) 041591846 (hardcover). — ISBN 0-415-91846-4 (pbk.)
        1. Women—Health and hygiene—United States—Sociological aspects.
    2. Women's health services—Political aspects—United States.
    3. Feminism—Health aspects—United States.   I. Clarke, Adele E.
    II. Olesen, Virginia L.
    RA778.R4426   1999
    362.1'082—dc21   98-9685
                                                                                          CIP

Virginia Olesen dedicates this book to Meg Stacey.
Adele Clarke dedicates it to Ruth Mahaney.
But it is mostly for our students past, present, and future
who have stimulated and taught us so much.
May their work go far beyond ours.

Contents

—◯—

(Re)Constructing Experience:
Searching the Self

Challenging New World Reproductive Orders

Revised and Disruptive Agendas for Women's Health

Acknowledgments

—◯—

In 1973, each of us taught our first course in women's health as the women's movement gained momentum and feminisms wended their way into the academy. Bringing critical social science perspectives to bear in new ways, Virginia Olesen organized the first research conference on women's health in the United States in 1975, held at the University of California, San Francisco. With Ellen Lewin, Sheryl Ruzek, Adele Clarke and others, she then went on to found the Women, Health and Healing Program in sociology there. To celebrate our "twenty-something" years in women's health, we decided to organize a conference.

We sought a radical revisioning of the entire domain of women, health, and healing—a fundamental reconceptualization rather than a conference-as-update-in-substantive-areas. We knew too well how very much had changed in feminism, in women, health and healing, in feminist theory, and what interesting new perspectives were being provoked by cultural studies and science and technology studies. We fantasized the conference we would most like to attend—whose voices we craved to hear revisioning women, health and healing. Our wish list of participants included many people we did not personally know and whom did not necessarily know us or our work. Nor had many ever focused on women's health. All they had in common was our belief that they had very important things to say in terms of theoretically reframing the very foundations of women's health. We did not request participants to address particular topics; instead we simply asked what they might contribute if they chose to join us.

Only one person turned us down and we suddenly had a stunning conference on our hands! Indeed, the area of women, health, and healing was itself a powerful draw for the contributors, pulling them in directions they already wanted to move, or were at least very open to moving. It has breadth, grounding, immediacy, the difficult powers of bodies and embodiment, the lived experiences of pain, fear, and joy. Women, health, and healing is a site where all kinds of feminisms meet the world—including all kinds of sciences and technologies through all kinds of cultures. The conference was truly a success, a site of powerful conversations and the kinds of intellectual engagements that have endured.

We are deeply grateful to the superb contributors, to the many volunteers who helped with the Conference, and to our patient editors at Routledge. The Conference on which this book is based was the fourth in the series sponsored by the University of California Systemwide Council of Women's Programs. We are also grateful for funding from the University of California Systemwide Humanities Research Institute, the Office of the President of the University of California and, at UC San Francisco, from the Department of Social and Behavioral Sciences, Dean Jane Norbeck of the School of Nursing, Vice Chancellor Dorothy Bainton, Dean Clifford Attkisson of the Graduate Division, the Department of the History of Health Sciences, and the Women, Health and Healing Program.

San Francisco, January 1998

Feminist Revisioning

Theoretical Speculations
and Interventions

Revising, Diffracting, Acting

ADELE E. CLARKE AND VIRGINIA L. OLESEN

About Revisioning

Diffraction patterns record the history of interaction, interference, reinforcement, difference. Diffraction is about heterogeneous history, not about originals.... Diffraction is a narrative, graphic, psychological, spiritual, and political technology for making consequential meanings. (Haraway 1997:273)

Despite decades of feminist research and theorizing in the social sciences, humanities, nursing, and related sites on the problematics of women's health and embodiment, probably the most common operant framing today in both the academy and society remains the biomedical model. This model centers on concepts of health status, health behaviors, and technoscience interventions. Gendered, cultured, historicized, classed, raced, and otherwise situated, women are routinely silenced or erased as actors in the production of health, in both the provision and receipt of health care per se as well as in health politics and policy.[1]

Yet a theoretical sea change has been occuring across many if not most segments of the social sciences and humanities in terms of fresh ways of conceptualizing multiplicities, multiculturalisms, cultural critiques, bodies, identities, marginalities, differences, women, subjects, objects, gender, communities, practices, and an array of other elements linked to modernity and postmodernity. This book draws deeply on these new approaches. We seek to again rupture increasingly biomedicalized frameworks of women's health, as feminists have notably ruptured these in the past, and to revision—and thus to retheorize—women, health and healing. Revisioning means letting go of how we have seen in order to construct new perceptions.

In many ways, the women's health movements of the last decades of the twentieth century in the United States have been exceptionally successful. There is considerably increased attention to women's health, increased attention to women in scientific and clinical biomedical research, an increase in women as providers of care, and even improved inclusion of women as consumers of health care in policy venues.

Yet at the same time, we also suffer from the increased biomedicalization of women's—and other people's—health, and increased co-optation of earlier feminist interventions now shorn of their feminist roots and epistemological and even ontological processes. Many of us share a painfully increased understanding that essentializing "women" and "men" often creates false universals that then work to erase significant differences *within* groups rather than address them seriously in health policy, practices, and caregiving. Moreover, "old" problems of access to care have been twisted and torqued by "managed care" and "health care reform" but remain ever with us, however unstable in their details.

We therefore see this historical moment as one beset by dilemmas, paradoxes, and contradictions—in both feminist theorizing and women's health situations—which cannot be ignored. We are reminded of the pointed comment made by Gloria Steinem in an early film on the women's movement that "feminism is not an unmixed blessing." Nor is the "success" of a social movement such as women's health. Our successes in both feminist theorizing and in women's health have themselves produced new problems—anticipated and unanticipated—which we are calling "complications." In this book, we set out many of these complications, seeking to place the dilemmas, paradoxes, and contradictions on the table for consideration and reflection.

What we hope to provide here is an occasion for rethinking the conceptual foundations of women's health, and perhaps troubling the concept itself. We want to provoke a retheorizing of women's health premised afresh upon the differences and complexities of women's knowledges, bodies, experiences, and situations, which the full range of feminist scholarship has been very busy revealing over the past two decades. We are no longer theoretically or politically naive—or at least, not in the same ways we were years ago. Our understandings are now considerably more nuanced both because we have paid profound attention to theory/theorizing and because we have lived through—or, perhaps more accurately, been battered by—the contradictions and the pseudo-privileging of "women's" agendas, the places and spaces where rhetoric has replaced action and activism, process and practice, deleting and diluting feminisms.

Our quest here is for fresh approaches and cross-disciplinary pathways rather than exploration of the many critical substantive topics in women's health (for example, breast cancer and violence). We in fact boldly argue that the destabilized methods and disruptive agendas generated here can be applied *in pursuit of* the substantive. This is not a dodge to get around the complexities in the topics of women's health (see Ruzek, Olesen, and Clarke 1997), but rather an argument for new conceptual and theoretical interventions found in the contributors' multiple approaches. Here, feminist theory writ large and women's health and healing writ large meet. We are decentering women, health, and healing from its long-standing cage in biomedicine, a process already begun in earlier feminist analyses (e.g., Arditti et al. 1985; Fisher 1986; McClain 1989; Ratcliffe 1989; West 1984; Lewin and Olesen 1985), and resituating it at the intersection of new theoretical frames that open new vistas, new horizons and—needless to say—new problems as well.

Our guiding metaphor for this project of revisioning women, health, and healing is Donna Haraway's concept of *diffractions*. Drawing from the optical metaphors and instruments so common in Western culture and technoscience, the concept of diffractions includes but goes beyond reflexivity as a critical practice because "reflexivity, like reflection, only displaces the same elsewhere, setting up the worries about copy and original and the search for the authentic and really real." Diffraction adds action after reflection: "Diffraction is an optical metaphor for the effort to make a difference in the world ... a device for considering how to make the end [of the millenium] swerve" (Haraway 1997: 16).

We take diffractions as close to what Blumer (1969) called "sensitizing concepts"—ideas to guide us toward fresh ideas and understandings. These are working concepts, pragmatically flexible to allow multipurpose use.[2] Diffractions allow us to attempt to see from multiple standpoints simultaneously, taking advantage of the poststructural deconstruction of woman/women into multiple lived subject positions through which differently situated knowledges, needs, and desires have been, are, and will continue to be constructed and articulated. Though we use the metaphor of re-*visioning* as path to the future, voice and other senses are, of course, also of importance. We need to hear multiple voices to see what to diffract. But voice, like vision, is not perfect. Contra Habermas, voice cannot necessarily carry a subject's meaning(s) or intention(s) unmediated. We must grapple with the inherently problematic politics and practices of representation.

Diffractions can allow tensions to be held simultaneously rather than "resolve" them—because they may not be "resolvable." Such tensions may instead be paradoxes and contradictions within which we must dwell. Such tensions are especially common around the difficult powers of bodies and embodiment, key sites where feminisms meet the world—including all kinds of sciences through all kinds of cultures. But again, and most important, diffractions are intended to provoke actions.

Thus we seek here to diffract new theoretical lenses through which fresh agendas and practices in women's health and healing can be forged. We do this because we believe now is the time for such reframing. Agendas of twenty-five years ago have been accomplished, discarded, co-opted, and/or now seem more than a little outdated. But laundry lists of women's health topics and issues will not suffice—though they are absolutely requisite as each issue has its own specificities.[3] The profound revolutions in feminist theorizing of women's extremely heterogeneous situations, identities, and desires absolutely must be taken into account if we are not to merely end up with more of the same defeminized and dehumanized biomedicalizations of women's health.

The theoretical lenses we draw upon for diffracting and revisioning women, health, and healing are feminist theory, cultural studies, and technoscience studies perspectives. We start by asking what has changed over the past quarter century in these areas and how these changes potentially relate to revisioning women, health, and healing. When second-wave women's health movements were gaining momentum in the early 1970s, feminist theory and women's studies were in their infancy, often simplistic, categorical, and universalizing. Then centered exclusively on women, feminist theory largely sought to explain women's oppressed positions in various social structures. Early theory produced three or four "kinds" of feminists: liberal, cultural, socialist, and/or Marxist, which could and did lead to different modes of political activism around women's health (e.g., Fee 1983). We often arrogantly thought we knew what liberation meant. Today the shelves of books and journals of feminist theory are overflowing. Almost nothing of our earlier understandings has gone uninterrogated and reframed, especially by the poststructural turn, but also by new feminist state theorizing, feminist legal theory, and often agonized yet highly productive and invaluable "global" confrontations. Gender studies are increasingly valued, if problematic and problematized.[4] It is through these theoretical "complications," described a bit more below, that revisioning women's health needs to occur.

In the 1970s, cultural studies as a field was largely confined to Britain. It sharpened its focus on popular cultural phenomena, from music to dress to movies and other especially visual cultures, examining these "bottom-up" phenomena through an array of critical means (Grossberg, Nelson, and Treichler 1992). Not necessarily feminist, early cultural studies also fixed its sites of study on education and labor (Gordon 1995; McNeil and Franklin 1991). Feminists working inside that approach then began challenging the male biases and the lack of gendered and raced analyses—including the limited choices of research topics.[5] Today cultural studies are quite global, vital, contentious, and productive of valuable understandings that can and should inform the future of women, health, and healing.

Technoscience studies barely existed before 1980. The term refers to the transdisciplinary field focused on examining the social and cultural interactions and consequences of sciences, technologies, and medicines. Like feminist theory and women's/gender studies, it includes scholars from sociology, history, anthropology, rhetoric, languages, communications, political science, cultural studies, and even literature (e.g., Hess 1997; Traweek 1993; Jasanoff et al. 1995). The term itself challenges traditional notions that "basic" scientific research *produces* "applied" technologies in a unidirectional fashion. Instead, the two are loosely viewed as coconstituitive, as hybrid (Latour 1987). The term also has a "specific historical meaning for fields where knowledge, and practice and the economy were intimately related," where science involves "the creation and sale of knowledge products"—technoscience (Pickstone 1993:438).

Over the past decade, exciting new work has been done in all three of these fields and, perhaps more important, they have begun to intersect with each other quite deeply. As we have come to examine the heterogeneities of women's lives and experiences, we have drawn increasingly upon understandings based on social and cultural frameworks. And we have been making increasingly explicit the relations among women, cultures, sciences, technologies, and medicines of many kinds. Women dwell in deeply technoscientific situations, not only but perhaps most intensely vis-à-vis health and healing. The work done through these perspectives and their intersections over the past decade provides new theoretical repertoires and resources for reinterpreting and revisioning women's health issues and, based upon thoughtful theorizing, setting new agendas for the next millennium. The substantive focus of this volume is largely on the United States, but many of the contributors have articulated transnational patterns and concerns. The goal of retheorizing is to think in ways complicated enough to cross all kinds of bound-aries. The saliences or lack of saliences of nation-states in the health and healing practices of women are questions to be explored rather than taken as given.

In the remainder of this introduction, we first elaborate what we see as the complications, the problematics that provoked us to have the conference that led to this book. We try to do this thoroughly enough to contextualize the papers that follow, but it is ultimately those papers which revision the future of women, health and healing. They reconceptualize our current situations in ways that we hope can help us move beyond the complications, providing new angles of vision—diffractions—and modes of action and reaction. They seek to build unique and important transdisciplinary bridges among the social sciences, human-ities, and health professions—what Foucault (1975) termed the human sciences—to create fresh meeting sites where new futures can be considered and created.

We are concerned here with two sets of complications of situated knowl-edges: those that have occurred around feminist theory and those that have occurred around women's health and healing in the past twenty years or so.

Feminist Theoretical Complications

> Challenging the material-semiotic practices of technoscience is in the interests of a deeper, broader and more open scientific literacy, which this book will call situated knowledges (Haraway 1997:11).

The need to destabilize the founding assumptions of modern theory, including modern feminist theory, has been with us for some years. Not only have "grand," "high," and "general" theories been critiqued (at least in part for ignoring gender as constitutive), but so too have "falsely universalizing, over-generalizing and over-ambitious models of liberalism, humanism and Marxism," including mod-ernist feminisms. In short, there is a "gulf between feminist theory of the 1970s and the 1990s" (Barrett and Phillips 1992:1), and the revisionings of women, health, and healing offered in this volume are predicated upon being within/against that gulf. This is very much a sketch of theoretical concerns, pieces toward a conceptual frame.

Complicating the Binaries

Perhaps the fundamental changes in theorizing women, sex, and gender can best be summed up in the phrase "complicating the binaries," which has by and large led to the interrogation of their analytic credibility and perhaps even utility. These binaries include:

male/female

straight/gay

sex/gender

subject/object

nature/culture

human/nonhuman

Loosely speaking, these were often initially construed as complementary, in dialectic (thesis, antithesis, synthesis). And they were transformed into continua and ideal types, yet ultimately retaining purity and distinctiveness. Further, they were deconstructed. Now each and all have been found coconstituitive—dialogic or multilogic rather than dialectic, because of the impossibilities of synthesis. That is, neither makes sense without the other, which therefore is part of, constituitive of it.[6] But each and all are also viewed as oversimplified, and simplification itself has become suspect. The binary is not enough.

Simplification often involves the deletion of the context or "situatedness" (Haraway 1991) of something and the erasure of the mundane and often messy work that has gone into creating it. Simplification can be naturalizing in the critical sense of rendering something as taken-for-granted and intrinsically accepted and acceptable (Star 1983, 1991). Simplification can be a strategy not of constructing conceptual access and bridges, but instead of engaging in practices of separation and reification. Thus in terms of the binaries, materially as well as symbolically and semiotically, the complicatedness of both sides and their interrelations and contexts must be deconstructed, analyzed, reconceived.

For example, the binary of male/female—"biological" sex—something ostensibly so obvious and self-evident, so "natural," has come to be understood instead as a nexus of continuous variables, properties, or attributes, many of which are studied in the life sciences but which cannot be understood solely in the terms presented by those sciences, themselves cultural phenomena of incredible import.[7] Recent challenges to the claimed simplicity of this binary and its anatomical enforcement in humans by surgical means have been mounted by heterogeneous hermaphrodites coming out of the closet.[8] In terms of sexualities, even the recent complication of straight/gay/bisexual/transgender is today understood or at least read as partial and inadequate.[9]

The sex/gender distinction, initially constructed by feminists to separate *biological* sex from *social/cultural* formations of gender, has also been found inadequate and problematic. Biological sex was long presumed by many feminists to be "real" rather than "socially constructed." A decade of feminist technoscience studies has laid that myth to rest, though we are forced to continue this project ad nauseam.[10] And gender too has recently come under an array of new critical gazes as problematic.[11] Historically, the feminist "impulse toward denying sexual difference came to be viewed as capitulation to a masculine mode" (Barrett and Phillips 1992:5). Butler's (1990) "critical genealogy of gender" seeks to displace the binary gender order and its fundamentalist assumptions of heterosexuality asserting in its place more fluid and temporary identifications and performativities.

Deeply important to this book are the complications of the nature/culture binary, site of much early feminist concern.[12] That is, not only is the biology of sex man-made (this term itself has its own complications), but our conceptions of nature are also deeply social, historical, cultural, and economic (e.g., Cronon 1995; Fine 1994). Nature had historically been exempt from the approaches of the sociology of knowledge—but no more (e.g., Aronson 1984; Hess 1997). Today "nature" and the life sciences included under the rubrics of biology and biomedicine that study it are taken, at least by feminists in technoscience studies and many others, as socially, historically, culturally, and economically constructed. Understanding the many ways in which this has been accomplished is fundamental to retheorizing women, health, and healing.

Nature does not exist outside of culture. This does *not* mean that what we might call trees don't compose what we might call forests or that you would not likely die if you walked out of a twenty-first story window. It *does* mean that trees and forests have distinctive historical, cultural, social, economic, and discursive meanings. Even death itself can be—and is—multiply construed (e.g., Karmaglin-pa 1987; Hogle 1999; Watson-Verran and Turnbull 1995). And multiple constructions bubble up through heterogeneous cultures and social organizations with varied and ever-changing repertoires and resources of social, cultural, sexual, and other meaning-making.

Two more binaries raise hackles and issues of concern. For a decade, Donna Haraway (1989, 1991, 1992) and Bruno Latour (1993) have insisted on our taking the nonhuman as well as the human seriously in our analyses. First, they draw our attention to the analytic salience of living and nonliving material entities in the worlds in which we and our objects of study are both situated. We are not alone. Nonhuman materialities, like all kinds of human organizational endeavors, configure our situatedness both in front of us and behind our backs. Yet we have insufficiently attended to these heterogeneities.

Second, Haraway and Latour problematize the distinction/binary of human/nonhuman, Haraway (1985, 1991, 1997) by talking about cyborgs, and Latour (1993) by talking about hybrids. That is, they introduce and then play with another binary: purity/miscegenation and the intensity of continuities with the nonhuman rather than the usually assumed disjunctions. Haraway's (1985, 1991) oft-cited and -reprinted "Manifesto for Cyborgs" articulated a critical and empowering approach to technoscientific devices and desires, attempting to provide us with the right tools for the job of living in the future-as-present and coming soon. Miscegenated/Hybrids-R-Us. Purity, like innocence, was a (witting or unwitting) pose. Latour (1993) places humans, nonhumans, and hybrids in a shifting amodern and offers an array of useful cartographies and mapping practices.

As we shall next see, concepts such as cyborg, hybridity, creolization, and *métissage* provide feminist theorizing with crucial bridges across divides of difference (Felski 1997:12). Binaries as two-sided frameworks have dissolved into multisided flexible but complicated cat's cradles. Maps are increasingly important.

Difference(s), Destabilized Identities, Subjectivities, Discourses

Recent reunderstandings of difference are predicated on the deconstruction and complications of the binaries but go far beyond these. They pursue and take seriously differences *within* groupings that heretofore were assumed to be homogeneous (sexes, races, ethnicities, sexualities, and any and all other bases of identities) and *within* individuals who were presumed to possess (if they were not somehow disenfranchised) a singular, authentic, coherent Enlightenment "self." Initiated by the profound critiques of white feminisms by African-American scholars and activists,[13] problematics of differences within groupings have led to efforts to perform integrated analyses of the inextricable and simultaneous dynamics of race, gender, and class. These have come to center stage this decade in both micro studies of, for example, labor processes, and in symbolic/semiotic/cultural studies.[14]

The destabilization of individual identity and subjectivity allowed space and place for multiple selves (rather than one authentic version and a series of false faces) and multiply experienced selves, subjectivities based on mutiple selves, multiple subject positionings in the heterogeneous cartographies of contemporary life.[15] King (1994:150) finds hopeful ironies in the ways in which "mutiple identities and nonunified subjects bring together political investments across several 'divides'" within feminisms that had been unbridged. Possibilities for coalitions multiply.

Ironically, some of these destabilizations were triggered by empirical work, but it involved qualitative/interpretive rather than quantitative and survey approaches to research.[16] In feminist qualitative work, the complicated articulations, the changes "of mind," and the historicized shifts (both fast and slow) were "performed" (Goffman 1959; Butler 1990) routinely in front of our eyes by the people we studied, becoming our data. In contrast, the positivist empiricism of quantitative and survey research is usually (but not always) profoundly challenged by multiplicities, and centers of such research are often key sites of resistance to the poststructural turn as much as they are sites of what Foucault termed surveillance. Research approaches are theory/methods packages, carrying their own epistemologies and even ontologies.[17] Our understandings of the ontological issues can only become increasingly important.

The Enlightenment ideal of a powerful and self-conscious political subject also dissipates. As it turns out, a "man" lurks within humanity and the state (Barrett and Phillips 1992:5; Brown 1995). Politics have come to be seen as the *constitution*, not merely the representation, of "interests." And the belief in the possibility of pure reason and rationality has come to be seen as naive and even dangerous in the vulnerabilities it promotes. In the age of cybersimulacra and political hyperhype, grand schemes of social reform such as the War on Poverty or the Great Society or even historical "progress" become ludicrous. But all is not lost.

Glimpsing New Directions

If we take difference(s) seriously, then what? A number of new directions have emerged: "Feminists have moved from grand theory to local studies, from cross-cultural analyses of patriarchy to the complex and historical interplay of sex, race, and class, from notions of a female identity or the interests of women towards the instability of female identity and the active creation and recreation of women's needs or concerns" (Barrett and Phillips 1992:6–7).

Sometimes inflected by, if exceeding, Foucault, feminists have taken up cultural and scientific discourse analyses with both vengances and enthusiasms. We have long been interested in how others construct us, women, the female, the feminine; new modes of discourse analysis have abetted this passion. Fraser (1997:381) notes that *hegemony* is "Gramsci's term for the discursive face of power ... the power to establish the 'common sense' or 'doxa' of a society, the fund of self-evident descriptions of social reality that normally go without saying.... [O]ne use of a conception of discourse for feminist theorizing is to shed light on the processes by which the sociocultural hegemony of dominant groups is achieved and contested." She then asks, "How do pervasive axes of dominance and subordination affect the production and circulation of social meanings? How does stratification along lines of gender, race, and class affect the discursive construction of social identities and the formation of social groups?"

Feminist analysts have answered loudly. Front and center have been studies of popular media.[18] The life sciences and biomedicine have also been major targets, and the new consumption studies are fascinating in how they address materialities (e.g., DeGrazia 1996).[19] Discourse concerns travel widely. Drawing on Dorothy Smith's work on institutional ethnography, Naples (1997) uses a new conception of discursive framing to analyze welfare reform.[20] Such frames, used in policy debates, employ themes that resonate with popular ideology and are woven through everyday practices of policy construction—key sites for diffraction. Certainly actions that challenge and destabilize destructive discursive constructions of women are in order.

But what of actions "for" something? Moira Gatens (1992) argued that French feminist theory of the "*écriture féminine*" does not take an essentialist position on difference, but rather makes the more radical move of destabilizing the binary of equality/difference. Felski (1997:12) has argued that "difference" has become an unassailable value, that there are dangers in the doxa of difference if conceived as fundamental, asserting in its stead the instabilities of hybridity, creolization and *métissage*; these have the advantage of "unseating difference from a position of absolute privilege." Braidotti and colleagues (1997) also seek to retain difference in less pure and rigid forms.[21]

A number of theorists are framing means through which we can with one hand hold on to the key differences difference makes while with the other find reasonable, if highly partial and temporary, sites on which to stand—and fight—*for* something. If there are no grand theories, there likewise can be no grand solutions to the complicated, inflected, and infected problems that beset us as women and as humans. How then to proceed? Some examples in brief:

In "Racism, Sexism and Homophobia," Audre Lorde (1984) insisted we must learn to relate across differences. Scott (1992) has argued that we as feminists should refuse the opposition between equality and difference in favor of a position for equalities that rest on differences rather than on their supposed erasure. In Evans's terms, "To treat people as equals may *require* that they not be treated the same way." That is, equality is not, and cannot be, about "sameness" (1995:4).

Spivak (1997) has emphasized the necessity of "building for differences." Spivak also used the helpful yet problematic term "strategic essentialisms," which was interpreted as allowing positive framings of woman/women to be used for political purposes without feminists making deep ontological commitments to them. Spivak asserts that instead she meant that persistent critique of *unavoidable* essentialisms is requisite, implying that practical politics—praxis—may demand both essentialisms and ongoing critique.

Paraphrasing Nicholson (1997:318–19), Alcoff (1997) takes the "idea of subjectivity positioned within specific discursive configurations" but also capable of reconstruction through reflexive (we would say diffractive) practices. She also takes the idea of women's needs as emanating not from anything essential but from socially (and we would add culturally) specific contexts. Alcoff then argues for "a historicized subjectivity that is capable of rearticulating itself," making possible an unstable but useful form of identity politics "where identity points to real patterns and needs but is also understood as 'relative to a constantly shifting context.'" It is *within* particular contexts that sites for political action exist. We would further assert that it is only within particular contexts that "solutions" to problems, however partial and temporary, can be attempted.

Fraser (1997) argues that feminist theory went over the edge into the sea of political paralysis because of insufficient criticality of the deletion of context and situatedness performed by structuralism in the first place, which was then rearticulated in poststructuralism in the second place. She faults *both* on these grounds, which are similar to Star's (1983) points about simplification. Further, Fraser seeks a pragmatic model of language that views language as manifest in diverse, contingent, and changing discourses. "It would enable us therefore to see individual identity and social group formation as complex and shifting. Thus it would also allow us to thematize conflict and power among social groups"

(Nicholson 1997:319). Discursive constructions and signifying practices can be handled as constituitive rather than determinative.

Contemporary feminist and antiracist legal theorists are at the forefront of articulating how equalities can rest on differences. Littleton (1987) and Minow (1987) lay out models of legal equality that account for difference. Cornell's concept of equivalence (1992) refers to something of equal value but not necessarily based on "likeness" or "sameness," while Crenshaw and others take up the problematics of the intersections of race and gender.[22] Given recent challenges to affirmative action as practiced, yet simultaneous wider social commitments on the part of the American populace to attempt to achieve justice and equality of opportunity, we can anticipate considerable diffraction and action on the legal front. This legal work should also contribute to new frameworks for greater equity which can rest on differences in health policy generally and women's health policy specifically.

Feminist postcolonial studies are also important sites of theoretical diffraction, and not necessarily comfortable or easy for either those who dwell there or those who seek to understand what that might mean. Narayan (1997) and Mohanty (1988), for example, urge Western feminists and others not to univeralize or essentialize non-Western nation-states and cultures. Universalizing and essentializing approaches are as suspect here as they are vis-à-vis gender or race. In (post)colonial contexts, both are forms of recolonization. Instead, acknowledging heterogeneities, histories, and cultural contestations counters hegemonic practices of old imperialisms and new globalizations, and refutes sexist practices of old and new nationalisms.

Thus in many sites, feminists are attempting to retheorize agency, to frame subjectivities that do not assume unified subjects, to retheorize politics beyond liberation of a "core" self, and to take discursive constructions into account without reification. How can we conceive—and enter—a politics without Enlightenment anchors? Can we have what Haraway calls "freedom projects"? What happens if we think of these as *practices* rather than events or beingness?

In sum, this most cursory of reviews serves to demonstrate that there are kinds of theoretical piecework going on, cobblings together of older and newer conceptual insights and modes of analysis into a theoretical carpetbag that may provide the right tools for some political jobsites. With these new insights and modes of analysis, we can presumably refigure "old" problematics, wrestle with "new" ones, and produce new practices of understanding, knowledge and, hopefully, situated activism. Women's health is one such highly political jobsite.

Complications of Women, Health, and Healing

Re-vision—the act of looking back, of seeing, with fresh eyes, or entering an old text from a new critical direction—is for women more than a chapter in cultural history; it is an act of survival. (Rich 1979: 35)

This book seeks to provoke entry into old texts of women's health in order to recast them. Complications discussed here include problematics of women's health movements and institutions, where certain successes have repositioned feminists in much more heterogeneous places than we were twenty-plus years ago. There is increased recognition of women's differences in health, and more is needed. Yet new processes of biomedicalization extend science, technology, and medicine further into our lives. Surveillance medicine is creating a new culture of risk and new burdens of health care consumption that particularly implicate women. And last but far from least, "the body" as feminist problematic—as "our bodies"—reappears, considerably rethought over the past decade. To address these, redefining "women," "health," and "healing" is in order.

Women's Health Movements and Institutions:

The past is always with us, but *how* this is so is neither simple nor direct. In feminist worlds, we must always remember that the histories of our work, activism, and institutions have not been told very often or very audibly. Those new to our worlds leap into an extant river of concerns and understandings that need some clarification. Hence a brief bit of history.[23]

In 1970 a newsprint booklet appeared that changed the framing of women's health across the globe. The Boston Women's Health Book Collective's *Our Bodies, Our Selves* (1970, 1976, 1984, 1994) marked the begining of the second wave of feminist activism in women's health in the twentieth century.[24] This branch of what would become the broader women's health movement intersected with related movements for better birthing, legalization of abortion, industrial health, and so on and inflected them with new feminist conceptions.

During the last decades of the twentieth century, a wide array of feminist organizations then pursued a wide array of women's health goals, from improved patient package inserts for contraceptives to informed consent and patient's rights, from better birthing practices to knowledgeable lesbian health care, from inclusion of women in clinical trials to increasing the numbers of women physicians.[25] There were three main kinds of feminist organizations. The first was autonomous and/or networked feminist women's health centers that have sought to provide direct care to women, such as the Federation of Feminist Women's Health Centers and hundreds of freestanding clinics. Education about women's health has been a key focus in such clinical settings, along with other forms of patient empowerment.[26] The second genre of women's health organization has been focused on feminist women's health policy and education. Here organizations such as the National Women's Health Network, the Boston Women's Health Book Collective, the Reproductive Rights National Network, and many local and state groups have been active. Third are the professional or semiprofessional reform organizations such as the American Medical Women's Association (AMWA) and less formal networks of women's health professionals, especially but not only in Washington.[27]

Perhaps the most important feature of such movements most recently is their globalization, composed of the emergence of new grassroots women's health movements, new extensions of feminist activism into explicit health issues, and densifying of the webs of connection among women health activists across national boundaries (e.g., Doyal 1996; Yanco 1996). This has been facilitated to some degree by the UN Decade for Women and by transnational nongovernmental organizations such as Health Action International and the International Congress on Women's Health.[28] In some countries, such as Australia, feminists in politics have been so successful in the governmental bureaucracies—including successes in women's health—that they are called "femocrats" (Broom 1991). In others, a particular event or women's health product such as Norplant has triggered major changes (e.g., Barroso and Corea 1995).

These movements have been amazingly understudied and are sites of sorely needed examination and comparison. What do we even think is/are women's health movements today? What counts and to whom? Hirsch and Fox Keller (1990) drew our attention to *Conflicts in Feminism*, but conflicts among feminists about reproductive and other women's health issues have just begun to be examined (e.g., Stanworth 1990; Clarke and Montini 1993; Ruzek, Olesen and Clarke 1997). Further, how can we analyze the breast cancer activism of very elite women and physicians' wives that made that disease the "cause" of the year 1996 for corporate as well as individual charity, sending the funds raised to a biomedicine that refuses to address cause and prevention? Assuming history has its own lessons, we need such work in order to understand the range of positions feminists and others have held, why they have held them, what goals they sought to achieve, and their own assessments of their efforts. All are requisite for diffraction.[29]

Among more recent movement successes, an outstanding achievement has been federal recognition of women's health as an important area of research and the building of governmental institutions to accomplish such projects. Many kinds of activism led to the Office for Women's Health Research at the National Institutes of Health (NIH) (first organized by executive decision and then through legislation), which in turn led to the establishment of such offices or coordinators in all key federal health agencies. The goal of all is to focus the attention of their agency on women's health issues and to facilitate exchanges. The Women's Health Initiative, a national network of Centers of Excellence in Women's Health through which federally sponsored research is organized, has significant potential. Among the initial accomplishments (and of course not without posing its own set of new problems) is the inclusion of women—even of childbearing age—in clinical trials and related health research. Moreover, the NIH Revitalization Act of 1993 requires not only that women be included in all grant proposals using human subjects (or a full explanation of why they are not included) but also that people of color be explicitly included. White men had been the literal as well as figurative/discursive "model" bodies (more below). Third, explicit research on women's health issues is being ambitiously undertaken. One of the first sponsored studies focuses on the long-term use of hormone replacement therapies in menopausal women. Sadly, a study of prevention strategies for osteoporosis, including vitamins and exercise, was canceled and many of the offices of women's health are also provisional and easily terminated.[30]

Yet these very successes also create new burdens and problems for feminists committed to improving women's health and healing—burdens of monitoring and attempting to influence directions of research, sponsorship, and the very doing of the research itself. Self-identified feminist women are involved across the board (though far from the only people involved). Indeed, feminists are quite differently positioned in the entire health and healing domain than we were twenty or so years ago, and multiply positioned inside and outside and on the margins of federal policy and research arenas, clinical settings, and scientific research per se. However, feminists do not necessarily agree about women's health issues, what research is desirable, what kinds of health insurance are most important, and so on.

For example, in the United States, one can read the key research of the Women's Health Initiative as the socialization of the costs of pharmaceutical testing. That is, the initial focusing of federal sponsorship of women's health research on pharmacological interventions in women's health seems to many of us like rehearsals of the old pacification stories of giving more drugs to women, which feminists critiqued decades ago (e.g., Prather and Fidell 1975). The difference here is that the federal government is paying for the research, rather than pharmaceutical companies themselves, as was the case with the Pill, for example. Pharmaceutical companies have long been trying to shift the burdens of drug research to the federal government (Djerassi 1981; Mastroianni, Donaldson, and Kane 1990). The Women's Health Initiative can be read as presenting a most viable opportunity.

Others read the Women's Health Initiative and Centers of Excellence as women physicians "doing it for themselves," to paraphrase Aretha Franklin's song, creating a female biomedical infrastructure in the NIH centered on women's health and considering a new separate specialty of primary care for women. There is an emerging and ambitious literature on women physicians compared to men physicians in terms of primary care, patient satisfaction, and so on.[31] What does it mean if it is the face of a woman at the other end of the Foucauldian speculum/panopticon? The larger feminist question is whether and to what degree women physicians now and in the future (when they will be much more of a critical mass in medicine) remain deeply within the biomedical model of medicine within which they were (and are still) trained, or whether they question and reconfigure that model in ways that feminists concerned with women's health (including feminist physicians) have long articulated.

But simple criticisms of corporate opportunism or professional aggrandizement assuredly will not suffice as an adequately theoretically informed analysis here. It is precisely at this juncture that theorizings of difference enter the conversation loudly and clearly. Krieger and Fee (1994) make a powerful argument that the historical constructions of "race" and "sex" as key *biomedical* terms, based deeply in nineteenth-century efforts to demonstrate the inferiority of Negroes and females, have naturalized these terms as biological categories. They argue that the health of women and men of color and the nonreproductive health of white women have been largely ignored. "It is critical to read these omissions as evidence of a logic of difference rather than an assumption of similarity" (Krieger and Fee 1996:21), difference here historically read as inferiority. Today these issues need fresh interrogation, the basis of which lies for Krieger and Fee in the "suppressed and repressed category" of social class and the complications of race and ethnicity.

Differences among women by race, class, and health/medical situation also shade our perceptions of research and treatment. Women have long been agents on their own behalf vis-à-vis biomedicine, sometimes ardently seeking biomedicalization of their conditions.[32] Some women need certain medications, such as estrogen replacement, as treatment and many of us may want the knowledge clinical trials promise. But we need to question why strategies for prevention are not also being pursued. Further, what insights does nursing have to offer and how does nursing knowledge—usually patient-identified, woman-generated knowledge—differ from biomedical knowledge?[33] Do women physicians and biomedical researchers, informed by feminism, generate kinds of knowledge that differ substantively from male knowledge production agendas? Are their research agendas different even if their methods remain the same?

As feminists, then, we are begining to confront the burdens of being "inside" biomedicine and attempting to change it from such relatively new and difficult sites of perception and action. The risks of co-optation are, of course, highest in these situations (Ruzek 1980). Gordon (1995:367) notes that "cooptation is not automatically a sign of political defeat but may register feminism's achievements. The flip side of the theoretical insistence that cooptation is necessary for social change is that social regulation can never be understood solely in terms of repression but also creates [new] arenas of struggle." How do we know the "when" of co-optation? And how do we both study and theorize it? Recently feminist historians and others have done exceptional work in attempting to understand where, why, and how earlier feminist activism succeeded and failed—even in its own terms. For example, Gordon (1994) and Quadagno (1994) have analyzed how progressive-era feminists reinscribed gender and racialized hierarchies in welfare and health policy. How will the Women's Health Initiative measure up in a decade or two? What will it reinscribe?

But also, how can we sustain feminist thinking from multiple standpoints— from outside centers of power (which, of course, are not powerless sites), from various marginalized sites, as well as from the hearts of federal bureaucracies? How can we continue to rehearse our stances at the periphery, which have long given us analytic bite? What do we stand to gain *and lose* by these new positionings? How do/can/will our modes of understanding and analysis change, given these shifts in positioning? If there are so many standpoints of feminists politically active and employed in women's health, what standpoints are taken by women not present but implicated through such politics?[34]

Doing Difference in Women's Health

"Late capitalism has fallen in love with difference" (Clarke 1995), and difference is moving into medicine—along with capital. What bell hooks (1992) refers to as "the commodification of difference" is frequently exemplified. For example, American social scientists and clinicians, especially but not only in urban areas, have long worked on developing what is now known as "culturally competent care"—health care that recognizes and is explicitly sensitive to the cultures of patients and their families and friends. While such care can be—and is—provided out of respect, it can also become commoditized in HMO competitions for racial/ethnic market segments. An array of other problems has also been discovered. Cultural *formulas* do not work well in clinical practices. Cultures are neither uniform nor static—nor are people. Some versions of culturally competent care (or some people attempting to provide it) are reinscribing traditions, including gendered patriarchal traditions. Reinscribing the old is being viewed by some feminists as recolonization (e.g., Mohanty 1988; Narayan 1997). A glaring example here occurred when a sex preselection clinic in the Pacific Northwest targeted Asian Indian communities for intensive niche advertising. Their services "allow" women to determine whether they are carrying male or female fetuses and, given traditional cultural male child preference patterns, "allow" them to seek abortions if the fetus is female.

The complications on this front, theoretically as well as practically, concern how we as feminists can respond to such situations. We know empirically that some women in such communities will want to pursue sex preselection because they, as agents of their own lives, desire to follow cultural traditions, especially in the diaspora. Others will be seeking newly gendered solutions (e.g., del Castillo 1993) for what they see as their own hybridity or *métissage*. And some physicians may have yet other agendas. For example, when a new physician provider saw that I (Adele Clarke) was a sociologist at UCSF, he said something on the order of, "Oh, great! We need to know which patients and families are patriarchal and matriarchal. We need to know who is responsible for the bill." Complications for us as feminists can indeed come from unexpected directions.

Inside feminist theory, there has been considerable debate about difference, working the edges where tensions lie between being marked and unmarked, speaking by choice from such standpoints (of color, female, fat, disabled, differently embodied) or being discursively constructed a priori so that nothing one can say can be heard, taking into account performativity or "doing" gender or race.[35] This is not the space to rehearse these debates. But what Zinn and Dill (1996) call "the difference project" in feminisms is and will continue to be central to revisioning women, health, and healing. The array of work on the health of women of color testifies to this.[36] As the book will demonstrate, for example, spaces where discourses meet agentic actors can be important sites of diffraction and revision. The theoretical point is that there are not only "identity" differences among women but also theoretical differences that are manifest in terms of what counts as health and healing.

There is also a most important new research area that takes up the project of making the fundamental distinction between *race* as a property of particular individuals reflected in their health status and behaviors and *racism* as consequential in the lives of people of color in ways that are manifest around both their health status (e.g., blood pressure) and behaviors (what people do and don't do). That is, racism as *causative* of health problems is finally being researched and demonstrated. In the past, health problems were *correlated* with being a person of a particular color or part of a particular community—demonstrating the kind of devaluing difference that Krieger and Fee (1994) referred to. Until recently, the possibility that racism, rather than racial difference, could in fact cause some of those attributes was only speculated about, and rarely.[37] Transdisciplinary working groups have formed in a number of biomedical settings to explore such phenomena, reflecting in part the development of a "critical mass" of concerned scholars. Their project in biomedicine parallels that of critical race theory in law.[38]

In taking difference(s) seriously in terms of health, further problems are of course posed. Difference has been and will likely continue to be a key site of surveillance, discussed below, making particular groups ever more vulnerable to various kinds of disciplining.[39] The fundamental question for the future is, what differences do differences now make, and how would we refigure them?

The New Biomedicalization

Perhaps the major complication we confront as feminists concerned about women, health and healing seeking to intervene around the legitimacy of differences is that this domain remains undertheorized and undercriticized while it becomes increasingly overbiomedicalized.[40] We are talking here not only of the need to resist co-optation of feminist approaches, but the need to reconceptualize biomedicine per se. It can certainly be argued that we need to begin from a fresh critique of biomedicine, because biomedicine itself has changed so very dramatically over the past several decades. Even the past few years have brought radical changes in health care delivery, dramatic reconceptualizations of genetic causality and possible interventions, shifts of caregiving from hospital to home and from professionals (back) to relatives and friends.

But let us begin with some definitions. We use the term *biomedicine* to signal that (techno)science is central in shaping medical worlds, along with the many other institutions of health care provision (e.g., hospitals, clinics, group practices, the medical supplies industry). One of the organizing premises of this book has been that the profound importance of sciences and technologies *within* medicine, past, present and future, has been ignored. Not only has it been ignored in medical anthropology, the sociology of health and illness, and even the history of medicine and the health sciences,[41] but it has also been ignored, until very recently, by feminists. However, we are now pioneering in making the linkages from science and technology worlds to the domain of application—the clinic. Our desire for knowledge about how certain diagnoses, treatments, visualizing technologies, and so on, came to be so sexist in their construction and use have driven such pursuits. And they have driven us into computer engineering and informatics to examine the very classification systems that structure the organization of biomedical knowledge.[42]

For example, the reproductive sciences or molecular biology or birth control need to be translated into biomedical applications. The biomedicalization of life itself (human, plant, and animal) is the key overarching, usually taken-for-granted, and often invisible *social* process here.[43] Biomedicalization means the ongoing extension of biomedicine and technology into new and previously unmedicalized aspects of life. This is often imaged as a juggernaut of technological imperatives (Koenig 1988), bearing distinctive Western biomedical assumptions (Gordon 1988). In the United States since World War II, state-supported institutions such as the National Institutes of Health have "pushed to integrate science, therapy and policy," becoming almost "the only [biomedical] research game in town" (Pauly 1993:137). Such integration over the past half century, as recent efforts to change health care organization revealed, constitutes a very robust biomedicalization of life indeed.

Many recent works on the body are concerned with these issues. Duden (1990:1,4) has argued that "to study the making of the modern body is to study the gradual unfolding of something that is now self-evident.... [T]he genesis of the modern body is consistent with other aspects of the modern image of man, the *homo oeconomicus*." Folbre (1994) has recently deconstructed and reconceptualized "Rational Economic Men" into "Imperfectly Rational Somewhat Economic Persons," reminding us of the messy and erratic ways in which cultures are practiced. Many of us who study the life sciences and biomedicine have noted that in the future, if not the present, "nature will be 'operationalized' for the good of society" (Lock 1993:48). Reproduction is being "enterprised up" (Strathern 1992). In the emergent industry of biotechnology, "the politics of fertility [now] extend from the soil to star wars" (Franklin 1995a:326). Our task is to continue to examine these processes.

One tool for understanding is the concept of a "[bio]medical industrial complex," put forward in the 1980s by Relman et al. (1987) to denote a parallel politicoeconomic institutional sector to the military industrial complex (and not unrelated to it). Moreover, this medical industrial complex is globalizing. By and large, the Western biomedical worldview is exported along with companies which can produce the many commodities—many of them technoscientific—which are requisite for proper health care within this worldview (Gordon 1988). HMOs and hospital companies are rapidly becoming multinationals.

But the traffic around biomedicine is complicated and goes in multiple directions. We do not (yet) include in our concept of biomedicine those traditions of healing that have not historically been part and parcel of Western framings of medicine. Often called "alternative" medicine, such practices as acupuncture, chiropractic, hydrotherapy, homeopathy, and others have been positioned since the early twentieth century on the margins as "other," foreign, exotic, and most often by "regular" medicine as quackery. But recently an article in one of the major journals of biomedicine, a journal intended to reach from science to policy to health care economics and organization, suggested that this might be made to change, given that "alternative" medicine received a high proportion of out-of-pocket health care dollars in the United States, compared with biomedicine. For example, herbal remedy sales exceed $3 billion per year in the United States, and one in three Americans has turned to nonconventional therapies (Pearlman 1998; see also Eisenberg et al. 1993). At the same time, many studies demonstrating the efficacy of many such practices, and their comparative cost-effectiveness, have appeared.[44]

There are now serious efforts at the federal level, the NIH Office of Complementary and Alternative Medicine, to include such practices in biomedicine—specifically in managed care institutions. And increasingly HMOs are offering services such as chiropractic and acupuncture (because they are often effective for pain management and much cheaper than prolonged Western treatment or surgeries). But how are these alternative practices to be integrated into Western biomedicine? How is Western biomedicine refigured as a result? We are reminded of the co-optation of feminist institutions, women's health clinics, which now appear in most medical centers, sometimes with "women's outreach clinics" based in the financial districts of large cities. Completely shorn of their feminist origins, intentions, and concrete practices, many of these "women's health" clinics simply hire women physicians, paint everything mauve, and open their doors.[45] There is even a UBS Women's Health Index on the stock market, made up of twenty-six companies in the field, and "Women's Health Stocks [are] Try[ing] to Be Darling Again" (Hays 1997). Does a similar fate await "alternative" modes of healing? While Western biomedical sciences often—perhaps even usually—seek to displace other sites and modes of knowledge production and healing, co-optation is another common response, another part of the biomedicalization of society and the selling of science (Nelkin 1987). But being shorn of epistemological and even ontological roots is a high price to pay for inclusion.

Questions for the future here include: What are the implications of biomedicalization for women's health? Can biomedicalization be controlled or regulated? As we go to press, the *New York Times* reports that the crisis in health care since Hillary Rodham Clinton's efforts to guide the reorganization of the health "system" has gotten so severe that it is building resistance on state and national levels, with increasing demands for regulation of HMOs, PPOs, and other insurance schemes. The *New York Times* reports we can anticipate getting some version of "Hillary Lite" (Passell 1997). Most feminists had found Hillary a bit lite to begin with and are, as we write, attempting to intervene to make such changes serve women better.[46] There will be many repeat performances.

Surveillance Medicine and New Burdens of Health Care Consumption

Part of the new biomedicalization includes what is now being termed "surveillance medicine," the creation of *potentially* diseased persons through risk analyses of individuals, communities and populations. Armstrong (1995), Lupton (1994), and others, drawing deeply on Foucault, argue that in addition to increased biomedicalization in terms of clinical medicine, a new kind of medicine is now being practiced which will expand dramatically in the future. Based on risk factors (derived from large-scale correlational data banks made possible by computing), the new surveillance medicine involves a fundamental remapping of the spaces of illness. In traditional Western clinical medicine, symptoms indicate an underlying pathological lesion within a specific individual patient's body— localized and specified. In contrast, surveillance medicine dissolves clinical categories of healthy and ill persons in favor of new categories of individuals-at-risk and at-risk communities and populations, via strategies of pathologization and vigilance.

In clinical medicine, diagnostic linkages are based on surface and depth symptoms (interior/exterior). In surveillance medicine, diagnosis is based on arrangements of predictive factors, and there may be no symptoms or disease whatsoever. "Surveillance medicine is read across an extracorporeal and temporal space. In part, the new space of illness is the community" (Armstrong 1995:401). Databases are the sites of monitoring and, in the United States, insurance companies are profoundly interested. "[I]llness becomes a point of *perpetual becoming* [as] surveillance medicine maps a different form of identity ... innovative spaces of *illness potential*" (Armstrong 1995:402, emphasis added). What Ogden (1995) has called "the risky self" is often a part of "risk groups" which can themselves be targeted. It is no accident that surveillance medicine is among the fastest-growing knowledge industries—medical informatics—on the planet. As we work on our own theoretical destabilizations, our potential materialities are concretized in binary bytes in silicon.

Obviously, the Human Genome Project and the many related projects it has spawned will be the major contributors to the development of surveillance medicine in the twenty-first century. Being "at risk" is now being transformed into "requiring biomedical prevention/intervention." For example, being diagnosed as having the "breast cancer gene" has led healthy women to have double mastectomies (Altman 1996). As sites of reproduction, women are also particularly implicated here (Rothenberg and Thompson 1994). Indeed, Rayna Rapp's paper in this volume takes up precisely such problems.

A related development, evidence-based medicine, is also dependent on major databases for what is becoming known as "outcomes research." Here the safety and efficacy of specific treatments are assessed based on data from very large numbers of patients and providers. Insurance companies and HMOs are already moving toward "allowing" only those procedures demonstrated as "valid" through such research. This development will likely cut in many different directions vis-à-vis women's health. For example, "unnecessary" hysterectomies and C-sections, so long criticized by feminists, will be highlit for deletion. However, provider discretion about individual case treatment, patient privacy, and patient involvement in treatment decisions will all likely be quite limited.

Evidence-based medicine is becoming yet another site feminists must patrol.

Surveillance medicine and genomics together have already begun to impose new burdens on health care consumers. There are incredible burdens of knowledge expectations—what lay people are expected to know and do about our health, especially in terms of prevention and especially if we have risk factors. As best we can determine, we all are at greater risk for something. Edgley and Brissett (1990) have called some aspects of this "health nazism" because of the fascist ways in which expectations of health behavior are imposed. Whatever this is, and whatever gets to count as "health," the most frightening aspect is that having a particular risk factor may well be construed as having a "preexisting condition" for insurance purposes, making large new subsets of people ineligible or, perhaps, having permanent caps placed on their overall health care coverage. Many of these issues are women's issues and adequately intersect with others to be sites for coalition, though notoriously difficult in terms of organizing (Clarke and Wolfson 1990).

(Re)Defining "Women," "Health," and "Healing"

This volume is premised on our belief that this is an important historical juncture at which to revision. A social and cultural (re)formation of women's health is being constructed within the American medical establishment and related healing domains—with concomitant contestations around HIV/AIDS, health care reform, and (endlessly) abortion. All these are, of course, women's and feminist health issues. AIDS activists patterned their work after earlier women's health activists (Epstein 1996), and today some breast cancer activists are taking fresh leads from AIDS activism. We might argue that, though largely unrecognized by the media, these movements are both distinctive and coconstitutive. A deep grasp of *all* of these and their interconnectedness is ultimately requisite for revisioning women, health and healing.

While we cannot fully anticipate the many new directions in which serious attempts at re/visioning will ultimately take us, certain themes are clear at this juncture. Probably most fundamental will be a rethinking of what the basic terms of our conversation—women, health, and healing—might mean. That is, as we come to understand that identities are simultaneously multiple and incorporate variation on all dimensions, we must frame how to attend to such complexities.

How can we begin to rethink women, health, and healing through the fresh lenses ground over the past decade in cultural studies, feminist studies, and gendered technoscience studies? What are the implications for health and healing of feminist and postcolonial "discoveries" that race, class, and gender are particularized, indivisible, and embedded in specific life situations? What messages are being sent from different standpoints, especially those developed by feminist women of color? And how can the diversities of situated knowledges be brought to bear on reconceptualizing health care toward the production of health rather than the amelioration of violence, disease, and devastation?

In our processes of redefining women to recognize differences important to health and health care, we need to move beyond simplistic and stereotypic notions. But the implications are much much deeper as we move to redefine/open up the right to re/define both health and healing as well. The word "health" is a simplified gloss. Can we reconceive health? What are the empirical parameters of "health" if not erased by normal curves? That is, could health be conceived plurally to allow for the ranges of variations of bodies and situations? We know the notions of health and illness are socially and culturally constructed.[47] Can we participate in their reconstruction to move against the homogenization of this domain of life?

Further, we are seeking to open definitions of women, health, and healing not only at the conceptual and practical level of the individual woman. We seek re/visioning within and among the meaning-making communities and collectivities through which we not only build our multifaceted identities but also where we live our lives and where we seek to make our lives and those of others better and "healthier." Refuting the atomized woman as the object of health care rather than the subject of her own and others' healing within the relational webs and frameworks of her broader yet situated social worlds is one of our goals.

Rather than be erased in favor of abstractions, "contexts" may be viewed as *situations* within which politics and policies may be forged. Our analyses need to be situated, at least in part context-driven. Commonalities among some women can be what those women face—commonalities of situation—rather than commonalities of identity or other aspects of their person. That is, women may share aspects of identities with multiple groups and aspects of situations with women of other identities. Thus identities need not be essentialized or erased to con-struct policies based on commonalities of situation. Such commonalities must, of course, be recognized and acknowledged by those involved, not merely attributed or imposed by others.

For example, many immigrant women, poor women and African-American women face personal/political situations where others want to control their childbearing. *Situated activism* here would include heterogeneous and dialogic efforts to enhance women's own control over their reproductive lives, however partial and contradictory. Moreover, discrediting discursive constructions, such as "welfare mother," could be handled as constituitive of situations and therefore requiring attention in terms not only of analysis but also in the formulation of policies to address specific situations. Again, while we have abandoned naive hopes of grand solutions to the complicated, inflected problems of women, health and healing, partial agendas of improved practices can be modest freedom projects.

Re-Visions: Overview of the Book

I think what binds the lumpy community of modest witnesses called feminist science studies together is what bell hooks called "yearning." Yearning in technoscience is for knowledge projects as freedom projects—in a polyglot, relentlessly troping, but practical and material way—coupled with the searing sense that all is not well with women, as well as billions of nonwomen, who remain incommensurable in the warped coordinate systems of the New World Order, Inc. (Haraway 1997:269)

Reflecting a sharing of concerns beyond what we had imagined at this historical moment, the conference and the book almost organized themselves. We begin with some more general *Theoretical Speculations/Interventions* that frame our project and provide a shared language for revisioning. Part of that project involves *Destabilizing Methods*, reflecting changes in how we ourselves go about producing knowledges about women's health (and anything else we care about). Here we find problems not only of epistemologies but also of ontologies, and confrontations with our cultural, social, and professional selves.

The section *(Re)Constructing Experience: Searching the Self* involves even more profound (because even more personal) confrontations with self. It involves openings of private interior worlds as parts of public professional work. In earlier years we sought analytic guidance from the feminist shibboleth that "the personal is political." Here several of our contributors use "the personal" as a site of diffraction to reexamine our own knowledge production processes—the personal as constituitive of the professional.

Reproduction holds an uncomfortable place in women's health domains, as women's health has traditionally been reduced to gynecology and obstetrics—reproductive health—while *nonreproductive* aspects of women's health have been ignored (e.g., Krieger and Fee 1994). Yet it was also among the earliest feminist concerns vis-à-vis *both* feminist theory and women, health, and healing. Reproduction has itself been so deeply transformed over the past decades that new projects *Challenging New World Reproductive Orders* abound. Reproduction has been culturally and scientifically diffracted, and our contributors examine these processes.

A number of our contributors also constructed newly *Revised and Disruptive Agendas for Women's Health,* focusing on key substantive areas and bringing recent theoretical insights to bear upon them. If "we" are now major producers of knowledge about women's health, what do we want to know about lesbian health? about health care reform? about midlife rather than "just" menopause? And last, how do we want to think about thinking about the future?

Feminist Revisioning: Theoretical Speculations/Interventions
Donna Haraway uses a "virtual speculum"—theory—to open up the New World Order for our collective examination and consideration. She raises the always complicated question of naming as part of seeing, because naming always has implications for the future, for action. This is a fundamental theme of the book as a whole. The incredible ruptures in feminist theorizing over the past two decades have ended whatever innocence we had about women and feminisms and futures—and language: "*Virtual Speculum* is diffractive and interrogatory. It

asks, 'Is this what feminists mean by choice, agency, life, creativity? What is at stake here, and for whom? Who and what are human and nonhuman centers of action? Whose story is this? Who cares?'"

From having named sometimes arrogantly and often inadequately and too partially, feminist theorizing has been leading us through complicated territories, encouraging us to see lived details of identities and selves and collectivities. We have learned to see difference. From simplifications we have moved to complications and reflections. But can we talk about them? Can we even design health policies that *account for* and *are accountable to* women in our heterogeneous life situations?

Ultimately this is the question Haraway asks—and answers. Future feminisms, she argues, must be predicated on multiply positioned women and take into account mutiple *and conflicting* vulnerabilities. Haraway urges us to foreground justice via new freedom projects. Through close readings of the work of Charlotte Rutherford and Nancy Scheper-Hughes, statistical analyses and ethnography both emerge as critical feminist technologies for producing convincing representations of the the reproduction of inequality.[48] Haraway asserts that social and health policies need to be constructed from the standpoints of those made most vulnerable by the sustained reproduction of inequalities.

Emily Martin presents us with a new woman, "The Woman in the Flexible Body." She articulates the North American social imaginary centered on health and the body which increasingly "has an international life, carried along with the global flows of goods, ads, images and people." The risk is that the flexible, adaptive, graceful, fluid, responsive, immunologically robust body/worker/person may well experience this new way of being-in-the-world as "liberation, even if one is moving across a tightrope." Yet few can successfully walk a tightrope, and no one can do so for long.

Rich with cultural images, Martin's paper demonstrates how these shift and change historically and in the present to reconfigure us to ourselves. This media-based imaginary of the flexible thus prefigures new sets of criteria for occupational and other kinds of stratification and normalization. Immune systems can be assessed like genetic maps: They can be found immediately "wanting" or "at risk" due to "preexisting conditions" or "predispositions." Martin worries about the seductiveness of the new metaphors of promise. In a provocative conclusion, she suggests, "While we are striving for the flexible, lean and agile, let us remember the virtues of the stable, the ample, the still."

Destabilizing Methods

A distinctive feature of feminist methodologies is how difficult they are to contain, how they bleed into everyday life. The borders between research and daily living are routinely and sometimes thoughtlessly crossed, only to reappear to us on the verge of publication, rupturing the pretense of some traditional scholarly claims requiring us again and again to open the black box of method. Rayna Rapp discusses how she came to see this clearly during her study of prenatal genetic counseling for amniocentesis in New York City.

Innovatively, Rapp chose to study one new reproductive technology across multiple sites. That is, she pursued an ethnographic understanding of this technology in many places among very divergent people—laboratory workers and technicians, genetic counselors, pregnant women and their partners—using very different kinds of medical services, geneticists, support groups for parents whose children have Down syndrome, and so on. She gradually pieced together a "layered picture of where some of the force fields of amniocentesis meet and resonate."[49]

In this age of information, she reeled it in as it came at her, asking more questions, referring people to newly discovered services, talking things over with respondents, colleagues, and friends, all of whom struggled for words for a new vocabulary with which to describe and engage the new situations in which they found themselves—a cross-cutting problem. Rapp gradually came to realize that ultimately she had located herself at the intersection of it all and there was no place to stand that was not "contaminated" with charged ethical and/or political issues. She had routinely violated research codes to fulfill moral/political commitments to be helpful to and empowering of respondents whenever possible. Some of her best data, she notes, was from her best friends and not respondents. And she had been called on to help improve the genetic counseling she' was studying for other purposes. She deals with these conflicts and "contaminants" by explicitly laying them out on the table for all to see. We become the jury and judge not only of a research report or product but of the very modes of working and a researcher's life itself. The research process and product are nonfungible.

In one of several moments in this book when the echos of different contributors became a chorus, Patti Lather titled her paper "Naked Methodology: Researching the Lives of Women Living with HIV/AIDS." The paper reflects—actually diffracts—her collaborative study of a support group (Lather and Smithies 1997), and her experiences in talking about this research in different venues. Here as there, she begins by baring process and product for all to see, starting from the premise that methodology is a ruin/rune. She seeks to delinete a theory of nakedness toward generating the theory of representation that itself structures her methodological imperatives. She seeks the vertigo produced by lifting layer after layer to get at "the naked truth," which is, of course, not there.

But the seeking is most productive in terms of delineating "methodological practices which work at the edges of what is currently available in moving toward *a social science with more to answer to* in terms of the complexities of language and the world." Her goal is not to do a better job at representing, but to explore how researchers can "be accountable to people's struggles for self-representation and self-determination" (Visweswaran 1988:39). Lather's recent published work, including her paper here, uses alternative textual practices as part of her effort to feature the voices and concerns of participants more clearly and distinctly from her own. She also explores the uses of and challenges posed by "response data"— what those studied themselves have to say about the research product (paper, book, whatever). Thus both Lather and Rapp are obsessed in productive ways with the risks of research, informing us that "do no harm" may be the key guiding tenet for contemporary human sciences researchers as well as for health care providers.

In contrast, the paper of Denise Segura and Adela de la Torre provides an in-depth critique of certain assumptions in quantitative research on Latina health in the United States. They focus most extensively on the static nature of empirical models of acculturation and how such models deny women's own agency in renegotiating and reinventing their identities and gender positions, especially through experiences of immigration. Worse, they argue that current U.S. health policy efforts to encourage recent Latina immigrants to maintain certain "good" health practices brought with them from "home" actually reinforce the exploitative and patriarchal elements of culturally idealized femininity captured in the icon *"La Sufrida"*—the one who willingly suffers on behalf of others in her family and her community. Instead of reinforcing *La Sufrida,* through examining recent ethnographic work Segura and de la Torre reveal a wide array of gender strategies being used today by Latinas to reconstruct their lives in new directions which they themselves view as more liberatory.[50] Cultural identities are and always have been fluid and contradictory, not icons to preserve at any cost. Western science and biomedicine can too easily collude with patriarchal cultural elements from elsewhere in its own interests.

Another critical methodological moment is provided by Marjorie DeVault, who argues that even feminist researchers have oversimplified and been categorically dismissive of so-called "women's professions" such as nutrition (and we would add nursing). Upon looking more closely, she finds such "intermediate" or "subordinate" professional sites to be much more complicated and, specifically, sites where revisioning and reform can bubble upward in daily practices through the active agency of women who live their professional lives under various male and other thumbs of oppression.

Becoming such a professional typically involves women in transformations of identity which are profoundly empowering for them. In turn, they may draw upon new strengths to nourish vulnerable social programs through difficult times, to start new ones, and to develop curricula that subvert others' agendas in favor of their own. As feminist scholars have carved out significant niches for our work, oftimes in hostile environments, so too have many women (feminist and other) in intermediate professional worlds.[51] Thus the paper by Segura and de la Torre and that by DeVault call upon researchers to attend more vociferously to the agency and actions of women negotiating their personal and professional lives far from the tops of Western hierarchies.

(Re)Constructing Experience: Searching the Self

The opening clip of *Dragnet,* an early television show with a long rerun shelf life, showed police detective Jack Webb on the phone, a disgusted look on his face, saying, "Please, just the facts, ma'am." His nasal voice dripped contempt for the emotional and the contextual, elements that feminists have been laboring to bring back into the human sciences. Sharon Traweek's paper demonstrates how searing "just the facts" can be. Like many things, facts can be deeply gendered, especially medical facts and experiences. Traweek searches herself and others, drawing on the biographies of a cohort of friends and colleagues as they intersected with the practices of obstetrics and gynecology in Japan, England, and the United States.

Traweek asks how can we live ourselves back into our research in conscious and explicit ways beyond Weberian "problem selection"—choosing to do research in areas we personally care about. How can we write and be present beyond the individual memoir form so very popular at this historical moment? Her startling answer is to write "just the facts" while we as readers "add back in" emotions and contexts.

Ruth Behar's "The Girl in the Cast" also explores the uses of lived experiences. She begins with a doubled perspective on a car accident in which nine-year-old Ruth's leg is broken—an erroneous newspaper report and her own recollections. A year in a body cast, her legs held apart by a rod between them which could be grasped to flip her over, a year of the bedpan every single time, a year in which her vision literally shrank because of her optical confinement. Yet it was also a year of a home tutor, "a teacher all to myself," and piles of books on her bed; the girl who returned to school was transformed into an English-speaking scholar-to-be. An old diary from this era becomes the path back into it, allowing Behar and us more direct access to this earlier time and self. Pieces of ourselves lay about us. We still confront the challenge of how to de-ghettoize such lived experiences, experiences we too bring with us to our sites of research—to work.

Françoise Verges searches the self from a critical stance in her paper on "(Post)Colonial Psychiatry." A series of distinctive moments in the history of psychiatry, positing different "selves" and different responsibilities of "culture(s)," has composed the making and unmaking of the colonized self. Despite changes and challenges within/out the postcolonies, postcolonial psychiatry today remains committed to the assimilation of non-Europeans into what is conceived as a higher order of psychological development—a modern Western "self." Global hierarchies dwell in psyches as well as markets.

Drawing on the work of Monnoni (who first directed the gaze onto the colonizers' psychology), Fanon (who studied the psychology of colonial racism), and Memmi (who sustained attention on colonizers' psychology), Verges examines colonizer male psychiatrists and their work on Reunion Island, a French Overseas Department in the Indian Ocean. She presents a case "in which diverse ethnic groups living in a society divided by class and race are pathologized, men feminized and women demonized," while *social and economic* conditions are transformed into *psychiatric* symptoms. Ultimately, in postcolonial psychiatry, non-European practices still "exist only as a support to the critique of Western psychiatry and not within their own logic." Psychiatry remains deeply colonial. Demonization of women, especially women of color, travels too easily.

Challenging New World Reproductive Orders

In feminist theory today, the argument is being widely made that reproduction has not been and certainly should be central to social theory. A long series of attempted erasures of the importance of women, reproduction, and even kinship produced these paucities of theory. Recent feminist work is both corrective and theoretically expansive, including Colen's (1989) concept of *stratified reproduction*, refering to the power relations by which some categories of people are encouraged to nurture and reproduce and are supported in doing so while others are disempowered.[52] Such *inequalities of reproduction* (Ginsberg and Rapp 1995:3) are often naturalized, made to appear inevitable, mirroring as they do other domains of social stratification, most notably, race and class.

In this volume, a series of papers takes up this theoretical challenge. They examine both material and discursive new world reproductive orders, exploring how these orders are co-constituitive. These orders have in some ways changed dramatically while in others have remained unchanged and still deadly. Anne Balsamo initiates the series by framing the cultural studies questions raised here: What are the relationships among cultural narratives and the social conditions of women? What are the material effects of discursive cultural representations? There are multiple feminist positions.

Balsamo's paper pursues the public nature of pregnancies and how cultural narratives of the surveillance of the pregnant body are now normative. (However, many pregnant material bodies are not surveilled due to lack of access to care.) "[N]ew reproductive technologies are used to discipline material, female bodies as if they were all potentially maternal bodies, and maternal bodies as if they were all potentially criminal." Balsamo pursues these themes through an analysis of *The Handmaid's Tale* as a speculative ethnography of the present. Significantly, she suggests that we think of reproductive technologies as *formations* in and of themselves, and that technological formations are distinctive *cultural formations*, requiring complex feminist analyses that take into account the highly divergent situations of involved and implicated women.

Such divergencies can be highlit through a technoscience studies approach. Balsamo examines the use of laparoscopy (a medical visualizing technology), which can turn problem pregnancies into public spectacles, constructing (selected, of course) cases of maternal "neglect" by "showing" how mothers-to-be have erred. Ingesting crack cocaine was clearly an error in the 1980s, and racialized caricatures of welfare mothers abounded.[53] Who is surveilled, when and for what purposes with the new reproductive technologies are key feminist questions.

Valerie Hartouni also uses a cultural studies approach to examine three seemingly unrelated cultural artifacts: an advertisement for bottled water showing a pregnant white woman, a Supreme Court ruling about abortion clinic picketing, and a CD-ROM titled *Nine Month Miracle*. "Situated in a reproductive landscape that has gradually been transformed over the course of the last decade through a proliferation of new forms and practices of life, these texts are also constituitive components of that landscape." Hartouni demonstrates how those components authorize particular forms of families, parents, pregnancies, babies, bodies, and—ultimately—worlds, while disenfranchising others. Illustrating hooks's (1992) concerns about "commodification of difference," some other products made by the producer of *Nine Month Miracle*, A.D.A.M. Software, Inc., allow the user to specify the race of the images to be viewed, shape-shifting hair and facial features to "fit" while the rest is merely retouched for color.[54] But the big news from all three artifacts is about gender. Women are natural if potentially dangerous mothers; uteruses are public spaces; and fetuses are now speaking subjects—in ads, in court, and on CD-ROMs. Such fetuses are, of course, all white, and their mothers are silenced.

Patricia Hill Collins's paper asks "Will the 'Real' Mother Please Stand Up?: The Logic of Eugenics and American National Family Planning." She asserts that traditional ideals about the family structure notions of "real" motherhood in American discourse, framing deeply racialized national identities and motherhood identities. This in turn feeds a logic of eugenics by which the nation-state seeks to "attend to its health" by reproductive policies that, through social engineering, enhance childbearing and rearing by the "fit" and decrease them among the "unfit."

Collins's argument is that there are separate and distinct American "national families" stratified by race and class; some are privileged by political and related discourses and social policies, while others are deprivileged and, in fact, attacked. All mothers are not created equal. In three contemporary cases examined, middle-class White families and mothers are viewed as "fit" biologically and culturally—able to fully reproduce desirable citizens—and are therefore privileged. Working-class White mothers are deemed "less fit"—biologically capable but culturally less so. While they are encouraged to have children, they receive much less support to raise them. Working-class African-American families and mothers are deemed unfit both biologically and culturally, and are therefore discouraged from having children and provided almost no support for raising them. Only some mothers are invited to stand up and be counted as "real" mothers.

Beth Richie takes us through the next step in her concern with how macro social structural elements of political economy themselves structure microsocial processes of parenting. These processes make poor and working-class Black mothers deeply vulnerable to stigmatization and marginalization as inadequate mothers, undermining them not only in the eyes of the dominant white culture—in popular discourse—but also in the eyes of their own families and communities—in their concrete material lives and local discourses and practices. Richie's paper is titled "The Social Construction of the Immoral Black Mother: Social Policy, Community Policing, and Their Effects on Youth Violence."

Richie documents a vicious circle: Poor Black mothers are limited in their abilities to parent by diminished economic and social resources; they therefore fear losing custody of their children (which children can manipulate); they are themselves vulnerable to the youth violence in their communities; their loyalties to family and community position them as both vulnerable to criticism and unable to defend against this without themselves criticizing family and community—especially around issues of sexism; last, if they do criticize and engage proactively in violence-prevention strategies, these women can and do feel even more more isolated, marginalized, and are at greater physical risk.

Far from the mommy track and soccer mom land, Richie documents how black women's mothering is constructed as responsible for a vast array of contemporary social problems: pathological family forms, draining social resources, breeding unwanted children who are themselves risks to society. Their very mothering is deemed somehow radically different and perverse.[55] Many of the postcolonial psychiatric constructions of creole mothers as demonized on the islands of Reunion that Verges documents elsewhere in this volume appear all too vividly in the popular and "scientific" discourses about Black mothers in the United States. Across race and class, contemporary discourses about mothers-to-be and mothers routinely undermine and degrade women. Only middle-class White mothers receive discursive validation and support, and even that is often trivializing, partial, and highly conditional.

Revised and Disruptive Agendas for Women's Health

In some ways, this entire book provides revised and disruptive agendas for women's health and should, in fact, be read as doing so. From Haraway's virtual speculum to Richie's mothers trying to survive in violent times, agendas for revisioning problems and revising policies abound. In this last section of the book, three more specific agendas are formulated.

First, Sheryl Burt Ruzek urges us to think seriously about and through women's interests in health reform. Her paper directly addresses some of the complicated cost issues and the radical changes in health care delivery mentioned above. Ruzek also provides an overview of the agenda of the feminist/women's health movement coalition, which responded to health reform efforts with the Campaign for Women's Health—representing over a hundred organizations and eight million women. Sophisticated feminist health activists have shown that women can be mobilized rapidly around health issues.

Yet Ruzek argues that this campaign did not take costs adequately into account and glossed over income and insurance differences among women. Echoing Harding's (1993:3) concept of "*over*advantaged elites," Ruzek cautions that some very difficult recommendations, trade-offs, and even sacrifices on the parts of some currently more privileged women may be requisite to have more just and equitable distribution of primary, preventive, and basic health care. Coverage for some "boutique" procedures may need to be eliminated or minimized to assure full access to the basics. Ruzek makes the painful point that boutique medicine should be paid for out-of-pocket and that "choice" beyond basic care is truly a luxury—even for American women.

Also looking ahead painfully, Jennifer Terry notes that her long experience studying the history of medical constructions of lesbians and their health and illness did not prepare her for the inadequacies of contemporary biomedical understandings and practices. From lesbian-feminist self-help politics in the 1970s to new forms of lesbian health activism in the 1990s, Terry elucidates both continuities and changes in terms of what counts as lesbian, as health, and as a satisfactory relationship between activism and expertise.

Terry's synoptic analysis of lesbians' health activist texts demonstrates the interelations of psychological, physiological, and societal factors that are central to an adequate understanding of lesbian health. The reclaiming of sexuality in the 1980s was also requisite.[56] Like Ruzek, Terry raises issues of costs and access in a time of retrenchment, noting that much of the work to date was done during a more expansive era. The challenges to lesbian and gay communities posed by HIV/AIDS are elaborated, along with the distinctive vulnerabilities of lesbians to breast cancer. Today the research era has arrived and lesbians themselves are more actively involved in knowledge production than ever before.[57]

There's more to midlife women's health than menopause is the fundamental argument put forward by Nancy Fugate Woods. What Coney (1994) has called *The Menopause Industry*[58] is composed of all the actors (human and nonhuman) involved in menopause, from midlife women to pharmaceutical research and development scientists, Premarin tablets, physicians, alternative health care providers, the makers of Depends, the National Institute on Aging, and so on.[59] Woods is concerned about the discursive as well as the material consequences: "At the same time the models of menopause organize an industry, they also function covertly to influence women's images of themselves and their bodies" in ways which can ultimately undermine women.

Biomedicine constructs midlife solely as menopause and menopause solely as disease *and* risk factor for disease, framing new surveillance medicine terms such as "endocrinopathy" to describe this. In sharp contrast, Woods and others' research has revealed that women's own constructions differ in profound ways and even conflict with such conceptions. Few women defined menopause as a medical event, but rather as cessation of periods, fertility, and bodily change. Women's own constructions seem to resist or perhaps dwell outside biomedicalized visions echoing Martin's (1987) earlier work. Woods argues that we need to produce new knowledge about this era of women's lives unencumbered by old categories of received theory and biomedicine.

Our last words are about "Resisting Closure, Embracing Uncertainties, Creating Agendas." In concluding, we attempt to diffract our mission for this book and create spaces for the kinds of destabilizations we hope it will provoke. It is our desire that this book will crack the conceptual carapace that has rigidified the very terms in which we can think about our lives, well-being, health, contentment, and even happiness. Today issues about women, health, and healing are not only applied, how-to questions, but also—and with considerable urgency— broader social, cultural and theoretical questions about the nature of the lives we lead and want to lead, and the very directions we think feminist social change should take.

Notes

1. Special thanks to Val Hartouni, Patti Lather, and Lisa Jean Moore for fast readings and conceptual help with this introduction.
2. See Star and Griesemer 1989 for another example, "boundary objects."
3. The goodness of practices lies in the details. See Ruzek, Olesen, and Clarke 1997; Dan 1994; Fee and Kreiger 1994; Fogel and Woods 1994; Moss 1996; Rosser 1994; Adams 1995; Bair and Cayleff 1993; White 1990; Apple 1990; Corea 1985; hooks 1994; de la Torre and Pesquera 1993; Smith 1995; Mastroianni, Faden, and Federman 1994a,b; Bayne-Smith 1996; Lorber 1997; McClain 1989; Olesen and Stacey 1993.
4. See, on gender issues, e.g., Hawksworth 1997; Annandale and Clark 1996; Butler 1990, 1993; Fraser 1989; Gatens 1996; McKenna et al. 1997; Visweswaran 1997; and Jaggar and Bordo 1989.
5. See Carby 1982; McNeil and Franklin 1991; Franklin, Lury, and Stacey 1991; Traweek 1993; Franklin 1995b; Balsamo 1996; and Gordon 1995.
6. We mean this here in both the Derridean and pragmatic philosophical senses of implicatedness through involvement. Practices are constitutive; opposition is a form of engagement. See Derrida 1991; Clarke and Fujimura 1992; Rorty 1991; Fraser 1989.
7. See, for example, Fausto-Sterling 1993, 1999; Oudshoorn 1994; Stone 1991, 1996; Gatens 1992; Jordanova 1989; Schiebinger 1989, 1993; Terry 1990.
8. See ISNA 1995–98; Angier 1997; Dreger 1997; Park and Daston 1995.
9. See e.g., Foucault 1978; Seidman 1996; Stone 1991, 1996; Rubin 1993.
10. See e.g., Bell 1995; Clarke 1998; Duden 1991; Harding 1991; Longino 1990; Jordanova 1989; Keller 1995; Martin 1987; Moscucci 1990; Oudshoorn 1994; Schiebinger 1989, 1993; and Stepan 1986.
11. See note 4 above.
12. See, e.g., Rosaldo and Lamphere 1974. Ortner's paper in that volume, "Is Female to Male as Nature is to Culture?" is a classic. In her argument that women are no closer to "nature" than men, one sees glimmerings of the idea that nature itself is a construct of culture.
13. See for example, Carby 1982; Collins 1990; Davis 1990; hooks 1992; Hurtado 1989; Moraga and Anzaldua 1981; Anzaldua 1987; Mohanty 1989; Segura and Pierce 1993; and James and Busia 1993.
14. See, e.g., Richie 1994, 1996; Hartouni 1997; Ong 1995. Ong (1995:1243), for example, examines how Asian-American clinicians and Khmer refugees are "equally caught up in webs of power involving control and subterfuge, appropriation and resistance, negotiation and learning that constitute biopolitical lessons of what becoming an American may entail for an underprivileged Asian group."
15. See, e.g., Mahoney and Yngvesson 1992.
16. On feminist qualitative research, see Olesen 1994; Behar 1997; Lather 1995; Lather and Smithies 1997; and Visweswaren 1994, 1997.
17. See Fujimura 1997; and Star 1991.
18. Popular media feminist discourse studies include Hartouni 1991, 1997; Penley 1997; and Bertin and Beck 1996.
19. See, e.g., Martin 1987, 1994; Schiebinger 1989, 1993; Oudshoorn 1994; Bell 1995; Bertin and Beck 1996; Duden 1991; Franklin 1995a, 1997; Hammonds 1994, 1997; Haraway 1989, 1991, 1997.
20. On institutional ethnography, see Smith 1990; and Campbell and Manicom 1995.
21. On difference, see e.g., Barrett 1987; Gatens 1992; Rhode 1990; Scott 1988; Felski 1997; Braidotti et al. 1997; Zinn and Dill 1996; and Terry and Urla 1995. On doing difference, see West and Fenstermaker 1995 and Collins et al. 1995. See also, on doing gender, West and Zimmerman 1987.

22. See e.g., Harris 1993; Littleton 1987; Minow 1987; Crenshaw et al. 1995; and Matsuda 1996.

23. In the first wave of feminist activism in the early twentieth century, the women's health issues taken up by divergent groups were birth control and maternal and child health; see, e.g., Chesler 1992; Marieskind 1980. The first and last full entitlement program for which all mothers and children were automatically eligible was framed in the Sheppard-Towner Act, passed very soon after women got the vote, and lasted from 1922 to 1929, when conservatives repealed it.

24. Recently a major professional journal in sociology generated a list of the ten most influential books to have appeared over the last quarter century. *Our Bodies, Ourselves* was on that list along with the work of such scholarly luminaries as Michel Foucault, Clifford Geertz, and Edward Said. See also Seaman 1969; and Ehrenreich and English 1979.

25. On the women's health movements, see Ruzek 1978, 1980; Dreifus 1978; Scully 1980; Simmons, Kay and Regan 1984; Zimmerman 1987; Worcester and Whatley 1988; Avery 1990; Boston Women's Health Book Collective 1994; Doyal 1994; Fee and Krieger 1994; Norsigian 1994, 1996; and Moss 1996.

26. See Federation 1981a,b. These are available only through the Federation, 633 East Eleventh Ave., Eugene, Oregon 97401 USA (503-344-0966).

27. For listings of major U.S. and other national and transnational organizations, see the Boston Women's Health Book Collective (1992:709–12,730–32). P.O. Box 192, Somerville, MA 02144 USA (617-625-0271), E-mail bwhbc@igc.apc.org See also National Women's Health Network, 514 Tenth St., Suite 400, Washington, D.C. 20004 (202-347-1140).

28. The latter group meets in 1998 in Cairo and in 2000 in San Francisco during the last week of January. For information on the San Francisco meetings, contact Professor Afaf Meleis, MHCAN, Box 0608, UCSF, San Francisco, CA 94143-0608 (415-476-1775), E-mail: meleis@itsa.ucsf.edu, fax 415-476-6042.

29. See on breast cancer, e.g., Altman 1996 and Belkin 1996; and for recent work by historians of women and the welfare state, e.g., Abramowitz 1988; Gordon 1994; Quadagno 1994.

30. For extensive discussion of the federal situation and initiatives, see Mastroianni, Faden, and Federman 1994a,b; Rosser 1988, 1994; Dan 1994; Dickersin and Schnaper 1996; Ruzek, Olesen, and Clarke 1997; and Benderly 1997.

31. See Part I of Dan 1994.

32. See Riessman 1983 and Figert 1996.

33. See, e.,g., Dan 1994 and Fogel and Woods 1994.

34. See, for recent formulations of standpoint theory, Heckman 1997 and Hartsock et al. 1997.

35. On difference, see note 21.

36. See, e.g., Adams 1995; Bair and Cayleff 1993; White 1990; hooks 1994; de la Torre 1993; and Smith 1995.

37. See, for example, Williams 1995; Williams and Collins 1995; Gamble and Blustein 1994; Krieger et al. 1993; and Krieger and Fee 1994.

38. See, e.g., Harris 1993; Crenshaw et al. 1995; and Matsuda 1996.

39. See Terry 1990; Terry and Urla 1995; Armstrong 1995; and Lupton 1994.

40. See, e.g., Estes and Binney 1989; Gordon 1988; Koenig 1988.

41. On medical anthropology, see Casper and Koenig (1996); on sociology of health and illness, see Lupton 1994; and Casper and Berg 1995; on the history of medicine, see Warner 1995.

42. See, for example, Forsythe 1992; and Bowker and Star 1994.

43. On biomedicalization, see Zola 1976; Conrad and Schneider 1980; Riessman 1983; and Estes and Binney 1989.

44. See, e.g., MacFarquhar 1997. A new journal titled *The Scientific Review of Alternative Medicine* just began.

45. See Worcester and Whatley 1988; Simmons, Kay, and Regan 1984; and Ruzek 1980.

46. See Norsigian 1994; and Part VII in Ruzek, Olesen and Clarke 1997; as well as Ruzek's article in this volume.

47. See Herzlich and Pierret 1986; Crawford 1985; Lupton 1994; and Armstrong 1995. On the concept of social suffering, see Green 1998.

48. History too offers an important technology for understanding the reproduction of inequality. David Kertzer's (1994) study of the liaison between the state and the Catholic Church in Italy and other parts of Europe into the twentieth century is exemplary. Through this liaison, a mode of organized and enforced infant abandonment by single women and others was authorized that accounted for up to half of all births in some areas. Poor women were coerced into serving as wet nurses in church/state creches, but the infant death rates were very, very high. The system, Kertzer argues, protected especially single but also married men from the burdens of unwanted marriage or children. Today, Italy has the lowest birth rate in the world.

49. See Marcus 1995; and Visweswaran 1994.

50. And such efforts at renegotiating gender are far from limited to the United States. See, for example, Adelaida del Castillo's (1993) work on Mexico. For fresh conceptualization of intercultures, see Heilemann 1996.

51. See also Stage 1997; and Tsing 1993.

52. On feminist approaches to reproduction, see Ginsberg and Rapp 1995; Franklin 1995a, 1997; Clarke 1995, 1998; Casper 1994, 1998; Strathern 1992; Rubin 1975; Cussins 1996; Dixon-Muller 1993; Greenhalgh 1995, 1996; Hartouni 1991, 1997; Kertzer 1994; Oudshoorn 1996; Petchesky 1990; Rothman 1984; Rapp 1998; and Stanworth 1987.

53. See also Young 1994; and Hartouni 1991.

54. See Moore and Clarke (in preparation).

55. See also Roberts 1995.

56. See also Rubin 1993.

57. See, for example, Ponticelli 1998.

58. This parallels what Estes (1979) called *The Aging Enterprise* some years ago, and Clarke (1998) discusses as the reproductive enterprise. On menopause, see also Vines 1994.

59. We extend both Coney and Woods here to take insights from technoscience studies about the fundamental importance of the nonhuman into account. Haraway (1992) and Latour (1993) both pioneered in such reconceptualizations, reminding us how much the material world "matters."

References

Abramowitz, Mimi. 1988. *Regulating the Lives of Women: Social Welfare Policy from Colonial Times to the Present.* Boston: South End Press.

Adams, Diane L. (ed.). 1995. *Health Issues for Women of Color: A Cultural Diversity Perspective.* Thousand Oaks, CA: Sage.

Alcoff, Linda. 1997. Cultural Feminism versus Post-Structuralism: The Identity Crisis in Feminist Theory. Pp. 330–55 in Linda J. Nicholson, (ed.), *Second Wave: A Reader in Feminist Theory.* New York: Routledge.

Altman, Roberta. 1996. *Waking Up/Fighting Back: The Politics of Breast Cancer.* Boston: Little Brown and Company.

Angier, Natalie. 1997. New Debate over Surgery on Genitals. *New York Times,* May 13:B7.

Annandale, Ellen, and Judith Clark. 1996. What Is Gender? Feminist Theory and the Sociology of Human Reproduction. *Sociology of Health and Illness* 18(1):17–44.

Anzaldua, Gloria. 1987. *Borderlands/La Fronters: The New Mestiza.* San Francisco: Spinsters/Aunt Lute.

Apple, Rima (ed.). 1990. *The History of Women, Health and Medicine in America: An Encyclopedic Handbook.* New York: Garland Press.

Arditti, Rita, Renate Duelli Klein, and Shelley Minden (eds.). 1984. *Test Tube Women: What Future for Motherhood?* Boston: Pandora/Routledge Kegan Paul.

Armstrong, David. 1995. The Rise of Surveillance Medicine. *Sociology of Health and Illness* 17(3):393–404.

Aronson, Naomi. 1984. Science as Claimsmaking: Implications for Social Problems Research. Pp. 1–30 in Joseph Schneider and John Kitsuse (eds.), *Studies in the Sociology of Social Problems.* Norwood: Ablex.

Avery, Byllye Y. 1990. Breathing Life into Ourselves: The Evolution of the National Black Women's Health Project, Pp. 4–10 in Evelyn White (ed.), *The Black Woman's Health Book.* Seattle: Seal Press.

Bair, Barbara, and Cayleff, Susan E. (eds.). 1993. *Wings of Gauze: Women of Color and the Experience of Health and Illness.* Detroit: Wayne State University Press.

Balsamo, Anne. 1996. *Technologies of the Gendered Body: Reading Cyborg Women.* Durham, NC: Duke University Press.

Barrett, Michele. 1987. The Concept of Difference. *Feminist Review* 26:29–41.

Barrett, Michele, and Anne Phillips (eds.). 1992. *Destabilizing Theory: Contemporary Feminist Debates.* Stanford: Stanford University Press.

Barroso, Carmen, and Sonia Corea. 1995. Public Servants, Professionals and Feminists: The Politics of Contraception in Brazil. Pp. 292–322 in Faye Ginsberg and Rayna Rapp (eds.), *Concerning the New World Order.* Berkeley: University of California Press.

Bayne-Smith, Marcia (ed.). 1996. *Race, Gender and Health.* Thousand Oaks, CA: Sage.

Behar, Ruth. 1996. *The Vulnerable Observer: Anthropology that Breaks Your Heart.* Boston: Beacon.

Belkin, Lisa. 1996. Charity Begins at . . . The Marketing Meeting, the Gala Event, The Product Tie-In. *New York Times Magazine,* December 22:40–57.

Bell, Susan. 1994. Translating Science to the People: Updating the New *Our Bodies, Ourselves. Women's Studies International Forum,* 17(1):9–18.

Benderly, Beryl Lieff, for the Institute of Medicine. 1997. *In Her Own Right: The Institute of Medicine's Guide to Women's Health Issues.* Washington, DC: National Academy Press.

Bertin, Joan E., and Laurie R. Beck. 1996. Of Headlines and Hypotheses: The Role of Gender in Popular Press Coverage of Women's Health and Biology. Pp. 37–56 in Kary L. Moss (ed.). *Man-Made Medicine.* Durham and London: Duke University Press.

Blumer, Herbert. 1993. *Symbolic Interactionism: Perspective and Method.* Berkeley: University of California Press.

Boston Women's Health Book Collective. 1970. *Our Bodies, Our Selves.* Boston: New England Free Press.

———. 1976. *Our Bodies, Our Selves.* New York: Simon and Schuster.

———. 1984. *The New Our Bodies, Our Selves.* Second edition. New York: Simon and Schuster.

———. 1994. *The New Our Bodies, Our Selves.* Third edition. New York: Simon and Schuster.

Bowker, Geof, and Susan Leigh Star. 1994. Knowledge and Infrastructure in International Information Management: Problems of Classification and Coding. In Lisa Bud-Frierman (ed.) *Information Acumen.* London: Routledge.

Braidotti, Rosi, Drucilla Cornell, Ien Ang, and Rita Felski. 1997. Comment and Response to Felski's "The Doxa of Difference." *Signs: Journal of Women in Culture and Society* 23(1):23–46.

Broom, Dorothy H. 1991. *Damned if We Do: Contradictions in Women's Health Care.* Sydney: Allen and Unwin.

Brown, Wendy. 1995. *States of Injury: Power and Freedom in Later Modernity.* Princeton: Princeton University Press.

Butler, Judith. 1990. *Gender Trouble: Feminism and the Subversion of Identity*. New York: Routledge.

———. 1993. *Bodies that Matter*. New York: Routledge.

Campbell, Marie, and Ann Manicom (eds.). 1995. *Knowledge, Experience and Ruling Relations: Studies in the Social Organization of Knowledge*. Toronto: University of Toronto Press.

Carby, Hazel. 1982. White Woman Listen! Black Feminism and the Boundaries of Sisterhood. Pp. 212–35 in Paul Gilroy/The Race and Politics Group (eds.), *The Empire Strikes Back*. London: Century Hutchinson, Ltd.

Casper, Monica. 1994. Reframing and Grounding Nonhuman Agency: What Makes a Fetus an Agent? *American Behavioral Scientist* 37(6):839–56.

———. 1998. *The Making of the Unborn Patient: Medical Work and the Politics of Reproduction in Experimental Fetal Surgery, 1963–1993*. New Brunswick, NJ: Rutgers University Press.

Casper, Monica, and Marc Berg. 1995. Constructivist Perspectives on Medical Work: Medical Practices and Science and Technology Studies. *Science, Technology and Human Values* 20:395–407.

Casper, Monica, and Barbara Koenig. 1996. Reconfiguring Nature and Culture: Intersections of Medical Anthropology and Technoscience Studies. *Medical Anthropology Quarterly* 10(4):523–36.

Chesler, Ellen. 1992. *Woman of Valor: Margaret Sanger and the Birth Control Movement in America*. New York: Simon and Schuster.

Clarke, Adele E. 1990. Women's Health Over the Life Cycle. Pp. 3–39 in Rima Apple (ed.), *The History of Women, Health, and Medicine in America*. New York: Garland Press.

———. 1995. Modernity, Postmodernity and Human Reproductive Processes c. 1890–1990, or "Mommy, Where do Cyborgs Come From Anyway?" Pp. 139–55 in Chris Hables Gray (ed.) with Heidi J. Figueroa-Sarriera and Steven Mentor, *The Cyborg Handbook*. New York: Routledge.

———. 1998. *Disciplining Reproduction: Modernity, American Life Sciences and the "Problems of Sex."* Berkeley: University of California Press.

Clarke, Adele E., and Joan H. Fujimura (eds.) 1992. *The Right Tools for the Job: At Work in Twentieth Century Life Sciences*. Princeton: Princeton University Press.

Clarke, Adele E. and Theresa Montini. 1993. The Many Faces of RU486: Tales of Situated Knowledges and Technological Contestations. *Science, Technology and Human Values* 18(1):42–78.

Clarke, Adele E., and Alice Wolfson. 1990. Reproductive Rights Organizing. Pp. 258–67 in Karen Hansen and Ilene Phillipson (eds.), *Women, Class and the Feminist Imagination*. Philadelphia: Temple University Press.

Colen, Shellee. 1989. "Just a Little Respect": West Indian Domestic Workers in New York City. In Elsa M. Chaney and Maria Garcia Castro (eds.), *Muchachas No More: Household Workers in Latin America and the Caribbean*. Philadelphia: Temple University Press.

Collins, Patricia Hill. 1990. *Black Feminist Thought: Knowledge, Consciousness and the Politics of Empowerment*. Boston, MA: Unwin Hyman.

Collins, Patricia Hill, Lionel A. Maldonado, Dana Y. Takagi, Barrie Thorne, Lynn Weber, and Howard Winant. 1995. Symposium on West and Fenstermaker's "Doing Difference." *Gender and Society* 9(4):491–513.

Coney, Sandra. 1994. *The Menopause Industry: How the Medical Establishment Exploits Women*. Alameda CA: Hunter House.

Conrad, Peter. 1992. Medicalization and Social Control. *Annual Review of Sociology* 18:209–32.

Conrad, Peter, and Joseph Schneider. 1980. *Deviance and Medicalization: From Badness to Sickness*. St. Louis, MO: C.V. Mosby.

Corea, Gena. 1985. *The Hidden Malpractice: How American Medicine Mistreats Women.* Updated edition. New York: Harper Colophon.

Cornell, Drucilla. 1992. Gender, Sex and Equivalent Rights. Pp. 280–86 in Judith Butler and Joan Scott (eds.), *Feminists Theorize the Political.* New York: Routledge.

Crawford, Robert. 1985. A Cultural Account of "Health": Control, Release and the Social Body. Pp. 60–105 in John B. McKinlay (ed.), *Issues in the Political Economy of Health Care.* London: Tavistock.

Crenshaw, Kimberly et al. (eds.). 1995. *Critical Race Theory: The Key Writings.* New York: New Press/Norton.

Cronon, William (ed.) 1995. Uncommon Ground: Toward Reinventing Nature. New York: Norton.

Cussins, Charis. 1996. Ontological Choreography: Agency Through Objectification in Infertility Clinics. *Social Studies of Science* 26:575–610.

Dan, Alice (Ed.) 1994. *Reframing Women's Health: Multidisciplinary Research and Practice.* Thousand Oaks, CA: Sage.

Davis, Angela Y. 1990. Sick and Tired of Being Sick and Tired: The Politics of Black Women's Health. Pp. 18-26 in Evelyn White (ed.), *The Black Women's Health Book.* Seattle: Seal Press.

deGrazia, Victoria, with Ellen Furlough (eds.). 1996. *The Sex of Things: Gender and Consumption in Historical Perspective.* Berkeley: University of California Press.

de la Torre, Adela. 1993. Key Issues in Latina Health: Voicing Latina Concerns in the Health Financing Debate. Pp. 157-68 in Norma Alarcon et al. (eds.), *Chicana Critical Issues.* Berkeley: Third Woman Press.

de la Torre, Adela, and Beatriz Pesquera (eds.). 1993. *Building with Our Hands.* Berkeley: University of California Press.

del Castillo, Adelaida. 1993. Covert Cultural Norms and Sex/Gender Meaning: A Mexico City Case. *Urban Anthropology* 22(3–4):237–57.

Derrida, Jacques. 1991. *A Derrida Reader.* New York: Columbia University Press.

DeVault, Marjorie L. 1991. *Feeding the Family: The Social Organization of Caring as Gendered Work.* Chicago: University of Chicago Press.

Dickersin, Kay, and Lauren Schnaper. 1996. Reinventing Medical Research. Pp. 57–78 in Kary L. Moss (ed.), *Man-Made Medicine.* Durham and London: Duke University Press.

Dixon-Mueller, Ruth. 1993. *Population Policy and Women's Rights: Transforming Reproductive Choice.* New York: Praeger.

Djerassi, Carl. 1981. *The Politics of Contraception: Birth Control in the Year 2001.* San Francisco, CA: W. H. Freeman.

Doyal, Lesley. 1994. Women, Health, and the Sexual Division of Labor: A Case Study of the Women's Health Movement. Pp. 61–77 in Elizabeth Fee and Nancy Krieger (eds.), *Women's Health Politics, and Power.* Farmingdale, NY: Baywood.

———. 1996. The Politics of Women's Health: Setting a Global Agenda. *International Journal of Health Services* 26(1):47–65.

Dreger, Alica. 1997. Ethical Problems in Intersex Treatment. *Medical Humanities Report* 19(1):1.

Dreifus, Claudia. 1978. *Seizing Our Bodies: The Politics of Women's Health.* New York: Vintage/Random House.

Duden, Barbara. 1991. *The Woman Beneath the Skin: A Doctor's Patients in Eighteenth-Century Germany.* Translated by Thomas Dunlap. Cambridge, MA: Harvard University Press.

Edgley, Charles, and Dennis Brissett. 1990. Health Nazis and the Cult of the Perfect Body: Some Polemical Observations. *Symbolic Interaction* 3l(2):257–80.

Ehrenreich, Barbara, and Deirdre English. 1979. *For Her Own Good: 150 Years of the Experts' Advice to Women.* Garden City, NY: Anchor/Doubleday.

Eisenberg, David, Ronald Kessler, Cindy Foster, Frances Norlock, David Calkins, and Thomas Delbanco. 1993. Unconventional Medicine in the United States. *New England Journal of Medicine* 328:246–52.

Epstein, Steven. 1996. *Impure Science: AIDS, Activism and the Politics of Knowledge.* Berkeley: University of California Press.

Estes, Carroll L. 1979. *The Aging Enterprise.* San Francisco: Jossey-Bass.

Estes, Carroll L., and Elizabeth A. Binney. 1989. The Biomedicalization of Aging: Dangers and Dilemmas. *The Gerontologist* 29(5):587–96.

Evans, Judith. 1995. *Feminist Theory Today: An Introduction to Second Wave Feminism.* Thousand Oaks, CA: Sage.

Fausto-Sterling, Anne. 1993. The Five Sexes. *The Sciences* (March–April):20–25.

———. 1999. *Body-Building: How Biologists Construct Sexuality.* New York: Basic Books.

Federation of Feminist Women's Health Centers. 1981a. *A New View of the Woman's Body.* New York: Simon and Schuster.

———. 1981b. *How to Stay Out of the Gynecologist Office.* Los Angeles: Women to Women Publications. [See address in note 26 .]

Fee, Elizabeth. 1983. Women and Health Care: A Comparison of Theories. Pp. 17–34 in E. Fee (ed.), *Women and Health: The Politics of Sex in Medicine.* Farmingdale, NY: Baywood.

Fee, Elizabeth, and Krieger, Nancy (eds.). 1994. *Women's Health, Politics, and Power: Essays on Sex/Gender, Medicine and Public Health.* Amityville, NY: Baywood.

Felski, Rita. 1997. The Doxa of Difference. *Signs: Journal of Women in Culture and Society* 23(1):1–22.

Figert, Anne. 1996. *Women and the Ownership of PMS: The Structuring of a Psychiatric Disorder.* New York: Aldine de Gruyter.

Fine, Gary Allen. 1994. Wild Life: Authenticity and the Human Experience of "Natural" Places. Pp. 156–75 in Carolyn Ellis and Michael Flaherty (eds.), *Investigating Subjectivity: Research on Lived Experience.* Thousand Oaks, CA: Sage.

Fisher, Sue. 1986. *In the Patient's Best Interest: Women and the Politics of Medical Decisions.* New Brunswick, NJ: Rutgers University Press.

———. 1995. *Nursing Wounds: Nurse Practitioners, Doctors, Women Patients and the Negotiation of Meaning.* New Brunswick, NJ: Rutgers University Press.

Fogel, Catherine Ingram, and Nancy Fugate Woods (eds.). 1994. *Women's Health Care: A Comprehensive Handbook.* Thousand Oaks, CA: Sage.

Folbre, Nancy. 1994. *Who Pays for the Kids? Gender and the Structures of Constraint.* New York: Routledge.

Forsythe, Diana E. 1992. Blaming the User in Medical Informatics. *Knowledge and Society: The Anthropology of Science and Technology* 9:95–115.

Foucault, Michel. 1975. *The Birth of the Clinic.* New York: Vintage.

———. 1977. *Discipline and Punish.* Harmondsworth UK: Penguin.

———. 1978. *The History of Sexuality. Volume I: An Introduction.* New York: Vintage.

Franklin, Sarah. 1995a. Postmodern Procreation: A Cultural Account of Assisted Reproduction. Pp. 323–45 in Faye D. Ginsberg and Rayna Rapp (eds.), *Conceiving the New World Order.* Berkeley: University of California Press.

———. 1995b. Science as Culture, Cultures of Science. *Annual Review of Anthropology* 24:163–84.

———. 1997. *Embodied Progress: A Cultural Account of Assisted Contraception.* London and New York: Routledge.

Franklin, Sarah, Celia Lury, and Jackie Stacey (eds.). 1991. *Off-Centre: Feminism and Cultural Studies.* London: Harper Collins Academic.

Fraser, Nancy. 1989. *Unruly Practices: Power, Discourse and Gender in Contemporary Social Theory.* Minneapolis: University of Minnesota Press.

————. 1997. Structuralism or Pragmatics? On Discourse Theory and Feminist Politics. Pp. 379–95 in Linda J. Nicholson (ed.), *Second Wave: A Reader in Feminist Theory.* New York: Routledge.

Fraser, Nancy, and Linda J. Nicholson. 1990. Social Criticism Without Philosophy: An Encounter Between Feminism and Postmodernism. Pp. 19–38 in Linda J. Nicholson (ed.), *Feminism/Postmodernism.* New York: Routledge.

Fujimura, Joan H. 1996. *Crafting Science: A Sociohistory of the Quest for the Genetics of Cancer.* Cambridge, MA: Harvard University Press.

Gamble, Vanessa Northington, and Bonnie Blustein. 1994. Racial Differentials in Medical Care: Implications for Research on Women. Pp. 174–91 in Anna C. Mastroianni, Ruth Faden, and Daniel Federman (eds.), *Women and Health Research,* vol. 1. Washington, DC: National Academy Press.

Gatens, Moira. 1992. Power, Bodies and Difference. Pp. 120–37 in Michele Barrett and Anne Phillips (eds.), *Destabilizing Theory: Contemporary Feminist Debates.* Stanford: Stanford University Press.

————. 1996. A Critique of the Sex/Gender Distinction. Pp. 3–20 in *Imaginary Bodies: Ethics, Power and Corporeality.* London: Routledge.

Ginsberg, Faye D., and Rayna Rapp (eds.). 1995. *Conceiving the New World Order: The Global Stratification of Reproduction.* Berkeley: University of California Press.

Goffman, Erving. 1959. *The Presentation of Self in Everyday Life.* Garden City, NY: Anchor Doubleday.

Gordon, Deborah A. 1995. Review Essay: Feminism and Cultural Studies. *Feminist Studies* 21(2):363–77.

Gordon, Deborah R. 1988. Tenacious Assumptions in Western Medicine. In Margaret Lock and Deborah Gordon (eds.), *Biomedicine Examined.* Dordrecht: Kluwer.

Gordon, Linda. 1994. *Pitied but Not Entitled: Single Mothers and the History of Welfare.* New York: Free Press.

Gordon, Linda, and Barrie Thorne. 1996. Our Bodies, Our Selves—A Book By and For Women. *Contemporary Sociology: A Journal of Reviews* 25(3):322–25.

Green, Linda. 1998. Lived Lives and Social Suffering: Problems and Concerns in Medical Anthropology. *Medical Anthropology Quarterly* 12(1):3–7.

Greenhalgh, Susan (ed.). 1995. *Situating Fertility: Anthropology and Demographic Inquiry.* Cambridge: Cambridge University Press.

————. 1996. The Social Construction of Population Science: An Intellectual, Institutional and Political History of Twentieth-Century Demography. *Comparative Studies in Society and History* 38(1):26–66.

Grossberg, Lawrence, Cary Nelson, and Paula Treichler (eds.). 1992. *Cultural Studies.* New York: Routledge.

Hammonds, Evelynn. 1994. Black (W)holes and the Geometry of Black Female Sexuality. *Differences* 6(2–3):126–45.

————. 1997. Toward a Genealogy of Black Female Sexuality: The Problematic of Silence. Pp. 170–82 in M. Jacqui Alexander and Chandra Talpade Mohanty (eds.), *Feminist Genealogies, Colonial Legacies, Democratic Future.* New York: Routledge.

Haraway, Donna. 1985. A Cyborg Manifesto: Science, Technology, and Socialist-Feminism in the Late Twentieth Century. *Socialist Review 80:65–107.*

————. 1989. *Primate Visions: Gender, Race and Nature in the World of Modern Science.* New York: Routledge.

————. 1991. *Simians, Cyborgs and Women: The Reinvention of Nature.* New York: Routledge.

————. 1992. Promises of Monsters. A Regenerative Politics for Inappropriate/d Others. Pp. 295–337 in Lawrence Grossberg, Cary Nelson, and Paula Treichler (eds.), *Cultural Studies.* New York: Routledge.

————. 1997. *Modest_Witness@Second_Millenium. FemaleMan©_Meets_Oncomouse™: Feminist and Technoscience.* New York and London: Routledge.

Harding, Sandra. 1991. *Whose Science? Whose Knowledge? Thinking from Women's Lives.* Ithaca: Cornell University Press.

———— (ed.). 1993. *The "Racial" Economy of Science: Toward a Democratic Future.* Bloomington: Indiana University Press.

Harris, Cheryl. 1993. Whiteness as Property. *Harvard Law Review* 106(8):1707–91.

Hartouni, Valerie. 1991. Containing Women: Reproductive Discourse in the 1980s. Pp. 27–56 in Constance Penley and Andrew Ross (eds.), *Technoculture.* Minneapolis: University of Minnesota Press.

————. 1997. *Cultural Conceptions: On Reproductive Technologies and the Remaking of Life.* Minneapolis: University of Minnesota Press.

Hartsock, Nancy, Patricia Hill Collins, Sandra Harding, Dorothy E. Smith, and Susan Hekman. 1997. Comment and Response on Hekman's "Truth and Method: Feminist Standpoint Theory Revisited." *Signs: Journal of Women in Culture and Society* 22(2):367–402.

Hawksworth, Mary. 1997. Confounding Gender. *Signs: Journal of Women in Culture and Society* 22(3):649–85.

Hays, Constance I. 1997. Women's Health Stocks Try to Be Darling Again. *New York Times,* May 18:1,6.

Heilemann, Mary Sue. 1996. Storied Health, Embodied Care: Mexican American Women in the Borderlands. Doctoral dissertation, University of California, San Francisco.

Hekman, Susan. 1997. Truth and Method: Feminist Standpoint Theory Revisited. *Signs: Journal of Women in Culture and Society* 22(2):341–65.

Herzlich, Claudine, and Janine Pierret. 1986. Illness: From Causes to Meaning. Pp. 73–96 in Caroline Currer and Margaret Stacey (eds.), *Concepts of Health and Illness.* Leamington Spa, UK: Berg.

Hess, David. 1997. *Science Studies: An Advanced Introduction.* New York: New York University Press.

Hirsch, Marianne, and Evelyn Fox Keller (eds.), 1990. *Conflicts in Feminism.* New York: Routledge.

Hogle, Linda. 1999. *Bodies as Materials: Culture, Memory and Medical Practice.* New Brunswick, NJ: Rutgers University Press.

hooks, bell. 1992. *Black Looks: Race and Representation.* Boston: South End Press.

————. 1994. *Sisters of the Yam: Black Women and Self-Recovery.* Boston: South End Press.

Hurtado, Aida. 1989. Relating to Privilege: Seduction and Rejection in the Subordination of White Women and Women of Color. *Signs: Journal of Women in Culture and Society* 14(4):833–55.

ISNA (Intersex Society of North America). 1995–96. *Hermaphrodites with Attitude: A Quarterly Journal.* E-mail: info@isna.org. P.O. Box 31791, San Francisco, CA 94131.

Jagger, Alison M., and Susan R. Bordo (eds.). 1989. *Gender/Body/Knowledge: Feminist Reconstructions of Being and Knowing.* New Brunswick, NJ: Rutgers University Press.

James, Stanlie, and Abena Busia (eds.). 1993. *Theorizing Black Feminisms.* New York: Routledge.

Jasanoff, Sheila, Gerald E. Markle, James Petersen, and Trevor Pinch (eds.). 1995. *Handbook of Science and Technology Studies.* Thousand Oaks, CA: Sage.

Jordanova, Ludmilla. 1989. *Sexual Visions: Images of Gender in Science and Medicine between the Eighteenth and Twentieth Centuries.* Madison: University of Wisconsin Press.

Karma-glin-pa. 1987. *The Tibetan Book of the Dead.* Boston: Shambhala Press.

Keller, Evelyn Fox. 1995. Gender and Science: Origin, History and Politics. *Osiris* 10:27–38.

Kelman, Sandor. 1975. The Social Nature of the Definition Problem in Health. *International Journal of Health Services* 5(4):625–41.

Kertzer, David I. 1994. *Sacrificed for Honor: Italian Infant Abandonment and the Politics of Reproductive Control.* Boston, MA: Beacon Press.

King, Katie. 1992. Local and Global: AIDS Activism and Feminist Theory. *Camera Obscura* 28:79–100.

———. 1994. *Theory in its Feminist Travels: Conversations in U.S. Women's Movements.* Bloomington: Indiana University Press.

Koenig, Barbara. 1988. The Technological Imperative in Medical Practice: The Social Creation of a Routine Treatment. Pp. 465–96 in Margaret Lock and Deborah R. Gordon (eds.), *Biomedicine Examined.* Boston, Dordrecht: Kluwer Academic.

Krieger, Nancy, D. Rowley, A. Herman, B. Avery, and M Phillips. 1993. Racism, Sexism and Social Class: Implications for Studies of Health, Disease and Well-Being. *American Journal of Preventive Medicine* 9(6, supplement):82–122.

Krieger, Nancy, and Elizabeth Fee. 1996. Man-Made Medicine and Women's Health: The Biopolitics of Sex/Gender and Race/Ethnicity. Pp. 1–30 in Elizabeth Fee and Nancy Krieger (eds.), *Women's Health, Politics, and Power.* Amityville, NY: Baywood.

Lather, Patti. 1995. The Validity of Angels: Interpretive and Textual Strategies on Researching the Lives of Women with HIV/AIDS. *Qualitative Inquiry* 1(1):41–68.

Lather, Patti, and Chris Smithies. 1997. *Troubling the Angels: Women Living with HIV/AIDS.* Boulder, CO: Westview.

Latour, Bruno. 1987. *Science in Action: Following Scientists and Engineers through Society.* Cambridge, MA: Harvard University Press.

———. 1993. *We Have Never Been Modern.* Translated by Catherine Porter. Cambridge, MA: Harvard University Press.

Lewin, Ellen, and Virginia Olesen (eds.) 1985. *Women, Health and Healing: Toward a New Perspective.* New York: Methuen/Tavistock.

Littleton, Christine. 1987. Reconstructing Sexual Equality. *California Law Review* 75(4).

Lock, Margaret. 1993. Cultivating the Body: Anthropology and Epistemologies of Bodily Practices and Knowledge. *Annual Review of Anthropology* 22:133–55.

Longino, Helen. 1990. *Science as Social Knowledge: Values and Objectivity in Scientific Inquiry.* Princeton: Princeton University Press.

Lorber, Judith. 1997. *Gender and the Social Construction of Illness.* Thousand Oaks, CA: Sage.

Lorde, Audre. 1984. Racism, Sexism and Homophobia. In *Sister Outsider: Essays and Speeches.* Trumansburg, NY: Crossing Press.

Lupton, Deborah. 1994. *Medicine as Culture: Illness, Disease and the Body in Western Societies.* Thousand Oaks, CA: Sage.

MacFarquhar, Larissa. 1997. Andrew Weil, Shaman, M.D. *New York Times Magazine* August 24:28–31.

Mahoney, Maureen A., and Barbara Yngvesson. 1992. The Construction of Subjectivity and the Paradox of Resistance: Reintegrating Feminist Anthropology and Psychology. *Signs: Journal of Women in Culture and Society* 18(1):44–88.

Marcus, George E. 1995. Ethnography in/of the World System: The *Emergence of Multi-Sited Ethnography.* Annual Review of Anthropology 24:95–117.

Marieskind, Helen I. 1980. *Women in the Health System: Patients, Providers and Programs.* St. Louis, MO: C. V. Mosby.

Martin, Brian, and Evelleen Richards. 1994. Scientific Knowledge, Controversy and Public Decision-Making. Pp. 506–26 in Sheila Jasanoff et al. (eds.), *Handbook of Science and Technology Studies.* Thousand Oaks, CA: Sage.

Martin, Emily. 1987. *The Woman in the Body: A Cultural Analysis of Reproduction.* Boston: Beacon Press.

————. 1994. *Flexible Bodies: Tracking Immunity in American Culture from the Days of Polio to the Age of AIDS.* Boston. Beacon Press.

Mastroianni, Anna C., Ruth Faden, and Daniel Federman (eds.) 1994a. *Women and Health Research: Ethical and Legal Issues of Including Women in Clinical Studies,* Volume 1. *Institute of Medicine.* Washington, DC: National Academy Press.

————. 1994b. *Women and Health Research: Ethical and Legal Issues of Including Women in Clinical Studies.* Volume 2: *Workshop and Commissioned Papers.* Institute of Medicine. Washington, DC: National Academy Press.

Mastroianni, Luigi Jr., Peter J. Donaldson, and Thomas T. Kane (eds.). 1990. *Developing New Contraceptives: Obstacles and Opportunities.* [National Research Council and Institute of Medicine.] Washington, DC: National Academy Press.

Matsuda, Mari. 1996. *Where Is Your Body? and Other Essays on Race, Gender and the Law.* Boston: Beacon.

McClain, Carol Shepherd (ed.), 1989. *Women as Healers.* New Brunswick, NJ: Rutgers University Press.

McKenna, Wendy, Suzanne Kessler, Steven G. Smith, Joan W. Scott, R. W. Connell, and Mary Hawksworth. 1997. Comment and Reply to Mary Hawksworth's "Confounding Gender." *Signs: Journal of Women in Culture and Society* 22(3):686–713.

McNeil, Maureen, and Sarah Franklin. 1991. Science and Technology: Questions for Cultural Studies and Feminism. Pp. 129–46 in Sarah Franklin, Celia Lury, and Jackie Stacy (eds.), *Off-Centre: Feminism and Cultural Studies.* London: HarperCollins Academic.

Minow, Martha. 1987. When Difference Has Its Home: Group Homes for the Mentally Retarded, Equal Protection and Legal Treatment of Difference. *Harvard Civil Rights–Civil Liberties Review* 22(1).

Mohanty, Chandra. 1988. Under Western Eyes: Feminist Scholarship and Colonial Discourses. *Feminist Review* 30:60–88.

————. 1992. Feminist Encounters: Locating the Politics of Experience. Pp. 74–92 in Michele Barrett and Anne Phillips (eds.), *Destabilizing Theory: Contemporary Feminist Debates.* Stanford: Stanford University Press.

Moore, Lisa Jean, and Adele E. Clarke. 1995. Clitoral Conventions and Trangressions: Graphic Representations in Anatomy Texts, c. 1900–1991. *Feminist Studies* 22(1):255–301.

————. In preparation. *Sex/Sexuality/Gender in Cyberanatomies: Clicking on Private Parts in Local and Global Formations.*

Moraga, Cherrie, and Gloria Anzaldua (eds.). 1981. *This Bridge Called My Back: Writings by Radical Women of Color.* Latham, NY: Kitchen Table/Women of Color Press.

Moscucci, Ornella. 1990. *The Science of Woman: Gynaecology and Gender in England, 1880–1929.* Cambridge, UK: Cambridge University Press.

Moss, Kary L. (ed.). 1996. *Man-Made Medicine: Women's Health, Public Policy and Reform.* Durham and London: Duke University Press.

Naples, Nancy. 1997. The "New Consensus" on the Gendered "Social Contract": The 1987–1988 US Congressional Hearings on Welfare Reform. *Signs: Journal of Women in Culture and Society* 22(4):907–45.

Narayan, Uma. 1997. Contesting Cultures: "Westernization," Respect for Cultures, and Third-World Feminists. Pp. 396–414 in Linda J. Nicholson (ed.), 1997. *Second Wave: A Reader in Feminist Theory.* New York: Routledge.

Nelkin, Dorothy. 1987. *Selling Science: How the Press Covers Science and Technology.* New York: W.H. Freeman.

Nicholson, Linda J. (ed.). 1990. *Feminism/Postmodernism.* New York: Routledge.

————. 1997. *Second Wave: A Reader in Feminist Theory.* New York: Routledge.

Norsigian, Judy. 1994. Women and National Health Care Reform: A Progressive Feminist

Agenda. Pp. 111–17 in Alice Dan (ed.), *Reframing Women's Health.* Thousand Oaks, CA: Sage.

———. 1996. The Women's Health Movement in the United States. Pp. 79–98 in Kary L. Moss (ed.), *Man-Made Medicine.* Durham and London: Duke University Press.

Ogden, J. 1995. Psychosocial Theory and the Creation of the Risky Self. *Social Science and Medicine* 40(3):409–15.

Olesen, Virginia (ed.). 1975. *Women and Their Health: Research Implications for a New Era.* Washington, DC: U.S. Department of Health, Education and Welfare.

Olesen, Virginia L. 1994. Feminist Qualitative Research. Pp. 158–74 in Norman Denzin and Yvonna Lincoln (eds.), *Handbook of Qualitative Research.* Thousand Oaks, CA: Sage.

Olesen, Virginia, and Ellen Lewin. 1985. Women, Health and Healing: A Theoretical Introduction. Pp. 2–23 in Ellen Lewin and Virginia Olesen (eds.), *Women, Health and Healing: Toward a New Perspective.* New York: Methuen/Tavistock.

Olesen, Virginia, and Margaret Stacey. 1993. Introduction to Special Issue on Gender and Health. *Social Science and Medicine* 36(1):1–5.

Ong, Aihwa. 1995. Making the Biopolotical Subject: Cambodian Immigrants, Refugee Medicine and Cultural Citizenship in California. *Social Science and Medicine* 40(9):1243–57.

Oudshoorn, Nelly. 1994. *Beyond the Natural Body: An Archeology of Sex Hormones.* London: Routledge.

———. 1996. The Decline of the One-Size-Fits-All Paradigm, or How Reproductive Scientists Try to Cope with Postmodernity. Pp. 153–72 in Nina Lyke and Rosi Braidotti (eds.), *Between Monsters, Goddesses and Cyborgs: Feminist Confrontations with Science, Medicine and Cyberspace.* London: Zed Books.

Park, Katharine, and Loraine Daston. 1995. The Hermaphrodite and the Orders of Nature: Sexual Ambiguity in Early Modern France. *GLQ* 1:419–38.

Passell, Peter. 1997. Backlash: In Medicine, Government Rises Again. *New York Times* December 7:1,4.

Pauly, Philip J. 1993. Essay Review: the Eugenics Industry—Growth or Restructuring? *Journal of the History of Biology* 27:131–45.

Pearlman, David. 1998. New Journal to Review Alternative Healing. *San Francisco Chronicle,* January 6:A2.

Penley, Constance. 1997. *NASA/Trek: Popular Science and Sex in America.* New York: Verso.

Petchesky, Rosalind Pollack. 1990. *Abortion and Woman's Choice: The State, Sexuality and Reproductive Freedom.* Second edition. New York: Longman's.

Pickstone, John V. 1993b. Ways of Knowing: Towards a Historical Sociology of Science, Technology and Medicine. *British Journal of the History of Science* 26:433–58.

Ponticelli, Christine (ed.). 1998. *Gateways to Improving Lesbian Health and Health Care: Opening Doors.* New York: Hayworth Press.

Prather, Jane, and Linda Fidell. 1975. Sex Differences in the Content and Style of Medical Advertisements. *Social Science and Medicine* 9:23–6.

Quadagno, Jill. 1994. *The Color of Welfare: How Racism Undermined the War on Poverty.* New York: Oxford University Press.

Rapp, Rayna. 1998. *Moral Pioneers: Fetuses, Families and Amniocentesis.* New York: Routledge.

Ratcliff, Kathryn Strother (ed.). 1989. *Healing Technology: Feminist Perspectives.* Ann Arbor: University of Michigan Press.

Relman, Arnold et al. 1987. Sounding Board: The Changing Climate of Medical Practice. *New England Journal of Medicine* 316(6):333–42.

Rhode, Deborah L. (ed.). 1990. *Theoretical Perspectives on Sexual Difference.* New Haven: Yale University Press.

Richie, Beth. 1994. Gender Entrapment. Pp. 219–32 in Alice Dan (ed.), *Reframing Women's Health*. Thousand Oaks, CA: Sage.

———. 1996. *Compelled to Crime: The Gender Entrapment of Battered Black Women*. New York: Routledge.

Riessman, Cathrine Kohler. 1983. Women and Medicalization: A New Perspective. *Social Policy* 17 (Summer):3–18.

Roberts, Dorothy E. 1995. Motherhood and Crime. *Social Text* 42:99–123.

Rorty, Richard. 1991. *Objectivity, Relativism and Truth*. New York: Cambridge University Press.

Rosaldo, Michelle Zimbalist, and Louise Lamphere (eds.). 1974. *Women, Culture and Society*. Stanford: Stanford University Press.

Rosser, Sue V. (ed.). 1988. *Feminism Within the Science and Health Care Professions: Overcoming Resistance*. New York: Athene/Pergamon.

Rosser, Sue V. 1994. *Women's Health: Missing from U.S. Medicine*. Bloomington: Indiana University Press.

Rothenberg, Karen H., and Elizabeth J. Thompson (eds.). 1994. *Women and Prenatal Testing: Facing the Challenges of Genetic Technology*. Columbus: Ohio State University Press.

Rothman, Barbara Katz. 1984. The Meanings of Choice in Reproductive Technology. Pp. 23–33 in Rita Arditti, Renate Klein, and Shelley Minden (eds.), *Test-Tube Women: What Future for Motherhood?* Boston: Pandora Press/Routledge and Kegan Paul.

Rubin, Gail. 1975. The Traffic in Women. Pp. 157–210 in Rayna Reiter (ed.), *Toward an Anthropology of Women*. New York: Monthly Review Press.

———. 1993. Thinking Sex. Pp. 267–319 in H. Abelove, M. Barale, and D. Halpern (eds.), *The Lesbian and Gay Studies Reader*. New York: Routledge.

Ruzek, Sheryl Burt. 1978. *The Women's Health Movement: Feminist Alternatives to Medical Control*. New York: Praeger.

———. 1980. Medical Response to Women's Health Activities: Conflict, Cooptation and Accomodation. *Research in the Sociology of Health Care* 1:335–54.

Ruzek, Sheryl Burt, Virginia L. Olesen, and Adele E. Clarke (eds.). 1997. *Women's Health: Differences and Complexities*. Columbus: Ohio State University Press.

Schiebinger, Londa. 1989. *The Mind Has No Sex? Women in the Origins of Modern Science*. Cambridge: Harvard University Press.

———. 1993. *Nature's Body: Gender in the Making of Modern Science*. Boston, MA: Beacon Press.

Scott, Joan. 1988. Deconstructing Equality-Versus Difference, or the Uses of Post-Structuralist Theory for Feminism. *Feminist Studies* 14(1):33–50.

Scott, Joan W. 1992. Experience. Pp. 22–39 in Judith Butler and Joan W. Scott (eds.), *Feminists Theorize the Political*. New York and London: Routledge.

Scully, Diana. 1980. *Men Who Control Women's Health: The Miseducation of Obstetrician-Gynecologists*. New York: Houghton Mifflin.

Seaman, Barbara. 1969. *The Doctors' Case Against the Pill*. New York: Doubleday.

Segura, Denise, and Jennifer A. Pierce. 1993. "Chicana/o Family Structure and Gender Personality: Chodorow, Familism and Psychoanalytic Sociology Revisited." *Signs: Journal of Women in Culture and Society* 19(1):62–91.

Seidman, Steven. 1996. *Queer Theory/Sociology*. Cambridge, MA: Blackwell.

Simmons, Ruth, Bonnie J. Kay, and Carol Regan. 1984. Women's Health Groups: Alternatives to the Health Care System. *International Journal of Health Services* 14 (4):619–34.

Smith, Dorothy. 1990. *The Conceptual Practices of Power*. Boston: Northeastern University Press.

Smith, Susan L. 1995. *Sick and Tired of Being Sick and Tired: Black Women's Health Activism in America, 1890–1950*. Philadelphia: University of Pennsylvania Press.

Spivak, Gayatri, with Ellen Rooney. 1997. "In A Word": Interview. Pp. 356–78 in Linda J. Nicholson (ed.), *Feminism/Postmodernism*. New York: Routledge.

Stage, Sarah. 1997. *Rethinking Home Economics: Women and the History of a Profession*. Ithaca, New York: Cornell University Press.

Stanworth, Michelle (ed.). 1987. *Reproductive Technologies: Gender, Motherhood and Medicine*. Minneapolis: University of Minnesota Press.

Stanworth, Michelle. 1990. Birth Pangs: Conceptive Technologies and the Threat to Motherhood. In Marianne Hirsch and Evelyn Fox Keller (eds.), *Conflicts in Feminism*. New York: Routledge.

Star, S. Leigh. 1983. Simplification in Scientific Work: An Example from Neuroscience Research. *Social Studies of Science* 13: 208–26.

———. 1991. Power, Technologies and the Phenomenology of Conventions: On Being Allergic to Onions. Pp. 26–56 in John Law (ed.), *A Sociology of Monsters: Essays on Power, Technology and Domination*. New York: Routledge.

Star, Susan Leigh, and James Griesemer. 1989. Institutional Ecology, "Translations" and Boundary Objects: Amateurs and Professionals in Berkeley's Museum of Vertebrate Zoology, 1907–1939. *Social Studies of Science* 19:387–420.

Stepan, Nancy. 1986. Race and Gender: The Role of Analogy in Science. *Isis* 77:261–77.

Stone, Sandy. 1991. The Empire Strikes Back: A Posttranssexual Manifesto. In Julia Epstein and Kris Straub (eds.). *Body Guards: The Cultural Politics of Gender Ambiguity*. New York: Routledge.

———. 1996. *The War of Desire and Technology at the Close of the Mechanical Age*. Cambridge, MA: MIT Press.

Strathern, Marilyn. 1992. *Reproducing the Future: Essays on Anthropology, Kinship and the New Reproductive Technologies*. New York: Routledge.

Terry, Jennifer. 1990. Lesbians Under the Medical Gaze: Scientists Search for Remarkable Differences. *Journal of Sex Research* 27(3):317–39.

Terry, Jennifer, and Jacqueline Urla (eds.). 1995. *Deviant Bodies: Critical Perspectives on Difference in Science and Popular Culture*. Bloomington: Indiana University Press.

Traweek, Sharon. 1993. An Introduction to Cultural and Social Studies of Sciences and Technologies. *Culture, Medicine, and Psychiatry* 17(1993): 3–25.

Tsing, Anna Lowenhaupt. 1993. *In the Realm of the Diamond Queen: Marginalities in Out of the Way Places*. Princeton: Princeton University Press.

Vines, Gail. 1994. *Raging Hormones: Do They Rule Our Lives?* Berkeley: University of California Press.

Visweswaran, Kamala. 1988. Defining Feminist Ethnography. *Inscriptions* 3/4:27–44.

———. 1994. *Fictions of Feminist Ethnography*. Minneapolis: University of Minnesota Press.

———. 1997. Histories of Feminist Ethnography. *Annual Review of Anthropology* 26:591–621.

Warner, John Harley. 1995. The History of Science and the Sciences of Medicine. *Osiris* 10:164-193.

Watson-Verran, Helen, and David Turnbull. 1995. Science and Other Indigenous Knowledge Systems. Pp. 115–39 in Sheila Jasanoff et al. (eds.), *Handbook of Science and Technology Studies*. Thousand Oaks, CA: Sage.

West, Candace. 1993. Reconceptualizing Gender in Physician/Patient Relationships. *Social Science and Medicine* 36(1):57–66.

———. 1984. *Routine Complications: Troubles with Talk Between Doctors and Patients*. Bloomington: University of Indiana Press.

West, Candace, and Sarah Fenstermaker. 1995. Doing Difference. *Gender and Society* 9(1):8–37.

West, Candace, and Don H. Zimmerman. 1987. Doing Gender. *Gender and Society* l(2):125–5l.

White, Evelyn (ed.). 1990. *The Black Woman's Health Book*. Seattle: Seal Press.

Williams, David R. (ed.). 1995. Special Issue on Racism and Health. *Ethnicity and Disease* 5.

Williams, David R., and Chiquita Collins. 1995. U.S. Economic and Racial Differences in Health. *Annual Review of Sociology* 21:349–86.

Williams, Raymond. 1985. *Key Words*. Second edition. New York: Oxford University Press.

Worcester, Nancy, and Mariamne Whatley. 1988. The Response of the Health Care System to the Women's Health Movement: The Selling of Women's Health Centers. Pp. 117–30 in Sue V. Rosser (ed.), *Feminism Within the Science and Health Care Professions*. .New York: Athene/Pergamon.

Young, Iris Marion. 1994. Punishment, Treatment, Empowerment: Three Approaches to Policy for Pregnant Addicts. *Feminist Studies* 20(1):33–57.

Zimmerman, Mary K. 1987. The Women's Health Movement: A Critique of Medical Enterprise and the Position of Women. Pp. 442–73 in Beth B. Hess and Myra Marx Ferree (eds.), *Analyzing Gender: A Handbook of Social Science Research*. Newbury Park, CA:Sage.

Zinn, Maxine Baca, and Bonnie Thornton Dill. 1996. Theorizing Difference From Multiracial Feminism. *Feminist Studies* 22(2):321–31.

Zola, Irving Kenneth. 1976. Medicine as an Institution of Social Control. *Sociological Review* 20:487–504.

The Virtual Speculum
in the New World Order

DONNA HARAWAY

These are the days of miracle and wonder
This is the long-distance call
The way the camera follows us in slo-mo
The way we look to us all
The way we look to a distant constellation
That's dying in a corner of the sky
These are the days of miracle and wonder
And don't cry, baby, don't cry
It was a dry wind
And it swept across the desert
And it curled into the circle of birth
And the dead sand
Falling on the children
The mothers and the fathers
And the automatic earth
       • • •
Medicine is magical and magical is art
The Boy in the Bubble
And the baby with the baboon heart

And I believe
These are the days of lasers in the jungle
Lasers in the jungle somewhere
Staccato signals of constant information
A loose affiliation of millionaires
And billionaires and baby
These are the days of miracle and wonder
This is the long-distance call

Paul Simon, "The Boy in the Bubble"[1]
Paul Simon/Paul Simon Music (BMI)

In its ability to embody the union of science and nature, the embryo might be described as a cyborg kinship entity.

—Sarah Franklin, "Making Representations"

The fetus and the planet Earth are sibling seed worlds in technoscience. If NASA photographs of the blue, cloud-swathed whole Earth are icons for the emergence of global, national, and local struggles over a recent natural-technical object of knowledge called the *environment,* then the ubiquitous images of glowing, free-floating human fetuses condense and intensify struggles over an equally new and disruptive technoscientific object of knowledge, namely "life itself." Life as a system to be managed—a field of operations constituted by scientists, artists, cartoonists, community activists, mothers, anthropologists, fathers, publishers, engineers, legislators, ethicists, industrialists, bankers, doctors, genetic counselors, judges, insurers, priests, and all their relatives—has a very recent pedigree.[2] The fetus and the whole Earth concentrate the elixir of life as a complex system, that is, of life itself. Each image is about the origin of life in a postmodern world.

Both the whole earth and the fetus owe their existence as public objects to visualizing technologies. These technologies include computers, video cameras, satellites, sonography machines, optical fiber technology, television, microcinematography, and much more. The global fetus and the spherical whole Earth both exist because of, and inside of, technoscientific visual culture. Yet, I think, both signify touch. Both provoke yearning for the physical sensuousness of a wet and blue-green Earth and a soft, fleshy child. That is why these images are so ideologically powerful. They signify the immediately natural and embodied, over and against the constructed and disembodied. These latter qualities are charged against the supposedly violating, distancing, scopic eye of science and theory. The audiences who find the glowing fetal and terran spheres to be powerful signifiers of touch are themselves partially constituted as subjects in the material-semiotic process of viewing. The system of ideological oppositions between signifiers of touch and vision remains stubbornly essential to political and scientific debate in modern Western culture. This system is a field of meanings that elaborates the ideological tension between body and machine, nature and culture, female and male, tropical and northern, colored and white, traditional and modern, and lived experience and dominating objectification.

The Sacred and the Comic

Sometimes complicitous, sometimes exuberantly creative, Western feminists have had little choice about operating in the charged field of oppositional meanings structured around vision and touch. Small wonder, then, that feminists in science studies are natural deconstructionists who resolutely chart fields of meanings that unsettle these oppositions, these setups that frame human and nonhuman technoscientific actors and sentence them to terminal ideological confinement (see, for example, Treichler and Cartwright 1992). Because the fruit issuing from such confinement is toxic, let us try to reconceive some of the key origin stories about human life that congeal around the images of the fetus. In many domains in contemporary European and U.S. cultures, the fetus functions as a kind of metonym, seed crystal, or icon for configurations of person, family, nation, origin, choice, life, and future. As the German historian of the body Barbara Duden put it, the fetus functions as a modern "sacrum," that is, as an object in which the transcendent appears (Duden 1993). The fetus as sacrum is the repository of heterogeneous people's stories, hopes, and imprecations. Attentive to the wavering opposition of the sacred versus the comic, the sacra-mental versus the vulgar, scientific illustration versus advertising, art versus pornography, the body of scientific truth versus the caricature of the popular joke, the power of medicine versus the insult of death, I want to proceed here by relocating the fetal sacrum onto its comic twin.

In this task, I am instructed by feminists who have studied in the school of the masters. Two feminist cartoons separated by twenty years, and a missing image that cannot be a joke, will concern me most in this chapter's effort to read the comics in technoscience. Set in the context of struggles over the terms, agents, and contents of human reproduction, all three of my images trouble a reduction-ist sense of "reproductive technologies." Instead, the images are about a specifi-cally feminist concept called "reproductive freedom." From the point of view of feminist science studies, freedom projects are what make technical projects make sense with all the specificity, ambiguity, complexity, and contradiction inherent in technoscience. Science projects are civics projects; they remake citizens. Technoscientific liberty is the goal. Keep your eyes on the prize.[3]

The first image, a cartoon by Anne Kelly that I have named *Virtual Speculum,* is a representation of Michelangelo's painting *Creation of Adam* on the ceiling of the Sistine Chapel[4] [Figure 1. *Virtual Speculum*]. *Virtual Speculum* is caricature in the potent political tradition of "literal" reversals, which excavate the latent and implicit oppositions that made the original picture work. In Kelly's version, a female nude is in the position of Adam, whose hand is extended to the creative interface with not God the Father but a keyboard for a computer whose display screen shows the global digital fetus in its amniotic sac. A female Adam, the young nude woman is in the position of the first man. Kelly's figure is not Eve, who was made from Adam and in relation to his need.[5] In *Virtual Speculum,* the woman is in direct relation to the source of life itself.

The cartoon seems to resonate in an echo chamber with a Bell Telephone advertisement that appeared on U.S. television in the early 1990s, urging poten-tial long-distance customers to "reach out and touch someone." The racial-ethnic markings of the cast of characters varied in different versions of the ad. The visual text showed a pregnant woman, who is undergoing ultrasonographic visu-alization of her fetus, telephoning her husband, the father of the fetus, to describe for him the first spectral appearance of his issue. The description is performative: that is, the object described comes into existence, experientially, for all the partic-ipants in the drama. Fathers, mothers, and children are constituted as subjects

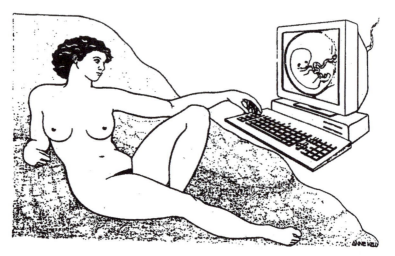

Figure 1. Cartoon from Norwegian Feminist Journal, *Nytt om Kvinneforskning*, No. 3, 1992.

and objects for each other and the television audience. Life itself becomes an object of experience, which can be shared and memorialized. Proving herself to be a literate citizen of technoscience, the pregnant woman interprets the moving gray, white, and black blobs on the televised sonogram as visually obvious, differentiated fetus. Family bonding is in full flower in Bell Telephone's garden of creation. Surrogate for the absent father, the mother touches the on-screen fetus, establishing a tactile link between both parents-to-be and child-to-be. Here are interactive television and video of a marvelous kind. The mother-to-be's voice on the phone and finger on the screen are literally the conduits for the eye of the father. These are the touch and the word that mediate life itself, that turn bodies and machines into eloquent witnesses and storytellers.

Through advertising, Bell Telephone puts us inside the dramatic scenarios of technology and entertainment, twins to biomedicine and art. In the ad, reproductive technology and the visual arts historically bound to the specific kinds of observation practiced in the gynecological exam and the life-drawing class come together through the circles of mimesis built into communications practices in the New World Order. Life copies art copies technology copies communication copies life itself. Television, sonography, computer video display, and the telephone are all apparatuses for the production of the nuclear family on screen. Voice and touch are brought into life on screen.

Kelly's cartoon works off the fact, which remains odd to women of my menopausal generation, that in many contemporary technologically mediated pregnancies, expectant mothers emotionally bond with their fetuses through learning to see the developing child on screen during a sonogram.[6] And so do fathers, as well as members of Parliament and Congress.[7] The sonogram is literally a pedagogy for learning to see who exists in the world. Selves and subjects are produced in such "lived experiences." Quickening, or the mother's testimony to the movement of the unseen child-to-be in her womb, has here neither the experiential nor the epistemological authority it did, and does, under different historical modes of embodiment. In Kelly's version, the bonding produced by computer-mediated visualization also produces subjects and selves; the touch at the keyboard is generative emotionally, materially, and epistemologically. But things work both similarly and differently from the way they do on the Sistine Chapel ceiling or in the Bell Telephone TV advertisement.

In *Virtual Speculum* the grayish blobs of the television sonogram have given place to the defined anatomical form of the free-floating fetus. Kelly's on-screen fetus is more like an *in vivo* movie, photograph, or computer-graphic reconstruction all of which are received at least partly within the conventions of post-Renaissance visual realism, which the bloblike sonographic image has great difficulty invoking. The televised sonogram is more like a biological monster movie, which one still has to learn to view even in the late twentieth century. By contrast, to those who learned how to see after the revolution in painting initiated in the fifteenth and sixteenth centuries in northern and southern Europe, the free-floating, anatomically sharp, perspectively registered fetal image appears self-evident at first viewing. Post-Renaissance anatomical realism and late-twentieth-century computer-generated corporeal realism still share many, although not all, viewing conventions and epistemological assumptions.

The fetus like the one in *Virtual Speculum* is the iconic form that has been made so familiar by the exquisite, internationally distributed images produced by the Swedish biomedical photographer Lennart Nilsson. Endoscopic intrauterine fetal visualization began in the 1950s, well before sonograms were part of the cultural terrain. The visible fetus became a public object with the April 1965 *Life* magazine cover featuring Nilsson's photograph of an intrauterine eighteen-week-old developing human being encased in its bubblelike amniotic sac. The rest of the Nilsson photos in the *Life* story, "The Drama of Life Before Birth," were of extrauterine abortuses, beautifully lit and photographed in color to become the visual embodiment of life at its origin. Not seen as abortuses, these gorgeous fetuses and their descendants signified life itself, in its transcendent essence and immanent embodiment. The visual image of the fetus is like the DNA double helix not just a signifier of life but also offered as the thing-in-itself. The visual fetus, like the gene, is a technoscientific sacrament. The sign becomes the thing itself in ordinary magico-secular transubstantiation.

Nilsson's images have spiked the visual landscape for the past thirty years, each time with announcements of originary art and technology, originary personal and scientific experience, and unique revelations bringing what was hidden into the light. Nilsson's photographs are simultaneously high art, scientific illustration, research tool, and mass popular culture. The 1965 "Drama of Life Before Birth" was followed by the popular coffee-table-format book, *A Child Is Born*

Figure 2. *The Creation of Adam,* **Sistine Chapel ceiling, 1511–12.**

(Nilsson 1977); the NOVA television special in 1983, "The Miracle of Life"; the lavishly illustrated book (Nilsson 1987) on the immune system, including images of developing fetuses, *The Body Victorious;* and the August 1990 Life cover photo of a seven-week-old fetus, with the caption "The First Pictures Ever of How Life Begins" and the accompanying story, "The First Days of Creation."[8] Finally, moving from conception through breastfeeding, *A Child Is Born* was issued in 1994 as a compact-disk adaptation whose content-rich multimedia design offers interactive features as part of the visual fetal feast (Nilsson and Hamberger 1994).[9] Truly, we are in the realm of miracles, beginnings, and promises. A secular terrain has never been more explicitly sacred, embedded in the narratives of God's first Creation, which is repeated in miniature with each new life.[10] Secular, scientific visual culture is in the immediate service of the narratives of Christian realism. "These are the days of miracle and wonder." We are in both an echo chamber and a house of mirrors, where, in word and image, ricocheting mimesis structures the emergence of subjects and objects. It does not seem too much to claim that the biomedical, public fetus given flesh by the high technology of visualization is a sacred-secular incarnation, the material realization of the promise of life itself. Here is the fusion of art, science, and creation. No wonder we look.

The Kelly cartoon is practically an exact tracing of its original. Looking at Kelly's cartoon returns the reader of comics to Michelangelo's *Creation of Adam* [Figure 2. *Creation of Adam*]. For "modern" viewers, the entire ceiling of the Sistine Chapel signifies an eruption of salvation history into a newly powerful visual narrative medium [Figure 3. *The Sistine Chapel Floor*]. Accomplished between 1508 and 1512 under the patronage of Pope Julius II, the ceiling's frescos mark a technical milestone in mastering the Renaissance problem of producing a convincing pictorial rendering of narrative. The gestures and attitudes of the human body sing with stories. Part of the apparatus of production of Christian humanism, which has animated the history of Western science,

Although history has long forgotten them, Lambini & Sons are generally credited with the Sistine Chapel floor.

Figure 3.   "The Sistine Chapel floor." © Gary Larson.

European early modern or Renaissance painting developed key techniques for the realization of man. Or, at least, such techniques provide a key way "modern man" tells his history.

Although I will not trace them, innovations in literary technology are also part of this story. Eric Auerbach (1953) places the critical mutation in Dante's *Divine Comedy,* with its powerful figurations of salvation history that locate promised transcendental fulfillment in the material tissues of solid narrative flesh. Figurations are performative images that can be inhabited. Verbal or visual, figurations are condensed maps of whole worlds. In art, literature, and science, my subject is the technology that turns body into story, and vice versa, producing both what can count as real and the witnesses to that reality. In my

Figure 4.   Albrecht Dürer, *Draughtsman Drawing a Nude*, 1538.

own mimetic critical method, I am tracing some of the circulations of Christian realism in the flesh of technoscience. I work to avoid the terms Judeo-Christian or monotheist because the visual and narrative materials throughout my book *Modest_Witness@Second_Millennium* are specifically secular Christian renditions of partially shared Jewish, Muslim, and Christian origin stories for science, self, and world. But I am also trying to trace the story within a story, within which we learn to believe that fundamental revolutions take place. I am trying to retell some of the conditions of possibility of the stories technoscientific humans continue to tell ourselves. It is doubtful that historical configurations conventionally called the "Renaissance," or in a later version of the birth of the modern, the "Scientific Revolution," or today's rendition, called the "New World Order," actually have been unique, transformative theaters of origin. But they have been narrativized and canonized as such cradles of modern humanity, especially technoscientific humanity with its secular salvation and damnation histories. Certainly, in this paper and my book, if only by opposition, I am complicit in the narrativization and figuration of the Scientific Revolution and the New World Order. *Modest_Witness@Second_Millennium* meditates on world making machines that are located at two ends of the story of modernity. Perspective techniques and the vacuum pump, at one end, and the computer and the DNA sequencing machine, on the other end, are the artifacts with which we convince ourselves our histories are true.

Metonymic for the entire array of Renaissance visual techniques, Albrecht Dürer's *Draughtsman Drawing a Nude* (1538) conventionally dramatizes the story of a revolutionary apparatus for turning disorderly bodies into disciplined art and science [Figure 4. *Draughtsman Drawing a Nude*]. In the drawing, an old man uses a line-of-sight device and a screen-grid to transfer point for point the features of a voluptuous, reclining female nude onto a paper grid marked off into squares. The upright screen-grid separates the prone woman on the table, whose hand is poised over her genitals, from the erectly seated draughtsman, whose hand guides his stylus on the paper. Dürer's engraving attests to the power of the technology of perspective to discipline vision to produce a new kind of knowledge of form. As art historian Lynda Nead argued, "Visual perception is placed on the side of art and in opposition to the information yielded through tactile perception. . . . Through visual perception we may achieve the illusion of a coherent and unified self" (1992:28). Here, as with Dürer's drawing, the disciplining screen between art and pornography is paradigmatically erected.

The gendering of this kind of vision is, of course, not subtle. Indeed, feminists argue that this visual technology was part of the apparatus for the *production* of modern gender, with its proliferating series of sexually charged oppositions condensed into the tension at the interface between touch and vision. Nead writes, "Woman offers herself to the controlling discipline of illusionistic art. With her bent legs closest to the screen, [Dürer's] image recalls not simply the life class but also the gynecological examination. Art and medicine are both foregrounded here, the two discourses in which the female body is most subjected to scrutiny and assessed according to historically specific norms" (1992:11). Obviously, it is only after the institutions of the life class and the gynecological exam emerged that Dürer's print could be retrospectively read to recall them.[11] As part of reforming her own self-making technology, Nead, the feminist art historian, is telling a story about the birth of the figure of Woman. As for me, the feminist analyst of technoscience attuned to artistic and biomedical visual delights, I see Dürer's majestic print and Bell Telephone's television advertising through the grid of Kelly's virtual speculum. In the life class and gynecological exam that is technoscience, critique caresses comedy. I laugh: therefore, I am . . . implicated. I laugh: therefore, I am responsible and accountable. That is the best I can do for moral foundations at the tectonic fault line joining the sacred, the scientific, and the comic. And everyone knows that end-of-the-millennium Californians build their houses, and their theories, on fault lines.

In Renaissance visual technology, form and narrative implode, and both seem merely to reveal what was already there, waiting for unveiling or discovery. This epistemology underlies the European-indebted sense of what counts as reality in the culture, believed by many of its practitioners to transcend all culture, called modern science. Reality, as Westerners have known it in story and image for several hundred years, is an *effect* but cannot be recognized as such without great moral and epistemological angst. The conjoined Western modern sense of the "real" and the "natural" was achieved by a set of fundamental innovations in visual technology beginning in the Renaissance.[12]

Twentieth-century scientists call on this earlier visual technology for insisting on a specific kind of reality, which readily makes today's observers forget the conditions, apparatuses, and histories of its production. Especially in computer and information sciences and in biotechnology and biomedicine, representations of late-twentieth-century technoscience make liberal use of iconic exemplars of early modern European art/humanism/technology. Current images of technoscience quote, point to, and otherwise evoke a small, conventional, potent stock of Renaissance visual analogs, which provide a legitimate lineage and origin story for technical revolutions at the end of the Second Christian Millennium. Today's

Figure 5. Diego Rodriguez de Silva y Velázquez, *The Toilet of of Venus* ("Rokeby Venus"), 1649.

Renaissance *Sharper Image catalogue*[13] includes the anatomized human figures in *De lumanis corporis fabrica* of Andreas Vesalius, published in Basel in 1543; Leonardo da Vinci's drawing of the human figure illustrating proportions, or the *Vitruvian Man* (ca. 1485–1490); Dürer's series of plates on perspective techniques; the maps of the cartographers of the "Age of Discovery"; and, of course, Michelangelo's *Creation of Adam*. Invoking this ready stock, a venture capitalist from Kleiner Perkins Caufield & Byers mutated the analogies to make a related historical observation, noting that biotech has been "for human biology what the Italian Renaissance was for art" (Hamilton 1994:85). In technoscientific culture, at the risk of mild overstatement, I think one can hardly extend an index finger (or finger substitute) toward another hand (or hand substitute) without evoking the First Author's (or First Author Substitute's) gesture.

In Michelangelo's version of authorship, Adam lies on the earth, and, conveyed by angels, God moves toward him from the heavens. An elderly, patriarchal God the Father reaches his right index finger to touch the languidly extended left index finger of an almost liquid, nude, young-man Adam. A conventional art history text concludes, "Adam, lying like a youthful river god, awakens into life" (Rubenstein et al. 1967:99; see also Jansen and Jansen 1963:359–60). Adam is a kind of watery, earth-borne fetus of humanity, sparked into life on a new land by the heavenly Father. Michelangelo's God, however, is also carrying another, truly unborn human being. Still in the ethereal regions above the earth, Eve is held in the shelter of God's left arm, and at the origin of mankind she and Adam are looking toward each other. It is not entirely clear whom Adam sees, God or Woman-exactly the problem addressed by the screen barrier between art and pornography. Maybe in innocence before the Fall and at the moment of the renaissance of modern vision, a yearning Adam can still see both at once. Touch and vision are not yet split. Adam's eye caresses both his Author and his unborn bride.

Anne Kelly's drawing suggests other screens as well, such as that between art and science, on the one hand, and caricature and politics, on the other. Like the transparent film between art and pornography, the interface between the medico-scientific image and the political cartoon unstably both joins and separates modest witnesses and contaminated spectators. In both potent zones of transformation, the reclining female nude seems suggestively common. Dürer's woman in *Draughtsman Drawing a Nude,* the *Venus d'Urbino* by Titian (1487?– 1576), the *Rokeby Venus* by Diego Velázquez *(1599–1660), Venus at Her Toilet* by Peter Paul Rubens (1577–1640), and Edouard Manet's *Olympia* (1863) are all ancestors for Kelly's first woman [Figure 5. *Rokeby Venus*]. Kelly's cartoon figure depends on the conventions in modern Western painting for drawing the recumbent nude female.[14]

Lynn Randolph's painting *Venus,* part of her *Ilusas* or "deluded women" series, is a more formal feminist intervention into the conventions of the female nude and her associated secretions and tools [Figure 6. *Venus*]. Scrutinizing the standard line between pornography and art, Randolph writes, "This contemporary Venus is not a Goddess in the classical sense of a contained figure. She is an unruly woman, actively making a spectacle of herself. Queering Botticelli, leaking, projecting, shooting, secreting milk, transgressing the boundaries of her body. Hundreds of years have passed and we are still engaged in a struggle for the interpretive power over our bodies in a society where they are marked as a battleground by the church and the state in legal and medical skirmishes" (1993).

Kelly, however, is drawing a female Adam, not a Venus. The story is different, and so is the optical technology. Kelly's woman looks not into the mirror that fascinates Rubens's and Valázquez's nudes but into a screen that is in the heavenly position of Michelangelo's God. The "venereal" women with mirrors in the history of Western painting have given way in Kelly's drawing to the "authorial" woman with keyboard and computer terminal. Kelly's woman is not in a story of reflections and representations. Whatever she sees, it is not her reflection. The computer screen is not a mirror; the fetus is not her double or her copy. First Woman in *Virtual Speculum* looks not into the normal reality established by Renaissance perspective but into the virtual reality given by a time called postmodernity. Both realities are technical effects of particular apparatuses of visual culture. Both realities are simultaneously material, embodied, and imaginary. Both realities can only be inhabited by subjects who learn how to see and touch with the right conventions. It's all a question of interactive visual technology. Reach out and touch someone; this is the long distance call.

Not under the arm of God but in computer-generated visual space, the fetus

Figure 6. Lynn Randolph, *Venus,* oil on masonite. 14 ¹/₂" x 10 ¹/₂", 1992. Photograph by Rick Gardner.

meets First Woman's gaze. Kelly's unborn fetus, not the Adamlike woman, is in the position of Michelangelo's still uncreated Eve. From the nonperspective of virtual space, the First Woman and the fetus confront each other as Adam and Eve did in Michelangelo's version of human creation. In that reading, the computer screen is the embracing arm of God. Had God's gender value been transmuted as Adam's has been? Is the computer womb now female, or is gender one of the many things at stake? Kelly's cartoon allows at least two readings of the fetus: It is either in the position of God or in that of the not-yet-created Eve. If the fetus is Eve, the computer itself, with keyboard, is the encompassing deity reaching out to the female Adam's extended but limp hand. That reading makes Kelly's Adam the effect of the computer, the effect of the "creative" technologies of cyberspace. On the other hand, the female Adam has her hand on the keypad; she seems to be in the position of author. Then the fetus is her file, which she is writing, editing, or, as one viewer suggested, deleting. Certainly, the politics of abortion are implicit in this cartoon. Maybe she is reaching for the "escape" key, or perhaps merely the "control" key.[15]

Like traditional masculine figures in the reproductive imagery of technoscience, who have brain children all the time,[16] Kelly's First Woman seems to have a pregnancy associated with the organs of cognition and writing. Her pregnancy is literally extrauterine. Or perhaps Kelly's Adam is not pregnant at all; she may be viewing a fetus with no further connection to her once the file is closed. Literally, the fetus is somehow "in" the computer. This fetus is a kind of data structure whose likely fate seems more connected to downloading than birth or abortion. Just as the computer as womb-brain signifies the superior creativity of artificial intelligence, the on-screen fetus is an artificial life form. As such, *Virtual Speculum*'s fetus is *not* disembodied. Rather, the specific form of embodiment inside the apparatuses of technoscience is the material conundrum presented by the cartoon. The computer is metonymic for technoscience, an inescapable materialization of the world. Life itself, a kind of technoscientific deity, may be what is virtually pregnant. These ontologically confusing *bodies,* and the practices that produce specific embodiment, are what we have to address, not the false problem of *dis*embodiment.[17] Whose and which bodies—human and nonhuman, silicon based and carbon based—are at stake, and how, in our technoscientific dramas of origin?

The proliferating readings of Kelly's cartoon make one conclusion inescapable: Reversals and substitutions undo the original, opening the story up in unexpected ways. Themselves forms of repetition, reversals and substitutions make the condition of all repetition obvious. The great stories of mimesis are undone. Caricature breaks the unspoken agreements that stabilized the original. Caricatures break the frame of salvation history. Perhaps that point gives the key for reading the multiple out-of-frame elements of Kelly's cartoon. The pregnancy is ectopic, to say the least; the fetal umbilical cord and barely visible placenta go off screen on the display terminal, and the electrical cords wander up and off screen from the whole cartoon with no point of attachment in view. The computer terminal, itself a work station, seems to be the metafetus in the picture. Further, this metafetus is an extrauterine abortus, with ripped-out umbilical cords like those in Lennart Nilsson's emblematic photographs of the beginnings of life itself. There is an odd kind of obstetrical art and technology at work here. it is not just Dürer's visual technology that makes a feminist "recall" the gynecological exam and the life class, those troubling and productive scenes of medical science and of art. In Kelly's meditation, the examination of both art and life is distinctly eccentric.

Fetal Work Stations and Feminist Technoscience Studies

If Kelly's fetus cannot be the woman's reflection, the unborn being might be her, or someone's, project. More likely, the fetus in cyberspace signifies an entity that is constituted by many variously related communities of practice. This fetus is certainly an object of attention and a locus of work, and Kelly's First Woman is at her work station.[18] Feminist scholars have also been at a "fetal work station." Like data processors at their video terminals in the information economy, feminists' positions at their analytical keyboards have not always been a matter of choice. Reproduction has been at the center of scientific, technological, political, personal, religious, gender, familial, class, race, and national webs of contestation for at least the past twenty-five years. Like it or not, as if we were children dealing with adults' hidden secrets, feminists could not avoid relentlessly asking where babies come from. Our answers have repeatedly challenged the reduction of that original and originating question to literalized and universalized women's body parts. It turns out that addressing the question of where babies come from puts us at the center of the action in the New World Order. With roots in local and international women's health movements as well as in various scholarly communities, since the early 1970s feminists have developed a rich toolkit for technoscience studies through their attention to the social-technical webs that constitute reproductive practice.[19] Idiosyncratically, I will inspect a small, recent inventory from this toolbox in order to pursue my inquiry into the optical properties of the virtual speculum.

In their powerful paper on the many constituencies who construct the French abortifacient called RU486, sociologist Adele Clarke and her former student Teresa Montini developed social worlds and arena analysis for feminist science studies (Clarke and Montini 1993).[20] Clarke and Montini are clear that their own analysis turns the volume up or down on some actors more than others; their own representations are part of the struggle for what will count as reproductive freedom, and for whom. Attention to this kind of point characterizes feminist science studies in general, whether generated from the academy or from policy-forming and community-action sites.

Using these tools, Monica Casper (1995b) studies human fetal surgery historically and ethnographically. Casper is developing the notions of the "technofetus" and the "fetus as work object." Casper's approach shows the fetus to be the site and result of multiple actors' work practices, including the mother's. Because Casper is necessarily a member of interdigitating communities of scholarly and political practice, her own positioning is neither invisible nor unaccountable. The many communities of practice that are held together around the technofetus are by no means necessarily in harmony. Their work tools—rhetorical and material—can make the fetus into very different kinds of entities. However, neither "multiplicity" nor "contestation" for their own sake are the point in feminist science studies. Joining analysts to subjects and objects of analysis, questions of power, resources, skills, suffering, hopes, meanings, and lives are always at stake.

In a similar spirit, Charis Cussins, trained in a science studies program, traces the continual "ontological choreography" that constructs subjects, objects, and agents at an infertility clinic (Cussins 1994). Subjects and objects are made and unmade in many ways in the extended processes of infertility treatment. Cussins shows that the different stakes, temporalities, trajectories, and connections and disconnections to women's and other's bodies and part-bodies—as humans and nonhumans are enrolled together in the practices of technoscience— require ethnographic, sustained inquiry.

Anthropologist Rayna Rapp's multiyear ethnographic study of women in New York City from many social classes, ethnicities, language communities, and racially marked groups also vividly describes the plethora of material-semiotic worlds in which fetuses and pregnant women have their being (Rapp 1994, 1997, this volume). Women who accept and who refuse the procedures of fetal genetic diagnosis, research geneticists, genetic counselors, family members, support groups for people with genetically disabled children—all these people, variously intertwined with machines, babies, fetuses, clinical materials, and each other, make up Rapp's research community. The consequences of all the actors' locations in these dynamic, differentiated worlds are crucial to her account, and her own profound mutations in the course of doing the work grow from and feed back into the research and writing.

In the linked interdisciplinary worlds of feminist accounts of technoscience, Valerie Hartouni, located professionally in a communications department, takes up the many contending discourses of maternal nature in contemporary reproductive cultures in the United States. In a subtle and incisive series of papers, Hartouni examines first how class, gender, and genetic parenthood interdigitate in the Baby M surrogate mother legal arguments; then how the judicial injunction not to speak of race in the case of the African American gestational surrogate Anna Johnson, who carried a child for a mixed-race (Filipina-Anglo) couple, was nonetheless part of the saturation of the case with racial and class markings; and finally how the performance video *S'Aline's Abortion,* despite explicit prochoice intentions, nonetheless was positioned by its visual rhetoric inside antichoice narratives for many audiences (Hartouni 1991; 1992; 1994; and 1997).[21] Hartouni's work is part of the broad feminist inquiry into how genetic relationship displaces other discourses of connection to a child in legal, biotechnical, familial, and entertainment worlds. Her writing contributes to the project of crafting the feminist visual literacy needed for working effectively inside a reproductive technoscience politics saturated with visual communications practices.

Reproductive politics are at the heart of questions about citizenship, liberty, family, and nation. Feminist questions are not a "special preserve" but a "general" discourse critical for science studies as such. Inaugural acts of chief executive officers in mid-1990s U.S. politics illustrate an aspect of this claim. After taking the oath of office as president of the United States in January 1993, Bill Clinton issued his first executive orders, which established his presidency symbolically and materially. His first acts did not concern war or other conventional domains of national interest and manly action. His first acts had to do with embryos and fetuses embedded in technoscientific contestations. Through embryos and fetuses, those orders had to do with entire forms of life—public, embodied, and personal—for the citizens of the state. Clinton began the process of lifting restrictions on providing information about abortion in federally funded clinics, permitting medical experimentation on aborted fetal tissue, and allowing the importation of the controversial abortifacient and potential cancer treatment RU486.

Similarly, but with opposite political intent, the first official act of Pete Wilson after he was reelected governor of California in 1994 was to order the closing of a state program that provided prenatal care to pregnant "undocumented" immigrant women. Wilson had staked his campaign on Proposition 187, which denied so-called illegal immigrants virtually all social services, especially public education and nonemergency medical care. Despite the denials of its backers, Proposition 187 was widely understood to have fundamental racial-ethnic, class, and national targets, especially working-class Latinos of color coming across the Mexican-U.S. border. The measure passed by a two-to-one margin. That is, Proposition 187 was overwhelmingly popular with the older, Republican, white, and economically affluent electorate who voted in the 1994 election—many of whom, including a candidate for U.S. Senate who supported Proposition 187, had recently hired "illegal" women of color to care for their white children while seeking to withhold social services from the children of these same employees. To withhold reproductive health care from "undocumented" women of color, whose children would be born U.S. citizens if their pregnancies came to term in California, was the first concern of the reelected executive. Fetal protection (and the health of women) suddenly looked like a bad idea, and fetal endangerment (and the endangerment of "illegal" women of color) was the direct implication of the governor's inaugural act. Biomedicine—where postnatal people, machines, fetuses, health beliefs, belief,s diagnostic procedures, and bodily fluids are enrolled together in potent configurations—was the arena of conflict. Biomedicine is where freedom, justice, and citizenship were at stake.

Finally, another of Clinton's first public acts as commander in chief threatened to queer the sacred site of the citizen-warrior by changing the U.S. armed forces' policy of excluding acknowledged gay men and lesbians from the military. The citizen-soldier's "manliness" has long been at the center of the political theory of the state and citizenship. However inadequately, color and gender were addressed in the U.S. military before the category of queer. The tragicomic panic that ensued in Congress and among the Joint Chiefs of Staff thwarted Clinton's intent to deal with the matter by executive order. My point is that discursive, embodied entities such as the fetus, the pregnant immigrant, and the homosexual are not the subjects of "social" issues, in contrast to "political" matters of state and public policy. Like the embryo or fetus and the "undocumented" pregnant woman, the queer is at the heart of contests to reconfigure precisely what public space is and who inhabits it. Technoscience is intrinsic to all of these struggles.

The work sketched here shows that to study technoscience requires an immersion in worldly material-semiotic practices, where the analysts, as well as the humans and nonhumans studied, are all at risk—morally, politically, technically, and epistemologically. Science studies that do not take on that kind of situated knowledge practice stand a good chance of floating off screen into an empyrean and academic never-never land. "Ethnography," in this extended sense, is not so much a specific procedure in anthropology as it is a method of being at risk in the face of the practices and discourses into which one inquires. To be at risk is not the same thing as identifying with the subjects of study; quite the contrary. And self-identity is as much at risk as the temptation to identification. One is at risk in the face of serious nonidentity that challenges previous stabilities, convictions, or ways of being of many kinds. An "ethnographic attitude" can be adopted within any kind of inquiry, including textual analysis. Not limited to a specific discipline, an ethnographic attitude is a mode of practical and theoretical attention, a way of remaining mindful and accountable. Such a method is not about "taking sides" in a predetermined way. But it is about risks, purposes, and hopes—one's own and others'—embedded in knowledge projects.[22]

Ethnography is not only a mode of attention, however. Textual analysis must be articulated with many kinds of sustained scholarly interaction among living people in living situations, historical and contemporary, documentary and *in vivo*. These different studies need each other, and they are all theory-building projects. No one person does all the kinds of work; feminist science studies is a collective undertaking that cultivates a practice of learning to be at risk in all the sorts of work necessary to an account of technoscience and medicine.

Under these conditions, looking for a feminist doctrine on reproductive technology, in particular, or on technoscience, in general, would be ludicrous. But understanding feminist technoscience scholarship as a contentious search for what accountability to freedom projects for women might mean, and how such meanings are crafted and sustained in a polyglot world of men and women, is not ludicrous. Preset certainties, feminist and otherwise, about what is happening in theaters of reproduction, or any theater of technoscience, stand an excellent chance of being flagrantly wrong. But feminist questions shape vision-generating technologies for science studies. Freedom and justice questions are intrinsic to the inquiry about the joinings of humans and nonhumans. Feminist technoscience inquiry is a speculum, a surgical instrument, a tool for widening all kinds of orifices to improve observation and intervention in the interest of projects that are simultaneously about freedom, justice, and knowledge. In these terms, feminist inquiry is no more innocent, no more free of the inevitable wounding that all questioning brings, than any other knowledge project.

It does not matter much to the figure of the still gestating, feminist, antiracist, mutated modest witness whether freedom, justice, and knowledge are branded as modernist or not; that is not our issue. We have never been modern (Latour 1993; Haraway 1994b). Rather, freedom, justice, and knowledge are—in bell hooks's terms—about "yearning," not about putative Enlightenment foundations. Keep your eyes on the prize. Keep our eyes on the prize. For hooks, yearning is an affective and political sensibility allowing cross-category ties that "would promote the recognition of common commitments and serve as a base for solidarity and coalition" (hooks 1990:27).[23] Yearning must also be seen as a cognitive sensibility. Without doubt, such yearning is rooted in a reconfigured unconscious, in mutated desire, in the practice of love,[24] in the ecstatic hope for the corporeal and imaginary materialization of the antiracist female subject of feminism, and all other possible subjects of feminism. Finally, freedom, justice, and knowledge are not necessarily nice and definitely not easy. Neither vision nor touch is painless, on or off screen.

The Right Speculum for the Job[25]

An inquiry into instruments of visualization, Kelly's cartoon can carry us another step toward understanding feminist science studies. *Virtual Speculum* is replete with signifiers of *choice*, a term that has been encrusted by colonies of semiotic barnacles in the reproductive politics of the last quarter century. What counts as choice, for whom, and at what cost? What is the relation of "choice" to "life," and especially to "life itself"?

Kelly's cartoon is not denunciatory. I do not see in it any stereotyped position on new reproductive technologies or pious certainty about supposed alienation and disembodiment. Nor is Kelly's cartoon celebratory. It does not reflect credit on the original; it does not announce a new scientific age in the image of an original Creation. The cartoon depends on signifiers of information and communications technologies. *Information* is a technical term for signal-to-noise discrimination; information is a statistical affair for dealing with differences. Information is not embedded in a metaphysics of reflection and representation. The pixel grid of the cartoon's screen will not yield a point-for-point emplotment of an original body, disciplined through an ontology and epistemology of mimesis, reflection, and representation. Kelly is not Dürer.

Instead, *Virtual Speculum* is diffractive and interrogatory: It asks, "Is this what feminists mean by choice, agency, life, and creativity? What is at stake here, and for whom? Who and what are human and nonhuman centers of action? Whose story is this? Who cares?" The view screen records interfering and shifted—diffracted—patterns of signifiers and bodies. What displacements in reproductive positioning matter to whom, and why? What are the conditions of effective reproductive freedom? Why are public and personal narratives of self-creation linked to those of pregnancy? Whose stories are these? Who is in the cartoon, who is missing, and so what? What does it mean to have the public fetus on screen? Whose fetuses merit such extraordinary attention? What does it mean to embed a joke about self-creation and pregnancy inside Western and "white" con-

ventions for painting the female nude? Kelly's cartoon is embedded inside signifiers of the Creation, Renaissance, Scientific Revolution, Information Age, and
New World Order. How does salvation history get replicated or displaced inside
technoscience? What are the consequences of the overwhelmingly Christian signifiers of technoscience. If Michel Foucault wrote about the care of the self and
the development of disciplinary knowledge in two different cultural configurations within Western history (classical Greek and modern European), Kelly is
sketching an inquiry into the apotheosis of the fetus and reproductive technoscience as a diagnostic sign of the end of the Second Christian Millennium. How
is care of the fetus today analogous to care of the self in classical antiquity—an
elite set of practices for producing certain kinds of subjects?

What is the right speculum for the job of opening up observation into the
orifices of the technoscientific body politic to address these kinds of questions
about knowledge projects? I want to approach that question by going back to the
eruption of the gynecological speculum as a symbol in U.S. feminist politics in
the early 1970s. Many feminists among my cohorts—largely young, white, middle-class women—"seized the masters' tools" in the context of the Women's
Liberation Movement and its activist women's health movement.[26] Armed with a
gynecological speculum, a mirror, a flashlight, and—most of all—each other in a
consciousness-raising group, women ritually opened their bodies to their own
literal view. The speculum had become the symbol of the displacement of the
female midwife by the specialist male physician and gynecologist. The mirror was
the symbol forced on women as a signifier of our own bodies as spectacle-for-
another in the guise of our own supposed narcissism. Vision itself seemed to be
the empowering act of conquerors.

More than a little amnesiac about how colonial travel narratives work, we
peered inside our vaginas toward the distant cervix and said something like,
"Land ho! We have discovered ourselves and claim the new territory for women."
In the context of the history of Western sexual politics—that is, in the context
of the whole orthodox history of Western philosophy and technology—visually
self-possessed sexual and generative organs made potent tropes for the reclaimed
feminist self. We thought we had our eyes on the prize. I am caricaturing, of
course, but with a purpose. *Our Bodies, Ourselves* was both a popular slogan and
the title of a landmark publication in women's health movements.[27]

The repossessed speculum, sign of the Women's Liberation Movement's
attention to material instruments in science and technology, was understood to
be a self-defining technology. Those collective sessions with the speculum and
mirror were not only symbols, however. They were self-help and self-experimen-
tation practices in a period in which abortion was still illegal and unsafe. The
self-help groups developed techniques of menstrual extraction, that is, early
abortion, that could be practiced by women alone or with each other outside
professional medical control. A little flexible tubing joined the mirror and the
speculum in more than a few of those sessions. Meanwhile, biomedical clinicians
were introducing the sonogram and endoscopic fetal visualization while Lennart

Figure 7.   Wonder Woman and the Doctors.

Nilsson's photographs spread around the medicalized globe. We had to wonder early if we had seized the right tools.

Still, the sense of empowerment experienced by the women in early-1970s self-help groups was bracing. The spirit was captured in a cartoon in the July 1973 issue of *Sister, the Newspaper of the Los Angeles Women's Center* [Figure 7. *Wonder Woman and the Doctors*]. Wonder Woman—the Amazonian princess from Paradise Isle, complete with her steel bracelets that could deter bullets; stiletto high heels; low-cut, eagle-crested bodice; star-spangled blue minishorts; and magic lasso for capturing evildoers and transportation needs—seizes the radiant speculum from the white-coat-clad, stethoscope-wearing, but cowering white doctor and announces, "With my speculum, I am strong! I can fight!"

Wonder Woman entered the world in 1941 in Charles Moulton's popular cartoon strips.[28] After falling into a sad state by the end of the 1960s, she was resurrected in several venues in the early 1970s. Wonder Woman's first female comic-book editor, Dorothy Woolfolk, brought her back to the mass market in

GLORIA STEINEM
ON HOW
WOMEN VOTE

MONEY FOR
HOUSEWORK

NEW FEMINIST:
SIMONE
DE BEAUVOIR

BODY HAIR: THE
LAST FRONTIER

WONDER WOMAN FOR PRESIDENT

PEACE
AND
JUSTICE
IN '72

Figure 8. *Ms.* **magazine cover, Vol. 1, No. 1, July 1972. Reprinted with Permission.**

1973. *Ms.* magazine put Wonder Woman on the cover of its first issue in July 1972 under the slogan "Wonder Woman for President" [Figure 8. *Wonder Woman Cover of Ms.*]. The Vietnam War was raging on one side of the cover and a "Peace and Justice in '72" billboard adorned the storefronts on a U.S. street on the other side. A gigantic Wonder Woman was grabbing a U.S. fighter jet out of the sky with one hand and carrying an enlightened city in her magic lasso in the other hand. The city might be a feminist prototype for SimCity 2000™.[29]

Wonder Woman's lasso outlined a glowing urban tetrahedron that would have made Buckminster Fuller proud.

In their groundbreaking 1973 pamphlet on medicine and politics, feminist academic and activist historians Barbara Ehrenreich and Dierdre English reprinted the *Sister* Wonder Woman figure seizing the speculum. The context was the chapter on the future, in which the authors emphasized that "self help is not an alternative to confronting the medical system with the demands for reform of existing institutions. Self help, or more generally, self-knowledge, is critical to that confrontation. Health is an issue which has the potential to cut across class and race lines.... The growth of feminist consciousness gives us the possibility, for the first time, of a truly egalitarian, mass women's health movement" (1973:84–85).[30] Ehrenreich and English emphasized that not all women had the same histories or needs in the medical system. "For black women, medical racism often overshadows medical sexism. For poor women of all ethnic groups, the problem of how to get services of any kind often overshadows all qualitative concerns.... A movement that recognized our biological similarity but denies the diversity of our priorities cannot be a women's health movement, it can only be *some women's* health movement" (1973:86; italics in original).

The speculum was not a reductionist symbolic and material tool that limited the feminist health movement to the politics of "choice" defined by demands for legal, safe abortion and attention to the new reproductive technologies. Nor was the speculum definitive of an exclusivist, middle-class, white movement. The women's health movement was actively built, and often pioneered, by women of color and their specific organizations as well as by mixed and largely white groups that cut across class lines.[31] That legacy is too often forgotten in the terrible history of racism, class-blindness, generational arrogance, and fragmentation in American feminism as well as in other sectors of U.S. progressive politics. However, the fullest meanings of reproductive freedom critical to feminist technoscience politics cannot easily be signified by the gynecological speculum or by the virtual speculum of the computer terminal, no matter how important it remains to control, inhabit, and shape those tools, both semiotically and materially. The networks of millionaires and billionaires from Paul Simon's song at the beginning of this chapter still determine the nature of the U.S. health system, including reproductive health, for everybody. The structure and consequences of that complex determination are what we must learn to see if "choice" is to have robust meaning. The last verse of "The Boy in the Bubble" reminds us that the relentless bursts of "information"—in transnational urban and rural jungles—are a long-distance call we cannot ignore. And Bell Telephone is not the only carrier.

The Statistics of Freedom Projects

A speculum does not have to be a literal physical tool for prying open tight orifices; it can be any instrument for rendering a part accessible to observation. So I will turn to another kind of speculum—statistical analysis coupled with free-dom- and justice-oriented policy formation—to find a sharper focus for describing what feminists must mean by reproductive freedom, in particular, and technoscientific liberty, in general. In this chapter, in relation to the goals of feminist technoscience studies, I have adopted the civil rights rallying cry, "Keep your eyes on the prize!" I mean my appropriation of this phrase to emphasize that conducting an analysis of reproductive freedom from the point of view of *marked* groups—groups that do not fit the white, or middle-class, or other "unmarked" standard—is the only way to produce anything like a general statement that can bind us together as a people. Working uncritically from the viewpoint of the "standard" groups is the best way to come up with a particularly parochial and limited analysis of technoscientific knowledge or policy, which then masquerades as a general account that stands a good chance of reinforcing unequal privilege. However, there is rarely only one kind of standard and one kind of relative mar-ginality operating at the same time. Groups that do not fit one kind of standard can be the unmarked, standard, or dominant group in another respect. Also, reproductive freedom is only one piece of what feminist technoscientific liberty must include, for women and men. Feminist technoscience studies are about much more than reproductive and health matters. Feminist technoscience studies are about technoscience in *general*. But, fundamentally, there is no way to make a *general* argument outside the never-finished work of articulating the partial worlds of *situated* knowledges. Feminism is not defined by the baby-making capacity of women's bodies; but working from that capacity, in all of its power-differentiated and culturally polyglot forms, is *one* critical link in the articulations necessary for forging freedom and knowledge projects inside technoscience.

Associate Counsel and Director of the Black Women's Employment Program of the NAACP Legal Defense and Educational Fund (LDF) Charlotte Rutherford (1992) provides the needed perspective. A civil rights lawyer, feminist, African American woman, and mother, Rutherford articulates what reproductive free-dom must mean and shows how both women's groups and civil rights organiza-tions would have to change their priorities in order to take such freedom into account. Her argument is the fruit of intensive meetings with many African American women's groups and internal debate in the LDF in 1989–1990 on Black women's reproductive health and the U.S. Supreme Court rulings on abortion restrictions. A group of nationally prominent African American women active in public policy issues "maintained that reproductive freedoms are civil rights issues for African American women" (Rutherford 1992:257). From that perspective, I maintain, reproductive freedom *in general* has a much sharper resolution.

Included in the LDF formulation of reproductive freedoms for poor women were, at a minimum, "(1) access to reproductive health care; (2) access to early diagnosis and proper treatment for AIDS, sexually transmitted diseases, and various cancers; (3) access to prenatal care, including drug treatment programs for pregnant and parenting drug abusers; (4) access to appropriate contracep-tives; (5) access to infertility services; (6) freedom from coerced or ill-informed consent to sterilization; (7) economic security, which could prevent possible exploitation of the poor with surrogacy contracts; (8) freedom from toxics in the workplace; (9) healthy nutrition and living space; and (10) the right to safe, legal, and affordable abortion services" (Rutherford 1992:257–58). It seems to me that all citizens would be better served by such a policy than from an approach to reproductive choice or rights that begins and ends in the well-insured, sono-graphically monitored, Bell Telephone system-nurtured uterus with its public fetus. These are the pulsating, relentless bursts of information in Paul Simon's song. These are "The Boy in the Bubble"'s long-distance message.

Not all African American women are poor, and not all poor women are African American, to say the least. And all the categories are discursively consti-tuted and noninnocently deployed, both by those who inhabit them (by choice, coercion, inheritance, or chance) and those who do not (by choice, coercion, inheritance, or chance). I believe that *learning* to think about and yearn toward reproductive freedom from the *analytical and imaginative standpoint* of "African American women in poverty"—a ferociously lived discursive category to which I do not have "personal" access—illuminates the general conditions of such free-dom. A standpoint is not an empiricist appeal to or by "the oppressed" but a cog-nitive, psychological, and political tool for more adequate knowledge judged by the nonessentialist, historically contingent, situated standards of strong objectiv-ity. Such a standpoint is the always fraught but necessary fruit of the *practice* of oppositional and differential consciousness. A feminist standpoint is a practical technology rooted in yearning, not an abstract philosophical foundation.[32]

Therefore, feminist knowledge is rooted in imaginative connection and hard-won, practical coalition—which is not the same thing as identity but does demand self-critical situatedness and historical seriousness. Situatedness does not mean parochialism or localism; but it does mean specificity and consequen-tial, if variously mobile, embodiment. Connection and coalition are bound to sometimes painful structures of accountability to each other and to the worldly hope for freedom and justice.[33] If they are not so bound, connection and coali-tion disintegrate in orgies of moralism. In the kind of feminist standpoint remembered and put back to work in this chapter, much important feminist knowledge must be technically "impersonal." Statistics have an important but fraught history in the crafting of authoritative, impersonal knowledge in democ-ratic societies. The history of statistics is directly related to the ideals of objectiv-ity and democracy.

In Theodore Porter's terms (1994; 1995), statistics is a basic technology for crafting objectivity and stabilizing facts. Objectivity is less about realism than it is about intersubjectivity. The impersonality of statistics is one aspect of the com-plex intersubjectivity of objectivity; that is, of the public quality of techno-scien-tific knowledge. Feminists have high stakes in the speculum of statistical knowledge for opening up otherwise invisible, singular experience to reconfigure public, widely lived reality. Credible statistical representation is one aspect of building connection and coalition that has nothing to do with moralistic "standing in the place of the oppressed" by some act of imperialistic fantasy or with other caricatures of feminist intersubjectivity and feminist standpoint. Demanding the competent staffing and funding of the bureaus that produce reliable statistics, producing statistical representations in our own institutions, and contesting for the interpretation of statistics are indispensable to feminist technoscientific politics. Providing powerful statistical data is essential to effective public representations of what feminist and other progressive freedom and justice projects mean.[34] Recording, structuring, processing, and articulating such data should raise at least as interesting scientific problems as any that have merited a Nobel Prize in economics so far.

Porter argued that "it is precisely the communicability of numbers and of these rules [for manipulating numbers] that constitutes their claim to objectivity.... The crucial insight there is to see objectivity as a way of forming ties across wide distances" (1994:48). Porter believed that this kind of objectivity inheres in specialist communities, which rely on expertise rather than on community and which substitute quantitative representations for trust and face-to-face interactions. He sees such modes of objectivity as ill adapted to express moral and ethical arguments (49). However, I believe that the history of struggle to recraft and stabilize public realities as part of learning to put together general policies from the analytical, imaginative, and embodied standpoint of those who inhabit too many zones of unfreedom and yearn toward a more just world shows "impersonal," quantitative knowledge to be a vital dimension of moral, political, and personal reflection and action.

Crafting a politics that refuses the constrictions of both the abortion and the new reproductive technology debates, with their inadequate discourse of choice, Charlotte Rutherford explores the requirements for reproductive freedom by means of statistical illustrations of the differential conditions that are experienced by women differently marked by race and class in the United States (Rutherford 1992). For example, in 1990, "29.3% of all African American families had incomes below the poverty level, compared to 8.1% of white families and 10.7% of families of all races" (1992:257n8). In 1985, because of the confluence of medically uninsured women's situations and the fact that 80 percent of private insurance policies did not include office visits or services for preventive, non-surgical reproductive health care, "at least 76% of all women of reproductive age must pay themselves for preventive, non-surgical health care" (258n11). "The maternal mortality rate (the number of deaths of mothers per 100,000 live births) for all African American women in 1986 was 19.3 compared to 4.7 for white mothers" (259n12). "In 1986, African American women were 3.8 times more likely than white women to die from pregnancy-related causes" (260). "Blacks were more than twice as likely as whites to have late (third trimester) or no prenatal care, ... and the frequency of late or no care among American Indians was at least as high as that for Blacks" (260n15).

"In 1991, almost five million working mothers maintained their families alone and 22.3% of them lived in poverty.... In 1988, of all poor African

American families, 75.6% were maintained by African American women alone, compared to 44% of poor white families and 47.8% of poor Hispanic families" (264n32). "In 1987, only 18% of the pregnancies to women under age 20 resulted in births that were intended, while 40% resulted in births that were not intended, and 42% ended in abortion" (265n38). "Among households headed by individuals between 15 and 24 years of age, the poverty rate is staggering: 65.3% for young African American families and 28.5% for young white families" (266n45). "The risk of infertility is one and a half times greater for African Americans [23% of couples] than for whites [15% of couples]" (267). "Whites and those with higher incomes are more likely to pursue infertility treatment than are African Americans and the poor" (168). "About 75% of low-income women in need of infertility services have not received any services. . . . Among all higher income women, 47% [in need of them] have received no services" (268n56). Among physicians who provide infertility services in the United States, only 21 percent accept Medicaid patients for such care (268n61). "By 1982, only fifteen percent of white women were sterilized, compared to twenty-four percent of African American women, thirty-five percent of Puerto Rican women, and forty-two percent of Native American women. Among Hispanic women living in the Northeast, sterilization rates as high as sixty-five percent have been reported" (273–74). Even in the 1990s, the federal government will pay for sterilization for poor women but not for abortions. The worst sterilization abuses of the recent past have been reduced by consent forms and procedures put in place since the 1970s, but the conditions leading poor women to "choose" sterilization more often because other options are worse are not acceptable. Meanwhile, "in 1985 eighty-two percent of all counties in the United States—home to almost one-third of the women of reproductive age—had no abortion provider" (280). To say the least, the situation has not improved in the 1990s. Restrictions on poor women's access to abortion mean later abortions. "In 1982, after the ban on federal funding was implemented, 50% of Medicaid-eligible patients had their abortions after nine weeks of pregnancy, compared with only 37% of non-Medicaid-eligible women" (280n128).

Rutherford also shows that toxins and other hazards in neighborhoods and workplaces differentially damage poor people and people of color because they get more intensive and long-term exposures. To be a houseworker or janitor, hospital worker, farm worker, dry-cleaning or laundry employee, chicken processor, tobacco worker, or fabric-mill worker is to experience a lifetime of toxic exposure that can damage reproductive cells and fetuses, not to mention adult bodily tissues. Pesticides, heat, noise, dust, mechanical hazards, poor nutrition, inadequate medical care, and high levels of stress lower life expectancies of adults, children, and fetuses. Those predominantly female occupations held disproportionately by women of color are especially dangerous to fetal and maternal health. The only thing that might be even more damaging to freedom and health is unemployment. Is anyone really surprised? "Who cares?" is the fundamental question for technoscientific liberty and science studies. Toxics are a civil rights issue, a reproductive freedom concern, and a feminist technoscience matter; that is, toxics are a general issue for technoscientific knowledge and freedom projects.[35]

The age of designer fetuses on screen is also the age of sharp disparities in reproductive health, and therefore of sharp disparities in technoscientific liberty. In the 1990s, fetuses are objects of public obsession. It is almost impossible to get through the day near the end of the Second Christian Millennium in the United States without being in communication with the public fetus. In these days of miracle and hype, the public fetus may be the way we look to distant galaxies. The fetus hurtling through space at the end of the movie *2001* is not a feminist image; neither is the long-distance touch of Bell Telephone. In alliance with the women meeting with Charlotte Rutherford at the Legal Defense and Educational Fund, both Kelly's First Woman with her finger on the divine keyboard and *Sister's* Wonder Woman seizing the gynecological speculum must work to make the general community of women publicly visible as movers and shakers in technoscience. That much, at least, is owed to the people who taught us all to keep our eyes on the prize. "With my speculum, I *am* strong! I *can* fight!" There is still a chance, barely, to build a truly comprehensive feminist technoscience politics.

The Invisible Fetus

> There are many lives and even more deaths to keep track of, numbering the bones of a people whom the state hardly thinks worth counting at all.
> —Nancy Scheper-Hughes, *Death Without Weeping*

It seems fitting to close this meditation on the virtual speculum with an image that is not there—with the *missing* representations of fetuses and babies that must trouble anyone yearning for reproductive freedom. In a world replete with images and representations, whom can we not see or grasp, and what are the consequences of such selective blindness? From the point of view of a barely imaginable, desperately needed, transnational, intercultural, and resolutely situated feminism—a feminism circulating in networks at least as disseminated, differentiated, and resilient as those of flexible capitalism's New World Order, Inc.—questions about optics are inescapable. How is visibility possible? For whom, by whom, and of whom? What remains invisible, to whom, and why? For those peoples who are excluded from the visualizing apparatuses of the disciplinary regimes of modern power-knowledge networks, the *averted gaze* can be as deadly as the all-seeing panopticon that surveys the subjects of the biopolitical state. Moreover, counting and visualizing are also essential to freedom projects. Not counting and not looking, for example in health and well-being, can kill the New World Order as surely as the avid seminal gaze of state curiosity, for example in the fixing of the criminal or the addict. Similarly, the assumed naturalness of ways of living and dying can be as intolerable as the monomaniacal construction and production of all the world as technical artifact. By now we should all know that both naturalization and technicization are equally necessary to the regimes of flexible accumulation.

Because my last image springs from a missing gaze, I have no picture to print, no reprinting permission to seek. In the demographers' language, this non-image is of human "reproductive wastage," that is, of the dead babies and fetuses, the *missing* offspring, who populate the earth's off-screen worlds in unimaginable numbers in the late twentieth century. These are fully "modern" or "postmodern" fetuses and babies, brought into invisible existence within the same New World Order that ordains bright lights, genetic gymnastics, and cybernetic wonders for the public fetuses of the better-off citizens of planet Earth at the end of the Second Christian Millennium. These missing fetuses and babies are not residues of some sad traditional past that can be scrubbed clean by the new brooms of modernity and its sequelae in postmodernity's regimes of flexible accumulation. Quite the contrary: The missing images, and what they represent, are precisely contemporary with and embedded in the same networks as the all-too-visible on-screen fetal data structures. If Anne Kelly's on-line fetus is postmodern, so is the uncounted fetus I am seeking in this essay. And vice versa, if "we" have never been modern, neither have "they."[36] Temporality takes many shapes in the wormholes of technoscience, but the least believable figures are the divisions of the world and its inhabitants into modern and premodern, progressive and traditional, and similar conventions. The solid geometry of historical time is much more troubling than that.

Of course, images of hungry babies and children, if not fetuses, periodically fill our television screens. The *mode* of presence and absence changes for differently positioned citizens in technoscientific public reproductive visual culture more than absolute presence or absence. The visual icons of hungry infants do not perform the same semiotic work as the icons of the highly cultivated onscreen fetuses favored by Bell Telephone. Here, I want to explore one form of off-screen, out-of-frame positioning for the children of contemporary, expanding, marginalized populations.

Nancy Scheper-Hughes is responsible for my missing visual text as I follow her through her search in the municipal records offices and *favelas*, or slums, of a town in a sugar-plantation region of the Brazilian Nordeste over the past twenty-five years. Besides drastically reducing the complexity of accounts in her book, my sketch adds analogies, renarrativizes, and uses parts of her story in ways she did not. But we are enmeshed together in webs spun by yearning and analysis.

Developing John Berger's image, Scheper-Hughes, an anthropologist, saw herself as a "clerk or keeper of the records"—listening, watching, and recording those events and entities that the powerful do not want to know about (Scheper-Hughes 1992:29).[37] For Scheper-Hughes, recording was a work of recognition and an act of solidarity. She attempted to count, to make statistically visible, the reproductive history, and especially the dead babies, of the poorest women in the Brazilian town. Moreover, she linked the existence and numbers of those dead babies to precisely the same global/local developments that led their richer sisters, living in the neighborhoods in which many of the impoverished *favela* women worked as domestics, to seek the latest in prenatal care and reproductive medicine. Undercounted and on screen: Those were the two states of being under examination.[38]

Caught in a nightmare, I am forced to remember another context in which offspring are counted in the regimes of technoscience. An equation in theroretical population biology has two variable quantities, r and K, which can be linked to different reproductive "strategies" adopted by species in the context of the theory of natural selection. "K-selected species" are said to "invest" tremendous resources in each individual offspring and to have rather few offspring over their lives. Each offspring, then, is a valued "reproductive investment," in the ordinary but nonetheless stupefying language of investment-portfolio management in which Darwin's theory has been developed in this century. On the other hand, "r-selected species" are said to adopt the strategy of spewing as many offspring into the world as possible, with little physiological or biosocial investment in any individual, in the hope that some offspring will survive to reproduce. For biologists, all human beings, with their large and expensive fetuses and infants who take many years to mature to reproductive age, are paradigmatic K-selected organisms. Dandelions or cockroaches, with their abundant offspring, none of whom get many nutritious goodies packed into their embryos or much parental attention during development, are typical r-selected creatures. Low infant mortality is the norm for K-strategists; high infant mortality is the normal state of affairs for r-strategists. As the sociobiological authors Martin Daly and Margo Wilson put it, the contrast is between "profligacy or careful nurture" (1978:124). [39] Careful parents with solid family values versus vermin and weeds: That seems to be the gist of the story in this reading of an equation. I translate this lesson in evolutionary theory into human reproductive politics in the New World Order: intensely cultivated fetuses, located at the center of national culture and portrayed as individuals from fertilization on, versus throwaway fetuses and dead babies, located "down there" and known only as "angels."

In the U.S. imperialist imaginary, societies "down there" relative to the United States, in the warm and sordid regions of the planet, seem to have lots of human beings who act like r-strategists. The colder, more cerebral, less genital climes to the north—if one discounts immigrants of color and other nonprogressive types common in racist imagery—are replete with good K-strategists.[40] The supposedly natural craving for a healthy child genetically related to the parents, which is said to drive reproductive heroics in contemporary wealthy nations or parts of town, seems almost to be a bad joke about K-selection. The fetus—and the child tied into lucrative markets of all kinds—becomes so important that media conglomerates and biomedical industries, who have much more money than mothers and fathers, seem to be the major reproductive investors. Meanwhile, literally many hundreds of millions of children experience serious deprivation, including 15 million hungry children in the United States in the mid-1990s.[41] The stereotypical rich people's lament that the poor have too many children seems to be an even worse joke about r-selection.[42] There is too much hunger, and hunger of too many types, independently of whether there are too many children of the rich or of the poor.

I strongly believe that there are too many people on earth, not just millions but billions too many for long-term survival of ourselves and incomprehensible numbers of other species. That belief in no way softens questions of justice and freedom about who survives and reproduces and how. The individual human beings matter; the communities matter. Counting matters. Further, reducing population growth rates and absolute numbers in every class, race, ethnicity, and other category on Earth will not necessarily reduce habitat destruction, urban or rural poverty, pollution, hunger, crime, agricultural land devastation, over-crowding, unemployment, or most other evils. Population levels are not causes in such a simple sense. The story of inter-relationship is much more complex, and it is hotly contested. I am convinced that the success of comprehensive free-dom and justice projects would do a much better job of alleviating suffering and reducing resource and habitat devastation than population limitation policies in the absence of such commitments. Those statements are also beliefs, ones deeply enmeshed in the fraught worlds of technoscience.

On the one hand, it seems that demographers and population specialists of every stripe do nothing but count human beings. United Nations reports, World Bank studies, national censuses, and innumerable reference works are full of data about population and reproduction for every spot on Earth. On the other hand, a clerk of the records—working out of the traditions of Catholic liberation theol-ogy, socialist feminism, medical anthropology, and risk-taking ethnography—was still needed to count missing children in the biopolitical age. In a time of crushing overpopulation, the perverse fact is that there are *too few* living babies among the poorest residents on earth, too few in a sense that matters to thinking about technoscience studies and reproductive freedom. These missing and dead babies are, of course, intrinsic to the ongoing production of overpopulation. The surplus death of the children of the poor is closer to a cause of overpopulation than one is likely to find by many other routes of analysis. The 1994 United Nations meetings on population and development in Cairo prominently advanced this proposition. Getting a grip on the motor of this surplus death is a problem of world-historical proportions. Wherever else this problem leads, it should take us to the center of feminist technoscience studies.

To pursue these claims, let us turn back to Nancy Scheper-Hughes's story. A U.S. white citizen, she first went to the *favelas* of the Nordeste of Brazil in 1964 as an idealistic twenty-year-old public health and community development worker. In those years, she came to know many women of a particular community, and she got involved in community action programs for child care and child health. Between 1982 and 1989, after an absence of fifteen years, Scheper-Hughes returned four times to the same community, this time as an anthropologist, an identity she had earlier disdained. The turbulent political and economic contexts of Brazil throughout those years were never far from the surface. In oral interviews and less formal interactions, Scheper-Hughes listened to the women living in this particular shantytown as they recounted reproductive histories and their meanings. She also haunted the records offices of the municipality and of hospitals, forcing recalcitrant institutions and bureaucrats to disgorge data on births and child deaths. Trying to get a grip on how many of which classes died in a year, she talked with the municipal carpenter, whose main job seemed to be making coffins for the children of the poor. His requisitions for the materials needed to make the boxes for dead "angels" gave her more numbers for her growing numerical testimony.

Scheper-Hughes's figures covered several years and allowed some sense of the trajectory of infant and child death and of the reproductive histories of women of different generations. Besides combing local, regional, and national data sources, Scheper-Hughes talked to pharmacists, grocers, priests, and anybody else who could cast some light on her questions about birth, life, and death among the very young and very poor. She talked to the better-off citizens and prowled through data on them, getting a grip on their different reproductive experiences. Across the period of her study, laws and practices governing registration of births and deaths changed substantially. There is no illusion of comprehensive data in Scheper-Hughes's accounting, but there is nonetheless an arresting ethnographic picture of infant birth and death in the flexible matrices of the New World Order.

There is nothing particularly modern about high rates of birth and infant and child mortality for our species. The opposite is supposed to be the case. The orthodox story of modernity has it that a demographic transition occurs more or less reliably with modern economic development, such that both death rates and birth rates decline, albeit rarely if ever in a neatly coordinated fashion. "Rates" themselves are a particularly modern sort of discursive object; knowledge about progress is inconceivable, literally, without knowledge of rates of change. Death rates go down first, followed at variously unfortunate intervals by birth rates. But whatever the fits and starts of different rates for births and deaths, modernity brings in its wake a greatly lowered rate of infant and child death as a fundamental part of the demographic transition to stable populations and low birth rates.

The people among whom Nancy Scheper-Hughes studied, however, experienced quite another sort of demographic transition. Scheper-Hughes called the pattern the "modernization of child mortality" and the "routinization of infant death" (1992:268 339). Scheper-Hughes emphasized the moral, social, and emotional relations of mothers and whole communities to the extreme levels of infant death among them.[43] Riveted by the form of modernity and postmodernity she describes, I highlight here only a limited part of her story. Over the period of the study, death rates for children over a year old did decline among the very poor as well as among the better off. Childhood infectious disease, the traditional "nonmodern" killer of the young, was reduced by immunization.[44] But death rates among children less than a year old went up, and the killer—drastic undernourishment, resulting in diarrhea and death from acute dehydration—was highly modern. The modernization of child mortality meant "the standardization of child death within the first twelve months of life and its containment to the poorest and marginalized social classes" (1992:296). In the town Scheper-Hughes studied, by 1989, 96 percent of all child deaths occurred in the first year of life.

In one sense, the cause of the increase in infant mortality seems obvious and easily remediable—loss of the practice of breastfeeding. Restore the practice of breastfeeding, which has continued to decrease in each generation in the "developing world" since about 1960, and the very poor will not see their infants die in such vast numbers. Promote breastfeeding, get the artificial infant formula-makers to cooperate, teach rehydration therapy, and watch death rates come down. Get poor women to "choose" breastfeeding as their grandmothers once did. These are neither new observations nor obscure solutions, and many people work hard to put them into action.

But Scheper-Hughes argues that the modernization of infant death through starvation and dehydration is *intrinsic* to the form of development practiced in the third world under the terms set by unleashed national and transnational market forces and structural adjustment policies enforced by world sources of capital. The drastically marginalized populations that teem all over the earth, including in U.S. cities, are the direct result of up-to-to-the-minute (post)modernization policies over the past thirty years, and especially the past fifteen years. In the current, acute, global forms of dependent capitalism, "marginalized" means anything but "rare." For Brazil, Scheper-Hughes narrates the complex patterns of the "economic miracle," World Bank versions of economic development in the 1980s, practices of structural adjustment, inflation, and the resulting falling real wage of the poorest classes. In the years following the military junta in Brazil in 1964, total national wealth increased in the context of the systematic relocation of wealth from the bottom 40 percent of the population to the top 10 percent. Progressively, in the context of mass dislocations and migrations, semi-subsistence peasants have become urban, temporary, day-wage workers in large numbers. Food has become a commodity everywhere and for everyone—including the newborn.

These are the critical determinants of reproductive freedom and unfreedom in the New World Order, with its up-to-the-minute, technoscientifically mediated systems of flexible accumulation. Labor patterns, land use, capital accumulation, and current kinds of class reformation might have more to do with the flow of breast milk than whether or not Nestle has adopted policies of corporate responsibility in its third world infant-formula markets. Artificial milk is a reproductive technology, without doubt, as is the human body itself in all its historical/natural/technical complexity. But agribusiness seed technologies, which come with packages of labor and resource use, or marketing systems for national and international customers are at least as much reproductive technologies as are sonograph machines, cesarean surgical operations, or *in vitro* fertilization techniques. Those seeds and those marketing patterns are central technoscientific actors, in which humans and nonhumans of many kinds are mutually enrolled in producing ways of life and death. It is high time that studies of reproductive technologies stop assuming that their central artifacts of interest are to be found only in the biomedical clinic. In several senses, computers in financial centers in Geneva, New York, or Brasilia are reproductive technologies that have their bite in the breasts of marginalized women and the guts of their babies. It shows in the coffin-maker's invoices; the shelves of local grocery stores, where "choice" is best studied; and, as we shall see, in (post)modern customs for establishing paternity among the poor.

Why do poor women stop breastfeeding in the New World Order? How does technoscientifically mediated capital flow affect paternity-recognition rituals? Why can't "rational choice" prevail in the *favelas* of the Nordeste, and perhaps also on the flatland of the East Bay near San Francisco in California? Scheper-Hughes tells an arresting story about the corporeal economy of breast milk, diarrhea, and family formation inside Brazil's economic miracle. With all its local themes and variations, the story travels globally all too well. It encapsulates one of the plot structures of postmodern narration—one left out of semiotics textbooks and psychoanalytical theory—in which gender, race, class, and nation get-up-to-the-minute remakes.

Loosely following Scheper-Hughes's map, let us explore the parameters of breastfeeding. In the 1960s the U.S.-sponsored Food for Peace program introduced large amounts of industrially-produced powdered milk into the third world. A food inscribed with a better technoscientific pedigree and radiating more enlightened purposes would be hard to find. International aid-promoted, packaged baby milk programs ended in the 1970s, but corporations like Nestle moved in to develop the infant-formula market. Much of this market depends on very small purchases at any one time, not unlike the soft-drink industry among the impovereished. Marketing infant formula to the poor is like marketing drugs—small, cheap packages are essential to hooking to customers and developing the mass market. Active organizing emerged against the aggressive, medically inflected marketing of artificial formula to women who could neither afford the product over the long haul nor count on conditions to prepare it hygienically. After a lot of denial and resistance, in response to an international boycott started in 1978, Nestle finally adopted codes for ethical practice and modified its marketing and advertising patterns. But breastfeeding continued to decline, and infant death continued to be modernized. "Ethics" turns out to have precious little to do with "choice" in vast areas of technoscience, including the yearning for reproductive freedom.

Four factors converge in this story. First, Scheper-Hughes found that the *culture* of breastfeeding unraveled over a brief period—including both the ability of older women to teach younger women and poor women's belief in the goodness of what comes from their own bodies, compared to what comes from "modern" objects such as cans or hypodermic needles.[45] To emphasize that breastfeeding is practice and culture, just as technoscience is practice and culture, is to stress that the body is simultaneously a historical, natural, technical, discursive, and material entity. Breast milk is not nature to the culture of Nestle's formula. Both fluids are natural-technical objects, embedded in matrices of practical culture and cultural practice. Women can lose, regain, or improve the natural-technical knowledge necessary to breastfeeding, just as young elephants can lose the ability to find water in long droughts when most of the older, knowledgeable animals are killed by poaching or by inexpert culling of herds. That comparison is not a naturalization of women but an insistence on the shared natural-technical matter of living as intelligent mortal creatures on this planet. Within the kind of feminist technoscience studies that makes sense to me, breastfeeding practices, elephant cultural transmission, and laboratory and factory knowledge and commodity production are ontologically and epistemologically similar. Historical ways of life and death are at stake in each of the natural-technical categories. The differences lie in the all-important specificities.

Second, and related to loss of knowledge about how or whether to breast-feed, poor women cannot breastfeed babies in the context of the jobs that they can get after the transition from semisubsistence peasant to urban casual day laborer, including current forms of domestic service. The issue goes way beyond the Brazilian *favela* that Scheper-Hughes studied. Just as right-wing California politicians can and do agitate for withholding medical and educational benefits from the children of the migrant women who take care of these same politician-employers' offspring, modern female employers of other women can and do discourage practices that the wealthy reserve for themselves in the interest of health and family. Breast-milk storage equipment notwithstanding, babies have to be with mothers in order to breastfeed consistently. On-the-job breastfeeding facilities, as well as other aspects of affordable and comprehensive child care, remain pie-in-the-sky labor demands in most places of employment in the United States. Discursively, such facilities are costly benefits, not natural rights. It is no wonder that poor women in and out of the "third world" have much less chance to "choose" breastfeeding, even if they continue, in spite of everything, to trust their own—disproportionately poisoned—bodies to give better nutrition than modern commodities can.[46]

Third, the shelves in the groceries that served the shantytown citizens were replete with every sort of scientifically formulated milk for infants. Literate or not, the mothers were well versed in all the varieties and their relative merits for babies of different ages and conditions. "The array of 'choices' was quite daunting, and the display of infant-formula powdered milk tins and boxes took up a full aisle of the local supermarket, more than for any other food product" (Scheper-Hughes 1992:319). Like the mandatory health warning on cigarette packages in the United States, packages that disproportionately fill the poorest areas of cities, all the infant-milk containers carried required warnings about proper use of the product, consulting a physician, and refrigeration. Consumer protection is such an illuminating practice in transnational capital's progressive regulatory regimes.

Fourth and last, let us turn to a scenario of family formation, to the kind of scene beloved in psychoanalytic contributions to feminist theory. I am particularly interested here in the material/semiotic rituals that create fathers and in the practices that relocate baby's milk from the breasts disdained by responsible, loving women to the packages—replete with corporate and state warnings—carried into the home by responsible, loving men. I am interested in the metonymy that marks the implantation of the name of the father in the *favela* and in what such substitutions do to the formation of the "unconscious" in feminist technoscience studies. I believe this kind of unconscious underlies practices of yearning, oppositional consciousness, and situated knowledges. The primal scene in the *favela* is established and signified by a gift of milk. Father's milk, not semen, is his means of confirming paternity and establishing the legitimacy of his child.

Scheper-Hughes writes that in the conditions of shantytown life, marriage becomes much more informal, consensual, and, in my ironic terms, postmodern. "Shantytown households and families are 'made up' through a creative form of bricolage in which we can think of a mother and her children as the stable core and husbands and fathers as detachable, circulating units. . . . A husband is a man who provides food for his woman and her children, regardless of whether he is living with them." The symbolic transaction by which a father "claims" his child and his woman is to bring the infant's first weeks' supply of Nestogeno, an especially valued Nestlé product in a lovely purple can. A woman who breastfeeds is thought of as an abandoned woman, or a woman otherwise unprovided for or sexually disdained by a man. Ideally, the equation is, "Papa: baby's 'milk'" (Scheper-Hughes 1992:323 25). Through that particular and historical milk, meanings of paternity circulate. In this specific narration of metonymy and substitution, a powerful version of feminist desire is born. The desire is not for a supposed natural mother over and against a violating father but for a new world order in which women, men, and children can be linked in signifying chains that articulate the situated semiotic and material terms of reproductive freedom.

· · ·

The missing babies of the *favela* are carried away in diarrhea, a "sea of froth and brine. . . . 'They die,' said one woman going straight to the heart of the matter, 'because their bodies turn to water'" (Scheper-Hughes 1992:303). Through the signifying flow of commodified milk—which links children and fathers, husbands and wives, first and third worlds, centers and margins, capital and bodies, milk and excrement, anthropologist and clerk of the records—we are recirculated back into the turbulent, heterogeneous rivers of information that constitute the embryo, fetus, and baby as a modern sacrum—or cyborg kinship entity—on the globalized planet Earth. The diarrhea of angels mixes with the amniotic fluid of on-screen fetuses. We are accountable for this material and semiotic anastomosis in the body politic and the clinical body of the "postmodern" human family. The longing to understand and change the fluid dynamics inherent in this kind of anastomosis is what I mean by yearning in feminist technoscience studies.

The signifying chains that make up these kinds of linkages are not, in any simple sense, about cause and effect. The multidimensional splices that bind together the New World Order, Inc., cannot be described in linear equations. But these higher-order linkages matter; they are not decorative flourishes. One task of feminist technoscience studies is to construct the analytical languages—to design the speculums—for representing and intervening in our spliced, cyborg worlds. In the Bell Telephone ad, paternity was channeled from the phone through the mother-to-be's touching the sonographic image of the fetus on the video monitor. In the *favela* of the Nordeste, paternity was channeled through the gift of scientifically-formulated, commodified infant milk. The signifiers of choice for Bell Telephone and for Nestlé parody feminist reproductive freedom and knowledge projects and the dispersed, disseminated, differentiated, "transnational" yearning that sustains them. In Kelly's cartoon, reproductive choice was interrogated in First Woman's authorial touch on the computer keyboard. In Charlotte Rutherford's arguments about reproductive freedom for African American women, the statistics of inequality bore eloquent testimony to the reproduction of unfreedom. All of these accounts are aspects of the inquiry into reproductive technology in the New World Order. As Wonder Woman put it in 1973, "With my speculum, I *am* strong! I *can* fight!" The right speculum for the job makes visible the data structures that are our bodies.

• • •

It was a dry wind
And it swept across the desert
And it curled into the circle of birth
And the dead sand
Falling on the children
The mothers and the fathers
And the automatic earth

And don't cry, baby, don't cry.
—© Paul Simon/Paul Simon Music (BMI)

Notes

1. The controversy over Paul Simon's relation to African musicians in his 1986 album *Graceland*, from which this song is taken, is part of the many layers of irony in my appropriating and recontextualizing the lyrics of "The Boy in the Bubble" in this chapter.
2. Anthropologist and science studies scholar Sarah Franklin (1993b) describes and theorizes the emergence of "Life Itself." Duden (1993) discusses the appearance of life as a system to be managed and women as an environment for "life." See also Laqueur 1990 and Terry 1989. Foucault's concept of biopower is braided into feminist histories of the body (Foucault 1978).
3. Technoscientific liberty is Michael Flower's (n.d.; 1994) concept. A rallying cry for the civil rights movement, *Keep Your Eyes on the Prize!* is the title of Henry Hampton's (1986–1987) famous television series, produced by Blackside, Inc., and the Corporation

for Public Broadcasting, on the African American freedom struggles of the 1950s and 1960s.

4. Kelly's cartoon illustrated an article in a special issue on reproductive technology of a Norwegian feminist journal (Stabel [1992:44]).

5. Teresa de Lauretis gave me a copy of an early-thirteenth-century "virtual speculum," called *The Creation of Eve*, from the Creation Dome in the entrance hall in the Basilica di S. Macro in Venice. In this flat, iconic, narrative painting, God is bending over the sleeping Adam in the Garden of Eden and extracting from his side the rib that will be formed into the First Man's wife and companion. This is not the creation scene that has inspired the iconographers of technoscientific advertising, conference brochures, and magazine-cover design. For these twentieth-century graphic artists, on the other hand, the touch between God and Adam depicted by Michelangelo has incited orgies of visual quotation. See magazine covers for *Omni,* April 1983, *Time,* November 8, 1993, and *Discover,* August 1992. For fans of Escher in the artificial life community, studied ethnographically by Stefan Helmreich (1995), the poster image for the second Artificial Life conference (Farmer et al. 1990) features a visual quotation from *The Creation of Adam* in the cyberspace mode. This creation scene takes place at night, with a quarter-moon shining through a window that is also a screen onto the starry universe. Describing the image, Helmreich writes, "The notion that Man replaces God and renders Woman irrelevant in the new creations of Artificial Life is vividly illustrated ... in a poster for the second workshop on Artificial Life, in which a white male programmer touches his finger to a keyboard to meet the waiting fingers of a skeletal circuit-based artificial creature (itself somewhat masculine)" (personal communication, May 18, 1995). The programmer himself is a kind of merman figure; the head and torso is of a human male, but the bottom half is a video display terminal whose nether end hooks into the eye of the circuit-skeletal figure. The Escheresque circular composition, full of arrows and fractal recursive shapes connoting self-organization, is a kind of uroborus, eating its own electronic tail in an orgy of self-creation. The men who got the conference together called themselves the "self-organizing committee." The conference was sponsored by the Center for Non-Linear Studies at the Los Alamos National Laboratory.

6. For comments on sonographic family bonding and on the pleasures of screen viewing and the terrors of needle assays in amniocentesis, see Rapp 1997. See also Hartouni 1994:79.

7. For discussion of U.S. fetal protection statutes and of 1981 Senate hearings on a Human Life Statute, see Hartouni 1991. For analysis of events in the United Kingdom, see Franklin 1993a. The sonogram is only one in a battery of visual artifacts that establish the fact of fetal life within political, personal, and biomedical discourse.

8. For analysis of this sequence of images in historical and political context, see Stabile 1992. The landmark feminist analysis of fetal visual culture was Petchesky 1987.

9. This project is reviewed by Gasperini, who assures the potential buyer, "Interactivity remains an option, never an interruption or a chore" (1994:198).

10. Susan Harding (1990) explores how God's creation and the first and second births of man work in the Christian right's innovative narrative technology that addresses abortion.

11. A visual gynecological examination by a male physician did not become common until the early nineteenth century in European societies; and manual touching of pregnant and birthing women was overwhelmingly a female practice at least through the seventeenth century—later in most places. Vision without touch could be mediated by the metal speculum, which also functioned as an instrument for opening the cervix to remove an obstructed fetus during childbirth. The gynecological speculum existed for many hundreds of years before debates emerging in the late-seventeenth and early-eighteenth

centuries in Europe foregrounded the complex gender struggles between male and female birth attendants and between gendered epistemological practices. The symbolic status of the metal speculum as a tool of male domination of women's bodies (and minds) emerged unevenly in the last couple hundred years in European-derived cultures. See Tatlock 1992:757 58. Thanks to Londa Schiebinger for calling my attention to this article. The complex history of gender conflict over the tools, practices, and people facilitating birth was crucial to the emergence of the plastic speculum as a symbol of women's liberation in self-help groups in the United States in the early 1970s. See Gerson forthcoming.

12. Gross and Levitt (1994) outrageously caricature the feminist science studies insistence on the contingency of "reality" and the constructedness of science. It is important that my account of reality as an effect of an observing interaction, as opposed to a treasure awaiting discovery, not be misunderstood. "Reality" is certainly not "made up" in scientific practice, but it is collectively, materially, and semiotically constructed—that is, put together, made to cohere, worked up for and by us in some ways and not others. This is not a relativist position, if by relativism one means that the facts and models, including mathematical models, of natural scientific accounts of the world are merely matters of desire, opinion, speculation, fantasy, or any other such "mental" faculty. Science is a practice, an interaction inside and with worlds. Science is not a doctrine or a set of observer-independent but still empirically grounded (how?) statements about some ontologically separate nature-not-culture. At a minimum, an observing interaction requires historically located human beings; particular apparatuses, which might include devices like the hominid visual-brain system and the instruments of perspective drawing; and a heterogeneous world in which people and instruments are immersed and that is always prestructured within material-semiotic fields. "Observers" are not just people, much less disembodied minds; observers are also nonhuman entities, sometimes called inscription devices, to which people have materially delegated observation, often precisely to make it "impersonal." (As we will see below, statistics can be one of those instruments for making reality impersonal.) "Impersonal" does not mean "observer-independent." Reality is not a "subjective" construction but a congealing of ways of interacting that makes the opposition of subjective and objective grossly misleading. These ways of interacting require the dense array of bodies, artifacts, minds, collectives, etc., that make up any rich world. The opposition of "knowing minds," on one hand, and "material reality" awaiting description, on the other hand, is a silly setup. Reality is eminently material and solid, but the effects sedimented out of technologies of observation/representation are radically contingent in the sense that other semiotic-material-technical processes of observation would (and do) produce quite different lived worlds, including cognitively lived worlds, not just different statements about worlds as observer-independent arrays of objects. I think that is a richer, more adequate, less ideological account than Gross and Levitt's insistence that science is reality driven (1994:234). Obviously, neither I nor any other science studies person, feminist or otherwise, whom I have ever met or read, means the "laws of physics" get suspended if one enters a "different" culture. That is a laughable notion of both physical laws and cultural, historical difference. It is the position that Gross and Levitt, in deliberate bad faith or else astonishingly deficient reading, ascribe to me and other feminist science studies writers. My argument tries to avoid the silly oppositions of relativism and realism. Rather, I am interested in how an observation situation produces quite "objective" worlds, worlds not subject to "subjective" preference or mere opinion but worlds that must be lived in consequence in some ways and not others. Mutating Hacking's title (1983), I am interested in "representing as intervening." For a theory of "agential realism," to which my arguments about "situated knowledges" is closely related, see Barad 1995.

13. The *Sharper Image Catalogue* is a lavishly illustrated advertising brochure for high-technology personal-fitness technology and related paraphernalia. With *Sharper Image* prod-

ucts, the shopper can recraft the body into a properly enhanced platform for supporting the upper-echelon citizens of technoscience.

14. Dürer's, Titian's, Velázquez's, Rubens's, and Manet's nudes all figure prominently in accounts of the emergence of modern ways of seeing. See Clark 1985. The relation between Manet's African serving woman and the reclining European nude also figures in the fraught racialized visual history of modern Woman. See Nead 1992:34–36; Harvey 1989:54–56.

15. An obstetrical nurse told me Kelly's First Woman might be replaying the sequential images of her pregnancy, which she was given on compact disc (CD) from the several sonograms recorded over the months of gestation. These CDs are narrative visual imagery that are solidly inside the conventions of Christian realism and its practices of figuration.

16. For a wonderful treatment of masculine self-birthing, see Sofia 1992.

17. Stefan Helmreich (personal communication) correctly insists that the "differently embodied" or materialized entities called information structures, which ALife researchers make and play with, must not be equated with "embodiment" as a point of reference for "locating situated and accountable lived experience." See Hayles 1992. Note also that AI and ALife are not the same thing. Langton argues that ALife uses "the technology of computation to explore the dynamics of interacting information structures. It has not adopted the computational paradigm as its underlying methodology of behavior generation, nor does it attempt to 'explain' life as a kind of computer program" (as AI has) (Langton 1988:38).

18. Monica Casper 1998 suggested the notion of the fetus as a work object, from which Kelly led me to extrapolate to the fetal work station. Casper was a graduate student in medical sociology at the University of California at San Francisco.

19. Ginsberg and Rapp 1991 provide a cogent, reflexive narrative and an invaluable 378-item bibliography for considering the historical, cultural, biological, technological, and political complexity that must inform any consideration of human reproduction.

20. The authors identify reproductive and other scientists' groups; pharmaceutical companies; antiabortion groups; feminist prochoice groups; women's health movement groups; politicians, Congress, and the Food and Drug Administration; and women users and consumers of RU486. For a discussion of the transition from a "modernist" focus on control of pregnancy and birth to programs of "postmodern" redesign, see Clarke 1995.

21. From her dissertation through her current book, *Cultural Conceptions*, Hartouni (1997) has shaped my thinking about feminist theories of reproductive freedom.

22. For these kinds of meanings of ethnographic practice in science studies, see the papers in Downey and Dumit 1997 and Escobar 1994. I adapt my discussion of being at risk as intrinsic to doing ethnography from conversations with Susan Harding, Anthropology Board, UCSC.

23. Quoted in Braidotti (1994:2). In her discussion of figuration as a "politically informed account of an alternative subjectivity," Braidotti (1994:1–8) recalled my attention to bell hooks's discussion of "postmodern blackness" in terms of that kind of consciousness called "yearning." Braidotti's nomadic subjects and hook's yearning are akin to Chéla Sandoval's notions of oppositional and differential consciousness (Sandoval forthcoming).

24. An examination of the perverse desires of the mutated, antiracist, feminist modest witness in technoscience can be advanced by adopting the reading practices of Teresa de Lauretis (1994).

25. This heading is in honor of Clarke and Fujimura 1992.

26. Remember Audre Lorde's famous warning from the 1970s: "The Master's Tools Will Never Dismantle the Master's House" (Lorde 1984).

27. Boston Women's Health Book Collective (1976; 1979). The Boston Women's Health Book Collective began putting out *Our Bodies, Ourselves* in newsprint form in the 1970s as an integral part of activist health struggles. See Gerson (forthcoming). For a bibliography of the early women's health movement and feminist science and medicine studies from the 1970s, see Hubbard, Henifin, and Fried 1982. Despite its extensive concern with instruments and tools, practices in and out of the laboratory, and science-in-the-making, the kind of activist-based material in Hubbard, Henifin, and Fried's bibliography is systematically excluded from professional, academic histories of science and technology studies. See, for example, Knorr-Cetina and Mulkay 1983.

28. Moulton was William Moulton Marston, psychologist, attorney, inventor of the lie-detector test, prison reformer, and businessman. Marston's conventional feminism ascribed force bound by love to women and opposed that to men's attraction to force alone. Despite her origins in the Amazon, Wonder Woman's ethnicity was unmistakably white. Her expletives ("Merciful Minerva!" and "Great Hera!") and her other cultural accouterments locate her firmly in the modern myth of Western origins in ancient Greece, here relocated to the New World. She could have easily joined a U.S. white sorority in the 1940s and 1950s, with their Greek-revivalist themes and rituals. The guiding goddesses of Wonder Woman's Amazonian matriarchal paradise were Aphrodite and Athena. See Edgar 1972. Thanks to David Walls and Lucia Gattone for the Ms. Wonder Woman issue and to Katie King for Wonder Woman lore.

29. SimCity2000 is one of a series of highly successful simulation games put out by the Maxis Corporation. See Bleecker 1995.

30. Thanks to Adele Clarke for pointing out the *Sister* cartoon and Ehrenreich and English's use of it.

32. See, for example, Committee for Abortion Rights and Against Sterilization Abuse 1979; Coalition for the Reproductive Rights of Workers 1980; Black Women's Community Development Foundation 1975; Davis 1981; Smith 1982; White 1990. This literature reflects the dominance of the black-white racial polarity of U.S. society and understates the presence and priorities of other racial-ethnic women in women's health and reproductive politics of that period. See Moraga and Anzaldúa 1981.

32. I am in permanent debt to Nancy Harsock's (1983) pioneering formulation of nonessentialist feminist standpoint theory. Standpoint theories are not private reservations for different species of human beings, innate knowledge available only to victims, or special pleading. Within feminist theory in Hartsock's lineage, standpoints are cognitive-emotional-political achievements, crafted out of located social-historical-bodily experience—itself always constituted through fraught, noninnocent, discursive, material, collective practices—that could make less deluded knowledge for all of us more likely. My arguments in this chapter also draw from Harding 1992 on strong objectivity as a mode of extended critical examination of knowledge-producing apparatuses and agents; Collins 1991 on the internally heterogeneous and insider/outsider locations that have nurtured Black feminist thought; Star 1991 on viewing standards from the point of view of those who do not fit them but must live within them; Butler 1992 on contingent foundations as achievements and agency as practice rather than attribute; Haraway 1988 on situated knowledges in scientific epistemology and the refusal of the ideological choice between realism and relativism; hooks 1990 on yearning—rooted in the historical experience of oppression and inequality but unimpressed by stances of victimhood—that can bind knowledge and action across difference; Sandoval forthcoming on the potential of learning and teaching oppositional consciousness across multiple and intersecting differentiations of race, gender, nationality, sexuality, and class; Bhavnani 1993 on feminist objectivity within a polyglot world; and Tsing 1993a and b on multiple centers and margins and on the stunning complexity and specificity of local-global cross-talk and circula-

tions of power and knowledge. That Hartsock, Harding, Collins, Star, Bhavnani, Tsing, Haraway, Sandoval, hooks, and Butler are not supposed to agree about postmodernism, standpoints, science studies, or feminist theory is neither my problem nor theirs. The problem is the needless yet common cost of taxonomizing everyone's positions without regard to the contexts of their development, or of refusing rereading and overlayering in order to make new patterns from previous disputes. I am recontextualizing all of this writing to make a case for how thinking about reproductive freedom should make its practitioners reconfigure how to do technoscience studies in general. Theory and practice develop precisely through such recontextualization. For learning to read the always topographically complex history of feminist theory (and theory projects broadly), see King 1994.

33. Adele Clarke (personal communication, May 16, 1995) reminded me of the history of recent feminist efforts to build reproductive policy from the standpoints of the most vulnerable, for example, the explicit program of the Reproductive Rights National Network ✳ in the 1970s and '80s. Clarke recounted the example of the passage of sterilization regulations in California, which applied to all sterilizations, not just those funded by Medicaid. Developed by Coalition for Abortion Rights and Against Sterilization Abuse (CARASA), national sterilization regulations applied only to Medicaid recipients. Shepherded by the Committee to Defend Reproductive Rights (CDRR), the California regulations—the only ones to pass on a state level—were the fruit of difficult coalition-building between middle-class, mostly white women from the National Organization for Women, who were more affected by inaccessible sterilization, and working-class and non-white women's groups, who were more impacted by abusive sterilization. In the 1990s, the ordinary situation of multiple and heterogeneous vulnerabilities and capabilities, which imply conflicting policy needs, demands urgent feminist attention in local and global dimensions. The International Reproductive Rights Research Action Group (IRRRAG) is a collaborative, multicountry research project on the meanings of reproductive rights to women in diverse cultural settings. See Petchesky and Weiner 1990. Petchesky is the coordinator of IRRRAG. Written by an international group of feminist activists and scholars, the papers in Ginsberg and Rapp 1995 put reproduction at the center of social theory in general and, through detailed and culturally alert analyses, show how pregnancy, parenting, birth control, population policies, demography, and the new reproductive technologies shape and are shaped by differently situated women. Nonreductive feminist reproductive discourse and policy can flourish in this context. For example, Barroso and Corrêa (1995:292 306) show how the difficult interactions of feminists and researchers around the introduction of Norplant into Brazil resulted ultimately in raised public consciousness, attention to informed consent in 'Norms of Research on Health' approved by the Ministry of Health, and effective local ethics committees. Nonfeminist approaches to reproductive technologies still abound everywhere. At the 1994 American Fertility Society's 50th Anniversary Meetings in San Antonio, Texas, a Norplant ad poster prominently features the words "Compliance-free contraceptive." Thanks to Charis Cussins for photographic evidence.

34. For the story of public health statistics intrinsic to freedom projects in the twentieth-century United States, see Fee and Krieger 1994. For a view of a feminist economics think tank, see the publications (e.g., Spalter-Rother et al. 1995) of the Washington, D.C., Institute for Women's Policy Research, cofounded by Heidi Hartman, winner of a 1994 MacArthur Fellowship for her work.

35. Following Rutherford, my point here is about toxics and reproductive freedom. In a related argument that has shaped my own, Giovanna DiChiro (1995a and b) shows how antitoxics movements, very often led by working-class and urban women of color, contest for what counts as nature and environment, what constitutes scientific knowledge, and who counts as producers of such knowledge.

36. My uses of the family of words around the signifier modern is in conversation with Bruno Latour, *We Have Never Been Modern* (1993). I continue to use the flawed, deceptive terms *modern* and *postmodern* partly to highlight the narratives about time in which we all still generally work and partly to insist on the dispersed, powerful, practical networks of technoscience that have changed life and death on this planet, but not in the ways most accounts of either progress or declension would have it. *Modern* and its variants should never be taken at face value. I try to force the words like all meaning-making tools to stumble, make a lot of racket, and generally resist naturalization. It's a losing battle.

37. Scheper-Hughes was tracking births and deaths that still escape the net of official national or international statistics late in the twentieth century. She points out that the statistic for infant mortality was first devised in Britain in 1875. The British Registration Act of 1834 required that all deaths be recorded and given a medical cause, thus replacing the "natural deaths" of children and the aged, at least in the intentions of the reformers. Pediatrics emerged as a medical specialty in Western medicine in the first decades of the twentieth century. Relative to other discourses critical to the regimes of biopower, child survival, much less fetal and infant survival, has a late pedigree everywhere as a problem requiring statistical documentation and action. Childhood malnutrition was first designated a pediatric disease in 1933 in the context of colonial medicine. "Protein-calorie malnutrition in children (of which there was an epidemic in nineteenth-century England) ... only entered medical nosology when British doctors working in the colonies discovered it as a 'tropical' disease" (Scheper-Hughes 1992:274 75). For the pioneering history of mortality statistics in France and their connection to class formations, production, residence, and contending political ideologies, see Coleman 1982.

38. Actually, for the middle- and upper-class Brazilian women in this town, modern scientific birth meant delivery by cesarean section rather than the "new reproductive technologies" favored by their Northern sisters. Scheper-Hughes recounts watching young girls play at giving birth by enacting the imagined surgical scenario. After the successful play-birth, the new "infant was immediately put on intravenous feedings"! Regional newspapers report that cesarean-section delivery rates among private maternity patients in northeastern Brazil approach 70 percent (Scheper-Hughes 1992:329).

39. See also MacArthur 1962. The mathematical equation need not carry the ideological interpretation that seems to proliferate so readily in the texts of some sociobiologists, but the interpretation is, so to speak, a natural. Stefan Helmreich summarized for me a particularly egregious racial-sexual rendering of r- and K-selection arguments, with people of African descent having more extramarital affairs, Black men having longer penises, Black women having shorter menstrual cycles, and a host of other racist-sexist pseudo-facts leading to the conclusion of different evolutionary strategies among (leaving aside the problem of the biological reality of the categories) white, Black, and Oriental populations. See Rushton and Bogaert 1987, and for an internalist response to their work as bad science, see Fairchild 1991. Without question, "good" and "bad" science are categories worth fighting for within the perspectives of strong objectivity, agential realism, and situated knowledge. It's just that the categories only do a bit of the needed critical work. How is it that sexual behavior, human and otherwise, as nonideologically represented by the best science, is solidly an instance of investment strategies, ontologically indistinguishable from other kinds of portfolio management, where the point is to stay in the game? How and why, materially-semiotically, did we make the world-for-us this way? Who are we? Are there still alternatives? The matter is hardly observer-independent, no matter what mathematical tools are in play! The matter is also not conceivably solved by individual choice of a different representational apparatus. Chic resistance talk will get one nowhere; material-cultural analysis might have a chance of providing consequential insight.

40. The blunt racist imagery of the warm, sordid, genital, fecund, and colored tropics contrasted to the cold, hygienic, cerebral, reproductively conservative, and white North is
officially disavowed and discredited, but I believe it still haunts U.S. popular and technical discourse on many levels and on many occasions, including elections and periods of
white middle-class frenzy about "welfare mothers."

41. "In the U.S., 30 million people suffer chronic under-consumption of adequate nutrients.
Almost half of the hungry are children . . . 76% of the hungry are people of color" (Allen
1994:2). In October 1994, in race-undifferentiated figures, the U.S. Census Bureau
reported that 15 percent of the population, that is, 39.3 million people, officially lived in
poverty in 1993. That year, the federal government defined poverty as a family of four
with a total annual income of $14,800 or less. The U.S. child-poverty rate is about double
that of any other industrialized nation.

42. Scheper-Hughes estimated that the shantytown women she worked with, or for whom
she could get records, had about six more pregnancies than their wealthier townswomen
living nearby but ended up with only *one* more living child. In her ethnographic account,
poorer women, especially in younger cohorts, expressed a preference for fewer children
than did more affluent women, not more. These preferences were not realizable in the
semiotic and material conditions that the women experienced.

43. Scheper-Hughes's descriptions and interpretations of parental reactions to child morbidity and mortality in the impoverished Brazilian Nordeste are controversial (see Nations
and Rebhun 1988), but the descriptions of malnutrition and infant mortality are not dis-
puted. Brazil has the eighth-largest economy in the world, but about 75 percent of its citizens in the Nordeste are malnourished.

44. Immunization was not the only way that contemporary allopathic medicine marked the
bodies of the extremely poor. In contrast to the infants and children of the rich, the poorest babies also ate a steady diet of strong antibiotics and many other types of medicine. In
this context, the marginalized poor might say, "We have never *not* been modern."

45. "In Brazil the decline in breast-feeding has been precipitous; between 1940 and 1975 the
percentage of babies breast-fed *for any length of time* fell from 96% to less than 40%. . . .
Since that time it has decreased even further" (Scheper-Hughes 1992:317). Breastfeeding
has also declined in the United States. In 1993, only 50 percent of all new mothers initiated breastfeeding while in the hospital, and only 19 percent persisted after six months. In
the United States, breastfeeding is also deeply differentiated by class and race, with the
most privileged groups "choosing" breastfeeding the most often, and their less-well-off
sisters "choosing" artificial formula. For example, 70 percent of college-educated mothers
breastfed their infants at birth, compared to 43 percent of those with a high school education and 32 percent of those with an elementary school education; 23 percent of Black
mothers breastfed their babies at birth, compared to 59 percent of white mothers (Blum
1993:299). Through its Women, Infants, and Children Program (WIC), the U.S. government purchases about $1.7 billion of formula per year for use by poor mothers, covering
about 40 percent of all U.S. babies (Baker 1995:25). Advertising by formula companies
remains a big issue, and it works in conjunction with the absence of child-care and
maternal support policies that would make breastfeeding feasible for economically disadvantaged people.

46. Lest we lose sight of biotechnology in this chapter, genetic engineering is on the way to
duplicating human breast milk. The product could be sold to affluent mothers (or
bought by taxpayers for the less affluent) whose own milk might not be quite the thing
or whose children might not thrive on current artificial milk. Dutch research with
cows involves bovine transgenics with milk-specific human genes so that the animal's
secretion mimics the human fluid. See Crouch 1995. I am not opposed to this research as

a violation of intimate female experience and cultural categories of nature, but, like Crouch, I am highly skeptical that this research would do as much to improve babies' and mothers' health as similar amounts of R&D money spent on maternal support policies that increased ordinary breastfeeding or on environmental policies that reduced the toxin burden in women's bodies all over the world.

References

Allen, Patricia. 1994. "The Human Face of Sustainable Agriculture: Adding People to the Environmental Agenda." Center for Agroecology and Sustainable Food Systems, University of California at Santa Cruz. *Sustainability in the Balance Series* (Issue Paper No. 4).

Auerbach, Erich. 1953. *Mimesis: The Representation of Reality in Western Literature.* Princeton: Princeton University Press.

Baker, Linda. 1995. "Message in a Bottle." *In These Times* 19 (20):24–26.

Barad, Karen. 1995. "Meeting the Universe Halfway: Ambiguities, Discontinuities, Quantum Subjects, and Multiple Positionings in Feminism and Physics." In *Feminism, Science, and the Philosophy of Science: A Dialog,* edited by L. H. Nelson and J. Nelson. Norwell, MA: Kluwer Press.

Barroso, Carmen, and Sônia Corrêa. 1995. "Public Servants, Professionals, and Feminists: The Politics of Contraceptive Research in Brazil." In *Conceiving the New World Order: The Global Politics of Reproduction,* edited by F. D. Ginsberg and R. Rapp. Los Angeles: University of California Press, 292–306.

Bhavnani, Kum-Kum. 1993. "Tracing the Contours: Feminist Research and Feminist Objectivity." *Women's Studies International Forum* 16 (2):95–104.

Black Women's Community Development Foundation (BWCDF). 1975. *Mental and Physical Health Problems of Black Women.* Washington, DC: BWCDF.

Bleecker, Julian. 1995 "Urban Crisis: Past, Present, and Virtual." *Socialist Review* #94/1+2:189–221.

Blum, Linda M. 1993. "Mothers, Babies, and Breastfeeding in Late Capitalist America: The Shifting Contexts of Feminist Theory." *Feminist Studies* 19 (2):291–311.

Boston Women's Health Book Collective. 1976. *Our Bodies, Ourselves: A Book by and for Women.* 2nd ed. New York: Simon and Schuster.

Boston Women's Health Book Collective. 1979. *Nuestros Cuerpos, Nuestras Vidas.* Somerville, MA: BWH Book Collective, Inc.

Braidotti, Rosi. 1994. *Nomadic Subjects: Embodiment and Subjectivity in Contemporary Feminist Theory.* New York: Columbia University Press.

Butler, Judith. 1992. "Contingent Foundations: Feminism and the Question of Postmodernism." In *Feminists Theorize the Political,* edited by J. Butler and J. Scott. New York: Routledge, 3–21.

Casper, Monica. 1998. *The Making of the Unborn Patient: A Social Anatomy of Fetal Surgery.* New Brunswick, NJ: Rutgers University Press.

Clark, Timothy J. 1985, 1984. *The Painting of Modern Life: Paris in the Art of Manet and His Followers.* New York: Knopf.

Clarke, Adele. 1995. "Modernity, Postmodernity and Reproductive Processes, c. 1890–1990." In *The Cyborg Handbook,* edited by C. H. Gray, H. Figueroa-Sarriera, and S. Mentor. New York: Routledge, 139–55.

Clarke, Adele, and Joan Fujimura, eds., 1992. *The Right Tools for the Job: At Work in Twentieth-Century Life Sciences.* Princeton: Princeton University Press.

Clarke, Adele, and Teresa Montini. 1993. "The Many Faces of RU 486: Tales of Situated

Knowledges and Technological Contestations." *Science, Technology, and Human Values* 18 (1):42–78.

Coalition for the Reproductive Rights of Workers (CRROW). 1980. *Reproductive Hazards in the Workplace: A Resources Guide.* Washington, DC: CCROW.

Collins, Patricia Hill. 1991. *Black Feminist Thought: Knowledge, Consciousness, and the Politics of Empowerment.* New York: Routledge.

Committee for Abortion Rights and Against Sterilization Abuse (CARASA). 1979. *Women Under Attack: Abortion, Sterilization Abuse, and Reproductive Freedom.* New York: CARASA.

Crouch, Martha L. 1995. "Like Mother Used to Make?" *The Women's Review of Books* 12 (5):31–32.

Cussins, Charis. 1996. "Ontological Choreography: Agency for Women Patients in an Infertility Clinic." *Social Studies of Science* 26 (3):575–610.

Daly, Martin, and Margo Wilson. 1978. *Sex, Evolution, and Behavior: Adaptations for Reproduction.* North Scituate, MA: Duxbury Press.

Davis, Angela. 1981. *Women, Race, and Class.* New York: Random House.

de Lauretis, Teresa. 1994. *The Practice of Love: Lesbian Sexuality and Perverse Desire.* Bloomington: Indiana University Press.

DiChiro, Giovanna. 1995a. "Local Actions, Global Visions: Women Transforming Science, Environment and Helath in the U.S. and India." Ph.D. diss., History of Consciousness Board, University of California at Santa Cruz.

———. 1995b. "Nature as Community: The Convergence of Environment and Social Justice." In *Uncommon Ground: Towards Reinventing Nature,* edited by W. Cronon. New York: Norton, 298–320.

Downey, Gary and Joseph Dumit. 1997. *Cyborgs and Citadels: Anthropological Interventions on the Borderlands of Technoscience.* Santa Fe: Santa Fe Institute Press.

Duden, Barbara. 1993. *Disembodying Women: Perspectives on Pregnancy and the Unborn.* Cambridge: Harvard University Press.

Edgar, Joanne. 1972. "Wonder Woman Revisited." *Ms.* 1 (1):52–55.

Ehrenreich, Barbara, and Dierdre English. 1973. *Complaints and Disorders: The Sexual Politics of Sickness.* Old Westbury, NY: The Feminist Press.

Escobar, Arturo. 1994. "Welcome to Cyberia: Notes on the Anthropology of Cyberculture." *Current Anthropology* 35 (3):211–31.

Fairchild, Halford. 1991. "Scientific Racism: The Cloak of Objectivity." *Journal of Social Issues* 47 (3):101–16.

Farmer, D., C. Langton, S. Rasmussen, and C. Taylor (self-organizing committee). 1990. "Artificial Life." Paper read at Artificial Life: Conference on Emergence and Evolution of Life-like Forms in Human-made Environments, February 5–9, at Santa Fe, New Mexico.

Fee, Elizabeth, and Nancy Krieger. 1994. "What's Class Got to Do with Health? A Critique of Biomedical Individualism." Paper read at Meeting of the Society for the Social Studies of Science, October 12–16, at New Orleans.

Flower, Michael. 1994. "A Native Speaks for Himself: Reflections on Technoscientific Literacy." Paper read at American Anthropological Association Meeting, November 30–December 3, at Washington, DC.

———. n.d. "Technoscientific Liberty." Unpublished paper, University Honors Program, Portland State University.

Foucault, Michel. 1978. *The History of Sexuality. Vol. 1: An Introduction.* Translated by Robert Hurley. New York: Pantheon.

Franklin, Sarah. 1993a. "Making Representations: The Parliamentary Debate on the Human Fertilisation and Embryology Act." In *Technologies of Procreation: Kinship in the Age of*

Assisted Conception, edited by J. Edwards, S. Franklin, E. Hirsch, F. Price, and M. Strathern. Manchester: Manchester University Press, 96–131.

———. 1993b. "Life Itself," paper delivered at the Center for Cultural Values, Lancaster University, June 9.

Gasperini, Jim. 1994. "The Miracle of Good Multimedia." *Wired* (February):198.

Gerson, Deborah. Forthcoming. "Speculum and Small Groups: New Visions of Female Bodies." Unpublished manuscript from dissertation-in-progress: "Practice from Pain." University of California at Berkeley.

Ginsberg, Faye, and Rayna Rapp. 1991. "The Politics of Reproduction." *Annual Reviews in Anthropology* 20:311–43.

Gross, Paul R., and Norman Levitt. 1994. *Higher Superstition: The Academic Left and Its Quarrels with Science.* Baltimore: Johns Hopkins University Press.

Hacking, Ian. 1983. *Representing and Intervening: Introductory Topics in the Philosophy of Natural Science.* Cambridge: Cambridge University Press.

Hamilton, Joan O'C. 1994. "Biotech: An Industry Crowded with Players Faces an Ugly Reckoning." *Business Week* (September 26):84–90.

Haraway, Donna J. 1988. "Situated Knowledges: The Science Question in Feminism as a Site of Discourse on the Privilege of Partial Perspective." *Feminist Studies* 14 (3):575–99.

———. 1994. "Never Modern, Never Been, Never Ever: Some Thoughts About Never-Never Land in Science Studies." Paper read at Meeting of the Society for Social Studies of Science, October 12–16, at New Orleans.

Harding, Sandra. 1992. *Whose Science? Whose Knowledge? Thinking from Women's Lives.* Ithaca: Cornell, University Press.

Harding, Susan. 1990. "If I Die Before I Wake." In *Uncertain Terms: Negotiating Gender in American Culture,* edited by F. Ginsburg and A. L. Tsing. Boston: Beacon Press, 76–97.

Hartouni, Valerie. 1991. "Containing Women: Reproductive Discourse in the 1980s." In *Technoculture,* edited by C. Penley and A. Ross. Minneapolis: University of Minnesota Press, 27–56.

———. 1992. "Fetal Exposures: Abortion Politics and the Optics of Allusion." *Camera Obscura: A Journal of Feminism and Film Theory* 29:130–49.

———. 1994. "Breached Birth: Reflections on Race, Gender, and Reproductive Discourse in the 1980s." *Configurations* 2 (1):73–88.

———. 1997. *Cultural Conceptions: On Reproductive Technologies and the Remaking of Life.* Minneapolis: University of Minnesota Press.

Hartsock, Nancy. 1983. "The Feminist Standpoint: Developing the Ground for a Specifically Feminist Historical Materialism." In *Discovering Reality: Feminist Perspectives on Epistemology, Methodology, and Philosophy of Science,* edited by S. Harding and M. Hintikka. Dordrecht/ Boston: Reidel, 283–310.

Harvey, David. 1989. *The Condition of Postmodernity: An Enquiry into the Origins of Cultural Change.* Oxford: Basil Blackwell.

Hayles, N. Katherine. 1992. "The Materiality of Informatics." *Configurations* 1:147–70.

Helmreich, Stefan. 1995. "Anthropology Inside and Outside the Looking-Glass Worlds of Artificial Life." Ph.D. diss., Department of Anthropology, Stanford University.

hooks, bell. 1990. *Yearning.* Boston: Southend Press.

Hubbard, Ruth, Mary Sue Henifin, and Barbara Fried, eds. 1982. *Biological Woman—The Convenient Myth: A Collection of Feminist Essays and a Comprehensive Bibliography.* Cambridge: Schenkman.

Jansen, H. W., and Dora Jane Jansen. 1963. *History of Art.* Englewood Cliffs/New York: Prentice-Hall and Harry N. Abrams.

King, Katie. 1994. *Theory in Its Feminist Travels: Conversations in U.S. Women's Movements.* Bloomington: Indiana University Press.

Knorr-Cetina, Karin, and Michael Mulkay, eds., 1983. *Science Observed: Perspectives on the Social Study of Science.* Beverly Hills: Sage Publications.

Langton, Christopher G. 1988. "Artificial Life." In *Artificial Life: SFI Studies in the Sciences of Complexity,* edited by C. G. Langton. Boston: Addison-Wesley, 1–47.

Laqueur, Thomas. 1990. *Making Sex: Body and Gender From the Greeks to Freud.* Cambridge: Harvard University Press.

Latour, Bruno. 1993. *We Have Never Been Modern.* Translated by Catherine Porter. Cambridge: Harvard University Press.

Lorde, Audre. 1984. "The Master's Tools Will Never Dismantle the Master's House." In *Sister Outsider: Essays and Speeches,* edited by A. Lorde. Trumansburg, NY: Crossing Press.

MacArthur, R. H. 1962. "Some Generalized Theorems of Natural Selection." *Proceedings of the National Academy of Sciences* 48:1893–97.

Moraga, Cherríe, and Gloria Anzaldúa, eds. 1981. *This Bridge Called My Back: Writings by Radical Women of Color.* Watertown, MA: Persephone Press.

Nead, Lynda. 1992. *The Female Nude: Art, Obscenity and Sexuality.* New York: Routledge.

Nilsson, Lennart. 1977. *A Child Is Born.* New York: Dell.

———. 1987. *The Body Victorious: The Illustrated Story of Our Immune System and Other Defenses of the Human Body.* New York: Delacorte.

Nilsson, Lennart, and Lars Hamberger. 1994. *A Child Is Born.* Philips. CD-I (compact disk).

Petchesky, Rosalind Pollock. 1987. "Fetal Images: The Power of Visual Culture in the Politics of Reproduction." *Feminist Studies* 13 (2):263–92.

Petchesky, Rosalind Pollock, and Jennifer Weiner. 1990. *Global Feminist Perspectives on Reproductive Rights and Reproductive Health.* New York: Hunter College/Reproductive Rights Education Project.

Porter, Theodore M. 1994. "Objectivity as Standardization: The Rhetoric of Impersonality in Measurement, Statistics, and Cost-Benefit Analysis." In *Rethinking Objectivity,* edited by A. McGill. Durham: Duke University Press, 19–59.

———. 1995. *Trust in Numbers: The Pursuit of Objectivity in Science and Public Life.* Princeton: Princeton University Press.

Randolph, Lynn. 1993. "The Ilusas (deluded women): Representations of Women Who Are Out of Bounds." Paper delivered at the Bunting Institute, Cambridge, MA, November 30.

Rapp, Rayna. 1994. "Refusing Prenatal Diagnostic Technology: The Uneven Meanings of Bioscience in a Multicultural World." Paper read at the Society for Social Studies of Science, October 12–16, at New Orleans.

———. 1997. "Real Time Fetus: The Role of the Sonogram in the Age of Monitored Reproduction." In *Cyborgs and Citadels: Anthropological Interventions on the Borderlands of Technoscience,* edited by G. Downey and J. Dumit. Santa Fe, NM: Santa Fe Institute Press.

Rubenstein, Nicolai, et al. 1967. *The Age of the Renaissance.* New York: McGraw-Hill.

Rushton, J. Philippe, and Anthony F. Bogaert. 1987. "Race Differences in Sexual Behavior: Testing an Evolutionary Hypothesis." *Journal of Research in Personality* 21:529–51.

Rutherford, Charlotte. 1992. "Reproductive Freedoms and African American Women." *Yale Journal of Law and Feminism* 4 (2):255–90.

Sandoval, Chéla. Forthcoming. *Oppositional Consciousness in the Postmodern World.* Minneapolis: University of Minnesota Press.

Scheper-Hughes, Nancy. 1992. *Death Without Weeping: The Violence of Everyday Life in Brazil.* Berkeley/Los Angeles: University of California Press.

Smith, Beverly. 1982. "Black Women's Health: Notes for a Course." In *Biological Woman—The Convenient Myth: A Collection of Feminist Essays and a Comprehensive Bibliography,* edited by R. Hubbard, M. S. Henifin, and B. Fried. Cambridge: Schenkman, 227–40.

Sofia, Zoë. 1992. "Virtual Corporeality: A Feminist View." *Australian Feminist Studies* 15 (Autumn):11–24.

Spalter-Roth, Roberta, Beverly Burr, Heidi Hartman, and Lois Shaw. 1995. *Welfare That Works: The Working Life of AFDC Recipients.* Washington, DC: Institute for Women's Policy Research.

Stabel, Ingse. 1992. "Den Norske Politiske Debatten om Bioteknologi." *Nytt om Kvinneforskning* 3:43–48.

Stabile, Carol A. 1992. "Shooting the Mother: Fetal Photography and the Politics of Disappearance." *Camera Obscura: A Journal of Feminism and Film Theory* 28:178–205.

Star, Susan Leigh. 1991. "Power, Technology and the Phenomenology of Conventions: On Being Allergic to Onions." In *A Sociology of Monsters: Power, Technology and the Modern World,* edited by J. Law. Oxford: Basil Blackwell, 26–56.

Tatlock, Lynne. 1992. "*Speculum Feminarium:* Gendered Perspectives on Obstetrics and Gynecology in Early Modern Germany." *Signs* 17 (4):725–60.

Terry, Jennifer. 1989. "The Body Invaded: Medical Surveillance of Women as Reproducers," *Socialist Review* no. 19 (July–Sept.):13–31.

Treichler, Paula, and Lisa Cartwright. 1992. *Imaging Technologies, Inscribing Science.* Special Issue, *Camera Obscura: A Journal of Feminism and Film Theory* nos. 28 and 29.

Tsing, Anna Lowenhaupt. 1993a. "Forest Collisions: The Construction of Nature in Indonesian Rainforest Politics." Unpublished manuscript.

———. 1993b. *In the Realm of the Diamond Queen: Marginality in an Out-of-the-Way Place.* Princeton: Princeton University Press.

White, Evelyn, ed. 1990. *The Black Woman's Health Book.* Seattle: Seal Press.

The Woman in the Flexible Body

EMILY MARTIN

My task in this paper is to elucidate some of the social "imaginaries'" that are relevant to concepts of health and the body in contemporary North American culture.[1] The nature of this task requires me to cover a range of topics that is wider than usual. The concepts of the right and proper life and death that make up social imaginaries are learned and developed in a multitude of diverse ways in families, organizations, communities, and institutions, but they are also developed in relation to (influencing and being influenced by) the vast and heterogeneous contents of the popular media. In part through such media, social imaginaries have an international life, carried along with the global flows of goods, ads, images and people. And in part through the force of media imagery, I will argue, social imaginaries have an important role within North America, in laying the groundwork for the oppression of disadvantaged groups in what amounts to a new incarnation of social Darwinism.

The Body as Machine

For some time now, I have been intrigued by the possibility that the science of reproductive biology includes in its inner core, its very language and concepts, deeply cultural assumptions about males and females (Martin 1991, 1992). Here I invite you to examine some words and images from medical and popular representations of women's bodies, with an eye and an ear to their poetry and artistry. A key to this task will be "waking up" or bringing to life some of the unseen or "dead" metaphors (as we were taught to call them in high-school English class) in scientific language. As long as they are "dead," Toni Morrison's words describe them:

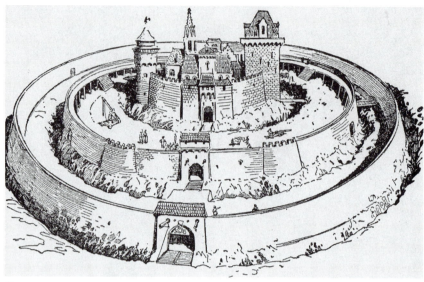

Fig. 1

A dead language is not only one no longer spoken or written, it is unyielding language content to admire its own paralysis.... Unreceptive to its own interrogation, it cannot form or tolerate new ideas, shape other thoughts, tell another story, fill baffling silences. (Morrison 1994:13–14)

If, in a productive synergy between biomedicine and the anthropology of medicine, the dead can be enlivened, perhaps the result could be a scientific language of the body that was receptive to its own interrogation, tolerant of new ideas and other thoughts, open to other stories and able to acknowledge the existence of, if not fill, baffling silences.

The standard medical accounts of a woman going through menstruation, birth, and menopause depict her body as metaphorically engaged in various forms of production on an industrial model: When she menstruates instead of getting pregnant, it is interpreted as a result of failed production. (Menstrual fluids, which one author of a standard text used in medical schools described as "the uterus crying for want of a baby," are seen negatively, as the result of breakdown, decay, or death of tissue.) When she gives birth it is regarded as successful production, but this production is often held to a rather strict timetable reminiscent of assembly line production. For example, a woman having her first birth after age twenty-five is called an "elderly primipara." When a woman reaches menopause, the main headquarters governing her body's reproductive system is thought to undergo a devastating breakdown leading to loss of the centralized control necessary to keep order (Martin 1992). The standard medical account of

Fig. 2

fertilization (at a metaphorical level) (as well as popular science) sees the egg as a damsel in waiting, or a damsel in need of rescue, and the sperm as her seducer, or rescuer, depending on whose account you read (Martin 1991).

All this imagery depicts a body of the machine age, specifically the post–World War II era of mass production (the 1950s), engaged in orderly assembly-line production on a rigid time schedule, divided into parts, each with a separate function. Even the courtship drama of the egg and the sperm is rigidly patterned, on a post–World War II model, machinelike in its inexorable conclusion in heterosexual union and fecundity.

In its machinelike solidity and concreteness, this body has definite edges. Where the body ends and the outside world begins is marked with precision, and is emphasized because this border is where the battle for health goes on. The "Castle of Health" image illustrated home health books in the 1920s and 1930s and shows how important the outer walls of the body's defense were. (See Figure 1.) The drawing "The Lilliputian Hordes," from *Life* magazine in 1950, shows the preoccupation at the time with body surfaces: All the action is taking place outside the body on the skin, where the germs are depicted as hordes of little devils trying to puncture the barrier of the skin with sharp objects like drill bits. (See Figure 2.) And of course this concern with the integrity of surfaces went along with the preoccupation of the times with hygiene, especially cleaning and protecting the surfaces of the body, as well as washing, dusting, airing, and disinfecting the surfaces of the home or the community.

I have portrayed this body of clear boundaries and machine-tooled parts as if it only lived in the 1950s. In fact, it is very much with us still. To mention just one domain, contemporary accounts of the immune system in both research and popular contexts see it as maintaining the health of the body through continuous warfare against the foreign enemy. This picture presupposes an absolute difference, and a clear way of defining, what is friendly "self" and what is unfriendly foreign "foe." This imagery of aggressive immuno-warfare against the foreign foe focuses on a body that is all of one kind, all purely self. This pure body is

THE BALTIMORE SUN, TUESDAY, OCTOBER 3, 1989

TO YOUR **HEALTH**

Lupus: when the body's defenses turn on you Page 4

Fig. 3

construed as the "normal" body, the desirable body to have. Once again, it is as if the body were a castle and its ramparts held stalwartly against anything foreign ever entering. Not only the bodies of persons, but also the bodies of other legal personages, corporations, have defended boundaries. Illustrations from current ads for financial firms convey this idea: Representing the strong, well-defended corporate "person," these ubiquitous ads feature photographs of huge, monolithic, and massively defended castles.

As Donna Haraway puts it, "The perfection of the fully defended, 'victorious' self is a chilling fantasy" 1992:320). She asks, "When is a self enough of a self that its boundaries become central to institutionalized discourses in biomedicine, war, and business?" Looking at the cover of a popular book about the immune system, *The Body Victorious,* by Lennart Nilsson (1985), gives us a very specific identification for this self, in terms of both race and gender. The cover shows a nude, muscular male figure, backlit so that the edges of his body are sharply outlined. Enough stray light escapes to show us that his facial features and hair type are Caucasian. Superimposed across his abdomen is a greatly enlarged color photograph of an immune system cell, a macrophage, in the act of eating up bacteria. This is a body whose boundaries are defined extremely clearly. Inside is only self; outside is only nonself. Should any foreign matter enter, it will be swiftly dispatched by the roving armies of the man's immune system.

Compared to the internal purity of this masculine self, women fall far short. When they are pregnant, they are truly hybrid, uneasily "tolerating" the foreign fetus. Technical immunological articles wonder why the mother does not mount an "attack" against the fetus, which immunologically is marked as nonself. An article in *The Economist* wonders, "Why Does the Body Allow Fetuses to Live?" (*Economist* 1985).

In addition to the "mixing" of self and other in pregnancy, women are statistically more prone to autoimmune diseases. These diseases are conceptualized as caused by the immune system mistakenly attacking self. In one illustration of a woman with lupus, an autoimmune disease, she is shown lying inside the ramparts of a castle. But instead of protecting her against threats to her health, the sharp spikes on the top and sides of the castle walls are turned inward; the castle of her body has literally turned against her. (See Figure 3.) The depiction of a woman in this illustration is no accident: The American Auto-immune Related Disease Association estimates there are fifty million Americans affected by eighty known autoimmune diseases, and most of them are women (Brody 1994). The chart on the following page shows the far greater incidence of autoimmune diseases in women than men.

In the August 1995 issue of *Science* (an issue entirely devoted to women's health), even though immunologist Noel Rose is quoted as saying, "It's a well-documented fact: Women are simply more immunologically talented than men" (Morell 1995:773), the bulk of attention is paid to women's immunological shortcomings. What the article in *Science* gives to women with one hand, it takes away with the other: While acknowledging that females' immune systems are

TABLE 1. Female/male ratios in autoimmune diseases

Disease	Female/male ratio
Hashimoto's disease	25–50:1
Hypothyroidism	6:1
Thyrotoxicosis	4–8:1
SLE	9:1
Rheumatoid arthritis	2–4:1
Sjögren's syndrome	9:1
Myasthenia gravis	2:1
Type I diabetes	5:1

From Ansar et al., Table 7, 272, 1985.

stronger than males', this strength is a double-edged sword. Women are "far more likely to contract an autoimmune disease ... indeed nine out of 10 lupus sufferers are women; overall, researchers estimate that 75% or more of autoimmune disease patients are women" (Morrell 1995:773). The same picture was replicated not long afterward in the popular magazine *American Health*. Here the culprit is the hormone estrogen: "'There is a fundamental problem with the immune system of women,' says Dr. Robert Lahita. ... He and other experts believe estrogen makes a woman's immune system so sensitive that it attacks the body's own tissues as well as genuine invaders" (Conkling 1995).

The greater sensitivity of women's immune systems becomes negatively tinged: Women's immune systems are so sensitive that they are apt to mix up self and nonself, painfully attacking self as if it were nonself. In another kind of immunological sensitivity (recently dramatically depicted in the movie *Safe*), the threat to the immune system is posed not by mistaken identity but by the twentieth century. The woman who is *Safe*'s main character is violently allergic to synthetic substances, fuel emissions, and all sorts of "fumes" from petroleum-based products. Also statistically more common among women than men, in "twentieth-century disease," or multiple chemical sensitivity, the immune system *over*reacts to chemicals, and thus fails to realize that products of industrial society are *not* harmful!

All forms of allergy and autoimmunity are understood to be a form of immunological *over*sensitivity. The immune system vigorously attacks things that don't need attacking: our own body parts, pollen, cat dander, wool, and so on. As a result, the afflicted person has to construct a self-contained environment and live within its walls. In both scientific and popular venues, gender differences in immune competence are stressed, but neither race nor class differences are even mentioned. Statistics on race and class dimensions of allergy and autoimmunity are almost nonexistent (our analyses are prisoners of the categories used to count cases), but one form of allergy (asthma) is documented to be 26 percent more common among African-Americans than among whites in the United States (Evans 1992). And African-Americans are three times more likely than whites to die from asthma (CDC 1995; Malveaux et al. 1993).[2]

Given all this, it might be argued that the model of the body as a fortress defended behind its ramparts in some ways casts women and minorities, with their mixed-up bodies and immunological oversensitivities, in a disadvantaged position.[3] What would happen if we started with a different set of assumptions about how the body works? Is there another way to think about the body and the immune system that might produce different questions and different endpoints?

The Body as a Complex Nonlinear System

A set of metaphors with implications quite different from "the body as machine" is currently exercising a significant amount of influence in some medical specialties. Scientists are deploying metaphors derived from chaos theory, also known as nonlinear dynamics or complexity theory. Cardiologists, for example, are coming to see the heart not as a pump, the quintessential mechanical body part, but as a self-organizing system that beats with a mechanical regularity only when the body is near death.

> Until recently, it was widely held that sudden cardiac death represented an abrupt change from the apparently periodic state of the normal heartbeat to one in which chaotic arrhythmias occur. Work from several sources has suggested that under *normal* conditions the heart has chaotic dynamics and that fatal disturbances of the cardiac rhythm are often preceded by a *decrease* in the degree of physiological chaos. This represents a reversal in the conventional usage of the term "chaos" when applied to the injured heart. (Skinner et al. 1990:1019); (see aslo Denton et al. 1990)

What would happen if, as a thought experiment, we described some of women's reproductive functions, such as menstruation and menopause, in terms of a chaos model, leaving aside the notion of the body as a mechanical factory or centralized production system? Our thought experiment might pose a question such as this: Have the periodic *regularities* of the female hormonal and bleeding cycle between puberty and menopause been overemphasized, just as the regularities of the heartbeat have been? In the current medical model, regular periodicity between well-defined limits is considered normal—estrogen, progesterone, and other hormones are produced (if all is normal) with machinelike regularity; menstrution occurs accurs (if all is normal) with the periodicity of a metronome. Disease produces irregularity, and shifts between stages of maturation (puberty and early menopause) produce irregularity. Regularity is normal, good, and valued; irregularity is abnormal and negatively valued.

Menstrual irregularity is often regarded medically as a pathology related to some organic dysfunction. The dysfunction is variously attributed to a "presumed" malfunction of the ovaries, or such problems as hyperandrogenism (Arai and Chrousas 1994), diabetes (Adcock et al. 1994), PMS (Khella 1992), or anorexia nervosa (Whitaker 1992). I do not mean to suggest that these correlations are spurious. *Rather, I want to call attention to the unexamined assumptions that normal equals periodically regular.* There is a sharp contrast set up in the typology of the normal and regular versus the abnormal and irregular. To begin to move toward a different view, one might ask: How regular are most women?

I know of no enthnographic study of the topic, but it seems very likely that women experiencing irregularity in their periods in puberty or during early menopause will be disturbed and anxious about the irregularity itself.[4] If the body is a machine, then a faltering or erratic pattern of behavior seems to portend its imminent failure. Women who are deemed irregular may be given medication to produce regular periods. (Epidemiologically, "correction" of irregularity is deemed a short-term benefit of oral contraception [Runnebaum 1992].) Women who are uncomfortable with their perceived irregularity may demand relief.[5]

In the machine model, regularity is a sign of health, irregularity a sign of disease or impending death. In the chaos model, it is just the opposite.

> The conventional wisdom in medicine holds that disease and aging arise from stress on an otherwise orderly and machinelike system—that the stress decreases order by provoking erratic responses or by upsetting the body's normal periodic rhythms. In the past five years or so we and our colleagues have discovered that the heart and other physiological systems may behave most erratically when they are young and healthy. Counterintuitively, increasingly regular behavior sometimes accompanies aging and disease. Irregularity and unpredictability, then, are important features of health. (Goldberger et al. 1990:43–44)

This new picture overturns the earlier notion of the heart as part of a stable homeostatic physiological system, in which the goal was to reduce variability and "to maintain a constancy of internal function. According to this theory ... any physiological variable, including heart rate, should return to its 'normal' steady state after it has been perturbed. The principle of homeostasis suggests that variations of the heart rate are merely transient responses to a fluctuating environment."[6] In contrast, the new finding suggests that "the mechanism that controls heart rate may be intrinsically chaotic. In other words, the heart rate may fluctuate considerably even in the absence of fluctuating external stimuli rather than relaxing to a homeostatic, steady state"(Goldberger et al. 1990:47).

> The reason chaotic organization might be an advantage to the heart is this:
> Chaotic systems operate under a wide range of conditions and are therefore
> adaptable and flexible. This plasticity allows systems to cope with the exigencies
> of an unpredictable and changing environment. (Goldberger et al. 1990:49)

If we were to rethink menstruation and menopause in the logic of a chaotic system, here are some possible shifts that could occur.

We could describe "irregularity" as an adaptive response to a changing internal and external environment. The young woman whose menstrual cycle is
affected by exercise, by stress, or by puberty could then think what a good job her
endocrine system is doing flexibly adjusting to her life, rather than worry unduly
about a pathological "irregularity." Epidemiological studies that have shown
greater menstrual irregularity in women who work at night (Miyauchi, Nanjo,
and Otsuka 1992) and women who are vegetarians (Lloyd, Schaiffer, and Demers
1991) could be taken to reveal the responsiveness of these women's physiological
systems to their particular environment, rather than a pathological deviation
from a putative norm of machinelike periodicity. The older woman whose menstrual cycle is affected by approaching menopause or other aspects of her life
could do the same. Here it would be particularly gratifying to see irregularity as a
sign of vigor and health instead of impending disease and death.

The change women undergo during menopause itself could be described as a
phase change of the sort complex systems often undergo. "Complex systems
sometimes behave discontinuously. Systems simply change states. In models of
complex systems, a controlling loop may reach a threshold state and transfer control to another loop altogether. The system appears to have experienced a discon-
tinuous jump from one set of apparent relationships dominating the action to
another" (Arney 1991:51). For a woman undergoing menopause, thinking of it
as a state change from reproductivity to maintenance of nonreproductivity
would constitute a far more positive view of her body than thinking of it as
breakdown of centralized control.

I am aware at this point that I may have offended readers who are medical
specialists by trespassing on a domain where I have no credentials. What hubris
for an anthropologist, of all people, to suggest alternative models to the way the
body is described in contemporary medicine! But actually, my suggestions are
based neither on ignorance nor on a purely theoretical, hypothetical logical possibility. They are based on ethnographic fieldwork in a wide variety of settings—
an immunology lab, clinics, a hospice for AIDS patients, support groups, urban
neighborhoods, and workplaces—which has convinced me that we are in the
midst of a profound sea change in how the body is conceptualized. Ordinary
people in all walks of life, my research has shown, quite commonly see their bodies as complex nonlinear systems (Martin 1994). This has happened in part by
way of an enormous cultural emphasis on the immune system, which has moved
to the very center of the way ordinary people now think of health (Martin 1994).

Let me illustrate with an example of how people talk about the immune system:

BILL WALTERS: I don't even think about the heart anymore, I think about the immune system as being the major thing that's keeping the heart going in the first place, and now that I think about it I would have to say, yeah, the immune system is really . . . important . . . and the immune system isn't even a vital organ, it's just an act, you know?

PETER: It's like a complete network . . . if one thing fails, I mean if—

BILL WALTERS [interrupting]: If something goes wrong, the immune system fixes it, it's like a backup system. It's a perfect balance.

STEVEN BAKER: The immune system is the whole body, it's not just the lungs or the abdomen, it's, I mean if I cut myself, doesn't my immune system start to work right away to prevent infection? So it's in your finger, I mean, it's everywhere.

From a mechanical body made up of simple components with different functions, these people have moved to a reconceptualization of the body based on a dispersed, fluid system. Like a fractal, the protective ordering functions of the immune system are present in every part of the body, no matter how different each appears. One woman we interviewed explained her conception of the immune system this way.

My visualization would be almost tides or something . . . the forces, you know, the ebbs and flows.

[Could you draw anything like that?]

I could.

[What is it that ebbs and flows?]

The two forces, I mean, the forces . . . imbalance and balance.

As she spoke, she drew the accompanying illustration, labeling it "the waves." (See Figure 4.) She was reaching for a way of imaging a fluid, ever-changing body, a body containing turbulence and instabilities, a body in constant motion, a body that is the antithesis of a rigid, mechanical set of parts. This new body is also in delicate relationship to its environment, a complex system nested in an infinite series of other complex systems.

It is not only men and women who are not professional scientists who are working with a conception of a fluid, flexible, ever-changing body. Although they are not yet in the mainstream, a subset of immunologists favors what they call a network theory of the immune system. Imagery of the dance replaces traditional imagery of the immune system in battle against external foes. The body positively reaches out into the world and takes it in:

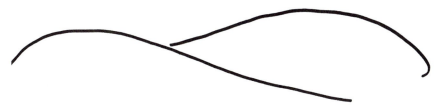

FIG. 4

> The dance of the immune system and the body is the key to the alternative view
> proposed here, since it is this dance that allows the body to have a changing and
> plastic identity throughout its life and its multiple encounters. Now the estab-
> lishment of the system's identity is a positive task and not a reaction against
> antigens [foreign substances]. (Varela and Coutinho 1991:251)

In this new kind of body, attuned to its environment, what counts for maintaining health is what goes on in interactions between the inside and the outside.
Thus, in striking contrast to the sharp-edged, closed images of the body in the
1950s and earlier, contemporary images more and more show us a body in
motion, not in repose, a body in action, not reclining passively, and a body with
no skin at all, exposing the inner workings of its protective system, opening the
body to its environment. (See Figure 5.)

Apart from images of the body in immunology and what my lab colleagues
came to call "immunology on the street," my research has also shown that flexibility, adaptability, and the ability to rapidly change in response to an ever-
changing environment with agility and grace are ideals that are "breeding"
widely in the culture, bubbling up in all kinds of different contexts. For example,
they are now well entrenched as ideal characteristics of work organizations, the
government, and educational institutions. "Flexibility" is enjoined of workers,
managers, teachers, and recent Ph.D.s.[7] Flexibility is used to characterize the
most desirable personality, the highest form of intelligence, and the species most
likely to survive. It labels countless products and concepts, from NordicFlex
Gold, an exercise machine, through "flex space," an architectural design, to the
light mask that "strengthens your immune system while you sleep." (See Figure 6
for another example.)

Flexibility has come to have such panache in connection with a major shift
in the forces of production that began in the 1970s along with the beginning of a
global economic system. This shift, which has been called flexible specialization
or flexible accumulation by David Harvey (1989) and others, has been characterized as "the signature of a new economic epoch" (Borgman 1992:75). It has
entailed flexibility of both labor and production: labor markets become more
variable as workers move in and out more rapidly; labor itself varies as workers
"job-shift" both within firms and among them, dictated by changing production

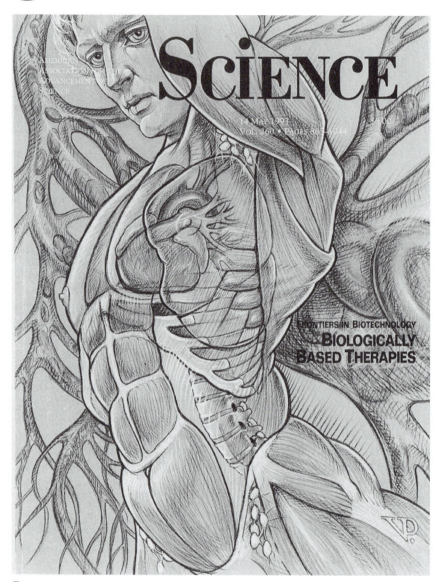

Fig. 5

conditions; products become more flexible as design and technology adapt quickly to the needs of production.[8]

Throughout, women and people of color have felt the brunt of these forces differentially. Following Doreen Massey (1991), we might say both "flexible sexism" and "flexible racism" have been present.

Returning to the thought experiment I undertook, to reimagine and revision

have a significant advantage over those tied down

by convention, bureaucracy and big-spending.

FLEXIBILITY

The varied demands of today's marketplace require small businesses to perform an increasing variety of functions.

Responsiveness to Change

Whether it's in sales or finance, realty or retail, flexibility is the new key to long-term success. In these days of doing more with less, the way in which companies allocate resources has changed. In the past, financial clout often determined who came out on top. Today, faced with competitive and market pressures unimagined ten years ago, companies must now find

Flexibility and a sense of adventure must be a part of any company's corporate culture if it is to succeed into the 21st century.

Large companies, of course, a greater challenge than small busin generally have an easier time impleme cies. But no matter what the size o companies with an adaptable struc outlook are better positioned to capture than their competitors; their ability to q cus, or even redefine, their business o sures their continued success.

Willingness to embrace c just the beginning of this reorientation. A response to rapidly evolving situations also a careful selection of business tools. Tool chosen for their versatility and dependabil

The new HP LaserJet 5P printer.
It specializes in everything.

$899

Estimated U.S. retail price. Actual price may vary.

From envelopes to index cards, letter-size to legal-size, the new HP LaserJet 5P tackles whatever comes its way. With two paper trays, the ability to print up to 10 wrinkle-free envelopes at one time, crisp 600-dpi print quality, and six-page-per-minute speed, it's the perfect printer for your business. Beyond all this, new wireless infrared printing ensures built-in flexibility into the future.

Imagine. Unsurpassed versatility. Legendary HP reliability. And now, surprising affordability. See your Yellow Pages for the HP dealer nearest you.

HP LaserJet Printers
Just what you had in mind.

HEWLETT®
PACKARD

FIG. 6

the processes of female physiology, we can now see that imagining the female body as I suggested would give women a flexible, adaptable, responsive physical self, one that is ideally suited to notions of the kind of self—agile, quick, graceful, in constant change, nimbly responsive to alteration in the environment—now thought necessary to survive in the contemporary world.[9]

But revisioning female physiology this way does not depend on the musings of an anthropologist. A biologist has recently described a flurry of new facts about menstruation. In place of the standard medical view of menstruation, that menstruation is the waste product of a failed conception, composed of debris, dead tissue, scrap material that is of no use, the Berkeley biologist Margie Profet (1993) substitutes the argument, which she bases on comparative evolutionary data, that "menstruation evolved as a mechanism for protecting a female's uterus and fallopian tubes against harmful microbes delivered by incoming sperm ... according to [this argument] the uterus is extremely vulnerable to bacteria and viruses that may be hitching a ride on the sperm, and menstruation is an aggressive means of preventing infections that could lead to infertility, illness and even death. In menstruation ... the body takes a two-pronged attack against potential interlopers: It sloughs off the outer lining of the uterus, where the pathogens are likely to be lingering, and it bathes the area in blood, which carries immune cells to destroy the microbes" (Angier 1993:1,5). Profet's account accomplishes two controversial but powerful reversals. The first is that sperm, instead of being gallant and virile rescuers of the hapless egg (our 1950s model), become unwitting carriers of harmful pathogens. The second is that women's menstrual flow, instead of being useless and disgusting debris, becomes an important part of her flexible and responsive immune system. Menstruation becomes "not a passive loss of unused uterine lining, but an aggressive way to prevent infection" brought in by sperm (Angier 1993: 1,5).

Sperm delivers germs; menstrual fluid washes them away. In Profet's reinterpretation, men's substances lose standing at the very same time that women's substances gain. Whether you are concerned about nutrition, exercise, toxins, stress, cancer, or AIDS, the health arena is saturated with immune system talk. The immune system has begun to function culturally as the key guarantor of health and the keymark of differential survival for the twenty-first century. Profet's model of female menstruation gives women a major new site for immune function.

However appealing and seductive to our contemporary sensibilities, imagining the body as a flexible, agile, adaptive system is not without its problems. To be flexible increasingly seems to be a good thing, but whose good does it serve?

Consider the employees of the Fortune 500 corporation where I did fieldwork, who were trained to become flexible, agile, and fearless, to "work without a net," thus making a reality of the book *Working Without a Net* (Shechtman 1994), which Newt Gingrich declares is "required reading for every American." All employees, from line worker to manager, were trained on ropes courses built specifically for the purpose at several sites on the East Coast. Belayed by moun-

So I'm not the most

AGILE

person.

I'm only ten months old.

BUT I DO HAVE PLANS.

Crazy, crispy, ambitious plans.

I want to be an athlete.
I want to kayak the Nile and pose by the pyramids.
I want to run and jump and

DANCE

and climb Mt. Kilimanjaro.

I WANT TO LIFT

three times my weight, like a worker ant.
I want to swim with the giant sea turtles.
I want to win the Tour de France

ON A TRICYCLE.

I want to be the first person to ever skip
around the world. And I want to

START A NEW ART MOVEMENT.

But before I can do any of that, what I really

NEED

now is a pair of Baby Conditioner *shoes with*
flexible soles and extra-wide toe-boxes.
For more information on Nike products call 1-800-462-7363.

FIG. 7

Anthropologist EMILY REED spends eight months a year deep within the AMAZON rain forest. For OBVIOUS reasons it's VITAL that she know the CUSTOMS AND LANGUAGES of the seven CANNIBALISTIC tribes who also inhabit the area. Choose a CRO that LACKS the FLEXIBILITY to do things many DIFFERENT ways, and YOU may ALSO find yourself TALKING TO THE HEADHUNTERS.

PHARMACO::LSR

FIG. 8

taineering ropes and harnesses, we climbed tall poles, crept across high wires, and slid down zip wires (Martin 1994). This training—exposing workers deliberately to fear and risk in a controlled environment—was to enable them to rapidly adjust to continuously changing conditions, especially if (or rather *when*) they were delayered (fired). According to the author of *Working Without a Net*, people who entered the work force around 1980 will have experienced, on average, five to seven job changes and three to five career changes by the time they retire. We need to realize the cost of being willing to change jobs many times, which may, through the route of part-time or self-employment, include loss of pensions, health insurance, and unemployment insurance. In the face of the incitement to be nimble and in constant motion, we need to realize the common human need for stability, security, and stasis.

Consider also the ads, from MCI to Nike shoes, that enjoin us to become "flexible folk" who will move fluidly through space and time to make ever-changing connections with our environment. These are the years of the flexible child, worker, computer programmer, and even anthropologist. (See Figures 7 and 8.) To whose good? Fresh from recent experiences of the body held to rigid postures, strict timetables, and limited movements, it is no wonder that moving gracefully as an agile, dancing, flexible worker/person/body feels like a liberation, even if one is moving across a tightrope. But can we simultaneously realize that these new flexible bodies are also highly constrained? They cannot stop moving, they cannot grow stiff and rigid, or they will fall off the "tightrope" of life and die.

Why not just join in the celebration of such an appealing way of life and enjoy being energized, alert, engaged, and active? For two reasons, and these will be my concluding thoughts. First is because this ideal image is based on a tiny portion of human capacities. It is an ideal some people will be able to achieve much better than others. While we are striving for the flexible, lean, and agile, let us remember the virtues of the stable, ample, and still. Second, even though the model of the body in constant change and adaptation might allow women's bodies to come closer to the new ideal than men's, I, for one, am reluctant to embrace uncritically any model that discriminates, even if it would reverse an age-old imbalance. Uncritical adoption of this alluring model risks making us think there is a *natural* basis why flexible, nimble men and women with responsive immune systems and resilient personalities survive in decent jobs, while others of us, with flawed or rigid immune systems, will slide into poverty and disease.

I began by suggesting that we "wake up" the dead metaphors in scientific language so it can become more receptive to its own interrogation. The point of waking the language up is not to *remove* metaphor from scientific descriptions, to sterilize them to abstraction. It is to open our minds to the presence of metaphor, the power of metaphor and to the possibility that scientific language awakened to its cultural powers might have more "nuanced, complex, mid-wifery properties" (to quote Toni Morrison [1994:15] once again) in relation to our contemporary concepts of the self.

Notes

1. The *Oxford English Dictionary* reports the use of the word *imaginaries* as early as 1709: "Mrs. Manley Secret Mem. (1736) III. 208 False glittering imaginaries."
2. Ironically, "management" of asthma, if successful, results in better "tolerance" of the air we have to breathe. Seeing the body as a fortress focuses attention on the integrity of the walls we can erect to separate us from the environment, not the content of the outside environment.
3. The question of why women and African-Americans have higher rates of these maladies would lead me too far afield here, but a place to start would be new research that ties the increasing incidence of allergy and autoimmune disease worldwide to the rise in the amount of airborne toxins from cars and industry (Matzinger 1994; Cone and Martin forthcoming).
4. Indirect evidence for this point is that when the birth control pill was first tested, women did not like that fact that they no longer had periods. Subsequently, the pill was redesigned to produce a regular, monthly period.
5. Canguilhem (1991:197–99) discusses the concept of regularity in physiology in relation to conceptions of the normal. Duden (1991:115) describes how in Germany in the eighteenth century, there was widespread concern about maintaining flows of various substances into and out of the body. What marked women off from men was "not their monthly bleeding as such but solely the periodic nature of their bleeding or discharge of fluids from the body."
6. It has often been pointed out that functionalist models in sociology and anthropology, whose heyday was in the 1950s, depended on a similar conception of homeostasis.
7. A recent report from the Committee on Science, Engineering and Public Policy argued

that there will not be enough jobs to go around, so even new Ph.D.'s will have to be able to nimbly shift and flexibly change jobs or specialties (Honan 1995).

8. Being flexible is not altogether new as a virtue for workers: it has long been a necessity for women and minorities, as well as the poor, marginal, and peripheral for whatever reason. Having more than one job, moving from job to job, and being adaptable and able to function in changing circumstances have long been a part of life in the inner city as well as remote rural areas (Weiss 1990; Williams 1988).

9. I do not have space to develop the point here, but corporate advertisements featuring flexibility often prominently feature women.

References

Adcock, C. J., L. A. Perry, D. R. Lindsell, A. M. Taylor, J. Jones, and D. B. Dunger. 1994. Menstrual Irregularities Are More Common in Adolescents With Type I Diabetes. *Diabetic Medicine* 11(5):465–70.

Angier, Natalie. 21 Sep 1993. Radical New View of Role of Mensturation. *New York Times,* September 21:C1, C5.

Arai, K., and G. P. Chrousas. 1994. Glucocorticoid Resistance. *Baillieres Clinical Endocrinology and Metabolism* 8(2):317–31.

Arney, William Ray. 1991. *Experts in the Age of Systems.* Albuquerque, NM: University of New Mexico Press.

Borgmann, Albert. 1992. *Crossing the Postmodern Divide.* Chicago: University of Chicago Press.

Brody, Jane E. 1994. "Hair of Dog" Tried as Cure for Autoimmune Disease. *New York Times,* October 18:C1.

Canguilhem, George. 1991. *The normal and the pathological.* New York: Zone.

CDC (Centers for Disease Control). 1995. Asthma–United States. *Mortality and Morbidity Weekly Report* 43(51–52):952–55.

Cone, Richard A., and Emily Martin. Forthcoming. The Immune System, Global Flows of Foodstuffs, and the New Culture of Health. In Paula Treichler and Constance Penley (eds.), *The Visible Woman.* New York: New York University Press.

Conkling, Winifred. 1996. Are Women the Weaker Sex? *American Health* 15(6):54–58.

Denton, Timothy A., George A. Diamond, Richard H. Helfant, Steven Khan, and Hrayr Karagueuzian. 1990. Fascinating Rhythm: A Primer on Chaos Theory and Its Application to Cardiology. *American Heart Journal* 120(6):1419–40.

Duden, Barbara. 1991. *The Woman Beneath the Skin: A Doctor's Patients in Eighteenth-Century Germany.* Cambridge, MA: Harvard University Press.

Economist. 1985. Why Does the Body Allow Foetuses to Live? *Economist* 296:89.

Evans, R. 1992. Asthma Among Minority Children: A Growing Problem. *Chest* 101(6):368s–71s.

Goldberger, Ary L., David R. Rigney, and Bruce J. West. 1990. Chaos and Fractals in Human Physiology. *Scientific* American 262(2):42–49.

Haraway, Donna. 1992. The Promises of Monsters: A Regenerative Politics for Inappropriate/d Others. Pp. 295–337 in Lawrence Grossberg, Cary Nelson, and Paula A. Treichler (eds.), *Cultural Studies.* New York: Routledge.

Harvey, David. 1989. *The Condition of Postmodernity: An Enquiry into the Origins of Social Change.* Oxford: Basil Blackwell.

Honan, William. 1995. Scientists and Engineers Need Broader Training, Report Says. *New York Times,* April 23:29.

Khella, A. K. 1992. Epidemiologic Study of Premenstrual Symptoms. *Journal of the Egyptian Public Health Association* 67(1–2):109–18.

Lloyd, T., J. M. Schaiffer, and L. M. Demers. 1991. Urinary Hormonal Concentrations and Spinal Bone Densities of Premenopausal Vegetarian and Nonvegetarian Women. *American Journal of Clinical Nutrition* 54(6):1005–10.

Malveaux, F. J., D. Houlihan, and E. L. Diamond. 1993. Characteristics of Asthma Mortality and Morbidity in African-Americans. *Journal of Asthma* 30(6):431–37.

Martin, Emily. 1991. The Egg and the Sperm: How Science Has Constructed a Romance Based on Stereotypical Male-Female Roles. *Signs: Journal of Women in Culture and Society* 16(3):485–501.

———. 1992. *The Woman in the Body: A Cultural Analysis of Reproduction.* Second edition. Boston, MA: Beacon Press.

———. 1994. *Flexible Bodies: Tracking Immunity in America From the Days of Polio to the Age of AIDS.* Boston, MA: Beacon Press.

Massey, D. 1991. Flexible Sexism: Environment and Planning D: *Society and Space* 9:31–57.

Matzinger, Polly. 1994. Tolerance, Danger, and the Extended Family. *Annual Review of Immunology* 12:991–1043.

Miyauchi, F., K. Nanjo, and K. Otsuka. 1992. Effects of Night Shift on Plasma Concentrations of Melatonin, LH, FSH and Prolactin, and Menstrual Irregularity. *Sangyo Igaku* [Japanese Journal of Industrial Health] 34(6):545–50.

Morell, Virginia. 1995. Zeroing in on How Hormones Affect the Immune System. *Science* 269:773–75.

Morrison, Toni. 1994. *The Nobel Lecture in Literature,* 1993. New York: Knopf.

Nilsson, Lennart. 1985. *The Body Victorious.* New York: Delacorte Press.

Paul, William E. (ed.). 1989. *Fundamental Immunology.* Second edition. New York: Raven Press.

Profet, M. 1993. Menstruation as a Defense Against Pathogens Transported by Sperm. *Quarterly Review of Biology* 68(3):335–86.

Runnebaum, B. 1992. The Androgenicity of Oral Contraceptives: The Young Patient's Concerns. *International Journal of Fertility* 37(suppl. 4):211–17.

Shechtman, Morris R. 1994. *Working Without a Net: How to Survive and Thrive in Today's High Risk Business World.* Englewood Cliffs, NJ: Prentice Hall.

Skinner, J. E. 1990. Neurocardiology: Brian Mechanisms Underlying Fatal Cardial Arrhythmias. *Neurologic Clinics* 11(2):325–51.

Varela, Francisco J., and Antonio Coutinho. 1991. Immunoknowledge: The Immune System as a Learning Process of Somatic Individuation. Pp. 239–56 in John Brockman (ed.), *Doing Science: The Reality Club.* New York: Prentice Hall.

Weiss, Chris. 1990. Organizing Women for Local Economic Development. Pp. 61–70 in John Gaventa, Barbara E. Smith, and Alex Willingham (eds.). *Communities in Economic Crisis: Appalachia and the South.* Philadelphia, PA: Temple University Press.

Whitaker, A. H. 1992. An Epidemiological Study of Anorectic and Bulimic Symptoms in Adolescent Girls: Implications for Pediatricians. *Pediatric Annals* 21(11):752–59.

Williams, Brett. 1988. *Upscaling Downtown: Stalled Gentrification in Washington, D.C.* Ithaca, NY: Cornell University Press.

Destabilizing Methods

One New Reproductive Technology, Multiple Sites

How Feminist Methodology Bleeds into Everyday Life

RAYNA RAPP

When I set out to map the social impacts and cultural meanings of amniocentesis, one of the new reproductive technologies, beginning in the mid-1980s, I began by interviewing twenty-five women who had received what is so antiseptically labeled a "positive diagnosis." They had discovered through chromosome testing that something was seriously wrong with the fetuses they were carrying; a decision to end or continue the pregnancy would therefore have to be made. Even now, the memory of how hard those women searched for words to describe their experiences with amniocentesis and selective abortion remains vivid to me; it impressed upon me the need to collectively construct new ways of talking appropriate to new ways of diagnosing. These women were working in a communicative system whose vocabulary is exclusively medical, whose grammar is technological, and whose syntax has yet to be negotiated. It was not always easy for them to frame alternative descriptions with which to more accurately represent their own experiences.

Attempting to both analyze the considerable discursive and practical powers of the biomedical framework and break away from it, I tried to follow as many constituencies as I could imagine with interests in prenatal diagnosis into the domains and arenas where they were socially rooted. Over the next several years, I eventually pieced together a layered picture of where some of the force fields of amniocentesis meet and resonate. I observed genetic counseling in medical centers, followed users and refusers of this technology to their homes, offices, or other community locations (wherever they had time to see me), interned in a cytogenetics lab to understand how diagnoses are made, queried geneticists and counselors about their work experiences and ethical practices, and spent time in a support group for parents whose children had Down's syndrome, the most commonly diagnosed chromosome anomaly, and one of the main conditions for which prenatal testing was developed. In the schools and programs serving those who bore hereditary disabilities, I learned that the social integration of a child with a diagnosed difference is not isomorphic with her medical history. I interviewed, I observed, I processed medical archives and attended health conferences. I played the student, the lab worker, and the sometimes stupefied television viewer. I made some new friendships and sorely tried some old ones. And I came to worry about the many intersections at which I was accumulating what used to be so unproblematically called "data."

This tracing of threads through multiple sites using a range of methodologies now has a name within anthropology: It has recently been deemed "multisited ethnography" (Marcus 1995; see also Gupta and Ferguson 1997a). The idea that many pieces of a cultural puzzle may be empirically localized and studied all over the place in open-ended fashion is, of course, a product of many discursive and practical conjunctures (cf. Morley and Robins 1995). Highly visible globalizing processes—in linked economies, media circuits, and political movements, for example—beckon us to tack back and forth between the construction of local and extralocal knowledge. Chaos theory (as Emily Martin so fruitfully shows us [Martin 1992]) provides compelling metaphors good for thinking about escalating and unbounded influences. Postmodernist theoretical perspectives suggest that cultural representations are uneasily and contradictorily cobbled together across seemingly unrelated terrains. And lengthy anthropological discussions of the analytics of complex cultural objects and the importance of breaking the space-place-culture link have been rich in the 1990s (Gupta and Ferguson 1997a; Gupta and Ferguson 1997b).

Multiple siting as a methodology surely owes a great deal to the enduring contributions of a political economy approach to culture, which has rightly insisted that the patterns anthropologists describe on the ground are localized traces of the uneven and internationalized flows of capital and its agents (Roseberry 1988). And in science studies, the persuasive powers of materialist explanation led some analysts to study "invisible colleges" (Crane 1972) and social interests undergirding knowledge construction and actor network enrollment, and to develop a view of science as politics by other means (Barnes, Bloor, and Henry 1996; Latour 1987). Where science studies and cultural studies conjoin, physical phenomena have been described as inherently heterogeneous and often unstable, hence open to contested meanings (Traweek 1991). Likewise, feminist analysts joined and often led interdisciplinary colleagues to examine the boundaries of science in general and biomedicine in particular as systems of knowledge construction in order to make visible the too-often "invisible and implicated actors" (Clarke and Montini 1993) who lived out its embodied and contested agendas (Keller 1995; Wajcman 1995).

Yet it was surely early second-wave feminist health research, much of it undertaken out of righteous indignation rather than theoretical positioning, which was first responsible for inventing some methods adequate to contests over power and health. *We* needed to track the dumping of Depo-Provera into third-world women's bodies far removed from the overdeveloped markets where pharmaceutical profits accumulated (Dixon-Mueller 1993). *We* noted that the original, high-dose birth control pill was tested on Puerto Rican women whose health status in no way approximated the fantasied modal female body of its North American designers' imaginary, even as their sterilization went uncontested by a Church that did not want them to become "effective contraceptors" (Mass 1976; cf. Meldrum 1996). Now we are tracking Norplant "under her skin" as it becomes a contraceptive of both choice and constraint in many countries (Mintzes, Handon, and Hanhart 1993) and worrying about the touted benefits of immunological contraception now under development (Richter 1993). We are also transmogrifying the boundaries surrounding international "human rights" to include "reproductive rights" (Correa 1994; Correa and Petchesky 1994). Moreover, such material discoveries and struggles have sparked the feminist cultural imagination in dystopic novels like Zoe Fairbain's *Benefits,* Marge Piercy's *Woman on the Edge of Time,* Margaret Atwood's *The Handmaid's Tale,* and the many novels of Octavia Butler (as Donna Haraway and others have been pointing out for some time).

In many dispersed-but-connected locations, U.S. feminist health activists were thus condemned to learn a lesson that is as open-ended as the problem it underlines: Our stories are unevenly and globally scripted. What may be perceived as "loose ends" in one national context or among one group of women become central dramas when reframed as transnational social and cultural flows. And it has taken an international women's movement to begin to imagine the diversity of struggles and aspirations that a revisioning of women's health might entail. (Imagine a book about multinational coalitions of women struggling against the Vatican in transnational meetings held in Cairo and Beijing. It sounds like a bad parody of a novel by Doris Lessing, rather than a thumbnail sketch of the second half of the UN's Decade for Women!) Learning to live with the benefits and burdens of multilayered nonclosure has thus been far from academic.

Emergent Methods

But such generalizations, of course, do not dictate a specific methodology: Rather, they influence structures of sentiment and desire within which the consciousness of individual researchers is, in part, shaped. This essay uses my own journey of enlightenment (which surely remains the dominant, if highly problematic, trope of anthropological investigation) as one illustration of this overdetermined and open-ended shift toward more layered methodologies in feminist health research. I hope to contribute to what Patti Lather in this volume so beautifully describes as the process of "troubl[ing] methodology ... work[ing] the ruins of a confident social science as the very ground from which new practices of research might take shape." After the fact (as Clifford Geertz entitles his autobiographic problematic [Geertz, 1995]), it is easier to retrospectively articulate a rational methodology. But here I hope to illustrate how the fragments of what later seems a usable tool kit emerge always and already delimited and limited by prior methodological and categorizing moves. Yet if we recognize our methodologies as partial but never impartial, we must also continue to explore how to take responsibility for the impacts of the contested knowledge they nonetheless construct.

The intersection, the coconstitutiveness, of methodology and responsibility was never far from my mind as I expanded my empirical research on the social impacts and cultural meanings of prenatal diagnosis in New York City. I was and remain particularly interested in how women of diverse racial-ethnic, national, class, and religious backgrounds experience the offer of genetic testing in their pregnancies, what they do and don't want from technology, how they understand childhood disabilities, what a fetus is, and what might be worth an abortion. I have constantly had to interrogate the connections and differences that linked me, and my research questions, to women from very different social locations, worrying over theoretical issues of representation in very concrete contexts. I have come to understand this new technology to provide an occasion in which every pregnant woman is interpolated into the role of moral philosopher: after all, you cannot confront the issue of the "quality control" of fetuses without wondering whose standards for entry into the human community will prevail and what the limits of voluntary parenthood might be.

And lurking inside the same issue is another big ethical concern characterized by the emergent discourse and practices of disability rights activists. This constituency has a lot to tell us all about the ways in which *social* discrimination, not simply absolute or natural physical or mental limitations, erect the barriers and fears that surround our cultural responses to disabled fetuses and children. So the problem of the new reproductive technologies as they intersect the lived diversity of women and the conversation we need to have between those championing disability rights and those committed to reproductive rights is central to the work I have undertaken. And the "we" of this political conversation is not always evident across enormous social diversity: It has to be imagined, and sometimes constructed in action, with all the attendant risks and potential failures of nerve or accomplishment.

Yet lest that sound too clear-cut a political location, I should rush to add that both the methods and ethics of my work emerged slowly. At the beginning I was struck by how the voices of experts in medicine, bioethics, health planning, and law dominated the published literature. The bodies from which these voices spoke were mostly male, overwhelmingly white, and highly professional. As a feminist researcher and health activist, as well as a woman trying to understand the complex consequences of having used amniocentesis in my own pregnancies, I thought I could help to wrest the discourse on new reproductive technologies from the hands of medical experts, turning it over to the women who used, might use, or might refuse to use them. Initially the women who had received distressing news from amniocentesis probably agreed to speak with me about a rather private and stigmatized subject because I was one of them: It was my own painful experiences with ending a pregnancy in which Down's syndrome had been diagnosed that first animated my research (Rapp 1984). Later, as I attempted to identify and query as many layers or constituencies of people who had interests in amniocentesis as I could imagine, I had to move beyond what I had already identified to be my own experience, constructing conversations across many social and cultural chasms. Sometimes I manipulated professional expertise to squeeze into tight corners within laboratories or science convocations. Often I was graciously tolerated by people who only vaguely understood or shared my agenda. And sometimes I connected with people who understood it better than I did.

I began in the cytogenetics lab run by the Health Department of New York City, learning how diagnoses are constructed—laboratory life, to use Latour and Woolgar's felicitous title (Latour and Woolgar 1979). I followed the lab's counselors through their peripatetic rounds at many hospitals in the city, observing hundreds of intake interviews where they explained prenatal testing to women of diverse race, class, ethnic, national, and religious backgrounds. I interviewed scores of women (and some men) across that diversity who had the test, or who refused it. But men were hard to come by; they rarely seemed interested, and sometimes it wasn't clear if the lack of interest was their own or a polite boundary-keeping mechanism set up by the pregnant women in their lives who wanted to keep this discussion to themselves. The meager presence of the exotic male potential parent in this research had to be problematized as one more site of contradictory cultural data collection that was not strictly "biomedical."

But it was not only the issue (or nonissue) of male participation in technological decisions surrounding pregnancy that alerted me to the nonmedical spaces which needed to be theorized and empirically marked. In 1984 I published an article describing my own experiences with "positive diagnosis" in Ms. Magazine, hoping to provoke a more public discussion among women of the benefits and burdens of this technology (Rapp 1984). I got far more than I bargained for, as is so often the case when one tries to imagine a political constituency and conversation. My article was anathematized on the front page of a right-to-life newsletter (where my "selfish lifestyle" was branded). I received scores of letters from women who also wanted to share their amniocentesis stories. And someone made a phone call that changed the course of my research dramatically. One of the founding members of a Down's syndrome parents' support group (Manhattan and the Bronx) and herself the mother of a child with Down's syndrome called me up to challenge some of my descriptions of disabled children and the social services available to them. I quickly joined the support group and, with her philosophical and practical guidance, began learning my way around the world of disability rights and educational services for children with special needs. I eventually interviewed twenty-eight families whose children had Down's syndrome, first through meeting activists in two parent support groups, later through the work I did on the educational committee of one of those groups, and then through a family-court–funded early-intervention program for developmentally-delayed children. On a more haphazard basis, I spoke with a dozen grown siblings of children with Down's syndrome, and interviewed a handful of parents whose offspring had other chromosomal or genetic disabilities. Over the years of this study, I have learned a great deal about the need to champion *both* the reproductive rights of women to accept or refuse to carry a pregnancy to term that will result in a baby with a serious disability, and the need to support adequate, nonstigmatizing, integrative services for all the children, including disabled children, that women bear.

And as the years of seemingly endless field research slogged on, I also became increasingly aware of the powerful and proliferating discourses on the state of being human that were rapidly seeping out of genetics laboratories onto the pages of *Time, Newsweek, Omni* and the airwaves of *Oprah.* This seepage flows both ways: Scientists too sometimes watch *Oprah,* and most admit to reading the Science Times section of the *New York Times* (Phillips, Kanter, Bednarczyk, and Tastad 1991). I started to worry about the multiple intersections of popular media representations of all the related issues—genetics, prenatal testing, abortion, childhood disability, and disability rights—on which my study touched.

In constructing a diagram of these overlapping, intersecting, but nonisomorphic layers, it is evident that pregnancy and the modern technologies that intervene to regulate it are not vested simply within the world of biomedicine. (Indeed, when I went to interview women and their supporters about a new pregnancy technology, we often ended up spending much of our time discussing religion, but that's another story.) Both pregnancy and its technologies occupy multiple and intersecting spaces in the social life of individual women and their supporters, in the lives of diverse medical, educational, religious, and activist constituencies, in modern globally proliferating media technologies, and, of course, in the politics of representation.

Anthropologists are obsessed with following all the scraps and edges of their problems, often preferring to view a central issue from multiple and oblique angles. In this case, my data proliferated wildly and richly, and there is always the ever-present temptation to conduct "just one more interview." No matter how many Haitian women accepting or refusing "the needle test" I interview, however many medical journals I process as cultural texts, regardless of the number of professional genetics congresses I attend, there will always be another mother of a child with Down's syndrome in East Harlem from whom I might learn a slightly different story, another geneticist who has thought deeply about the ethical implications of piloting cystic fibrosis carrier screening, another educational TV program on the Human Genome Project, or a new sitcom featuring an "older" pregnant woman as trickster-heroine. Engagement with all would enrich my cultural understandings of a new technology. This study thus has no obvious theoretical or temporal limits.

Moreover, the topic is marvelously and maddeningly reflexive. Everyone I run into has an amniocentesis or disability or abortion story, and so do I; geneticists and genetic counselors are highly literate colleagues, and they constantly read over my shoulder as I write, suggesting additional questions and endless black holes of data collection. And, in the worlds of feminist scholarship and social theory, interest in the new reproductive technologies has intensified dramatically in the last decade, as have sophisticated and multidisciplinary discussions of the history, social construction, and philosophical importance of the body, and embodied differences, especially those marked through sex, sexuality, and race. This volume bears ample testimony to that process. Almost by definition, then, this is a work without boundaries, in which I meet Donna Haraway's cyborg constantly coming and going, sometimes worrying, sometimes celebrating the simultaneously eugenic and liberatory nature of her technologically embodied social self.

Category Problems

After all this layered hand-wringing over endlessly expanding and troubling one's methodology, what has been gained? Ultimately, that is a question to which answers can only be forged collectively, call-and-response fashion, among audiences and constituencies who use, reject, or transform this work. But at the very least, methodologically, I have learned to let my categories fall apart again and again, only to see them reconstituted, sometimes for better and sometimes for worse.

This problem of categories is most glaringly apparent in my attempts to build racial-ethnic and class diversity into my work. Initially, I intended to contrast observations and interviews with patients from white, Hispanic, and African-American backgrounds, distinguishing middle-class, working-class, and working-poor groups. With some effort, I managed to collect my comparative sample by observing and interviewing in seven city hospitals serving diverse catchment areas. But the diversity I encountered *within* groups quickly underlined how static such sociological classifications can become. Ethnic identity is, of course, far more complex than such census categories indicate; and while occupation and payment plan yield good approximations of socioeconomic status, they barely touch the experiential meanings of social class. Moreover, microvariation across New York's hospital catchment areas is profound: "Hispanic" on Manhattan's West Side virtually stands for Puerto Rican and Dominican; in the parts of Brooklyn where I worked, it was also likely to cover people from Honduras, Nicaragua, Guatemala, or Panama, and in Queens, Ecuadorian, Colombian, Peruvian, and Argentinean women and their families fell under this label. Sometimes socioeconomic standing varied throughout an individual's lifetime, as was true of many Colombians, Argentineans, and

Ecuadorians who had middle-class educations by the standards of their home country but found themselves in working-class jobs after migrating to New York. Thus the diagram I had hoped to construct, in which class differences could be distinguished from as well as overlapped with ethnic and cultural resources, was muddied by variations in micro experiences as well as macro economics.

Yet over the course of several years of research, I came to pick out patterns that *did* reflect the resources and boundaries of the class and ethnic identities to which people were assigned, or assigned themselves. There is thus an analytic tension in my texts and other presentations between labeling individuals and trying to indicate the rich array of cultural resources from which they draw their health beliefs and family aspirations. When I generalize about "white, middle-class professionals" or "Hispanic service workers," I also attempt to attach concrete stories belonging to "Iliana Mendez, Ecuadorian baby-sitter," or "Linda Scott, U.S.-born theatrical set designer." I intend these labels to signal the routes and life trajectories within which an individual's consciousness is forged, without creating pigeonholes into which people are too easily slotted. Individual consciousness is always complex and cannot be reduced to the analytic categories within which positivist social investigators are most comfortable working. Yet we cannot do away with such categories, even as we interrogate them, for they provide not only sorting devices, but signposts on the way to understanding socially significant differences.

And throughout this research, different differences took on heightened salience, according to context. Matters of class, for example, figure large in problems of scientific literacy, confidence, and agency in medical settings. Thus working-class and working-poor women and their families are quite likely to act deferentially when speaking with medical professionals, even when they do not understand their language or necessarily share their worldview. But among middle-class professional patients, interrogation of genetic counselors and the authority of their statistics is common; white professional men, especially, express their anxiety by "fighting with numbers," attempting to show genetic counselors (who are almost inevitably master's-degree–holding women) that their facts don't apply to the anxious man's wife.

But if class is deeply intertwined with knowledge/power interactions, religion and community background are more likely to shape attitudes toward disability and abortion. Latina women spoke confidently, for example, about maternal/fetal fusion, and their authority to accept or end what they imagined to be childhood suffering. The maternal and Catholic authority of Mary to protect and even sacrifice a child figured large for them, even among evangelical Protestants. But white native-born women of all classes seemed much more tortured about the stigma of making a "selfish" decision to end a pregnancy in which a disability had been diagnosed. Surely their vulnerability to this label owes a lot to the shifting political demography of female labor-force participation and divorce rates as well as to the national dramas being played out around abortion. And ethnicity and class resources resonate throughout the family stories I heard concerning children with disabilities. Paradoxically, kids with developmental delays may have more stimulating environments when they come from larger families; such families are, on average, less likely to be middle-class than the more privileged homes in which a child with a disability is likely to be a first or only child. So while educational and medical professionals recommend universal enrollment in early-intervention infant services (which are often very important sites for the transmission and contestation of values around "health" and "normalcy"), the more middle-class families who use these programs may have relatively more to learn than their less privileged peers when it comes to infant stimulation. Tracking such different differences became a central concern of this project. But our descriptive tools to mark the specificity and accuracy of differences of gender, ethnicity, class background, national and religious community, and ablebodiedness are always incomplete. Such categories can permeate the problems we attempt to understand, helping to clarify them, but their effects are quite partial. And the form of their partialness is never impartial, for they bring with them the possibility of (re)creating stereotypes as well as illuminating generalizations.

My awareness of this tension evolved as I moved from hospital to hospital, discovering the sameness and differences among the people from whom I was learning. My initial observations took place in a hospital with a robust mix of private and clinic patients, and I eventually conducted field work at seven hospitals which ran the gamut of services and populations that characterize healthcare in New York City's hospitals. Each hospital staff and patient population had its own characteristics, depending on the racial-ethnic and class mix of housing and immigration in specific city neighborhoods. In all seven hospitals, I realized again and again that New York's population receiving prenatal health services is a rainbow of Filipinos, Greeks, Haitians, Mexicans, Hawaiians married to Lebanese, Mormons married to Buddhists, Iranians married to Poles, Colombians married to Egyptians, and single mothers with and without partners whose roots lie all over the globe, as well as the more predictable ethnic varieties. And some city hospitals serve an almost exclusively working-poor clinic population, overwhelmingly funded by Medicaid; the future of this group's health care is now up for grabs despite the history of New York's many progressive attempts to build some access and accountability into health services for the poor (Rosner 1986, 1995). Depending on locale, such populations tend to be African-American, African-Caribbean, and/or new or old immigrants who are Spanish-speaking. Such intercutting diversity toppled the neat census categories around which I had initially designed my sample. Thus, as the methods and locales of this study kept expanding, so did my comprehension of the challenges that large and diverse urban populations pose for accurate description. Moreover, "accurate" description implies many things: a historical understanding of the lack of closure to almost any population, especially an urban population in the United

States at the end of the twentieth century; a commitment to interrogate how categories are constructed and used by bureaucrats and the people who "choose" to inhabit them, and the consequences of those uses; and a willingness to locate myself and what I am studying in the relations of knowledge and power that are in part shaped by the deployment of such categories.

When Methodology Bleeds into Daily Life

In the ruins and revisions of my sociological categories, data is potentially everywhere. I began to write the introduction to my book on prenatal diagnosis on the day that the development office at the New School, hoping to use my grant to raise additional institutional funds, sent a new employee to do a story on my research. In preparation for the interview, I had sent her some of my recent articles. The young reporter has a sister who is mentally retarded; preparing to write university publicity on my research then led her to interview her own mother on the impact her sister's life had had on the rest of the family. In such a situation, we agreed that it is unclear who is interviewing whom, and I incorporated her story into my own.

Much of what I have learned about family life with disabilities is highly personal knowledge, culled from a couple who are among my best friends and whose daughter has a genetic disability. Having (rather scrupulously, I imagined) protected the confidentiality of my friend, her husband, and her child over a decade of shooting my mouth off in public about this issue, I was rather unprepared to hear her casually come out as my informant when we shared a panel on something more-or-less cyborgian at a large conference several years ago. And so it goes. Working "at home" has methodological, ethical, and interpretive consequences that would have been hard to foresee from the places I was initially trained to explore as an anthropologist. "Home" now entails not only the repatriation of my work from more conventional anthropological locations in other people's countries to working in the society in which I also permanently live, but also working close to the bone on a topic of deep personal salience and almost obsessive concern. And the escalating recognition of the multiple sites at which the "personal is political" foundational credo of feminist health research is challenged ethically and reciprocally when we take the diversity of women seriously.

When conducting fieldwork at home, the "outer reaches" of the sample bleed into daily reality. This constitutes both a great advantage for enforced wisdom and a confusion for sampling parameters. We can no longer picture DNA, genes, or bodies as bounded units; nor are scientific, medical, or political interventions into the people bearing them any less open-ended. Intersections and boundary crossings provide material locations where emergent social phenomena such as prenatal testing can best be studied. While this is all to the good, it leaves the problem of methodology wide open at its edges.

It also constitutes ethical problems that bear some discussion. The problems of ethics in anthropological fieldwork, in feminist research, and in medically based social science investigations that have at least an implicit (and sometimes a quite explicit) applied and policy edge have been well discussed (Agar 1980; American Anthropological Association 1996; Enslin 1994; Oakley 1981; Gluck and Patai 1991; Stacey 1988). In recent years, much of the anthropological discussion of ethics has been resituated inside a discussion of the politics of text construction: Who is represented, who does the representing, what symbolic violences are associated with citation and silence (Clifford 1988; Fox 1991; Narayan 1993; Visweswaran 1994; Wolf 1992)? Patti Lather's contribution to this volume does a particularly good job at taking these complex issues on board in a sophisticated, ethical, and enormously creative fashion. I therefore leave them in her very capable hands while retaining a rather old-fashioned focus on "ethics," because I want to emphasize that field-based research in anthropology is much broader than the process of "writing ethnography." The daily problems and choices with which the fieldworker is confronted have practical consequences for the people whose lives she touches, as well as for her own data collection and interpretation. They include such mundane problems as the protection of confidentiality; language translation and power; the contamination of evolving but lopsided relationships through continuous intervention; and paradoxes of feedback and consulting. Each deserves a book of its own but will receive only a few words now.

The problem of confidentiality is something of an obsession among anthropologists. But styles, of course, change. Whereas once it was considered de rigueur to disguise "my village" but claim "my people," many of us now think that the claims of historical accuracy and the delineation of power relations (theirs and ours, in interaction) override the conventions of both masking and owning subjects. The topic on which I am working is highly charged. Because I was asking people to tell me stories that often felt like crucibles of tough decision making, I promised, and have delivered, confidentiality via pseudonyms for any pregnant woman, mother, child, or supporter I have interviewed. It has been harder to provide anonymity for genetic counselors and other medical service providers, many of whom have discussed hard ethical situations and personal values with me both on and off the record. Moreover, some service providers and scientists may want recognition for their work, rather than confidentiality. Nor can confidentiality be completely guaranteed in a highly literate and information-obsessed culture such as our own.

A second ethical problem concerns the subject of language. I have constructed a story using medical vocabulary, the words of people I interviewed, and a political language intended to intervene in policy debates and practical pregnancy and child-rearing services available to women and their supporters. Sometimes, I use the language of "polymerase chain reaction," "proband," and "balanced translocation" as aspects of native text construction in the genetics community, explaining what I have learned of their meanings as I do so. At other times, I have gone to some lengths to write out the vernacular cadences of West Indian women's anxiety over "choosing" amniocentesis, or the subtle distinctions Spanish-speaking women use to describe their pregnancies and abortions in the context of themselves as "older" women. Social movements for both reproductive rights and disability rights have so influenced my thinking that I cannot use phrases such as "birth defect," "defective fetus," "termination," or "positive diagnosis" without putting them in quotation marks, insisting on the alternative understandings such words muffle and the biases they project.

Attention to the power of language immediately raises unsettling questions that range from the practical to the abstract. Practically, can there be "informed consent" without funding interpreters for low-income patients whose first language is not English? How can resistance to building second-language training into the curriculum of genetic counselor training programs be overcome, given the overwhelming and ever-expanding amount of scientific expertise students truly need to acquire? More abstract issues are also embedded in an analysis of the politics of language. For example, can the specialized vocabularies of science, especially genetics, ever be popularized and democratized, or is this discourse overdetermined to remain highly specialized, hence secret and hegemonic? When should we interpret a pregnancy story self-consciously told in the language of the streets as "resistant" to medicine or social control, and when is it "merely" reproducing the relative powerlessness of its teller? The power of speech and silence, technical and popular vocabularies, English and its translations all enter into the ethics of the research and its interpretation discussed here.

The ethics of language choice became immediately clear to me when I began observing at a hospital which serves a predominantly African-Caribbean patient population. There I sometimes found myself translating the genetic counselor's explanations and questions into Spanish or French for recent migrants from the islands. In translating, I was performing a "payback" service for the pregnant women and counselors who were allowing me to observe their interaction; I was also contaminating my own data collection process. Moreover, my translation choices were exquisitely baroque, often paralyzing, and had to be made in a split second. Was my agenda to make sure the counselor's technical information had been passed on as perfectly as possible? Or was I translating "a woman's right to choose" to use or refuse the test, based on whatever I could glean from the patient herself? Might my goal be to evoke an active, articulated response to the complex issues raised by prenatal testing, so that I might pursue this as part of my own research agenda, despite how unsettling this might well be for the patient? There was no neutral space from which translation could occur.

This lack of neutrality ran through my interactions at every level. It was hard to listen to myself on the early, taped interviews: I talked too much, identified too much of my own experience, reiterated too much of the technical information in what I took to be its most practical format each time I spent a few hours with a woman awaiting amniocentesis results. For many months I practiced silencing myself on tape, thinking I might lessen the contamination of the stories I was collecting.

But I was also learning an obvious and painful lesson. I had located myself at the intersection of all the discourses I was studying and was overcommitted to two contradictory goals. The first, more scholarly and distanced, was witnessing and interpreting the clash of scientific thinking, maternalism, and social analysis inherent in how women recounted their amniocentesis stories. This task was easiest to perform when working with women "like me": well-educated, secular, most likely to be middle-class, white, and relatively empowered, even in the world of medical services of which they might have significant criticisms. With them, I had at least the illusion that their understandings of biomedical discourse and its complex resources were consonant with both those of health care providers and my own.

The second goal was more activist and engaged and was often brought into play in interactions with women I perceived to hold less power in the world than I do: women who were poorer, often lacking in privileged education, and coming from ethnic, national, religious, and racial communities that were as likely to have been the guinea pigs as the beneficiaries of scientific and medical research. Under these circumstances, I was laboring to put medical and scientific resources into a social perspective, and to ensure that the women I was interviewing fully understood the benefits and burdens of the services they were being offered, and the choices they were being forced to make. My role as a teacher was overdetermined.

Identifying the contradictions and conflicts in my own role was, of course, one of the hardest lessons I had to learn. College professors don't abandon their lecterns without great effort, and activists always need an audience. While I painfully learned when to hold myself back and when to intervene to give "information" or suggest how a woman might gain access to needed resources, I also came to accept the inevitable contamination of data that serious interactive feedback entails. The issue was not simply establishing rapport with informants. The issue was how might I contribute, in whatever small ways were possible, to their empowerment in a world where scientific and medical services are inequitably distributed. Similar ethical problems lie at the heart of many anthropologists' fieldwork experiences. They are necessarily heightened when working at home, in a culture as fraught with discrimination and inequality as our own.

Contamination of my data also occurred less dramatically (and perhaps more productively) in my interactions with health care providers. It is a truism of fieldwork that if you hang out long enough, the majority of the population on whom you are imposing your research agenda eventually comes to accept and trust you. I remember with both pain and appreciation the afternoon on which a genetic counselor whom I'd been observing said, "I'm learning a lot from having you watch me. I respect you as a social scientist and a mother. It makes me more conscientious, having to respond to your questions, knowing you're thinking about what the patient is getting out of all of this." Her compliments signaled the palpable presence of the Heisenberg uncertainty principle—the contamination of the process under observation by the presence of the observer—inside my research terrain.

Over years of participant observation, genetics team members have come to feel free to ask for feedback, and sometimes quite a bit more. I have therefore occasionally been called in to speak with crisis-wracked patients who were in shock and in grief, to advise counselors on how to improve their services, and to provide criticisms of the lack of cultural sensitivity built in to some kinds of provider-patient interactions. While in principle I might have demurred, insisting that I would provide feedback "once the study is over," in a case like this the study seemed unending. And the practical needs of service providers and patients are immediate. I know that my interventions have sometimes been incorporated into counseling protocols and influenced things said or unsaid to patients. Such interventions have real effects on both my interactions with health care providers and on the services whose impact I am observing. I hope they have been modestly effective, as well as effectively contaminating. The ethics of giving feedback in a real-world situation where access to resources and the conditions of choice are everywhere at stake had to be resolved in a way that was biased toward what I considered responsible application of my accumulating knowledge.

The problems of ethical feedback easily escalate when working in one's home society, accumulating knowledge that bridges the powerful world of highly literate science workers and their often less literate and almost always less powerful clients. Soon after my publications on amniocentesis began appearing in medical anthropology and gender studies journals, they were abstracted by the genetics community. I have been privileged to be asked to report on aspects of this study at medically-oriented conferences, workshops, and policy meetings of institutions such as the National Society of Genetic Counselors, the Federal Bureau of Maternal and Child Health, and the National Institutes of Health. At first I was a bit overwhelmed to find myself on the genetics speaking circuit and always tried to coauthor whatever I presented with colleagues in genetic counseling so that I would not be perceived solely as a critical outsider. Gradually I have learned to stand up for my own interpretations, asking health professionals to examine the scientific assumptions that form a part of their own cultural backgrounds. I am honored that my work has seemed valuable, if only to raise controversies and debates, within the world of health services and policy.

But I have also come to be wary of the available slots into which anthropological analyses can be placed in the world of biomedical science. When I began observing counseling intake interviews, for example, I was immediately struck by the neo-Freudian working assumptions many counselors seem to use. When a patient from a radically different linguistic, social, and cultural background than their own was silent, or refused the test, or wouldn't engage in probablistic thinking, some counselors would say, "She's denying," "She's passive," "She's regressive," rather than looking for the chasms that were separating their own communicative concerns from those of their client. Over time, as I unearthed some of the complex meanings behind silences or refusals, especially as articulated by women whose cultural backgrounds were very different from those of their counselors, some counselors came to rely on the new, culturalist interpretations I was providing them. But what does it mean to have a counselor now say, when discussing a noncompliant patient, "She's Haitian" or "She's Chinese," rather than "She's fatalistic," as an explanation of behavior the counselor does not quite understand? Has my hard work only served to re-create what Michel-Rolph Trouillot called "the savage slot" (Trouillot 1991), a role impatiently awaiting a cultural occupant, as the new, poor, ethnic immigrants of America's cities become anthropological stand-ins for the tribal peoples my professional tribe once studied? The ethics of fieldwork must include a constant assessment of the limited benefits and possible harm researchers can do in situations where racial, ethnic, national, and religious stereotypes are built into communicative and social service interactions across class differences.

In speaking about the ethical tensions that shadowed this study, I have, of course, been speaking about power. Power is inscribed in all aspects of this study: It resides in the increasingly well funded and metaphor-producing world of molecular genetics (Heath and Rabinow 1993; Fleising and Smart 1993; Martin 1992; Rabinow 1992; Suzuki and Knudson 1989; Bishop and Waldholz 1990). It is shot through the world of biomedicine, where the cutting edges of genetic research converge with social policy and its translation into health services. It blasts communicative chasms between health care providers, already stratified amongst themselves by differences attached to gender, educational level, and often ethnic or national background, and their multicultural, multiclass patient populations. Powerful discrimination segregates the hard-earned knowledge of families raising disabled children with stigmatized differences from much of civil society. And power exquisitely stratifies public, media representations of the complex issues surrounding prenatal diagnosis, abortion rights, prejudice against disabled people, and access to scientific literacy and medical services. Power differences are everywhere represented and enacted in the anthropological methods, data, interpretations, and ethics whose limits I have tried to suggest. It is the multilayered discursive and practical consequences of such power differences that we need to address as we collectively revision women, health, and healing.

Acknowledgments

Funding for this study was provided by: the National Endowment for the Humanities, the National Science Foundation, the Rockefeller Foundation's "Changing Gender Roles Program", the Institute for Advanced Studies, the Spencer Foundation, and a semester's sabbatical from the Graduate Faculty, New School for Social Research. I am deeply grateful for their support, and absolve them from any responsibility for the uses to which I have put it. I especially thank the scores of pregnant women, health care providers, and family members who took the time and energy to engage my research questions. Protecting the confidentiality of their collaboration has meant providing pseudonyms for anyone I quote. Faye Ginsburg applied her usual and quite extraordinary humor and editorial insight to a nascent draft of this essay; I am, as ever, extremely lucky to have her friendship and collaboration. Adele Clarke's editorial guidance was inspirational, enabling me to think more deeply about aspects of my own work that I take for granted.

References

Agar, Michael. 1980. *The Professional Stranger.* New York: Academic Press.

American Anthropological Association. 1996. The New Code of Ethics. *Anthropology News-letter,* April:13–17.

Barnes, Barry, David Bloor, and David Henry. 1996. *Social Studies of Science.* Chicago: University of Chicago Press.

Bishop, John E., and Waldholz, Michael. 1990. *Genome.* New York: Simon and Schuster.

Clarke, Adele, and Theresa Montini. 1993. The Many Faces of RU486: Tales of Situated Knowledges and Technological Contestations. *Science, Technology, and Human Values* 18:42–78.

Clifford, James. 1988. *The Predicament of Culture.* Cambridge, MA: Harvard University Press.

Correa, Sonia. 1994. *Population and Reproductive Rights: Feminist Perspectives From the South.* London and New Delhi: Zed/Kali for Women.

Correa, Sonia, and Rosalind Petchesky. 1994. Reproductive and Sexual Rights: A Feminist Perspective. Pp. 107–23 in G. Sen, A. Germain, and L. C. Chen (eds.), *Population Policies Reconsidered: Health, Empowerment, and Rights.* Cambridge, MA: Harvard University Press.

Crane, Diana. 1972. *Invisible Colleges: Diffusion of Knowledge in Scientific Communities.* Chicago: University of Chicago Press.

Dixon-Mueller, Ruth. 1993. *Population Policy and Women's Rights: Transforming Reproductive Choice.* Westport, CT: Praeger.

Enslin, Elizabeth. 1994. Beyond Writing: Feminist Practice and the Limitations of Ethnography. *Cultural Anthropology* 9(4):537–68.

Fleising, Usher, and Alan Smart. 1993. The Development of Property Rights in Biotechnology. *Culture, Medicine and Psychiatry* 17:43–58.

Fox, Richard. 1991. *Recapturing Anthropology: Working in the Present.* St. Louis, MO: School of American Studies, Washington University.

Geertz, Clifford. 1995. *After the Fact: Two Countries, Four Decades, One Anthropologist.* Cambridge, MA: Harvard University Press.

Gluck, Sherna, and Daphne Patai (eds.). 1991. *Women's Words: The Practice of Feminist Oral History.* Bloomington: Indiana University Press.

Gupta, Achil, and James Ferguson (eds.). 1997a. *Anthropological Locations: Boundaries and Grounds of a Field Science.* Berkeley: University of California Press.

Gupta, Achil, and James Ferguson (eds.). 1997b. *Culture, Power, Place: Explorations in Critical Anthropology.* Durham: Duke University Press.

Heath, Deborah, and Paul Rabinow. 1993. Bio-Politics: The Anthropology of the New Genetics and Immunology. *Culture, Medicine and Psychiatry* 17(1):1–26.

Keller, Evelyn Fox. 1995. The Origin, History, and Politics of the Subject Called "Gender and Science": A First-Person Account. Pp. 80–94 in S. Jasanoff, G. Markle, J. Petersen, and T. Pinch (eds.), *Handbook of Science and Technology Studies.* Thousand Oaks, CA: Sage.

Latour, Bruno. 1987. *Science in Action.* Cambridge, MA: Harvard University Press.

Latour, Bruno, and Steven Woolgar. 1979. *Laboratory Life: The Construction of Scientific Facts.* Beverly Hills: Sage.

Marcus, George. 1995. Ethnography in/of the World System: The Emergence of Multi-Sited Ethnography. *Annual Review of Anthropology* 24:95–117.

Martin, Emily. 1992. The End of the Body? *American Ethnologist* 19: 121–40.

Mass, Bonnie. 1976. *Population Target.* Toronto: Latin American Working Group.

Meldrum, Marcia. 1996. "Simple Methods and "Determined Contraceptors": The Statistical Evaluation of Fertility Control, 1957–1968. *Bulletin of the History of Medicine* 70:266–95.

Mintzes, Barbara, Anita Hardon, and Jannemieke Hanhart (eds). 1993. *Norplant: Under Her Skin.* Amsterdam: Women's Health Action Foundation (WEMOS).

Morley, David, and Kevin Robins, 1995. *Spaces of Identity: Global Media, Electronic Landscapes, and Cultural Boundaries.* London: Routledge.

Narayan, Kirin. 1993. How Native Is a "Native" Anthropologist? *American Anthropologist* 95:671–86.

Oakley, Ann. 1993. Interviewing Women: A Contradiction in Terms? Pp. 221–42 in *Essays on Women, Medicine, and Health.* Edinburgh: Edinburgh University Press.

Phillips, D. P., E. J. Kanter, B. Bednarczyk, and P. L. Tastad 1991. Importance of the Lay Press in the Transmission of Medical Knowledge to the Scientific Community. *New England Journal of Medicine,* October 17:1180–83.

Rabinow, Paul. 1992. Artificiality and Enlightenment: From Sociobiology to Biosociality. Pp. 234–52 in J. Crary and S. Kwinter (eds.), *Incorporations.* New York: Zone.

Rapp, Rayna. 1984. The Ethics of Choice. *Ms.* April:97–100.

Richter, Judith. 1993. *Vaccination Against Pregnancy: Miracle or Menace?* Amsterdam: Health Action International.

Roseberry, William. 1988. Political Economy. *Annual Review of Anthropology* 17:161–85.

Rosner, David. 1986. *A Once and Charitable Enterprise: Hospitals and Health Care in Brooklyn and New York, 1885–1915.* Princeton, NJ: Princeton University Press.

Rosner, David (ed.). 1995. *Hives of Sickness: Public Health and Eidemics in New York City.* New Brunswick, NJ: Rutgers University Press.

Stacey, Judith. 1988. Can There Be a Feminist Ethnography? *Women's Studies International Forum* 11(1):21–27.

Suzuki, David, and Peter Knudson. 1989. *Genethics: The Clash Between the New Genetics and Human Values.* Cambridge, MA: Harvard University Press.

Traweek, Sharon. 1991. Border Crossings: Narrative Strategies in Science Studies and Among Physicists in Tsukuba Science City, Japan. Pp. 429–66 in Andrew Pickering (ed.), *Science as Practice and Culture.* Chicago: University of Chicago Press.

Trouillot, Michel-Rolph. 1991. Anthropology and the Savage Slot: The Poetics and Politics of Otherness. Pp. 17–44 in Richard G. Fox (ed.), *Recapturing Anthropology: Working in the Present.* Santa Fe, NM: School of American Research Press.

Visweswaran, Kamela. 1994. *Fictions of Feminist Ethnography.* Minneapolis: University of Minnesota Press.

Wajcman, Judith. 1995. Feminist Theories of Technology. Pp. 189–204 in Sheila Jasanoff, Gerald Markle, James Petersen, and Trevor Pinch (eds.), *Handbook of Science and Technology Studies.* Thousand Oaks, CA: Sage.

Wolf, Marjorie. 1992. *A Thrice-Told Tale.* Stanford, CA: Stanford University Press.

Naked Methodology

Researching the Lives of Women with HIV/AIDS

PATTI LATHER

—◯—

In January of 1992 I was invited to serve as a "chronicler" for women living with HIV/AIDS. My coresearcher, Chris Smithies, and I have since interviewed twenty-five women, largely in meetings with Women and AIDS support groups in four major cities in Ohio, but also, as is not atypical of even quasi-ethnographic work, at holiday and birthday parties, on camping trips and retreats, in hospital rooms, and at funerals, baby showers, and picnics.

We desktop-published the results in late 1995 and mailed copies to the participants, with whom we met in their support groups in early 1996 in order to revise toward what the women called "a Kmart book." By this, they meant a book widely accessible to themselves, those they care about, including other HIV-positive women, and the wider community. The revision was published in trade book format in 1997, entitled *Troubling the Angels: Women Living With HIV/AIDS* (Lather and Smities 1997).

This paper is about methodological learnings from the instructive complications of this project. After short overviews of what opens up when inquiry is situated as a ruin/rune and a brief survey of Levinas, Irigaray, and Nietzsche on nakedness as a methodological practice, I focus on three areas of methodological learning: getting lost in textwork, textuality as praxis, and the role of "response data" (St. Pierre 1997) in not getting paralyzed in a project that gestures toward a less comfortable social science.

Methodology as a Ruin/Rune

As a point of departure, I situate this project as a ruin/rune, permeated by limit and spoils, where much is refused, including abandoning the project to such a moment (Haver 1996). Against the grain of research traditions that fabricate inquiry as a triumphal continuity, I look for breaks and jagged edges as a place from which to read the practices that my coresearcher and I have devised. Here inquiry is a rune from which we might draw useful knowledge for the shaping of present practices of feminist inquiry.

What opens up when inquiry is situated as a ruin? In a 1992 address to the American Historical Association, Judith Butler drew on Walter Benjamin's (1968) "Theses on the Philosophy of History" in order to gesture toward the value of taking the failure of teleological history, whether Marxist, messianic, or, in its most contemporary formulation, the triumph of Western democracy (e.g., Fukuyama) as the very ground for a different set of social relations. It is the ruins of progressivist history, naive realism, and transparent language that allow us to see what beliefs have sustained these concepts; only now, at their end, Butler argued, does their unsustainability become clear. Hiroshima, Auschwitz, My Lai, and AIDS, for example, make belief in history's linear unfolding unsustainable. None of the usual recourses can save us now: God, the dialectic, reason (Haver 1996).

In such a time and place, terms understood as no longer fulfilling their promise do not become useless. On the contrary, their very failure becomes provisional grounds, and new uses are derived. The claim of universality, for example, "will no longer be separable from the antagonism by which it is continually contested" in moving toward a configuration of ethics and sociality that is other to the Hegelian dream of a reconciliation that absorbs difference into the same (Butler 1993:6). Butler terms this "the ethical vitalization" (1993:7) of the failure of certain kinds of ideals, a Nietzschean transvaluation of working the pathos of the ruins of such ideals as the very ground of what playwright Tony Kushner has termed "non-stupid optimism" in struggles for social justice (de Vries 1992).

Moving across levels of the particular and the abstract, trying to avoid a transcendent purchase on the object of study, we set ourselves up for necessary failure in order to learn how to find our way into postfoundational possibilities. The task becomes to throw ourselves against the stubborn materiality of others, willing to risk loss, relishing the power of others to constrain our interpretive "will to power," saving us from narcissism and its melancholy through the very positivities that cannot be exhausted by us, by the otherness that always exceeds us. To situate inquiry as a ruin/rune is to foreground the limits and necessary misfirings of a project, problematizing the researcher as "the one who knows." Placed outside of mastery and victory narratives, inquiry is a kind of self-wounding laboratory for discovering the rules by which truth is produced as we attempt to be accountable to complexity. Here, thinking the limit becomes our task and much opens up in terms of ways to proceed for those who know both too much and too little.

Let's Be Nude: Levinas, Irigaray, Nietzsche

> We no longer believe that truth remains truth when the veils are withdrawn; we have lived too much to believe this. Today we consider it a matter of decency not to wish to see everything naked, or be present at everything and "know" everything. (Nietzsche, quoted in Kofman 1988:194)

To situate an inquiry as a kind of self-wounding laboratory for discovering the rules by which truth is produced is to risk reinscribing the potentially fully conscious, individualized, humanist subject. Attempting to move such reinscription more toward disloyal repetition than its mindless variant, I briefly survey the possibilities of nakedness as a methodological posture via the theories of Levinas, Irigaray, and Nietzsche.

My particular interest in nakedness comes from the very material practice of spending time in hot tubs, which has characterized my methodological wrestling in this project.[1] Grounded in the hours spent in my coresearcher's hot tub, where we discussed the project, my interest in nakedness also comes out of a small research retreat in Wisconsin when this project was at its beginning. There, structured around the concept of each of seven women having two hours of "exquisite attention" for her work in any way she wanted, I stripped and sat in a Jacuzzi, surrounded by six dressed women who fired questions at me about the ethics and politics of what I was undertaking in my research on women living with HIV/AIDS.

As was evident at that session, this work pushes a lot of buttons for those invested in the politics of knowing and being known. This is as it should be, and I will present some of these concerns in the section on methodological learnings about using response data. Before turning to those learnings, I want to delineate a theory of nakedness by juxtaposing Levinas, Irigaray, and Nietzsche as a way to sketch the theory of representation that structures my methodological imperatives.

Levinas argues that a direct encounter with another is by way of "a being becoming naked" (Robbins 1995:280). "Naked—that is, without clothing, covering, or mask—it signifies without attributes, outside any categories, not across its generality, but by itself" (p. 282). Levinas sees this as a kind of destitution, "absolute poverty," "wretchedness," absence and exile from the world, some relation of absolute frankness (p. 283). For Levinas, to speak at the level of nudity is to expose oneself to vulnerability, but it is the very nakedness of the face that stymies violence. Questions about the registers of impossibility of Levinas's relation of absolute frankness become more focused when juxtaposed with Irigaray and Nietzsche.

Against Levinas's grounding in a metaphysics of prerhetorical presence (Robbins 1995:284), Irigaray counsels the "risky method" of affecting hysteria as a way for a woman to break free of "*'the fabric [of discourse], reveal her nakedness, her destitution in language, explode in the face of them all, words too'*" (Chisholm

1994:275, emphasis in original). As a means to explode out of indifference, objectivity, or critical or theoretical distance, hysterical defiance is constructed out of an excess, out of an overcompliance that works as a parody of the representability of female sexual difference. Seeking not healing but dis-ease, Irigaray stages her text in order to provoke resistance in her readers to male inscription of women's sexuality.

Using Nietzsche against Freud, Irigaray interrupts Levinas's ideas about the possibilities of nakedness. Nietzsche believed that the way to whatever "truth" was possible was via the unconscious and forgetting. "Every opinion is also a hiding-place," he wrote, "every word also a mask" (quoted in Kofman 1993:91). For Nietzsche, "unmasking is not about removing from the text a cloak that veils the truth, but rather showing the clothing which an apparent 'nakedness' conceals" (p. 92). Here the text functions as a perspectival reinscription of the will to power, enacting Nietzsche's critical project: to make the perspective appear, denaturalize it, see it as the expression of a hierarchical relationship between forces.

Nietzsche invites us to a difficult task: to learn to read well, to decipher the text in order to discover the drives toward mastery. He counseled self-estranging breaks where one could hardly recognize oneself in past productions, a strategic, deconstructive indulgence in the surface, not because there are no depths but because under each layer is another layer where we revaluate and subvert "the naked truth." There is a vertigo produced by such a practice. After the death of God, all concepts change their meaning, lose their meaning, become dislocated, are fragments of wreckage, cease to be a foundation. How does one manage to live in such a place, fuller of future by risking not being understood as one writes outside traditional norms, fearing being understood by those without ears to hear?

Nietzsche's big question is, what does the will that wants the truth want (Kofman 1993:24)? His best answer was an affirmation of the will that wills itself to illusion, knowing it will not perish without absolute knowledge. The necessary multiplication of perspectives can work toward the solution of the problem of value, "a pragmatism directed toward a use which is yet to come" (p. 127). Hence, the discipline of science becomes the rigor of staging and watching oneself, turning life into a means to knowledge without being able to overcome it. In Bruno Latour's words, "There are no more naked truths, but there are no more naked citizens, either"; it is time to begin again "when new words are needed" (Latour 1993:144–45).

Troubling the Angels: Women Living With HIV/AIDS

Finally moving to the heart of this paper, I delineate methodological practices that work at the edges of what is currently available in moving toward a social science with more to answer to in terms of the complexities of language and the world. My particular interest is in the possibilities and limits of a recharged methodology that forces one to reach, to stretch, and to push the limits of reflexivity in the examination of one's research practices.

Fleshing out the web of contradictions within which feminist researchers work, given the indignity of being studied, the violence of objectification (Karamcheti 1992), what are the ethics of such pursuits? What work do we want inquiry to do? To what extent does method privilege findings? What is the place of procedures in the claim to validity? What does it mean to recognize the limits of exactitude and certainty, but still to have respect for the empirical world and its relation to how we formulate knowledge? What is left for science in an era of blurred genres? Such questions are about the politics and ethics of feminist research with/in the postmodern, research that probes questions of narrative authority and the possibilities of generative research methodologies. To address such questions, I turn to the research practices of our study of women living with HIV/AIDS.

Textwork: Getting Lost

In her 1992 book *The End(s) of Ethnography*, Patricia Clough recommends that we give up on data collection and "the defenses and compulsions of method-ology" and turn, instead, to decoding representations (Clough 1992:137). On the contrary, like Nietzsche, my turn is not away from but into the grounds of science, respecting the limits of language and interpretation in what I presently term feminist efforts toward a double science, both science and not-science, a version of what Nietzsche has called the "unnatural sciences" (Nietzsche 1974:301).

Having wanted to never be an armchair methodologist, I am much about the seductions of fieldwork. My interest is precisely in the grounds of science and the attachment to its procedures that rub us up against the sort of stubborn materiality that Benjamin (1968) was so interested in rescuing from abstraction. While there is a myriad of topics to be addressed—such as the particulars of emergent design, group interviews, the dynamics of coresearching, the issue of subjectivities that refuse to stand still, and researcher theorizing of other people's lives—it is only the last that will be dealt with here.

Theoretically situated in poststructural theories of meaning-making and subject formation, this project focuses on how the participants construct them-selves in relation to the categories laid on them—indeed, demanded of them—as women with HIV/AIDS. Methodologically grounded in qualitative/ethnographic research approaches, the study enacts an interest in what it means to tell the lives of others, an interest much pursued across poststructural anthropology, feminist methodology, and critical ethnography. Both within and against conventional notions of social science research, the goal is not so much to better represent the researched as to explore how researchers can "be accountable to people's strug-gles for self-representation and self-determination" (Visweswaran 1988:39). What follows are a few pages from *Troubling the Angels* that gesture toward such a practice in data reporting.

Story Series 3: Making Meaning

"I'd Probably Be Dead if It Wasn't for HIV"

CHRIS: How has being HIV+ changed your life?

RITA: Well, I liked something that Lori said. This is a gift for me to take a second look at life, at what the value of life really is. I'd probably be dead now if I didn't have HIV. At first, I used it as an excuse; I'm dying anyway. Then my family invited me back home; it was a shock and a relief. I got on methadone and off of the heavy coke and heroin I was on. I sold drugs to support it and the other things you have to do to support your habit. Here was a chance to wipe the slate clean and start over. I just went for it completely. It was just such a relief to go back to being the person I was 15–20 years ago. It was a slice out of my life and then I got to come back and be the person I was when I left here. So, I'd probably be dead if it wasn't for HIV, as crazy as that sounds.

CHRIS: What would your life be like if you didn't have the virus?

CR: When I think of the rocky marriage, the rocky childhood, and then going into adult life, I've always given. I became a mother at 12 and I never had time to be young. If I hadn't contracted the virus, I'd still probably be in some shit relationship and taking care of kids. Now I have time for myself. About three months ago these religious women that live next door to me asked me if I'd like to come live with them, because people aren't coming to live in the convent anymore. And I said no, this is the first year of my independence and I ain't sharing a toilet with nobody. *[much giggling]* And when I don't want to make up the bed, I don't make up the bed, if I don't want to sleep in the bed, I sleep on the floor, I sleep on the couch, I mean, it's fun. If I hadn't had the virus, I

PATTI: Early in our reading of the literature about living with HIV/AIDS, we were at first disappointed when we saw that our findings from this research study were "nothing new". For example, in a movie called *Living Proof: HIV and the Pursuit of Happiness,* a woman who had been a drug addict says, "If I hadn't found out I was HIV-positive I'd probably be dead." This repeats a quote that is used for the title of one of the story chapters in this book, a repetition that initially dismayed us. Then we decided that this repetition of themes is a kind of validity—if our findings were being repeated across various sources on dealing with AIDS as well as other terminal illnesses, then we must be on the right track. Another example of this is John Clum's essay on how HIV+ people tell their stories, "'And Once I had It All': AIDS Narratives and Memories of an American Dream." In *Writing AIDS: Gay Literature, Language, and Analysis,* edited by Timothy Murphy and Suzanne Poirier (Columbia University Press, 1993), 220–24. This is similar to Louisa's story at the end of Story Series 4, "We Had a Real Nice Life."

mean, I'm two steps from eating pork and beans out of the can just to say I can do it. I'd have been worried about whether some man is gonna call, did I say something to make him mad, I mean all that shit. Before the virus I didn't think I could live without a man.

CHRIS: I have heard some people who have the AIDS virus say that it has been a gift, an opportunity to change and grow. What do you think about this?

MELODY: You have to believe in yourself. You have to get to know yourself through this disease. I've had to look at me and where I'm at and get a perspective on where I want to be and yet actually be where I am at. It's hard to explain, but this disease makes me look consciously and subconsciously every moment because I don't take the moments for granted. I don't procrastinate and just let them slip away. I just want to seize everything. It's brought back the child in me and the wonderment when everything is like doing it for the first time, because it's a different moment. It might be the same people and the same type of situation, but yet it's a different moment. And that's what makes me grateful for being diagnosed with AIDS. Because I wouldn't have done that; I would have procrastinated until the day I died.

LORI: I think it would be surprising to people to hear that infected women's self esteem has risen.

PATTI: That is a surprising statement; how do you explain that?

LORI: Well, look at Rita and how she abused her body and womanhood for so many years and this one little sentence changes her life and now she's on a campaign to make herself wonderful. My life hasn't really significantly changed and I don't think my self-esteem has changed but I think we all now, we are very self absorbed. I think, looking in the mirror, you wouldn't look at stuff like we do

Another example of how our research findings cut across other contexts is the work of Bill T. Jones who conducted survival workshops for those, including children, with life-threatening illnesses in the construction of his dance performance *Still/Here*. Jones, an African-American, HIV+, gay choreographer, emphasizes that this work is "not about AIDS" as he focuses on the issues involved in living with deadly diseases: the loss of easy belief, the fear of loosing one's ability to care for oneself, the facing of death. "Through these workshops, I'm learning to talk about hope in a hopeless world," Jones says (*Columbus Alive*, Dec. 5, 1993). The nationwide workshops allowed participants to create theatrical and movement vocabularies about hope, will and survival in the face of mortality. The video-documentary of these sessions were combined with newsreels, talk show tapes, and still photographs into a full-length work which is followed by a post-performance symposium entitled *Managing*

and you have to take people and things that are said in two ways. How do I respond to that, do I process that as a positive woman or just as a woman? Just like women in general, do I respond as a woman or as an American. There's a lot of different ways that you have to process information but this adds one more that makes you very protective of yourself, not getting hurt, not getting physically ill. Like Robyn talked about this woman at work coughing, well I have never noticed people coughing like I do now. You're just more aware of this kinda of stuff.

LINDA B: Right! You want to get your Lysol out!

CHRIS: Rita, Lori used you as a reference for self-esteem.

RITA: I probably would have kept going and going until I overdosed and then this. When I found this out, I don't know why that was the point that made me stay with treatment. At first I thought why should I quit now, I'm dying anyway. I had a friend who has it that decided that, but I kind of think like maybe God gave this to me to help someone, maybe myself. I sure wasn't worth a damn. I didn't even know what the word self-esteem was. The methadone lady started a group for women and she asked me if I wanted to join that group down there and I said no, I got this other group I go to. No offense, but I don't want to get to know any of your people. And she said well there are people here who don't do drugs, but I have no interest in cultivating any relationships with those people.

CHRIS: You made some real strong decisions.

RITA: Yeah, finally, finally, I've started making those kind of decisions. I have no desire whatsoever to even look where the drugs are in this city.

CHRIS: You're doing well and you mentioned earlier that you don't care to have romantic relationships.

Mortality. "A victim is someone who has been diminished," said Jones after the OSU Wexner Center performance. "My experience in the survival workshops is that the circumstance of the participants has given them an opportunity to become more whole" (*Ohio State Quest,* Spring, 1995:11).

What does this mean in terms of understanding how the women in our study make sense of their HIV experiences? The most important thing I've learned is the doubled need for hope when the languages of hope that we have are no longer broadly persuasive. Especially for those outside of traditional religious thinking about death, the lack of philosophical options, of secular resources to think about death is a situation of at once too little and too much knowledge.

Largely struck dumb by the data, in spite of the preceding efforts to make some interpretive sense of it, largely unable to even be descriptive let alone

RITA: That's the biggest thing, not looking for dates. I had no friendships with women, because it was a competition. I didn't look at women as friends. Now, with guys, I feel I would have to tell him about HIV. Some of the people I told, I found out afterwards, would say things like, she came in my bathroom, she gave me a hug, she talked to my kids. It's like people were so ignorant about it. And then I thought that's too much to even invest. I'm not interested in investing that much emotional energy. I like being by myself. I'm very selective. I've got a lot of acquaintances, but only a couple of friends. People in this group, I've learned more about them than I've known people in my life.

CHRIS: So what's it like having this group?

RITA: Learning how to be a friend to a woman. I like it; it's something I've never done before. And it's not for anything other than wanting to.

CHRIS: Is that related to self esteem?

RITA: Yeah, 100%. Now I'm finding out that I've got something to say that's worth listening to.

analytical, I am left feeling that no one has the right to take away hope, whether it be through participation in experimental drug trials or the succor of traditional religion or investments like my own in social justice struggles. The task is to proceed in a way that works against what *Angels in America* playwright Tony Kushner has termed "the stupidly optimistic" (de Vries 1992) by focusing on the ruins of history and the fragmentation of agreed upon meaning toward, not some victory narrative couched in the very conquering optimism that has lost its credibility, but some sense of what it means to use the now-time of a crisis of otherness to struggle toward a more just social order.

In a May 1993 reaction to an early talk I gave about this research, Herb Simons wrote the following:

> There's something troubling to me about that paper, a refusal to deconstruct the remarks of the HIV/AIDS [women], in the same way, for example, that you deconstructed the classroom essay by the student who wrote on [the film] *Killing Us Softly*. No problems of "persuasion to consensus" in your writings on this; you were "blown away" and so should the reader. All talk of pomo notwithstanding, isn't that the message of the paper? Allow yourself to be "totally engulfed and cognitively overwhelmed." Accept the "gift of witness." No commentary after [the] informant[s] on "all representations as misrepresenta- tions," on the dangers of "praxis putting itself in place of theory," on invidious hierarchies and suspect binaries. No, this, after all, is research "for social jus- tice," a concept that remains essentialized and unproblematized. No Fou- caultian reading of the discourse "writing" [the informants'] remarks. No Freudian reading of [their] palpable rationalizations. Instead, seduction. First, of Patti, then by Patti of the reader—both now visited by Angels. Yes: a rhetoric of excess. Romanticized. A wallowing in sisterhood, multiversity, and possibili- ties for logological, angelic transcendence. A tale, finally, of family: of Benjamin the grandfather, Felman and Eagleton the passers of Benjamin's seed, and of Lather the appreciative child. How precious!
>
> But I don't blame you for your gaps, your silences, your caring. After all, I too was moved by [the] narrative. What your paper tells me most of all is that there's only so much pomo a truly caring person can take before it begins to taste like sandpaper on the tongue. In proportion to our immersion in pomo skepticism and languacentricity, to that extent do we need an emotional cathexis. You got one.[2]

My interest here is not so much in Simons's understanding of "pomo," nor even, at this point, in the uses of emotionality and pathos in writing up qualita- tive data. Wanting to take the crisis of representation into account in practices of data analysis, my interest here is in what poststructural anthropologist George Marcus, has referred to as a move toward evocative portraits, a type of data reporting that "emphasizes a direct exposure to other 'voices' . . . unassimilated to given concepts, theories, and analytic frames" (Marcus 1993:13). "We are," he says, in a moment "when the need to chronicle the world seem[s] to outstrip the capacity to theorize it. . . . What we're saying . . . is kind of old-fashioned: that it is possible to present the voices of others in a more or less unmediated way" (pp. 14–15).

The preceding excerpts from *Troubling the Angels* mark my getting lost in the relations of text work, turning both into and away from the conventional move of researchers positioned "behind [the] backs [of informants] to point out what they could not see, would not do, and could not have said" (Britzman 1995:237). To struggle against omnipotence in making sense of participant efforts to make sense of their experiences of HIV/AIDS, I trouble the ethics of reducing the fear, pain, joy, and urgency of people's lives to analytic categories. Exploring the textual possibilities for telling stories that situate researchers not so much as experts "saying what things mean" in terms of "data," the researcher is situated as witness giving testimony to the lives of others.

Britzman (1995) raises the dangers of such a posture: the reification of experience and identity, agency and voice, and unmediated access to something "real." Simons's words, in reading my practices as reverting back to humanist pathos, empathic caring, and a longing for transcendence, some way out, in the face of human struggle, give me a way out that I don't want to accept. There is no exit from the lack of innocence in discursive stagings of knowledge. With a deconstructive goal of keeping things in process, keeping the system in play, fighting the tendency for our categories to congeal, my textual practices move toward some place of both/and and neither/nor, where I trouble the very categories I can't think without.

Textuality as Praxis

This work is beyond me. (Blanchot 1982:126)

In *Troubling the Angels*, Chris and I attempt practices that move across different registers into a sort of hypertext that invites multiple ways of reading. Given that our task, to produce a Kmart book, is in tension with my gnomic and abstruse ways of knowing, what practices have I developed in my task of being of use to these women who brought me into this project?

Quoting from the advance flier for the book:

> Based on an interview study of twenty-five Ohio women in HIV/AIDS support groups, *Troubling the Angels* traces the patterns and changes of how the women make sense of HIV/AIDS in their lives. Attempting to map the complications of living with the disease, the book is organized as a hypertextual, multilayered weaving of data, method, analysis, and the politics of interpretation.
>
> Because of the book's unconventional narration, it invites multiple entries and ways of reading. Interspersed among the interviews, there are inter-texts, which serve as "breathers" between the themes and emotions of the women's stories; a running subtext where the authors spin out their tales of doing the research; factoid boxes on various aspects of the disease; and a scattering of the women's writing in the form of poems, letters, speeches, and e-mails.
>
> Enacting a feminist ethnography at the limits of representation, *Troubling the Angels* mixes sociological, political, historical, therapeutic, and policy analysis along with the privileging of ethnographic voice.

Decisions about textual format grew out of many factors: my interest in nonlinear, many-layered textuality, the practical need for a format that would allow Chris and myself to write separately and then combine parts, our desire to include whatever the women themselves wanted to contribute in the way of writing, and, finally, my interest in the angel as a means of addressing what Rilke terms the "Too Big" or "too great, too vast" (1989:317) in an accessible way to a broad-based audience.

What is effected by such a complicated and complicating text? My goal is to capture what is already at work in the future, to work the interstices of reason and feeling, to displace the concept and hostile interrogation as ways of knowing. This is a hyptertextual pastiche that is a "warping of comfort texts" (Meiners 1994), aimed at opening up possibilities for displaying complexities. Like Rilke's *Duino Elegies*, in a text that accumulates meaning as it progresses, a reader must move across the different registers of a text which has become a series of reflections and retractions, propositions and rejections, models and deflation of models, back-tracking to issues that can't be settled for long, ruminations that dramatize the construction of a poetics as well as an ontology, canceling the distance between subject and object, reader and writer and written about (Komar 1987). Here, the text turns back on itself, putting the authority of its own affirmations in doubt, an undercutting that causes a doubling of meanings that adds to a sense of multivalence and fluidities in constructing an audience with ears to hear.

Given the critical practices at work in this text that require more of readers, why couldn't this have been a "simple" text, a "realist tale" (Van Maanen 1988)? Such a tale would tell the stories that the women want to tell, and not risk displacing their bodies and their stories with High Theory, committing the "academic krime" of eliding material contexts, vanity research that loses the women's stories.[3] Why did I feel I had to read Nietzsche in order to proceed? How do I reconcile myself to palpable costs in terms of time and the ethics involved in using the site of this inquiry to wrestle with what it means to move toward a less comfortable social science? As one of the women involved in the study wrote, "Will you guys get this done soon? I can't wait to see this! Some of us are on a time line, you know!" And as Simon Watney notes, much writing on AIDS in the social sciences is "taking the scenic route through an emergency" (Watney 1994:221).

In order to both locate myself in the problematic of this text and push my own motives in this project, in which I wish to be "of use" (Piercy 1973), what helps me to navigate the (necessarily) troubled waters of this inquiry? Of primary use has been the writing and reactions of those who have read parts of the manuscript or heard me talk to it. Hence I offer a montage of their reactions.

Role of Response Data: "With Ears to Hear"

What follows are reactions from various readers of parts of the book, including some of the women in the study, couched within an argument that an ending commensurate with the complications of such a study is enriched by the "fold" (Deleuze 1993) of this sort of "response data" where "the audience teaches you something," perhaps particularly that "we need other people to help us think."[4]

I call on my friend, Marilyn, the first person to read an early version of the manuscript. She noted how the "spectator" voice of Chris and myself in the subtext let her identify with another outsider. This took the edge off the voyeurism, she said, and forced her as reader to deal with her "denial, horror, and respect" as she is plunged into the difficulties of the women's lives, feeling "almost jealous of their hold on what matters" by the end. And I think of my HIV-positive friend, Rex, the next person to read an early version, having to take to his bed for the rest of the day, writing me later: "I long for angels. I need their comfort, their doubt. I feel part of 'big concepts,' human struggles repeated throughout history, touched and comforted. Facing death is a very personal experience. Here everything that can be said has been said, but I feel joined to these women as I explore its aspects and feel ennobled in being simply human in an experience that is alone but doesn't have to be lonely." And finally I think of a student I had in a recent course who was moved by reading parts of the manuscript to get tested for HIV: "After I found out that I was negative, I didn't feel so connected to those women. I didn't feel that I would use their words to help me live my life. And I'm embarrassed to say it, but I feel privileged over them. At one point I could have been them. I hoped I could be so strong. Now I feel separated from them and I feel sorry for them."[5]

From my research journal, November 4, 1994:

I handed out the table of contents page plus sections from the story series to which this group of women had made particularly visible contributions. It took almost an hour to get through the overview, with many questions and many stories bubbling out, especially from the new women who seem sad to miss the opportunity to get their stories in the book. Those who had participated seemed thrilled to see their own and one another's words, corrected some of the attributions, wanted to know where some of their own words had gone, commented on what a long way I had come, how I was so much smarter now then when they had first met me at the retreat, over and over "confirmed" the pertinence of the major themes we had featured, and were much more interested in the sexuality section than the death and dying one.[6] I asked what they thought of the angels, and one woman answered, "It's what holds us. I think it's beautiful." Another said that spirituality is such a part of this, that it makes sense. The facilitator showed her guardian angel pin that was on the inside of her collar and talked of how she was formerly pretty uninterested in spiritual matters, but that this work had led her to great interest in—angels! One woman wanted to know, "But why 'troubling'?" I said: because these are not the romantic ladies tripping around in nighties that are so popular right now. These are angels who trouble our sense that all is right with the world, that AIDS is something "out there," unrelated to each one of us, that we can afford to distance from. The biggest learning of this trip for me was that they want to read the whole thing and how much they trust that we will do the "right thing" by them. This underscored our earlier decision to do the desktop publishing in order to get a "real book" into their hands in a timely fashion.

From my research journal, February 7, 1995:

I joined the group the last half hour, overviewed the table of contents, walked them through handouts from selected story series to which their group had made a large contribution, and passed around the angel images, which drew some interest, but not much. One woman couldn't stop reading; she gulped it down, talking about how much she liked the format. She said the angel images were good, "not fat little white babies," but images that "fit the topic." She said the format catered to a general reader, but also breaks the conventional style, a different style that will get attention. A doctoral student, she noted that the split text was "postmodern" with its multiple voices, dialogue within dialogue, its "not presenting a master narrative." "It's not just one woman's story, but a playing back and forth across the stories, stories that break into each other, providing relief. I think it's great. I'm proud of you. Who would have thought when we did the taping [for the interviews] that it was really going to be a book." I talked to this woman about writing a few pages of her reaction to the text; she responded with how busy she was. The facilitator noted that the format, in not being just one person speaking at a time, captured the support group motif and was "feminist" in the way we took a "backseat" with our researcher narratives and worked collaboratively with one another and the research participants. Again, I was struck with all the stories we're not telling, both the shifts in the lives of the women we have interviewed and the stories of women who have newly joined the group.

Not nearly as copacetic as the member checks have been some of the reactions of academic audiences to which I have presented various parts of the manuscript. For example, a January 1995 presentation at the Ontario Institute for Studies in Education evoked the following comments: I did not give a real sense of the women's lives and what it was like to be a woman living with HIV/AIDS, particularly as I, in my talk, displaced these "real" stories with the work of the angels in the text. There was "too much style" and not enough substance, too much "ease" or lightness with a topic that called for the greatest seriousness. There was too little control on the part of the women and a too easy calling on their resistance to greater involvement, practices of mine that amplified the mysteries of research and the effects of a research elite versus "real egalitarianism in research." The writer of the E-mail message that summarized this reaction went on to note that "the people who loved" my presentation said that the title clearly indicated it was about "the validity of angels" in the study rather than a summary of the data. He wrote, "I agree with this and I wonder about a kind of voyeurism in that kind of expectation anyway. With the issue of seriousness (which can be tied to the 'tell the women's story' trope) I think it was appropriate that you dealt with the issues in such a way that they remained open to interrogation." He went on to comment on the importance of presenting such material in a way that doesn't become silencing.[7]

The following excerpts from student writing elaborate on such contradictory reactions. From a 1994 summer course I taught at University of British Columbia, they are written in reaction to my paper, "Troubling Angels" (Lather 1995). On the one hand, there was resistance to the seduction into angelizing and concerns about latent New Age triggers, the dangers of seeming to point to a way out, the deflection of the "main" task, and the reinforcing of binaries and romanticizing in a way that elides material contexts.

> The discussion of how to "do" science differently raises important questions, but not with women who are dying.... The philosophy of the research has overtaken the bodies of the women with HIV/AIDS.... I have seen so much of this in Educational Psychology: the loss of children for the sake of the design, the hypothesis, the ethnographer in the classroom, video-taping, technologizing the scene beyond the players.... I have seen the children disappear in educational research and perhaps I am resisting seeing the women disappear in feminist research.... I am so overwhelmed with questions about ethnography and the contradiction of Social Science.... I am excited about the philosophy and am seduced by its radical freedoms; I am skeptical of its abrogations and its recklessness at the same time. More than before I am thinking about responsibility—as a writer, a researcher, and as a woman in the institution. (Diane Hodges)

On the other hand, my insisting (on) angels in this study was read as a dedemonizing discourse that worked to decenter the "main" topic in a way that parallels the lack of an epicenter of the pandemic itself. "Here, conventional stories of science and praxis won't do" (Cliff Falk). Working toward some different concept of (dis)ease, the economy of troubling angels posits "in-your-face" angels who are about the lack of social resources and workable spirituality and the lack of control over death that so troubles a society used to controlling through science.

> As a First-Nations person ... I am familiar with the notion of the unknowable or uncontrollable.... I like the terms you use because they trouble the notion of the human ability to contain and control the uncontrollable.... What this means is that I like your use of troubling angels because it troubles the space between life and death, the material and the un-material. (Elaine Herbert)

Another student wrote:

> The angel [works] as a means of writing the unwritable. I do like the idea of not creating a "simple" story, whatever that may be. These women are not living a single story although we have, as a society, constantly attempted to write one for them and for us around the issue of AIDS. And the angel, as you have presented, holds the possibility of the telling in excess of our frames of reference, as Felman puts it. Be that as it may, the angel is still a troubling choice, I guess because of the enormous cultural baggage with which it/he/she/they have been saddled.... The redemption angel is so present in our culture, especially right now. Are these stories which to attempt to redeem the angel or trouble the angel? Will that obscure the stories and perhaps create a "cooling comfort" from the troubling we may experience in sharing their stories? ... The kind of angel you are attempting to evoke seems a metaphor for AIDS and how it brings us up against so much of what we attempt to avoid in this society: death,

our lack of control over death and our struggle to make sense of that which does not make sense. The angel as a critical gesture is very powerful if somehow you, and the reader, can generate an angel such as Benjamin's in the context of these women's stories. (Robin Cox)

Finally, another student, Millicent Delphine Brake, wrote a poem based on her reading of a transcript from the aforementioned jacuzzi scene where I was grilled by other feminist researchers as this project was beginning. All words in the poem are from that transcript.

FACE TO FACE
Face to face with the limits of my work,
 I wrestle in a feminist movement,
 To draw from HIV+/AIDS Women
 The stories they want to tell.

Face to face with the limits of my work,
 I wrestle in a feminist movement,
To save myself from emancipatory intentions
Of what it means to use other people's lives as DATA.
. . .
To not kill them with my high theory but to create a space
Where their stories are about us and women surviving with
 AIDS.
. . .
To think about what it means to be an ACADEMIC
 Poking around in other people's lives.
. . .
Poking around myself as DATA and what it means
 IN RELATION TO OTHERS
. . .
As I draw from myself the stories I would tell,
 If I were not just one blood cell away,
Being faced with the knowledge of being HIV+,
 At this moment, in this place.

How then, would my politics of knowing and being known
 Be understood in a crisis of representation,
Forcing us to take stock of our ways of doing difference,
 Without SILENCING the stories of OTHERS?

How am I to hear such commentary? Refusing textual innocence and an untroubled realism, I have moved to what Deborah Britzman terms ethnography as "a site of doubt" where the focus is on how poststructuralism fashions interpretive efforts, "the disagreements, the embarrassments, the unsaid, and the odd moments of uncertainty in contexts overburdened with certain imperatives"

(Britzman 1995:236). Here representation is practiced as a way to intervene, even while one's confidence is troubled, by calling upon multiple voices who keep refashioning themselves in language across existential time. Here the task becomes to operate from a textual rather than a referential notion of representation, from persuading to producing the unconscious as the work of the text (Lather 1996).

Such a move troubles the sort of reflexive confession that becomes a narcissistic wound that will not heal and eats up the world by monumentalizing loss. My interest is, rather, in Derrida's ethos of lack when lack becomes an enabling condition, a limit used (Butler 1993). Surely Daphne Patai's "solution" to the problem of vanity ethnography, what she calls "nouveau solipsism," is not best addressed by reversion to a pragmatic realism (Patai 1994). Instead, my efforts are to work the ruins of a confident social science as the very ground from which new practices of research might take shape.

Conclusion

The effects of *Troubling the Angels* as a book and the process of its making are and will continue to be knowings based in an uncompromising insistence that the truth cannot be spoken directly. Moving well outside of formerly comfortable holds on sense making and toward some other sense that what sets us on a straight path leads us astray, Chris and I have constructed a text whose significance will not be exhausted by the meaning attributed to it by any one person, ourselves included. This leaves us in need of an audience we cannot create and cannot do without, an audience only history can make possible, as we move toward a solution that deconstructs itself in the face of history's sedimentations and our urge to some beyond. Going down and inside our "'heart's double will'" (Nietzsche, quoted in Pippin 1988:56), we continue to use the laboratory of this project to address what it is that we have come to this project to understand and what it means to know more than we are able to know and to write toward what we don't understand.

Notes

1. A precedent for such practice is Judith Butler's thanking Donna Haraway for response to an earlier draft of Butler's paper "in a hot tub in Santa Cruz" (Butler 1994:173).
2. Keynote address, the Ethnography and Education Research Forum, February, 1993, sponsored by the University of Pennsylvania. For my research into student reaction to liberatory curricula, to which Simons refers, see Lather 1994.
3. Diane Hodges, from summer 1994 course I taught at the University of British Columbia, "Analyzing Data in the Crisis of Representation."
4. Bettie St. Pierre, E-mail correspondence, July 5, 1995, in response to a presentation of her dissertation research (St. Pierre 1994).
5. This and other student writing is used with permission.

6. The one exception to this was my statement that most of the women did not want to spend their energy being angry at their infectors. Both of the women new to the group took issue with this. A 40-something African-American woman who was both recently infected and recovering from a death's-door hospitalization said, "I would have killed him if he weren't already dead." The other, a sixty-seven-year-old African-American woman, diagnosed in 1984 but still quite healthy, talked of her great struggles to not be consumed with anger at her long-dead husband for infecting her.

7. Handel Wright, E-mail message, March 7, 1995. Used with permission. This maps on in interesting ways to the debate around reviewing Bill T. Jones's dance *Still/Here*, about living with death-threatening illness. In the December 1994–January 1995 issue of the *New Yorker*, Arlene Croce ignited a firestorm by refusing to review what she called "victim art," claiming that it left no viable position for the reviewer. Unfortunately, what could have opened up interesting issues of how to position oneself in response to bone-shattering testimony has been deflected by her unfortunate decision to take her stand without seeing the production.

References

Benjamin, Walter. 1968. *Illuminations: Essays and Reflections*. Edited by Hannah Arendt. New York: Schocken Books.

Blanchot, Maurice. 1982. *The Space of Literature*. Translated by Ann Smock. Lincoln: University of Nebraska Press.

Britzman, Deborah. 1995. The Question of Belief: Writing Poststructural Ethnography. *Qualitative Studies in Education* 8(3):233–42.

Butler, Judith. 1993. Poststructuralism and Postmarxism. *Diacritics* 23(4):3–11.

Butler, Judith. 1994. Bodies That Matter. Pp. 141–74 in C. Burke, N. Schor, and M. Whitford (eds.), *Engaging With Irigaray: Feminist Philosophy and Modern European Thought*. New York: Columbia University Press.

Chisholm, Dianne. 1994. Irigaray's Hysteria. Pp. 263–84 in C. Burke, N. Schor, and M. Whitford (eds.), *Engaging with Irigaray: Feminist Philosophy and Modern European Though*. New York: Columbia University Press.

Clough, Patricia. 1992. *The Ends of Ethnography*. Thousand Oaks, CA: Sage.

Deleuze, Gilles. 1993. *The Fold: Leibniz and the Baroque*. Translated by T. Conley. Minneapolis: University of Minnesota Press.

de Vries, Hilary. 1992. A Playwright Spreads his Wings. *Los Angeles Times*, October 25.

Haver, William. 1996. *The Body of This Death*. Stanford: Stanford University Press.

Karamcheti, Indira. 1992. The Business of Friendship. [(Review of *Friends, Brothers and Informants: Fieldwork Memoirs of Banaras,* by Nita Kumar.] *Women's Review of Books* IX(12):16–17.

Kofman, Sarah. 1988. Baubo: Theological Perversion and Fetishism. Pp. 175–202 in M. A. Gillespie and T. Strong (eds.), *Nietzsche's New Seas: Explorations in Philosophy, Aesthetics, and Politics*. Chicago: University of Chicago Press.

———. 1993. *Nietzsche and Metaphor*. Translated by Duncan Large. Stanford: Stanford University Press.

Komar, Kathleen. 1987. *Transcending Angels: Rainer Maria Rilke's Duino Elegies*. Lincoln: University of Nebraska Press.

Lather, Patti. 1994. Staying Dumb? Feminist Research and Pedagogy with/in the Postmodern. Pp. 101–32 in H. Simons and M. Billig (eds.), *After Postmodernism*. Thousand Oaks, CA: Sage.

————. 1995. Troubling Angels: Interpretive and Textual Strategies in Researching the Lives of Women with HIV/AIDS. *Qualitative Inquiry* 1(1):41–68.

————. 1996. Troubling Clarity: The Politics of Accessible Language. *Harvard Educational Review*, 66(3):525–45.

Lather, Patti, and Chris Smithies. 1997. *Troubling the Angels: Women Living With HIV/AIDS.* Boulder, CO: Westview/HarperCollins.

Latour, Bruno. 1993. *We Have Never Been Modern.* Translated by Catherine Porter. Cambridge, MA: Harvard University Press.

Marcus, George. 1993. [Interview.] *Lingua Franca,* July–August:13–15.

Meiners, Erica. 1994. [Course writing for Education 508B, "Data Analysis in the Crisis of Representation," University of British Columbia, summer.]

Nietzsche, Friedrich. 1974. *The Gay Science.* Translated by Walter Kaufmann. New York: Vintage.

Patai, Daphne. 1994. Sick and Tired of Scholars' Nouveau Solipsism. *The Chronicle of Higher Education,* February 23:A52.

Piercy, Marge. 1973. *To Be of Use: Collected Poems.* Garden City, NY: Doubleday.

Pippin, Robert. 1988. Irony and Affirmation in Nietzsche's *Thus Spoke Zarathustra.* Pp. 45-71 in M. A. Gillespie and T. Strong (eds.), *Nietzsche's New Seas.* Chicago: University of Chicago Press.

Rilke, Rainer. 1989. *The Selected Poetry of Rainer Maria Rilke.* Translated and edited by S. Mitchell. New York: Vintage.

Robbins, Jill. 1995. Visage, Figure: Speech and Murder in Levinas's *Totality and Infinity.* Pp. 275–98 in C. Caruth and D. Esch (eds.), *Critical Encounters: Reference and Responsibility in Deconstructive Writing.* New Brunswick: Rutgers University Press.

St. Pierre, Bettie. 1997. Methodology in the Fold and the Irruption of Transgressive Data. *Qualitative Studies in Education* 10(2):175–89.

Van Maanen, John. 1988. *Tales of the Field: On Writing Ethnography.* Chicago: University of Chicago Press.

Visweswaran, Kamala. 1988. Defining Feminist Ethnography. *Inscriptions* 3–4:27–46.

Watney, Simon. 1994. *Practices of Freedom: Selected Writing on HIV/AIDS.* Durham: Duke University Press.

La Sufrida

Contradictions of Acculturation and Gender in Latina Health

DENISE A. SEGURA AND ADELA DE LA TORRE

Research in women's health has recently uncovered significant disparities in access and health status among ethnic women and women of color. For Latina and Chicana/Mexicana women, acculturation, as one of the most important predictive factors in both health access and health status measures, tends to frame empirical research and inform health policy. What is problematic in these empirical models, however, is the assumption that acculturation is a static process that can be captured and measured by specific attributes such as language, ancestry, behaviors, and attitudinal preferences. Overreliance on assumptions of static acculturation objectifies the immigrant woman subject by denying her power in the decision-making process. This results in descriptive attributes becoming "objective" criteria that predict good or bad health outcomes.

This paper challenges the static modeling design used in empirical studies of Chicana/Mexicana women's health that depict these women as objects who acquiesce to the environment rather than subjects who transform their environments. After reviewing the standard models that predict "good health outcomes" based on lower rates of acculturation, we will juxtapose these findings with more recent qualitative studies of Mexican immigrant women that illustrate how women reinvent their cultural identities within the process of migration, wherein class and gender locations are problematized. By examining the dynamic nature of Chicana/Mexicana cultural identity as part of the larger process of cultural identity reconstruction in the United States, we propose an alternative model to understand this group's observed health behaviors. We argue that the health behaviors examined empirically and accounted for within the aegis of a static acculturation model may mask a critical renegotiation of gender position for recent Mexican immigrant women. The items typically used to measure cultural identity and acculturation in much of the health services research form at best crude measures of immigrant status for specific Latina/o subpopulations but provide little understanding of the fluid and contradictory nature of cultural identity across immigrant categories. This understanding is essential if we are to provide more effective health policy and services to this group.

A major conclusion of this study is the need to reformulate current acculturation scales to incorporate the dynamism of cultural identity and cultural transformation of immigrant Mexican women as processes rather than outcomes. Furthermore, we argue that the current popular trend of promoting the "good" health behaviors of recent Mexican immigrants should be challenged as ignoring the cultural contradictions that exist and are often rooted in patriarchal family structures.

La Sufrida

La Sufrida, the long-suffering, self-effacing, ever-present self-sacrificing mother-image is present in many Chicano/Mexicano households. *La sufrida* is a virginal archetype that maintains and reproduces Chicano/Mexicano culture. She is the woman who will not eat so her children and husband can eat. She is the woman who will not adorn her face or body, the woman whose happiness is integrally bound to her family's well-being. As Gloria Anzaldua states, "The welfare of the family, the community, and tribe is more important than the welfare of the individual. The individual exists first as kin . . . and last as self" (1987:18).

Today we begin to deconstruct this culturally heroic icon of Chicano/Mexicano womanhood and family ideology. We contend that the ideological "presence" of the self-sacrificing Chicana/Mexicana martyr-mother within Chicano/Mexicano family research lays a foundation for much of the way health care services and delivery are constructed. This stereotype interjects itself into acculturation frameworks, obscuring the complexity of gender as a social construction among Chicanas/Mexicanas in favor of a static moment in a population's history and culture. We argue that deconstructing the image of *la sufrida* is essential both to retire stereotypes and to identify transformative elements of Chicano/Mexicano culture that might be accessed to improve the health care situation of this population. Ultimately, we propose the development of theoretical and policy approaches that analyze gender strategies among Chicanas/Mexicanas in order to develop (among other things) more effective intervention strategies.

Deconstructing *la sufrida* begins by understanding real and perceived differences between Chicanas/Mexicanas and other American women. Socioeconomically and culturally, these differences include language, ideological configurations, preferred behaviors, customs, and so on. How "difference" is represented and evaluated, however, has profound implication for Chicana/

Mexicana health treatment and policy development. Here we present just a few portrayals of "difference" from the academic and popular presses:

> The difference between Anglo and Mexican-American women may be related to the fact that Mexican Americans have more positive views of housewives than Anglos. (Hurtado 1995:45)

> Some of the hottest new imports from Latin America—to replace "intimidating and materialistic American women"—are marriage-minded Latin ladies ... from good families where respect for husband and marriage are taught at an early age. *Hispanic Link Weekly Report* 1989

> The women's movement has opened opportunities, she says, but it hasn't shown the Latina how to be whole. From 9 to 5, she sees herself as a career woman, from 5 to 8 as a mother; from 8 to 11 as a wife. (Alvarado 1991)

> In summary, the stereotyped Mexican-American family has a high regard for authority, an adherence to tradition, a philosophy of acceptance and resignation, and a religious orientation. (Padilla 1971:67)

These excerpts speak to the popular image of *la chicana* or *la mexicana* as family-centered, marriage-minded, and respectful. This one-dimensional Chicana/Mexicana *la sufrida* stereotype encompasses an idealized set of characteristics associated with "traditional" Chicano/Mexicano culture. The image of *la sufrida* wearing a black dress, entering the church to kneel reverently at the feet of the Virgen de Guadalupe to light a candle with money she has scraped together by denying herself any number of unnamed diversions or pleasures, and praying for her family is a picture reified in film (those few that have Latinas in them), novels, or calendars. The stereotype of the "good" Chicana/Mexicana as sacred and holy, self-sacrificing, familistic, and fatalistic frames much of the literature accessed by health care professionals today. Most important, these stereotypes have operated within acculturation models developed in the social sciences to explain behavioral differences between Anglo women and Chicanas/Mexicanas.

Acculturation Models Used in Health

Research that examines health behaviors of Mexican-origin women increasingly focus on the role of acculturation and health care outcomes. Typically these applied behavioral models attempt to explain why women of more recent immigrant origins are more likely than native-born and more acculturated Chicana/Mexicana women to exhibit health behaviors that are "protective factors" for these women and their families. This particular finding has gained prominence in part by countering the conventional wisdom on the primacy of socioeconomic factors in determining health outcomes. In the case of Chicanas/Mexicanas the more recent immigrants, despite their horrendous poverty and lack of access to health care, continue to have good birth outcomes, have low rates of alcohol and tobacco consumption, and maintain sexually monogamous lifestyles more often than their more acculturated counterparts. The effects of an evolutionary, linear acculturation process on health behaviors suggests negative impacts; Markides et al. (1990) argue that acculturation and alcohol consumption are positively related to younger stressors that affect Hispanic women's decisions to consume alcohol. Research on single mothers (Stroup-Benham, Trevifio, and Trevifio 1990) illustrates the economic stress among less-educated Mexican-American women. However, it is noted that the influence of acculturation on consumption is very complex and depends on variations such as age, sex, and type of measure of alcohol consumption.

Indeed, several studies on alcohol consumption indicate that multiple incomes combined with the restructuring of the family unit, increases the probability or alcohol consumption for these women. Acculturation, therefore, cannot explain why single female heads of household consume more alcohol than women in dual-female-headed households or women in dual-parent households. As Stroup-Benham and her colleagues argue, the stressors associated with being a single female head of household may be better indicators of health behaviors than acculturation.

Other studies that focus on the effects of acculturation on health seek to explain illicit drug use. Amaro et al. (1990) suggests that acculturation into U.S. society, as reflected by language use, is related to higher rates of illicit drug use. In this model, acculturation was measured simply by identifying the respondent's place of birth and language use, without attempting to access the social and economic context.

Underlying these static models of acculturation are psychometric constructs that assume the key cultural attributes of Mexican-origin women are defined by descriptors such as English-language fluency, ethnic identity, values, ideology, and cultural customs (Cuellar, Harris, and Jasso 1980). In the highly regarded Cuellar Acculturation Rating Scale, substantial explanatory power is derived from the language component. Yet Cuellar admits that "obviously, the 20 items contained in [the scale] do not tap all of the components of acculturation. It is acknowledged that perhaps the more important constructs of acculturation may not even be measured by this scale" (Cuellar, Harris, and Jasso 1980:209). Despite this caveat from the author himself, the acculturation scale is nonetheless used as a critical predictor for health behaviors among Mexicana/Chicana women, even though it captures at best only the immigrant status of these women, much as a snapshot fixed in time. Since few studies acknowledge the limitation inherent in the use of such fixed acculturation scales, they subsequently tend to reify the knowledge acquired from these discrete scales. Worse, overreliance on these scales obscures an appreciation of acculturation as a dynamic and continuous process that cannot possibly be captured by models that rely on discrete variables. Nonetheless, tacit acceptance of this discrete variable permeates the health behavior literature on Chicana/Mexicana women.

The following chart illustrates the use of acculturation scales as a predictor of health behaviors.

Author	Acculturation Index	Acculturation Var. Design (Yes)	Acculturation Var. Design (No)
Mainous 1979	Self-concept as a variable	Relation between self-concept and accult.	
Cuellar, Harris, and Jasso 1990	Defines accult. model (multidimensional)	Relation between host culture and accult.	
Markides et al. 1990	Accult. stress model and accult. model	Relation between health risk behaviors and accult.	
Stroup-Benham, Trevifio, and Trevifio 1990	Sociocultural	Relation between drinking behavior and accult.	
Mainous III 1989	Self-concept as a variable	Relation between self-concept and accult.	
Olmedo and Padilla 1978	Sociocultural	Relation between sociocultural factors and accult.	
Olmedo 1979	Diachronic and synchronic		
Rodriguez 1983	Sociocultural		
Scribner and Dwyer 1989	Sociocultural		No variable design mentioned
Ginzberg 1991	Socioeconomic		No variable design mentioned
Marin et al. 1993	Research infrastructure		No variable design mentioned
Moore and Hepworth 1994	Socioeconomic		Acculturation was not a predictor

The first six examples demonstrate empirical research in which the acculturation variable design was utilized, while the remaining six either did not mention a variable design or concluded that acculturation was not found to be a predictor.

In the first example, Mainous (1979) investigated self-concept in relation to acculturation. An acculturation variable design was applied in which the respondent's self-concept as an insider or an outsider to his/her native culture was examined. Results indicated that the respondent's self-concept was an important element in determining their level of acculturation. Cuellar, Harris, and Jasso (1990) also utilized an acculturation scale in which the study measured the amount of acculturation to the host culture the subject had adopted. The study attempted to attain a holistic picture of the acculturation process through developing a gauge to calibrate the amount of acculturation that had taken place. Thus, acculturation was based on a multidimensional approach.

The subsequent application of an acculturation design was measured by Markides et al. (1990) in which acculturation influences were examined in relation to the health risk behavior of Mexican-Americans (consisting of health service utilization, cigarette smoking, alcohol consumption, and diet). In relation to alcohol and acculturation, for example, the author found a positive correlation.

In the case of Stroup-Benham, Trevifio, and Trevifio (1990), the consumption of alcohol was found to be influenced by the level of acculturation the participant had attained over his or her lifetime. In the example of Olmedo and Padilla (1978), acculturation was affected by sociocultural characteristics. Subjects who were exposed to the host culture for a longer period of time were expected to rate higher on the acculturation scale.

In the final example in which acculturation was focused on, Mainous (1989) reexamined the relation between self-concept and the respondent's level of acculturation. Results similar to those of the previous study in 1979 were found—self-concept appeared to influence the measurement of acculturation.

Half of the twelve articles that examine health behaviors and outcomes for Latina/Chicana/Mexicana women identify acculturation as having a significant impact on the health and well-being of these women and/or their children. That is, Latina/Chicana/Mexicana women who are less acculturated have better health outcomes. The immediate policy implication of these findings is that acculturation is bad for your health. The focus, therefore, in this kind of research is to identify the moment when acculturation becomes disadvantageous to health behaviors. But this linear model obscures the complexity of both acculturation and health behaviors. Moreover, it diminishes Chicana/Mexicana agency.

Revisioning Culture and Gender Identity for Mexican Immigrant Women

Research on Chicana/Mexicana health behaviors often assumes that their actions are best understood within the context of a unique set of ethnic and cultural traditions. To ascertain the degree of adherence to Chicano/Mexicano culture, many researchers (as we have seen) rely on acculturation scales. However, the multidimensional process of acculturation is all too often reduced to the simplest measurable component, that is, Spanish-language use. Although language loyalty may be a good indicator of immigrant status, its utility for understanding acculturation is limited. If we think of acculturation as a process of acquiring knowledge to enhance one's ability to survive and prosper in a new society, clearly Spanish-language use can be viewed as one item in a woman's knowledge reservoir, as opposed to a "barrier" to full social participation. The local opportunity structure and lack of human capital are also important. Spanish, as the "home" of a woman's expressions of self and the means through which she interprets reality and opportunity, cannot be underestimated as a source of strength, survival, and betterment as she explores her changing environment in interaction with others. As a proxy for acculturation, however, it is limited, especially when we consider differences among Chicanas/Mexicanas that flow from their class, gender roles, sexual orientation, and immigrant status.

Instead of relying conceptually and methodologically on acculturation we might delve into what Renato Rosaldo calls the "cultural borderlands" and move beyond cataloguing shared patterns and meanings to problematize survival tools and social expressions among women (Rosaldo 1989:26–38). If we accept the premise that culture is not just a system of shared patterns and behaviors but includes continuous performance and conflicting ideologies, then it is vital to reject reductionism in models of acculturation inasmuch as they render invisible critical components of Chicana/Mexicana identities.

Recent scholarship reveals important differences between U.S.-born women of Mexican descent and women raised in Mexico who now reside in the United States. Socioeconomically, Mexicana immigrants' educational levels are lower (fifth or sixth grade, on average) than those of U.S.-born Chicanas (tenth or eleventh grade, on average); their language use varies; and their employment is distinct (e.g., more Mexicanas labor in blue-collar occupations, whereas Chicanas tend to work in white-collar jobs) (Ortiz 1995). If we consider sexual and fertility behaviors, foreign-born Latinas and Mexicanas tend to be more sexually conservative regarding the number of sexual partners and age at first intercourse as well as more likely to have planned their pregnancies and be married or living with a partner (Becerra and De Anda 1987; Rapkin and Erickson 1990). Foreign-born Latinas are also less likely to have knowledge of or experience with birth control and are more likely to begin their prenatal care later in pregnancy or eschew it altogether (Becerra and De Anda 1987; Rapkin and Erickson 1990). Other research argues that birth outcomes are more favorable for Mexican-born women residing in the United States vis-à-vis U.S.-born women of Mexican descent (Guendelman et al. 1990). This research lends additional support to the theory that an inverse relationship between acculturation and good health among Mexican women exists, caused by a more protective lifestyle among less-acculturated women, regardless of socioeconomic status or age. This study notes possible measurement error, since foreign-born Mexicana women are prone to a reporting bias. For example, Mexico-born women are less likely to receive a pregnancy examination which can result in lower reporting of miscarriages and induced abortions.

Underreporting of medical problems and conditions can easily skew research directions and distort the effects of acculturation. The National Latina Health Organization states, "Latinos are less likely to receive preventive or regular health care than other Americans." Moreover, a "larger percentage of Latinas than white women had never heard of or received a Pap smear, breast exam, or mammogram. Almost twice as many Latinas as white women had never heard of breast exams and nearly three times as many had never heard of mammograms" (National Latina Health Organization 1996). Thus, underreporting may contribute to the development of a false image of better health among less acculturated Mexicana women. This possibility argues for the need for research studies to carefully delineate acculturation effects from those that may be more closely aligned to income and education.

Other evidence contradicts acculturation theses concerning patterns of educational attainment and social mobility among women and men of Mexican descent. Third-generation Chicanos tend to be overrepresented among low educational achievers than their first- and second-generation counterparts (Hayes-Bautista, Schink, and Chapa 1988; Chapa and Valencia 1993). Similarly, mobility patterns in general rise markedly for the second generation (children of adult immigrants) and either stabilize or move downward with the third generation. These socioeconomic realities must contextualize an understanding of the process of culture and identity among Chicanas and Mexicanas today.

Feminist-based research on Chicana and Mexicana women emphasizes the dynamism within their cultural adaptation and identity formation. Immigrant women experience continuous shifts in cultural identity formation as renegotiation of gender roles occurs with changes in their economic or family status. Until recently, much of the research on Mexicano migration was male-certified and documented the economics of immigration. In this literature, examinations of Mexicana women and immigration were anchored within the family nexus. That is, Mexicana women typically were viewed as migratory appendages to the breadwinner Mexicano man. Recent research contests this view and asserts that often Mexicana women have their own reasons for emigrating that sometimes include reuniting with an absent husband, but at other times reflect motivations to escape abusive spouses, seek a freer environment to express one's sexuality (Arguelles and Rivero 1993), and/or gain a better life (Hondagneu-Sotelo 1994). Whether the reason is to reunite the family or to enact individualistic needs, Mexicana women's innovation in immigration is only now becoming visible to researchers and policy makers.

As members of a racial-ethnic minority whose political, economic, and cultural uniqueness has been historically undermined and devalued, Chicanas have maintained and affirmed a distinct set of values and behavior that emphasize familism, *compadrazgo,* and a collectivist orientation (Griswold de Castillo 1979; Segura and Pierce 1993). Research on Chicanas is shifting to emphasize both an analysis of gender role attitudes and behaviors as well as the contradictions posed by contestation and agency within families and their communities. For example, the existence of alternative mothering models within Chicano communities that utilize women in the kinship network to provide physical and affective care for children and emotional and economic support for parents (Segura and Pierce

1993) offers insight into potential health care intervention strategies. Pesquera's study of professional, blue-collar, and white-collar Chicana workers explores women's recasting of traditional cultural values to reconcile the "competing urgencies" of family and paid employment. She finds a positive relationship between women's class locations and economic contributions to the household vis-à-vis their spouses and their ability to successfully renegotiate the household division of labor (Pesquera 1993:181). The creativity of Chicanas to reinvent culturally prescribed traditional motherhood by renegotiating parenting with partners is finding voice in other feminist scholarship (Lamphere, Zavela, and Gonzales 1993). This research illustrates that gender roles are dynamic and subject to renegotiation as part of the process of facilitating the economic survival of the household and a woman's own sense of self.

The complexity of gender in Mexicano households intersects with economic opportunity. Recent research on Mexicano immigrants observes that with employment, women often assert themselves more directly in family decision-making. In some cases, as Hondagneu-Sotelo shows (1994), patriarchal authority is hotly contested. In other cases, patriarchal control is subverted covertly and bolstered by the relative economic strength of the woman (Segura 1994). The contradictory pressures of migration on "Traditional gender roles and practices" is also highlighted in de la Torre's study of Mexican agricultural migrants (1992). De la Torre found that the pressures of paid employment required these women to shift away from the traditional practice of breast-feeding infants and toward bottle-feeding. This renegotiation of traditional health practices exemplifies how migrant women can (and do) adapt their behavior to accommodate both the economic and health needs of their families as they cross new employment boundaries.

Conclusion

So what does all this mean? Chicanas and Mexicana migrant women often desire to affirm traditional practices and values. These preferences are often ideological and subject to change. In the case of Chicanas, the local context—the contradictions of race-ethnicity in inner cities and suburbs, where expressions of cultural heritage constantly shift and vary by class—is critical to explore, rather than "measure" by a static acculturation measuring stick. For Mexicanas, affirmation of traditional practices and values reverberates with the pressures of migration and settlement. Thus, what is "traditional" is adaptation and innovation, both of which flow from Mexicana/Chicana agency.

Acknowledgments

Adela de la Torre would like to acknowledge graduate assistant Arli Eicher for her help in completing this paper.

References

Anzaldúa, Gloria. 1987. *Borderlands/La Frontera: The New Mestiza.* San Francisco: Spinsters.

Alvarado, Y. 1991. Title TK. *Vista,* date TK:14–20.

Amaro, Hortensia, Rupert Whitaker, Gerald Coffman, and Timothy Heeren. 1990. Acculturation and Marijuana and Cocaine Use: Findings from HHANES 1982–84. *American Journal of Public Health Supplement* 80:54–59.

Arguelles, Lourdes, and Anne M. Rivero. 1993. Gender/Sexual Orientation, Violence, and Transnational Migration: Conversations with Some Latinas We Think We Know. *Urban Anthropology* 22(3–4):259–75.

Becerra, Roscina M., and D. DeAnda. 1984. Pregnancy and Motherhood Among Mexican American Adolescents. *Health and Social Work* 9:106–23.

Chapa, Jorge, and J. Valencia. 1993 Latino Population Growth, Demographic Characteristics, and Educational Stagnation: An Examination of Recent Trends. *Hispanic Journal of Behavioral Sciences* 2:199–218.

de al Torre, Adela, and Beatriz M. Pesquera (eds.). *Building with Our Hands: New Directions in Chicana Studies.* Berkeley: University of California Press, 1993.

Cuellar, Israel, Lorwen C. Harris, and Ricardo Jasso. 1980. Acculturation Scale for Mexican American Normal and Clinical Populations. *Hispanic Journal of Behavioral Sciences* 15:165–87.

Ginzberg, Eli. 1991. Access to Health Care for Hispanics. *Journal of the American Medical Association* 265:238–41.

Goodwon-Lawes, Julie. 1993. Feminine Authority and Migration: The Case of One Family from Mexico. *Urban Anthropology* 22ª3–4):277–97.

Griswold de Castillo, Richard. 1991. *Chicano Art: Resistance and Affirmation, 1965–1985.* Los Angeles: Los Angeles Wight Art Gallery.

Guendelman, Sylvia, Jeffrey Gould, Mark Hudes, and Brenda Eskenazi. 1990. Generational Differences in Prenatal Health Among the Mexican American Population: Findings from the HHANES 1982–84. *American Journal of Public Health Supplement* 80:61–65.

Hayes-Bautista, David E., Wemer O. Schink, and Jorge Chapa. 1988. *The Burden of Support: Young Latinos in an Aging Society.* Stanford, CA: Stanford University Press.

Hispanic Link Weekly Report. 1989. Sin Pelos en la Lengua. *Hispanic Link Weekly Report,* August 14:3.

Hondagneu-Sotelo, Pierrette. 1994. *Gendered Transitions: Mexican Experiences of Immigration.* Berkeley: University of California Press.

Hurtado, Aida. 1995. Variations, Combinations and Evolutions: Latino Families in the United States. Pp. 40–61 in Ruth Zambrana (ed.), *Understanding Latino Families: Scholarship Policy and Practice.* Thousand Oaks, CA: Sage Publications.

Lamphere, Louise, Patricia Zavella, and Felipe Gonzales, with Peter B. Evans. 1993. *Sunbelt Working Mothers: Reconciling Family and Factory.* Ithaca, NY: Cornell University Press.

Mainous, Arch G. III. 1989. Self-Concept as an Indicator of Acculturation. *Hispanic Journal of Behavioral Sciences* 11:178–89.

Marin, Gerardo, Hortensia Amaro, Carol Eisenberg, and Susan Opava-Stitzer. 1993. The Development of a Relevant and Comprehensive Research Agenda to Improve Hispanic Health. *Public Health Reports* 198:546–50.

Markides, Kyriakos S., Laura a. Ray, Christine A. Stroup-Benham, and Fernando Trevifio. 1990. Acculturation and Alcohol Consumption in the Mexican American Population of the Southwestern United States: Findings from HHANES 1982–84. *American Journal of Public Health Supplement* 80:42–46.

Moore, Patricia, and Joseph T. Hepworth. 1994. Use of Perinatal and Infant Health Services by Mexican-American Medicaid Enrollees. *Journal of the American Medical Association* 272:297–304.

National Latina Health Organization. 1996. Essential Principles for Responsible Health Reform. HTTP:www.gopher://latino.sscnetuc/9.edu:70/00/R. . .s%20for%20Responsible %20Health%20Reform. Accessed July 10.

Olmedo, Esteban L., and Amado M. Padilla. 1978. Empirical and Construct Validation of a Measure of Acculturation for Mexican-Americans. *The Journal of Social Psychology* 105:170–87.

Ortiz, Vilma. 1995 Labor Force Position of Latino Immigrants in California. Berkeley: Chicano/Latino Policy Project, University of California.

Padilla, Amado M. 1971. Psychological Research and the Mexican American. Pp. 65–77 in Margaret M. Mangold (ed.), *La Causa Chicana: The Movement for Justice.* New York: Family Service Association of America.

Pedraza, Silvia. 1991. Women and Migration: The Social Consequences of Gender. *Annual Review of Sociology* 17:303–25.

Pesquera, Beatriz M. 1993. In the Beginning He Wouldn't Even Lift a Spoon: The Division of Household Labor. Pp. 181–95 in Adela de la Torre and Beatriz M. Pesquera (eds.), *Building with Our Hands: New Directions in Chicana Studies.* Berkeley: University of California Press.

Rapkin, A. J., and P. I. Erickson. 1991. Acquired Immune Deficiency Syndrome: Ethnic Differences in Knowledge and Risk Factors among Women in an Urban Family Planning Clinic. *AIDS* (August) 184–94.

Rodriguez, Josie. 1983. Mexican Americans: Factors Influencing Health Practices. *The Journal of School Health* 53:136–39.

Rosaldo, Renato. 1989. *Culture and Truth: The Remaking of Social Analysis.* Boston: Beacon Press.

Scribner, Richard, and James H. Dwyer. 1989. Acculturation and Low Birth Rate Among Latinos in the Hispanic HHANES. *American Journal of Public Health* 79:1263–67.

Segura, Denise A. 1994. Working at Motherhood: Chicana and Mexican Immigrant Mothers and Employment. Pp. 211–33 in Evelyn Nakano Glenn, Grace Chang, and Linda Rennie Forcey (eds.), *Mothering: Ideology, Experience and Agency.* New York: Routledge.

Segura, Denise, and Jennifer L. Pierce. 1993. Chicana/o Family Structure and Gender Personality: Chodorow, Familism, and Psychoanalytic Sociology Revisited. *Signs: Journal of Women in Culture and Society* 19:62–91.

Stroup-Benham, Christine A., Fernando M. Trevifio, and Dorothy M. Trevifio. 1990. Alcohol Consumption Patterns Among Mexican American Mothers and Among Children from Single- and Dual-Headed Households: Findings from HHANES 1982–84. *American Journal of Public Health Supplement* 80:36–41.

Whose Science of Food and Health?

Narratives of Profession and Activism from Public-Health Nutrition

MARJORIE L. DEVAULT

Scientific knowledge of food and nutrition is organized around a paradox—or at least the appearance of a paradox. Science, in its traditional construction, claims to produce knowledge that is abstract, timeless, replicable, and universal.[1] The social activities of producing, distributing, and using food, on the other hand, are more obviously relational, contextualized, politicized, and embodied activities. As in many health-related fields, this disjuncture is managed, and at least partially obscured, by a gendered division of labor (Smith 1987:83–84). Nutritional scientists—historically, mostly men—develop "basic" knowledge of food and human sustenance, while professional dietitians and public health nutritionists—mostly women—are given the complex and often frustrating tasks of using the findings of nutritional science to solve problems in particular material settings. Authorized knowledge moves in one direction, from scientists "down" to practitioners, whose broader knowledge of food in the life-world is typically understood as mere application of general principles.

I begin with this contrast in order to call attention to the work of "intermediate" or "subordinate" professionals in the health care system—nurses, social workers, health educators, science and medical technicians, for example—workers who are mostly women and who are often left out of analyses of science and the production of scientific knowledge. This essay draws from my studies of one such group, dietitians and community nutritionists, in which I explore how these professionals are positioned in a complex network of institutions that organize the production and distribution of food (see also DeVault 1995a, b). I am interested in how they are drawn into these networks, how they are trained in the "authorized" knowledge of food and nutrition, and what they might have to contribute as actors at the margins of the institutions that organize and control food systems.

One of my difficulties has involved finding a comfortable stance toward this group. I became interested in food and nutrition work because it seemed like undervalued work; even before I knew very much about it, I was interested in taking this field seriously—and that is still my intention. I wish to avoid the dismissive, humorous, or hostile tone that characterizes much writing on the less prestigious professions (see, for example, Shapiro 1986, whose history of home economics is billed on the book jacket as a "droll" and "amusing" text that "deconstructs the marshmallow"). I believe that the pervasive sexism in societal views of professional work sometimes creeps into feminist writing as well, rendering us too ready to criticize women in the so-called women's professions, and too easily inclined to see them in caricatured ways, simply as carriers and enforcers of dominant ideologies. As I learned more about this field, I did find grounds for critique. In fact, I would argue that dietitians and nutritionists do work in institutions where they are drawn into practices that carry and enforce dominant views of nutritional science (and a larger social order). But I will also argue that this observation captures only part of the practice and thought one can find among nutrition professionals.

In this paper, I propose a feminist rationale for renewal of the long-standing sociological concern with professional socialization and work, especially in the so-called women's professions. In doing so, however, I wish to pay particular attention to the disciplinary lens of sociology, considering how the traditional concerns of the field have shaped approaches to these topics, and how we might see these concerns differently, bringing "subordinate" groups more fully into analyses of professional work. I will suggest that feminist studies in this area can work against the traditional sociological view—and thus supplement it—by calling attention to the gendered diversity of professions and to significant heterogeneity within professional fields.[2] I will illustrate such an approach with an analysis of how some public health nutritionists negotiated professional identities in a particular moment, the decade that spanned the late 1960s and early 1970s, when food and hunger were widely if only briefly understood as political issues. Their stories raise questions about professional socialization in the "women's" professions—about the selves that form during professional training, the curious mix of authority and deference that characterizes professional identities in these fields, and the possibilities for practice that challenges professional subordination. In pursuing these questions, I will rely on feminist methodological strategies that provide a foundation for the analysis: I will attend to the emotional dimensions of social organization and to dynamics of participation and exclusion.

Profession as a Topic in Feminist Studies

Feminist scholars enter the academic world with an oppositional purpose. We bring new perspectives, and we intend to challenge the dominant modes of scholarship that have too often left women's experiences unexplored. In spite of considerable success in that project, we often find that becoming professional is an enterprise that leads in other directions, to some peculiar dilemmas. As we learn to be sociologists, nutritionists, historians, lawyers, theorists—as we accept the discipline of any field—we often find that we must struggle to sustain and act upon the feminist insights and intentions with which we began.

This observation points to the powerful effects of professionalism as a form of work organization. Becoming a professional means gaining a particular kind of authority; a professional is warranted to do particular kinds of work, to speak as an expert, to set policy. For these reasons, becoming a professional promises—for many of us—the opportunity to bring new ideas into public discourses, and perhaps the power to make change. But the process of becoming professional is inherently conservative. One is trained in the established paradigms of a profession, gains the competences associated with the field, and becomes a practitioner of a craft with its own canons and traditions. One also learns about disciplinary and professional boundaries and etiquette—one learns that the professional warrant to act depends on adherence to established modes of thought and practice.

In an early second-wave feminist essay, Mary Howell wrote about these potential contradictions in an article entitled "Can We Be Feminists and Professionals?" (1979). Professionalism, she argued, teaches elitism and can lead to arrogance toward "clients," while feminism begins with solidarity among women in all kinds of positions and aims at the elimination of oppressive relations. Professionalism assumes that experts should control others, while feminism assumes that women should be in control of their own lives. And professional frameworks dictate particular, established agendas, while feminism calls for a focus on change and liberation. Howell did not insist that we leave professions; she noted that there are very few ways for women to work effectively outside of patriarchal institutions. She did suggest that we need to develop a keen awareness of our professional contexts, and that thinking through the difficulties of feminist action within established conventions, collectively, is a process essential to maintaining feminist understandings of these contradictory situations.

Berenice Fisher (1990), a feminist educator who teaches in a school for human service professionals, has also written about the experience and effects of professionalism, with special attention to fields that are predominantly female. Fisher is interested in the contradictory experiences of women who enter the human service professions, such as social work, nursing, and teaching. She points out that many women are drawn to these fields by the promise of economic independence and the chance to perform work they understand as socially valuable. As they move into these "women's professions," however, they discover that these promises are not fully met: They usually receive relatively low pay, they may have little control over their own work, and they are often located in bureaucracies that regulate their activities but provide little support for the work they want to do. Fisher's discussion of this phenomeonon is titled "Alice in the Human Services"; by calling on the story of Alice in Wonderland, she calls attention to an aspect of the subjective experience of professional training and entry into a career—the sense we may sometimes have that we've entered a rather strange world, where things are not quite what they should be. In part, Fisher points to features of the women's professions that are widely recognized, related to their subordinate status relative to the "classic" professions such as medicine or law (see Stromberg 1988). But Fisher also urges that feminists look beyond these features of the women's professions and examine respectfully the perspectives and activities of women committed to these fields of work. She points out that, too often, these traditionally female professions are devalued by feminists as well as nonfeminist observers (though perhaps for different reasons). And her discussion suggests that women professionals respond actively to the constraints of their positions, and may resist or transcend conservative aspects of professional training in their actual practice.

Sociologists have produced a vast literature on the professions, characterized by particular ways of thinking about this form of work organization. While these studies are often useful, it seems important to notice the boundaries that are implicitly drawn by sociological studies of professional work. The theoretical apparatus that highlights some aspects of professional work leaves out others. For example, most sociological studies focus on the professional as autonomous expert, leaving out all those who support professional work. Even studies of women in "supportive" professions, such as nursing or social work, often overlook "other women" in the lives of these professionals—women whose labor underwrites professional activity (e.g., domestic workers, paraprofessionals, and clerical staff).[3] Clients' perspectives are often left out of research on professional work. Sociological frameworks also seem to encourage analyses of the abstracted, formal features of professional work such as questions of status and control—characteristics of the work that can be compared across professions. Sociologists less often tie these formal features of professional work to their substantive aspects, considering the products and consequences of professional work as well as its organization. (I saw this effect in my own writing when one of my informants read an early paper from this study and exclaimed, "But there's nothing about food in here!")

Most important for this analysis, sociological studies of professional socialization typically proceed from the profession itself, asking, "How are good professionals produced?" Feminists are often more interested in the production of professionals who will resist the demands of male-centered professional standpoints. Indeed, as I have thought about these issues, I have begun to collect a "counterliterature" on professional socialization that reads the process rather differently, with a concern for its darker side and for individual struggles for authenticity and multiple allegiances as well as professional identity.

Virginia Olesen and Elvi Whittaker (1968), for example, in an early study of nursing students, provide an account of professional socialization as an intensely emotional process. Shulamit Reinharz addresses both the shaping effects of professional training and resistance to those effects in her autobiographical account, *On Becoming a Social Scientist* (1979). Susan Krieger's autobiographical essays in *Social Science and the Self* (1991) deal with similar struggles, compounded by the homophobia woven into the practices of professional institutions. Cheryl Townsend Gilkes (1983) writes about the careers of African-American women activists who think of career mobility in terms of "going up for the oppressed," and who conduct careers that are organized by allegiances to their communities of origin rather than professional communities. Patricia Hill Collins's (1990) discussion of the work of black feminist intellectuals points less directly to this kind of strategic use of the powers conferred upon individuals through professional education and credentialing. And in a review of Krieger's book (perhaps because she is writing less formally), Barrie Thorne shares a dream that vividly expresses an aspect of professional socialization that rarely shows up in sociological studies.

> One night when I was in the throes of finishing my Ph.D. dissertation, I dreamed that I was in a line of people slowly marching toward a guillotine wielded by my advisor. As he chopped off each head, he declared, "I pronounce you my colleague." Just before it was my turn, I jolted out of the dream. It left me with disturbing thoughts about professional socialization as loss, conformity, even as a kind of violence to the learner. (Thorne 1994:138)

These writings represent a feminist, "oppositional" strand in studies of professional socialization. While mainstream studies examine the process as one that fits the individual to the professional mold, these feminist writers treat the process as more problematic and variable, making more room for questions about the endpoint in the process, and taking account of individual or collective goals that might conflict with institutional ones. This approach makes the notion of profession itself problematic.

I did not plan my study of the nutrition professions with all these ideas in mind. However, I have come to see that my interest in the work of nutritionists is rooted not only in theoretical questions, but also in my personal and practical concerns—my own struggles to operate as a "feminist professional." These insights into my own feelings have helped me to read my informants' stories of becoming professional more closely, with greater attention to their hopes and struggles along the way. In the next section I begin an analysis of some of those stories.

Narratives of Entry

I have collected career narratives from thirty-five dietitians and nutritionists. Nearly all of them received undergraduate training in food and nutrition, usually in schools of home economics (though sometimes these programs are found in schools of agriculture or health studies). Most informants were certified as registered dietitians, and some had graduate training as well. They worked in the range of occupational settings available to those with such training—most in hospitals or community health centers, and a few in food companies, commodity boards (food industry organizations formed to promote particular agricultural products), health clubs, and their own practices.[4] All but one were women.

I began each interview by requesting a career history. To most interviewees, I said something like, "I usually start by asking if you'll tell me the story of your career." I used the familiar term *story* partly out of a relatively unconsidered personal inclination toward informality; as I consider how the interviews unfolded, however, I believe the term also signaled my openness to complex and grounded narratives. Stories are entertaining, plotted, and full of contextual detail. They begin at the beginning, wherever that may be.

Informants sometimes seemed surprised that I asked for a story. In many interviews, I find in the transcript an opening "dance" of sorts as we orient to each other as teller and listener, negotiating a way to begin. Often, I noticed signs that the teller was preparing: a deep breath or contemplative pause. Sometimes there was clear indecision and an appeal for help: "You mean—way back?" I learned to help out with a gentle nudge: "Long story?"

Many narrators started in childhood, telling of interests and aspirations, family contexts, and their first thoughts and feelings about meaningful work and future lives. They talked about interests in food and its significance, sometimes in the context of a rich ethnic heritage, or about the importance of food in family lives, sometimes as an aspect of family illnesses. These stories of early interest must be interpreted with care; they are, of course, constructed retrospectively, and I do not mean to take them as unproblematic causal accounts. But they may reveal some of the meanings of a nutrition career that are not easily expressed elsewhere.

Informants' stories were told with emotion—pride, regret, affection for family and teachers, and sometimes anger, uncertainty or disappointment—and the depth of feeling in these accounts took me somewhat by surprise. I feel now that I should not have been surprised by the feeling in these narratives; after all, my interest in these lives stems in part from my desire to understand my own too often submerged feelings about career and profession.

Two Worlds

My aim in interviewing was to elicit stories without imposing a structure. I asked many clarifying questions along the way, but I did not plan specific questions in advance. As the interviewing proceeded, I learned about the class and family backgrounds of my informants. Telling their stories, they provided the contexts those stories required, explaining along the way who they had been and where they had come from. The portraits that emerged hint at travel between two worlds: the richly social world of their families and communities, and a relatively unfamiliar world of professionalism.

As a group, these professionals came from stable, upwardly mobile, but not particularly affluent families. Raised primarily in the northeastern United States, they were mostly white, and the white women who mentioned ethnicity were of European descent (e.g., German, Irish, Italian). One of the thirty-five interviewees was African-American, and three were immigrants from Asian or Caribbean countries. Many of their parents held working-class or middle-class jobs that were relatively secure; they were bakers, government workers, nurses, and salesmen. Informants' families were relatively comfortable economically, and expected them to go to college (sometimes as the first family members to do so), but they were careful about money. One woman recalled that she came from a family "that thought eating well was important"; then she laughed gently and added, "And eating economically, too."

The accounts convey a distinctive texture of family life. Several informants spoke of a closeness to family and community that was both comforting and confining. Gina Falcone explained, "I had been very protected in a family unit, in my little neighborhood in [a large city]—it was very neighborhood-oriented."[5] Parents were very much involved in the women's decisions about education and work, and urged them to consider professions in part because they thought very practically about work as a means of survival. One father "felt that his daughter should have a definite career. You know, a definite earning potential." And several informants reported that their parents advised them to choose fields where the pay is good and "there's always work." They also spoke of relatively traditional families, telling somewhat ruefully at times of their parents' views on appropriate work for women, and how they were quite explicitly directed toward "women's" professions.

When they talk of high-school years (and even earlier experiences), many of these people describe themselves as school achievers, and they often mention an early interest in science. As they tell of moving toward college, they often convey the sense of entering a new world that is characteristic of social mobility stories. Dorothy Mancini remarked, "I had no notion what a college was." Another woman described herself as "the baby of the family" and "not a trailblazer," but also indicated that one factor in choosing a college was her desire to move away from the family. And another explained that her small college was a good choice because it gave her the chance to "feel secure."

Gina Falcone's story gives the most vivid sense of movement from one world to another. Her Catholic high school provided little career counseling, and when she began to think about a career, she sought advice from "my teacher that I trusted." Then, she explains:

> I went to the public library in [the city], myself, and looked up lists of colleges. And I didn't even know about the library at that point. . . . I squeakily asked someone whether—if they had such a thing.

Telling the story as an experienced professional, she wishes she had gone to Cornell University, a place that was "too intimidating" at the time. Instead, she relates:

> I found a little college in [a small town], which is where my family—my mother's family is originally from. It's a small Catholic college, I was not feeling very adventurous. And, well, maybe it was adventurous in a way *[laughing]*, in retrospect.

Her choice was indeed "adventurous" for the young girl she was then; and it began to move her away from family and into a wider professional world.

These young women move from family and community toward the promise of professional work. But they enter a profession with a particular character, and the roads they travel do not always lead to the destinations they expect. They enter a "women's" profession, leading to positions with relatively limited authority and very short career ladders. Indeed, their comments about gender tracking often emerged as they talked of feeling blocked, or wondering whether to leave the field. They learn that pay is low and caseloads high; that respect and adequate resources are hard to come by; and that "teamwork" means, in most settings, that they will do whatever is needed.

These young nutritionists also enter a field that is marked by continuing (if often relatively muted) tension between competing conceptions of the aims and scope of nutrition work. I entered the field as a researcher, in the mid-1980s, through contacts with nutrition educators who had an explicitly political and often activist orientation toward their professional work. As I expanded my view of the field, I began to see that these women operated in a larger professional environment whose strongest and most pervasive themes were quite different. As I read journals and attended professional conferences, I saw that the field relied heavily on a science mediated by agricultural interests and the food industry. At professional meetings, much of the research presented is subsidized by corporate funding; "snack breaks" and luncheons are sponsored by groups such as Pepsi, Kraft Foods, and the Pork Council. Those working in the field are not unaware of these corporate connections: They notice them, joke about them, and sometimes raise these issues for sustained debate (see, e.g., Tobin, Dwyer, and Gussow 1992). But these connections are mostly accepted as part of the landscape of the field, and they coexist with an understanding of "science" as the source of "objective knowledge."

Much of the work that these professionals do—and believe in—is work that they insist would not get done without support from industry. Thus, they "make do" with what they can secure: Jobs are always vulnerable to shifting currents of politics; program planning is driven in part by agricultural policy and the supplies of surplus commodities it produces; and nutrition education often relies on materials produced by food corporations and commodity boards promoting particular products. Dietitians and nutritionists are aware of these dilemmas and compromises and come to understand them in various ways. Their standard practices, constructed in various times and settings in fragile niches on the margins of the powerful institutions of medicine, industry, and agriculture, are formed through both historical and moment-to-moment negotiations between nutritionists' own visions and intentions and their sense of what is possible (for more on this theme, see the case studies of professional practice in DeVault 1995a). They carry on with the day-to-day work of feeding, educating, managing—doing their best to deliver food to patients and clients in need.

Networks of Resistance

Within the larger professional field, there are pockets of resistance to dominant constructions of professional work, which provide other ways of seeing the landscape and conceiving of meaningful practice. Some people enter the field with commitments to other communities, and struggle to work in ways that honor those commitments that arise outside the profession. Some of those people find professional mentors who help them in that project and train them in a countertradition within the profession. The networks that sustain these countertraditions grow and shrink in different historical moments. When I conducted career-history interviews in the early 1990s, students just entering the field were drawn most often by the promise of new developments in high-tech medicine and a cultural emphasis on "fitness." But a number of the midcareer women I talked with, especially those working in public health settings, talked of coming to the field with a strongly political orientation, born out of the political movements of the 1960s that, for a while at least, made food a political issue. Political activism outside the profession gave nutritionists the opportunity to expand a network of public-health programs and institutions inside their field that they believed could provide sites for productive work with communities in need.

We can see how individuals encounter these networks by examining several moments in the career histories of three of these women. All three studied nutrition as undergraduate students between 1964 and 1974, a decade of political activism and possibility. Their stories show how a collective sense of doing nutrition work differently was woven into their careers. They give some sense of these women's struggles to find professional work that is meaningful, and also show how meaning is constructed collectively, with like-minded colleagues and the institutions (however fragile) they create together.

Dorothy Mancini, for example, recounts a turbulent time in her college years. Her story is told haltingly, with much laughter marking her references to politics and the near "slip" in her career path, when she almost became an English major:

> I was much more together, I think, when I was in high school. When I got to college, everything fell apart. *[laughing]*

> MLD: Yes, it's sort of a shock. What do you mean by that?

Well—I was quite sure what I wanted to do before I got to college. *(laugh)* I got to college, I was no longer quite so sure, and almost became an English major. *(laugh—for several seconds)* Decided I did not like science. Um—that I much preferred to write and be on picket lines, *(laugh)* if I was in school. This was in the mid-sixties, and so I almost dropped out at the end of that first year. And I was going to transfer to arts and sciences. Um—I decided to stay.

Why did she decide to stay? As the story proceeds, Mancini's college years are told as a continuing struggle to stay on track. Basic science courses seemed less engaging than literature and politics, but those focused on food and nutrition were more promising, somehow.

I finally started taking some of the nutrition courses, and biochemistry, and really liked that. *[I ask why.]* Well, the nutrition. I wasn't taking—I was sick of all these courses that didn't seem to make any sense, in any way, to—the kinds of things that I was interested in at that point, which was, you know, *[laugh]* civil rights, stuff like that.

She does not spell out exactly how things begin to come together, but the implication, I believe, is that nutrition courses deal with things that matter for people. In her senior year—in 1968—Mancini takes a course in public health nutrition, and here she encounters the beginning of a network of professional activism.

My senior year they started teaching a course in public health nutrition, and—that was like magic. And that combined what I loved about nutrition, and what I loved about people, and communities, and sort of grassroots teaching. . . . I got a very broad exposure to public health nutrition, because this was the first time they were teaching this course, and so, they were trying everything out. And we got out to elderly programs, and Head Start programs, and community health center programs . . . they got us to everything that was possible. . . .

So that's how I learned about public health and community nutrition. And it really—that made sense to me, in terms of, well, I mean do I—I really liked it.

She goes on to say that the course was never again taught in quite the same way; in subsequent years, the teacher had formal credentials and didn't try to pack so much into the course. She doesn't use the words, but we can hear that the new political perspectives in the field have begun to be institutionalized. In that initial moment, however, public-health nutrition is "like magic" for Mancini, and gives her professional life a clear direction.

For Gina Falcone, a similar struggle developed in the late 1960s, during the internship that typically follows a college degree and leads to professional certification. She too refers rather obliquely to politics as an element in her story; its significance emerges slowly and quietly. She begins by talking about the intense, continuing work—"abuse," she calls it—required in her "old-style" internship:

> We worked, one time, nine weeks in a row without a weekend off. And a lot of times I—one time I worked twenty-one days in a row without a day off . . . that was real student abuse. I mean, if they needed a potwasher, you washed pots. It's not bad to—I mean, everyone needs to pitch in, I really believe in teamwork. But I felt so abused, in a lot of ways. It was a real tug-of-war inside me between wanting to be a good student and learn things, and wanting to just run off, and explore my own life. And it was real hard to balance those two things, that growing up stuff.

She talks then about her teachers, stern but understanding; she appreciates that "they could have tossed me out, and I could have said, 'Well, I'll be a secretary.' [laughing] And be back at square one or something." And she talks about the other students, a highly qualified group, and "quite a mix of people."

Then, very quietly, and with a comment that she is somewhat uncomfortable being taped, she mentions her involvement with a political group working in a newly established community clinic.

> I got involved in that. It was—again, trying to go beyond myself, get out of the four white walls, get to meet different people, of color, and experience. [softly] And, put my nutrition into action. You get to do that a little bit in your internship. But this was much more meaty, and [softly] I don't know.

In fact, her internship produced a crisis, and for a while she wasn't sure she could continue. She felt herself being drawn into a model of hospital dietetics—a model in which "counseling" can only mean a fleeting contact at a time of crisis—that seemed wrong in several ways.

> That's when I really realized that [pause] hospital dietetics was very limited. When people are scared, they take in a little bit. And that I noticed that doctors would give you discharge orders, right before the patient was discharged. And I spent so much time handing out menus, and making sure that things were in order. Aaaghhh. I felt like what I went into it for was such a small piece of—of the pie, that it wasn't worth it to me. And I saw a lot going on in the kitchens [softly] that, I didn't really like. The way people treated each other.

Falcone's reference to how people "treated each other" alludes to the pervasive hierarchies of hospital life, organized not only through physicians' control of nutrition work but extending as well to the layers of support staff who contend over the conduct of more mundane aspects of institutional life. Her comment about the kitchen deserves closer examination.

> I saw a lot going on in the kitchens *[softly]* that, I didn't really like. The way people treated each other.

The kitchens are a site where nutritionists are required to exercise a particular kind of class-based (and in most settings ethnically charged) authority. In the kitchens they cannot merely help and advise clients; instead they must be supervisors of a low-paid workforce. Had I heard it only once, I would have been puzzled by this fleeting reference to this kind of discomfort; it is rarely discussed explicitly in terms of class and cultural relations. However, the kitchen appears, fleetingly, in many career stories—it points to the part of the job that many of these young women do not enjoy, because, as they explain, it is often difficult to work with nonprofessional staff. Given this charged context, I believe we can read Falcone's soft aside as evidence of her resistance to the expectation that she will exercise this kind of authority. Her next sentences suggest that she is interested in another kind of authority, perhaps equally uncomfortable, but more worth pursuing:

> I was really observing a lot, and at the same time verbalizing what I was feeling. Those were very new and different things for me—[from] being in a small little family unit, where you didn't criticize authority *[smiling]*. So, for me that was— I just wanted to do other things with my life. I wasn't sure what that was, but I knew that hospital dietetics was not [it].

Falcone endures a period of confusion and uncertainty. A friend who is both professionally and politically active provides a sense of what might be possible. But she must try out several uncomfortable positions before she finds a community health center where she feels comfortable with the work she is asked to do.

Mary Ann Walter encountered the developing network of new public health nutrition programs during the early 1970s, in her first jobs in the rural communities of a southern state:

> The first thing was starting up the elderly feeding—you know, the elderly feeding programs.

> MLD: That must have been fairly new then.

> It was, it was brand-new. 1976. And—here I am, a—let's see, 1976. So I was twenty-five years old. And they give me this grant proposal, and about a hundred and twenty-five thousand dollars *[laughing]*. And—here get these feeding sites going *[laughing]*. You know, luckily, I'm the kind of person that, I don't know why, I'll take on anything. I usually don't—I have enough confidence, that I can do it. So I did. And um—I did that for two years, and it was a very good experience, I learned a lot.

Though she enjoyed this work, she "burned out" and, missing the personal contact of nutritional counseling, moved to a newly established WIC program.[6]

If you know anything about the history of WIC, WIC was just starting back then. They'd finally got funds allocated. So it was a very exciting time, because [the state] was one of the ten states they originally surveyed, and said, major nutritional problems, you know, let's implement all these federal programs. And [this area] was one of the ten surveyed, so there was a lot of pressure to get [it] on the WIC program, as much as possible. So I was able to—being, again, the only RD [registered dietitian] in this eight-county program—I was able to *really* do a lot. And I've always liked jobs like this, where I can kind of—given the lead, just go do it *[breath, and a little laugh]*.

Working at these jobs, she met other public health professionals who had come to the area with the National Health Service Corps. They mentored her in a broader vision of public health practice:

These folks had all gotten their master's degrees, so they had kind of a . . . a broader scope on public health, public health nursing, public health nutrition. And—how it can impact on—well, eventually on the family, but—you know, just how it can impact on other health professionals, and the whole area, the region, you know, providing services, to groups. Which I've always found fascinating.

MLD: So by a broader scope, you mean sort of taking all of the—the whole system into account? Or—

Right. And seeing how your piece fits in. And where you—what you really need to do to make an impact. I mean, one-on-one counseling's nice. But, you know—in the scope of things, you probably need to move up a level, in terms of policy, decision making, you know, implementing training, you know, whatever it might be. Um—so it really expanded my horizons beyond direct service.

All three of these women have continued working in various community health settings for over twenty years. They have sought and found ways to contextualize their work with individuals, broadening the scope of their professional practice. Their commitments to the work were nurtured and sustained because they found groups of like-minded professionals who were building fresh visions of meaningful work.

The community health networks these women encounter do not, of course, solve the problems of hunger and inequality. Indeed, the professional orientation of these programs—and the political trade-offs that produce them—tend to support definitions of these problems in terms of education rather than inequality (see DeVault and Pitts 1984). But there were some significant gains. Commodity food programs, the expansion of food stamps, and new programs to aid the elderly and pregnant women and their children did help to get food to people who needed it. And many community health centers provided sites in which professionals could work with community advocates to improve nutrition and health services.

This network did not stay in place, however. By the time I began these investigations, in the mid-1980s, the Reagan administration had forced deep cuts in these programs. (Indeed, community nutritionists, based in the Society for Nutrition Education, were battling the American Dietetic Association, whose leaders approved the "fiscal responsibility" they saw in the administration's cutbacks.) It was no longer easy to find any job in a community setting, and certainly less inspiring to work there. By the 1990s there was even deeper pessimism about the future of these programs.

Under these difficult conditions, some of these practitioners continue their work in local communities. Some are fortunate enough to work in programs that give them considerable autonomy; they can do things such as helping to obtain the equipment mothers need to feed their children more easily—a high chair, for instance. Others simply take charge of their own activity, giving advice about food and also making referrals to the public library or a GED program. Some are bound by tightly regulated programs that mandate only particular kinds of help in particular circumstances. In these situations, they may sometimes step beyond the bounds of professional propriety. An African-American community nutritionist told me that she gets angry about the commercial foundations of the program she must implement, which she feels encourages some clients to believe that particular kinds of formula are essential for their infants' health. At times she speaks very directly to her clients:

> Sometimes I come right out and say, "You know, I just hate this." [Hitting a spoon against the table, and emphasizing each word] I say, "I hate this, I say, you don't need all this stuff."
>
> MLD: You say that to them?
>
> Yes, sometimes. I say, "You see this food guide. Most of our food guides—all of our food guides—have milk as the first thing." I say, "You know, the dairy industry is a powerful lobby." I say, "Milk is important." But I say, "Everybody can't even drink it, because people of color sometimes can't—you know, have that lactose intolerance."

She wants her clients to learn not only that milk is nutritious, but more important, "to manage their own stuff": to make their own informed decisions about how to keep their children healthy, rather than learning to depend unthinkingly on the products promoted through the program. Finally, some community nutritionists I interviewed during the 1980s and 1990s continue their political work outside of their occupational settings, by working with local groups, helping to run food banks and emergency pantries, testifying at legislative hearings, and organizing within professional organizations. These activities are organized by their conceptions of the professional mandate; they can be seen as individual expressions of a collective challenge to the dominant view of the profession.

My analysis of these stories highlights a challenge to one conception of science, an attempt by those working in local communities to "own" nutritional science. Toni Liquori's (1995) study of changing views of science and practice in the nutrition department at Teachers College provides another examination of a local version of this generational shift. She shows how, in some periods, faculty and students have been able to conceptualize food as "nurturance" (as opposed to more science- or industry-based conceptions of food as "nutrients" or "marketable products"). The challenges posed over these decades seem, in the 1990s, to have largely been absorbed and managed by dominant constructions of science and a medical model of nutrition work. Yet that dominant view itself is continually reconstructed in response to shifts in scientific and political contexts. Perhaps, then, we should see such changes in terms of an ebb and flow that includes the periodic reappearance of countertraditions within the professions, nurtured through periods of "doldrums" by networks of professionals who sustain alternative views.[7]

Conclusion: Claiming Our Own Professional Practice.

The career stories analyzed here point to recruitment and socialization to professional work as a process involving keenly emotional transformations of self. Though it has not been the dominant way of conceiving professional socialization, this idea is not entirely new. Virginia Olesen and Elvi Whittaker (1968) wrote about emotions in the professional socialization of nursing students; they suggest that an inner dialogue, in response to a series of depressions and elations, is key to the students' adjustment to the demands of nursing. More recently, feminist philosophers and social scientists have argued that emotion is always significant for knowledge production, and ought to be treated in a more focused way as a signpost to knowledge (e.g., Jaggar 1989; see de Montigny 1995 for a powerful account of becoming a social worker).

Feelings are rarely explicitly made part of the official curricula of professional training. Individuals living through the process of training and socialization often experience these moments in relative isolation. Furthermore, professional training often produces, structurally, a kind of isolation from family and community. Thus, as new recruits to professional life, we learn to suppress many emotions. If we are lucky, we find networks of colleagues and create spaces—more or less formally—where we can work on reconciling our hopes and fears with the demands of professional work.

My intention here is to effect a small version of such a reconciliation, both in my own writing and in my analysis of those I studied, by examining professional work in a way that opens the concepts of sociological study to admit more of the complex lived experience of women professionals. I have attended to aspects of professional socialization that I believe are too often overlooked: the actual pathways from women's lives and communities into professional identities—pathways that are always more complex than they might appear, as well as more contingent and more deeply infused with emotion.

I hope that this approach represents at least a step toward developing an honest and useful stance toward the group I study. I mean to suggest that my researcher's attitude toward the field of dietetics and community nutrition must include an openness to the heterogeneity of the field, and the various ways that nutrition professionals position themselves within it. Rather than conceiving practitioners one-dimensionally, as mere carriers of the dominant ideologies of their field, such a view would provide for analyses that hold in our range of vision the landscape of the field, the competing views of subgroups within it, and the struggles of individuals to locate professional selves within the constraints of both that larger terrain and their local situations. Further, and extending the metaphor of "mapping," it seems necessary to consider my own location in a neighboring county. The point is not just that nutritionists and sociologists operate in similar environments because we are professionals, but that our practices connect us: just as these community nutritionists "work on" the food lives of their clients, I "work on" their stories. We hope that our work will benefit those we "work on," but we are also tied to professional settings, with their particular constraints and demands. Acknowledging these connections does not provide any direct route to better practice, but it may help us to think more usefully about agendas and coalitions, and how our concerns might be aligned with those of women positioned differently in this complex of social relations.

Acknowledgments

Julia Loughlin, Linda Shaw, and Arlene Kaplan Daniels provided useful comments on an early draft of this paper. I am also grateful to Adele Clarke, Virginia Olesen, and other participants in the "Revisioning Women, Health, and Healing" conference for helpful responses to my work and the inspiration of theirs.

The question in my title alludes to the work of philosopher Sandra Harding (1991), who has been a leader in recent thinking about how feminists and other liberatory thinkers might transform science for their purposes.

Notes

1. Recent work in social studies of science, however, has revealed that this claim obscures a considerably "messier" and more complex practice and product (see, e.g., Latour and Woolgar 1979; Haraway 1989).

2. There are several ways in which existing feminist work on the professions has accomplished this kind of revision. Simply calling attention to the differences between historically "male" and "female" professions puts one kind of heterogeneity on the agenda (see, e.g., Stromberg 1988). Analyses of segregation and stratification within professions have also shown the differentiating effects of gender (Rossiter 1982) and race (Hine 1989). And studies that emphasize the struggle and contentiousness that always mark the process of professionalization (e.g., for nursing, Melosh 1982, Reverby 1987, Fisher 1995) work against monolithic accounts of any professional field.

3. For exceptions to this pattern, however, see Griffith (1995) and Biklen (1995) on connections between teachers and mothers.

4. Typical jobs in hospital settings involve individual diet counseling or food service management (though this part of the work is often, and increasingly, outsourced). Jobs in public health settings, usually community clinics, involve individual counseling as well, but may afford more opportunities for sustained nutrition education and community outreach. In nearly all settings, staffs are small and career ladders short; in a midsized hospital or a community clinic, for example, a "working director" might supervise a staff of three to six dietitians. Features of these "typical" jobs, as well as the range of less common settings for nutrition work, are discussed in more detail in DeVault 1995a.

5. All names are pseudonyms. I have provided individual identification for the three women whose stories I analyze closely here; there are also occasional references to others included in the study, who are not identified by name.

6. The WIC program (Special Supplemental Food Program for Women, Infants, and Children) is a U.S. government nutrition program that provides food subsidies and nutrition education for low-income women who are pregnant and for their infants and children.

7. I have borrowed this characterization from Rupp and Taylor's (1987) account of U.S. feminism during its relatively quiescent period from World War II until the 1960s.

References

Biklen, Sari Knopp. 1995. *School Work: Gender and the Cultural Construction of Teaching.* New York: Teachers College Press.

Collins, Patricia Hill. 1990. *Black Feminist Thought: Knowledge, Consciousness, and the Politics of Empowerment.* Boston: Unwin Hyman.

de Montigny, Gerald A.J. 1995. *Social Working: An Ethnography of Front-Line Practice.* Toronto: University of Toronto Press.

DeVault, Marjorie L., and James P. Pitts. 1984. Surplus and Scarcity: Hunger and the Origins of the Food Stamp Program. *Social Problems* 31: 545–57.

DeVault, Marjorie L. 1995a. Between Science and Food: Nutrition Professionals in the Health Care Hierarchy. *Research in the Sociology of Health Care* 12: 287–312.

———. 1995b. Ethnicity and Expertise: Racial-Ethnic Knowledge in Sociological Research. *Gender and Society* 9: 612–31.

Fisher, Berenice. 1990. Alice in the Human Services: A Feminist Analysis of Women in the Caring Professions. Pp. 108–31 in Emily K. Abel and Margaret K. Nelson (eds.), *Circles of Care: Work and Identity in Women's Lives.* Albany: State University of New York Press.

Fisher, Sue. 1995. *Nursing Wounds: Nurse Practitioners, Doctors, Women Patients, and the Negotiation of Meaning.* New Brunswick, NJ: Rutgers University Press.

Gilkes, Cheryl Townsend. 1983. Going Up for the Oppressed: The Career Mobility of Black Women Community Workers. *Journal of Social Issues* 39: 115–39.

Griffith, Alison I. 1995. Mothering, Schooling, and Children's Development. Pp. 108–21 in Marie Campbell and Ann Manicom (eds.), *Knowledge, Experience, and Ruling Relations: Studies in the Social Organization of Knowledge.* Toronto: University of Toronto Press.

Harding, Sandra. 1991. *Whose Science? Whose Knowledge?: Thinking from Women's Lives.* Ithaca, NY: Cornell University Press.

Haraway, Donna J. 1989. *Primate Visions: Gender, Race and Nature in the World of Modern Science.* New York: Routledge.

Hine, Darlene Clark. 1989. *Black Women in White: Racial Conflict and Cooperation in the Nursing Profession, 1890–1950.* Bloomington: Indiana University Press.

Howell, Mary. 1979. Can We Be Feminists and Professionals? *Women's Studies International Quarterly* 2:1–7.

Jaggar, Allison M. 1989. Love and Knowledge: Emotion in Feminist Epistemology. Pp. 145–71 in Allison M. Jaggar and Susan R. Bordo (eds.), *Gender/Body/Knowledge: Feminist Reconstructions of Being and Knowing.* New Brunswick, NJ: Rutgers Univ. Press.

Krieger, Susan. 1991. *Social Science and the Self: Personal Essays on an Art Form.* New Brunswick, NJ: Rutgers Univ. Press.

Latour, Bruno, and Steve Woolgar. 1979. *Laboratory Life: The Social Construction of Scientific Facts.* Beverly Hills, CA: Sage.

Liquori, Toni. 1995. Food Matters: The Influence of Gender on Science and Practice in the Nutrition Profession: An Institutional Ethnography. Ed.D. dissertation, Teachers College, Columbia University.

Melosh, Barbara. 1982. *"The Physician's Hand": Work Culture and Conflict in American Nursing.* Philadelphia: Temple University Press.

Olesen, Virginia L., and Elvi W. Whittaker. 1968. *The Silent Dialogue: A Study in the Social Psychology of Professional Socialization.* San Francisco: Jossey-Bass.

Reinharz, Shulamit. 1979. *On Becoming a Social Scientist.* San Francisco: Jossey-Bass.

Reverby, Susan. 1987. *Ordered to Care: The Dilemma of American Nursing, 1850–1945.* Cambridge: Cambridge University Press.

Rossiter, Margaret W. 1982. *Women Scientists in America: Struggles and Strategies to 1940.* Baltimore: Johns Hopkins University Press.

Rupp, Leila J., and Verta A. Taylor. 1987. *Survival in the Doldrums: The American Women's Rights Movement, 1945 to the 1960s.* New York: Oxford University Press.

Shapiro, Laura. 1986. *Perfection Salad: Women and Cooking at the Turn of the Century.* New York: Henry Holt and Company.

Smith, Dorothy E. 1987. *The Everyday World as Problematic: A Feminist Sociology.* Boston: Northeastern University Press.

Stromberg, Ann Helton. 1988. Women in Female-dominated Professions. Pp. 206–24 in Ann Helton Stromberg and Shirley Harkness (eds.), *Women Working: Theories and Facts in Perspective* Second edition. Mountain View, CA: Mayfield.

Thorne, Barrie. 1994. [Review of *Social Science and the Self*, by Susan Krieger.] *Gender and Society* 8:138–40.

Tobin, Debra S., Johanna Dwyer, and Joan D. Gussow. 1992. Cooperative Relationships Between Professional Societies and the Food Industry: Opportunities or Problems? *Nutrition Reviews* 50: 300–6.

(Re)Constructing
Experience

Searching the Self

Warning Signs

Acting on Images

SHARON TRAWEEK

Most of the people doing research on biomedicine and technoscience during the past twenty-five years have also been subjects of biomedical diagnosis. Our research has shaped how we live with our own diagnostic images and it has shaped how we intervene in their interpretations; those experiences and actions have shaped our research and writing. We diagnose technoscience and biomedicine; in turn, we are diagnosed. We are subject and object to ourselves; we have been objects of study for our research subjects. Our subjectivity as knowers and as objects of study is paralleled by our knowledgeable inquiries into the ways of knowing in biomedicine and technoscience; we are multiply informed. We know our subject intimately; we are knowing subjects.

We are in an excellent position to demonstrate and investigate just how knowledge is necessarily embodied and how embodiment shapes human knowledge. I am interested in why we have so steadfastly avoided writing about this intriguing intimacy. Why do we write and even conduct our research as if we did not know "in the biblical sense"? Pondering this denial has led me to rethink imaging, representation, strategic discourse, and engagement in technoscience/biomedicine and in our own research.

I have learned from speaking on this subject that many of us still want to insist that the distinctions between subjectivity and objectivity are simultaneously natural, normal, and obvious, and that they require vigilant defense. Many still believe that subjectivity is the name for unreflected experience and that objectivity is the proper name for carefully investigated claims adjudicated by qualified researchers. I must say that I am quite uninterested in writing to you here about anyone's unreflected experience, including mine, and I am quite eager to explore with you how we actually construct and investigate our claims and seek the adjudication of qualified experts. I think we could do it better.

Over the last twenty-five years our work has come to be read as authoritative, we have come to be seen as experts, and the fields of inquiry we launched have been situated in the curriculum for the next generation. We have challenged the assumption that patients, clients, and users have no useful knowledge. We have challenged the assumption that there is only one way of doing things right, that there is only one way to investigate our social worlds or to investigate the earth and the universe where we live. We have challenged some fundamental assumptions about the way knowledge is crafted. Some among us have made profoundly important and disturbing interventions in the very notion of what knowing is.

We have done all that without yet challenging the conventions about how we researchers go about convincing our peers about the veracity of our work. Specifically, I am exploring how our ways of knowing are constrained by our ways of writing. We have successfully learned to think and write in the passive voice and in the third person; we teach and enforce that, even as we know that those literary conventions have a very specific history, as does their enforcement. Obviously, I know that until variations in discursive strategies are better received by researchers, we and our students must perform those conventions. I am asking why and how we might begin to challenge such rules.

Exemplars

I offer two sets of exemplars from my current work. One is the tradition in anthropology of "life history studies" and "generational cohort studies" which focus on either one individual or one group to explore the ways changing political, economic, cultural, intellectual, gender, and related discourses and practices are embodied and enacted in one person's life or one cohort's history and vice versa. A Japanese friend and I decided in the late 1970s, while we were in graduate school in the United States, to begin doing a set of life history studies on ourselves, exploring our cohort. We have considered publishing a progress report on the first twenty years of this research during the late 1990s. Now at midcareer, we also decided to engage in a collaborative, comparative study of our own cohort, women physical, biological, and social scientists in Japan and the United States; we began that project in 1996. Later in this essay I will be reporting from life histories collected from such scientists.

My second set of exemplars includes Paul Fussell's *The Great War in Modern Memory* and Raymond Williams's *Keywords*. Fussell argues that popular narratives of the times, including songs, powerfully shaped both the experiences of soldiers during World War I and their memories of those experiences. Our generation, like any other, has used local cultural narratives to craft and to recognize ourselves and our bodies; recent generations have also used narratives that circulate globally. We Americans have scavenged from Dick and Jane readers to

Marilyn Monroe movies and Wonder Woman comics, from consciousness-raising groups nearly thirty years ago to the new NIH clinical studies of women's bodies, from films about Marie Curie to stories about Eleanor Roosevelt, as we make and remake ourselves and our work.

Raymond Williams noted that the political, cultural, and intellectual language of his friends changed so much during his absence in World War II that he could not engage in discussions with them until he had learned the new meanings for several hundred words. Since the late 1960s many women have been reading the research on medical practices, reproductive technologies, the comparative political economy of health care and its distribution, the social construction of knowledge in the health sciences, the dialogics of patient-caregiver talk, the use of images in the biological sciences, and the deployment of contested discursive strategies. The representation of women and our bodies in those images and discourses has shaped our understanding of our bodies. Furthermore, our bodies and their meanings have changed powerfully during the last thirty years because we learned new languages to explore our new bodies, just as Raymond Williams learned a new language to explore his familiar yet changing world.

There are other exemplars, too, for this project, including the massive research literature in cultural studies of bodies, situated knowledges, standpoint theories, subject positioning, feminist studies of narratives and language, and subaltern studies. To cite all that research would run to several thousand entries. There is also a very extensive literature on how our grammars, arguments, narrative forms, and literary styles are inescapably intertwined, whether we are writing for research journals, television, poetry, or our diaries. We know too the literature on how biomedicine and technoscience require institutions and infrastructures; we know how knowledge can be power. We know that facination with images and metaphors from science, technology, and medicine saturates public culture, and that those circulating images and metaphors also shape research, including our own.

Intimate Knowledge

Many women of my generation in science, technology, and medical studies have done research on the techniques and technologies, knowledges, and practices of reproduction. They include anthropologists, historians, sociologists, and philosophers, among others; a serious bibliography also would include several thousand entries. Some of these researchers are constructing new modes of inquiry and new modes of theorizing and new modes of writing for their work. It is often less well known to those who do not know them personally that they are, in addition to their considerable research, also working from what is usually called personal experience. If we thought about it for a few seconds, it would be clear that women between the ages of twenty and sixty-five would be likely to have some personal experience with obstetrics and gynecology. Of course, these researchers rarely note this so-called personal fact in their scholarly writing and speaking. We all learned long ago that in our formal writing and speaking we should never refer to the person doing research, the author, the speaker.

Why "of course"? Well, we all know that to mingle the personal and the intellectual, the experience of reproduction with the knowledge about reproduction, would be to violate some very old taboos of our trade. What are those taboos we absorbed so long ago? I know, you know, he knows, she knows, we know, and they know that for many of us it is our job to separate objectivity and subjectivity, our publics and our privates, the social and the personal, universals and particulars, the third person masculine generic and the first person singular. To be on one side of the line is to be in the right place to make knowledge and facts and methods and theories; to be on the other side is to be at home. We rarely ask ourselves what would happen if we were to theorize at home and with a different grammar.

Before continuing, I would like to offer two caveats. First, this essay is an attempt to pose questions; it is not a review of the literature. For that reason there will be few citations, although I do mention many research fields. Second, there are no confessions in this essay. I have come to realize that some readers and some audiences believe that when the first and second person pronouns are used that the text is somehow "confessional." There are no references in this text to any informant's emotions about our life events. However, in two narratives below there are diagnoses of "hysteria" by physicians; one is elicited by a joke and the other is an effort to explain physical symptoms as a psychosomatic manifestation of stress.

Actually, there is a separate argument that the content of our so-called personal, private, interior states, our sentiments and emotions, draws strongly from the social and cultural milieu in which we live our lives, just as our other kinds of thoughts do. There is considerable research literature on this point; one part of that research concerns the social construction of emotions. I have written, for example, about how at different stages of their careers, through a long process of sentimental education, American high-energy physicists come to have specific, strong emotions, such that they very much want to do what they should do, and do not want to do what they should not.

I am arguing here that we are conditioned by our education to believe that any violation of the canons of "objective" discourse means that the account is "personal" or "confessional." In what follows I have deliberately avoided using any references to emotional states of mind simply to expose the power of our own minds to supply those references and to believe that they are in the text. In this essay, I have explicitly used this strategy to emphasize that we academic researchers have been quite powerfully socialized [or acculturated] to be very uncomfortable even raising the question of how we differentiate subjectivity from objectivity. The intensity of our socialization is strongly correlated with the intensity of our desire to avoid this subject. It is almost impossible, paradoxically, for a fully initiated academic researcher to be willing to explore this subject rationally. This essay is about the intellectual constraints of that canon and the implications for our research; it is not about me.

I shall be writing here of "her body" and "our bodies," and I shall write of "his voice" and "her voice" as much as I will write about "their bodies" and "their research." I will write in the first person singular and plural; I will write in the second person singular and plural; I will write in the third person singular and plural. Try to notice which subject speaks the voice of theory and which subject has the voice of method. Where is the universal and where is the personal? Imagine a narrative composed of these words in the first person plural. Consider it a story of our cohort or a story of some friends. Or rewrite the story with these words in the third person plural, a story of another generation. Read these words in the third person singular as a singular case study or a story about your daughter, your sister, or your mother. Imagine these words spoken in the first person singular, as your story. Which voice has the theory? Where is the method? Where is the data? What are the images? What is the moral? What is lost? What is gained? What is our subject? What is our object? Who, then, speaks?

In what follows I will write of many research subjects: of violence and rape, poverty and plenty, mythical narratives circulated in films and reenacted by adolescents, welfare and shame, schooling for social security, birth control, clinical trials, infertility workups, Clomid, divorces and marriages, England, the United States, Japan, obstetrical devices, abnormally long fallopian tubes and tubal pregnancies, amniocentesis and chorionic villi sampling [CVS], ultrasound devices, uterine monitoring, pregnancy surveillance, positive results, negative results, genetic counseling, miscarriages, statistics, second trimester abortions, menopause mistakenly induced, induced labor, gynecological drapes, stirrups, cervical injuries, hemorrhaging, hysterectomies, hysteria, elderly primiparas, pregnant faculty, resident aliens, private clinics, university research hospitals, colonial medicine, geneticists, Down's syndrome, a fetus expelled, daughters and sons born dead, diagnostic debates, pregnancy losses, mammograms, biopsies, excessive success, multiple sclerosis, rituals, autoimmunity, histories of diseases and diagnoses, health benefits denied, images, monitoring, surveillance, physical sciences, biological sciences, and social sciences. We could include an extensive research bibliography for each of these topics. In the following cohort case history you will learn how people aware of all this research also encountered these researches as they were used by experts to narrate their bodies and their lives. In that site doubled with knowledge, could they think? Didn't you?

Cohort Biographies of (Re)Productive Lives

Most middle-class Americans thirty-five to sixty-five years old have had our bodies routinely monitored our entire lives, unlike our parents' Depression-bred cohort. All our lives we have lived with diagnostic images of our bodies; many of us have brain, dental, gynecological, intestinal, kidney, obstetric, skeletal, and spinal images of ourselves; we have X rays, CAT scans, MRIs, graphs, tables, and charts of ourselves, our parents, our children, our friends, our partners. We try to understand them and we act upon them. We are immersed in an unending history of interpretations of body images and stories of moral acts without closure. Our parents came to this surveillance late in life; our cohort could easily fill family albums with our diagnostic images and charts. (See the emerging histories of imaging in medical diagnosis.)

Rape

His mother's family suffered during the Depression of the 1930s; losing most of their property and most of their possessions, they fell several social classes. (From socioeconomic histories of the 1930s, we know that this family history was not unusual.) Later his mother reported that she had imagined herself traveling far, becoming rich, and then returning home to restore the family's property. (From the history of American depression-era films, we now know that this was a common cultural narrative.) Just before graduating from high school, she and a cousin sneaked away and drove west in his car. (From histories of the cultural politics and representations of cars in the United States we know this is another common American cultural narrative.) The informant is not entirely certain, but as best as he can tell, shortly after she arrived in the new city, his mother was raped; nine months later he was born. (From histories of rape we know that his mother's politics of silence were and are rather common around the world; so too is vulnerability in transit.) She avoided her family; her obstetric care was provided by public health services. The mother did not want her child born "on welfare," so her brother was summoned to pay for its delivery. (We now know that there was considerable stigma associated with welfare during the Depression.) She thought that if she had stayed at home and finished high school, none of this would have happened to her; she resolved that all her children would finish college. (See histories of the image of higher education in American culture.)

During the 1960s, while they were college students, two of her roommates were raped. (At the time they did not know how normal that was, nor did anyone around them; we now know that the college years are the most dangerous time in an American woman's life.) They did not get pregnant, because they were using birth control pills. They had gotten them very cheaply at a Planned Parenthood clinic in Oakland. (Having read Marcia Meldrum's history of contraceptive clinical trials, we know that they must have been part of those trials, their time using that pill translated into "woman-years" and situated somewhere in those statistics.) They did not know they were part of a research project; the idea of informed consent came later.

Infertility

Beginning in the 1970s, many in my generation got what are called full infertility workups. (See histories of U.S. infertility research and clinical practices.) Quite a few were diagnosed with a thick skin on their ovaries and were told to take

Clomid, widely characterized in the media as triggering multiple births. (See histories of infertility techniques and technologies.) We joked with the doctors that we wanted babies, not litters; they felt we had an attitude problem. (See studies of the representation of U.S. women patients as noncompliant, hysterical, "douchebags," and so on in the nineteenth and twentieth centuries.) In another infertility workup, an eminent specialist concluded that an informant's fallopian tubes were abnormally long; he wanted to surgically shorten them, so they would be statistically normal. When she refused, the physician wanted to send her to a psychiatrist. Many of us in the United States were divorced within a year of these infertility diagnoses. (See statistical studies of the correlation between serious reproductive difficulties and divorce for this generation in the United States; the rate has been between 75 and 95 percent over the past twenty-five years. A child's serious illness or death often has similar consequences in the United States.)

Self-Help

We joined self-study groups at public health clinics; we paid twenty-five cents for our own plastic speculums and we finally saw our own cervixes and our friends' too. (See the history of U.S. public health clinics and the history of U.S. women's self-help health groups.) Reading Nancy Henley, they learned the politics of their physicians' touch and learned how to remove the sheet over their knees that hid their gynecologists' gaze from them.

During the mid-1980s I was a patient at a private obstetrics and gynecology clinic near Tokyo in Japan. During my several visits there, all the other clients appeared to be Japanese middle-class women. Many Japanese women subsequently have told me that the examination procedure I am outlining describes their experience, too; that is, this is considered the normal procedure for gynecological examinations. I was led into a large room with other women; there were several examination tables. We all changed into cotton shifts, got onto the tables, and put our feet into the stirrups. There was a curtain hanging from the ceiling halfway to the floor; it bisected the room. We women were each wheeled up to the curtain by nurses until the bottom half of each of our bodies was on the other side of the curtain. We heard the doctor arrive on the other side of the curtain; he examined each of us in turn, speaking to each one. We could hear and see each other and we could hear the doctor talking to each of us and to the nurses, but we could not see the doctor. Later this resident alien explained to the doctor how unlike an American gynecological exam setting this had been, mentioning that in the United States doctors see patients in private rooms, perhaps with one nurse attending. He remarked that Japanese women were too modest for that U.S. practice.

Ultrasound

During the mid-1970s another informant in the United States chose the new amniocentesis procedure. She received the then-new genetic counseling and had the procedure done. Her scientist partner, who had accompanied her, was quite surprised at the low quality of the ultrasound imaging technology being used. (See histories of ultrasound technologies; see also research on the technological infrastructure of U.S. clinical practice and its funding.) Later her obstetrician, doing the then-new ultrasound monitoring of her pregnancy, found no movement in the image, and after a few more days of finding no movement in the image he said the baby was dead.

After hearing the alternatives she decided to wait until her body delivered the baby "naturally." (See histories of the various natural childbirth movements in the United States.) Some people told her she was morbid to carry a dead baby, now that it was legal to have the fetus aborted. Without the then-new imaging and other diagnostic technologies, of course, no one would have known the baby was dead until the miscarriage. (See the research literature on how ultrasound images have changed cultural discourses about pregnancy and pregnancy loss.) Home from the hospital, she got a call from the research hospital telling her that her baby boy was healthy, that the test results were "negative." (See the research on genetic counseling for different diagnostic outcomes.) Her obstetrician said he was confident the amniocentesis had killed the baby, but it would not contaminate the fine research statistics; they only counted miscarriages that began within seventy-two hours of the procedure. Within a couple of years three of her close friends had the same experience. (See the history of risk assessment and the history of statistical analysis of clinical practices. Can what counts be counted?)

Pregnancy Loss

Another informant lost her pregnancy after an amniocentesis. Her mother said, "I bet you are sorry you wrote those books when you should have been having babies." Her sister-in-law agreed. Many in the cohort of women under sixty have lived lives that are very different from their mothers'; we are just begining to write the histories of the shift in subjectivities that has accompanied the vastly larger opportunities in public life for middle-class women since the 1970s. We are also beginning to study the distribution of choices made in this cohort and the implications of the variation in their choices for the next cohort.

That informant's considerable grief for her lost pregnancy was then considered excessive by her friends, her partner, her family, and her doctors. She was having an experience that few before her could have had. Prenatal genetic testing became available at U.S. teaching hospitals about the same time that second-trimester labor inductions became legal. Research on the physical and psychological effects of second-trimester pregnancy loss became available about fifteen years later. By now there is a great deal of research on second-trimester pregnancy loss; it is now known that bodies can take eighteen or more months to recover from labor induced during the second trimester and that many women take about five years to recover emotionally. Most American obstetricians in urban areas now recommend that couples attend ongoing preganancy-loss support groups. (See the cross-cultural research on these support groups and their discourse.) The cohort of women who took those genetic tests between the early

1970s and the late 1980s and who experienced second-trimester pregnancy losses during those fifteen years did not know how common their difficulties were until the research began to be published in the 1980s. That pioneering cohort in the United States, the group whose decisions were not guided by research and whose experience had no authoritative narratives, would now be between about forty and sixty years old.

Genetic Testing

During the mid-1980s, after receiving a "positive" diagnosis for a genetic abnormality in her child, one informant asked for the proportion of Down's syndrome chromosomes in the results, since she knew that if only a few cells were affected, the child might have few problems. She seriously considered carrying the pregnancy to term, based upon her observations a few years earlier of a support group for parents with Down's syndrome. (See research on genetic counseling and on support groups for "affected communities" such as families with Down syndrome children.) However, her husband, a university-based researcher, was extremely opposed to raising a Down's syndrome child. He would not discuss this, but expressed his feelings by repeatedly imitating the movements of a child with cerebral palsy and speaking gibberish. She chose abortion and then divorce. (See the research on changing U.S. attitudes and laws concerning people with different physical abilities; see also statistics on the U.S. divorce rate among parents of children diagnosed with major physical difficulties.)

Prenatal genetic testing means that people now are presented with the necessity of making moral decisions in an utterly new moral domain. With the new diagnostic tests parents learn about possible genetic abnormalities before their child's birth, and they are offered the possibility of abortion. Generations before them did not face these choices, choices triggered by accessible diagnostic images; the very language of how to talk about this kind of choice had to be invented. By the 1980s many people were being confronted with another new moral choice: whether or not to prolong life for people who are not likely to recover from profoundly disabling injuries and illnesses. The language for exploring those choices also had to be invented. We are beginning to see the research on these inventions of new moral discourses in many different cultures. It is not often that the world gets new cultural discourses about birth and death, that one generation's experience of birth and death can differ so much from the last that a new way of talking about it must be invented.

Barren Mothers

Following a "positive" CVS result, an informant and her husband decided she should have an abortion. Her induced labor lasted a day and a half before the fetus was expelled. In Japan they would not say "the fetus was expelled"; they explained instead that her daughter would be born dead. You see, in Japan she had a baby and she has her daughter's death certificate. By law the baby had to be cremated or buried. Later she went to a Buddhist temple that specialized in prayers for never-born children. The reason the children were not born alive is irrelevant at the temple; they are to be remembered; they are counted among a woman's children statistically, socially. In Japan, then, she is a mother with three children, a son, a daughter, and a "water child" (born too early to know its sex), all dead. While teaching in the United States, one of her graduate students referred to our subject as "barren," and the teacher, startled by the agricultural metaphor in her postindustrial world and not yet adjusted to thinking like an American, said she was surprised that the label could be used to describe a woman who had borne three children. ("Barren" and "fertile" clearly refer to agricultural modes of production. See histories of later representations of women's bodies as mechanized manufacturing sites; in this discourse non-production, whether through infertility, miscarriage, abortion, stillbirths, or menopause, is regarded as malfunction.)

Hemorrhaging

While writing her dissertation she became pregnant. The options were bleak; abortion was now legal, and she chose one. Her heavy bleeding after the abortion led to hemorrhaging. After receiving her Ph.D. and getting a faculty position, she began to spend a lot of time in London. She woke one morning in her apartment there to discover she was having heavy vaginal bleeding, quite similar to that she had experienced after her abortion; her partner took her to the "National Health," where she encountered, for the first time, a woman gynecologist; the doctor's family was from India. (See histories of transnational circulations of public health personnel, such as the emigration of Filipino nurses to the United States and Indian physicians, especially women, to England.) The doctor said the bleeding could be a normal response to stress, but it could be more serious, so she suggested monitoring. The doctors at the American university where she was on the faculty suggested a hysterectomy; she went back to London, got monitored, and got better. (See histories of the significant national and regional variations in the rate of surgical interventions, particularly for breast cancer, hysterectomies, and Cesarean sections.)

Policies and (Re)Producing Careers

Many in my generation reentered graduate school and professional school when the climate for women students improved in the mid-1970s. As we built careers we asked our employers about their policies for pregnant faculty, doctors, and lawyers; they usually had considerable difficulty responding to what they took to be an oxymoron. Even now, early careers in the professions are still modeled on the image of a young man giving everything to his work, eighteen hours a day, from his undergraduate days until he gets tenure, joins a practice, or joins the firm; that usually happens between the ages of thirty-five and forty. The years from eighteen to forty are a woman's major reproductive years, as they are for men. (See the research on the so-called mommy track and the stigma associated with it; see also the research comparing men's and women's "productivity" in the sciences.) As more women entered demanding careers at the same age as men, the assumptions about reproduction and productivity in the workplace have become volatile issues.

Inducing Menopause

An informant was given drugs to control pain. Later, in consultations with a gynecologist about her menstrual periods having suddenly stopped, she learned that the neurologist had prescribed the same drugs gynecologists use to suppress ovulation. (The neurologist asked, incredulously, why gynecologists try to suppress ovulation.) She was also having hot flashes; they determined that the drugs had induced menopause; it was not reversible.

Cervical damage

While still a graduate student, an informant was told by doctors at a major research hospital that she had permanent cervical damage to her neck from an earlier car accident. Some advised that the deterioration could be slowed by wearing a brace the rest of her life; the head of the department said that if she were to train herself to have perfect posture at all times, she could go without the brace. About ten years later, while giving lectures at another university, she found herself numb on one side but able to move. A prominent neurologist at a major research and teaching hospital diagnosed her problem as hysteria, explaining to his students that this hysteria was due to what he called the stress on a middle-aged woman suffering from "an excessive level of success." (See research on representations of middle-aged women patients.) Another neurologist who knew the informant called the first doctor to say that the patient did not "somatize stress"; with this new information, the first doctor then ordered further diagnostic tests: CAT scans, MRI, spinal taps, and so on.

According to the doctors, those first tests and ones done two years later revealed that her neck, or cervical region, was damaged, just as the doctors had argued twelve years earlier after her serious car accident; furthermore, they said she had two of four signs of multiple sclerosis, now known to be exacerbated by the stress of pregnancy. Her neck's cervical region had joined her reproductive cervical region as a contested discursive site. (See the literature on contested discourses and discursive strategies.) Her current doctor is a young Asian-American woman at a prominent university research hospital who thinks this patient might be an interesting research subject, so she wants more diagnostic images and tests, but the patient's HMO requires that new symptoms emerge before the tests will be authorized. Her new doctor remains eager to enter the diagnostic discursive debates about the body with so many images.

Warning Signs

Do you think these accounts could be read as the autobiography of a scientist? Do they read like a medical record? Did you think that these informants have "confessed" something "personal"? Did you think these are just "stories"? There is a major problem with narrativizing lives and bodies and using those narratives to build theory among people who have been severely disciplined to use only the passive voice and the third person plural in their work, among people who have been strongly socialized to believe that all epistemological complexity is lost when one writes in the active voice and with first, second, and third person singular pronouns or even first person plural pronouns. If you are one of them, this narrative might have brought to mind whatever pop psychologies and do-it-yourself Freudianisms that are lodged there. The story might have elicited your sympathy; it might have triggered your anger; you might have felt a great distance from the subject. You might want to tell your narratives and show images of your body.

The narratives are from a cohort study, a study of people, a study of a generation. Consider my uses of the first, second, and third person singular and my uses of the first, second, and third person plural. The report was written in declarative, short sentences, hardly a compelling style of writing. Consider the research texts about bodies and resistance that are written in this body's story and that narrativize that life. Consider that my "report" contained absolutely no information about what anthropologists would call interior (psychological) states. All that you thought you read about "personal" responses to the social facts of these lives were projected from your own minds; it did not come from my textual accounts. Meanwhile, did you notice the theories, methods, data, and images in this account?

Acting on Images

I remember meeting an Aboriginal filmmaker in Houston at an event sponsored by the city's biannual international festival; that year Australia was being celebrated. He thought my research on physicists was a startling and very amusing reversal of anthropology. Besides filmmaking, his own work was the collection of all the data, including films and photographs, generated by anthropologists about Aborigines; these data were to be preserved in a museum run by Aborigines on Aborigine lands. As I mentioned earlier, most of us now realize that a great deal of knowledge has been generated in colonial settings; historians of science, technology, and medicine are just now beginning to write the history of the way colonies and colonized peoples were surveyed and scrutinized and revised in the name of European and North American science, technology, and medicine. We have many studies, too, of the way women everywhere have been surveyed, scrutinized, and revised in the name of European and North American science, technology, and medicine. I think it is about time we asked why we refuse to speak in passionate voices about what we have learned from our research and what we have done about it.

The people I have studied during the past twenty-five years talk all the time about passion, commitment, intuition, style, and their pleasures in the work they do. In fact, if people do not display enough of these qualities as they do physics and make ideas about the physics they do, they are not taken very seriously. As I have written elsewhere, those physicists bring their bodies to their labs; they need them to think. Many anthropologists have written a great deal about how people all over their world use sex for thinking; in particular, we use local ways of differentiating our sexuality as metaphors for other kinds of distinctions we want to make. Along with many others, I suggest that we begin to notice how we embody our theories and theorize our bodies, just as I ask how physicists embody their theories and theorize their bodies. I even think we should be methodical about these investigations of our embodied rationalities.

Through my body I have learned a very great deal about technoscience and biomedicine; so have you. Our third-person accounts in the passive voice do not allow us to report on what we have learned. That intellectual politics of silence constructs artificial barriers among our multiple ways of knowing. If we rejected that politics of silence, we would be obliged to report on what we have learned, how we have learned, and how our multiple ways of knowing are related to each other. We would have to write and think more carefully. We would have to raise the standards of research and argument. Our subject is too important to use the old conventions and traditional practices. In our current canonical ways of writing we must not and cannot ask these questions. I have deliberately written this as an essay in order to avoid the intellectual constraints required by the literary form of the journal article. As we feel our way through all these dilemmas and as we learn to write about our imaged, monitored, discursive bodies, I think we must explore how we can find patterns, make theories, write across the rules, and take action. Our research will be better; it will become more powerful and more important, too.

We need to write histories of those gaps in our arguments, those silences. Why have we slashed our minds from our bodies; why do we compulsively separate our ways of knowing; why do we deny that knowers have subjectivities? What did we think was at risk? The construction of those barriers and the containment of our risk are moral economies and personal questions and intellectual issues. Should we not investigate that activity? We all know our discursive sites are unstable and without closure; our lives are inconclusive discourse sites and they are without predicable endings. Does that mean that we are unable to think? How do we learn to make narratives about new kinds of images? What are our narrative ethics? Whose stories are we telling? As I construct my interpretations about these scientific, technical, and medical images, whose stories am I entitled to tell and whose images can I show? What are the research ethics and the narrative ethics if I ask whose story am I telling? Whose stories am I entitled to tell? Are there theories somewhere in my narratives of embodied images?

How are knowledge, politics, bodies, statistics, gender, race, and class made together? Knowing how to theorize memory, how do we challenge the politics of silence about the sexual violence in our lives and our mothers' lives? Who needs to know if there are theories and methods somewhere in the diagnostic images of our bodies? How do we all deal with the politics of expertise in the monitoring of our bodies? How do we go about constructing authoritative voices as researchers, as patients, as physicians? How do we make decisions about our bodies, as we must, when we can hear contested discourses and unstable interpretations without end? How do we console each other if we think we are living in an epistemologically and morally ambiguous world? How do we get access to the health care we want? How could we reconstruct the multiple political economies of health care constituting the practices in these stories?

As I feel my way through all these challenges, do research in new ways, and learn to write differently about diagnostic images and texts, I am theorizing messy worlds, transnational bodies. These can never be worlds of isolated and controlled variables, even if all those well-made images, monitoring devices, fluorescent lighted waiting rooms, clinical trials, and authoritative commentaries about our bodies lull us into thinking otherwise. We know how to make sense of the mess we are in; let's do it.

Postscript:

I am eager to acknowledge the detailed and thoughtful suggestions I received from Adele Clarke, Amelie Rorty, Merritt Roe Smith, and Sherry Turkle; this essay has certainly been strengthened by them.

The press has discouraged us from using footnotes; they probably prefer that the same format be used throughout this book, and most of the authors here are accustomed to a form that I do not use. I work in an academic tradition that finds text interrupted by bracketed proper names and dates quite tiresome, to put it mildly. Rather than collude with the press on this point, I have chosen to write here some very brief bibliographical notes, in lieu of footnotes, endnotes, or bracketed names and dates in the text.

Vincent Crapanzano's *Tuhami: Portrait of a Moroccan* (University of Chicago Press, 1980), Marjorie Shostak's *Nisa: The Life and Words of a !Kung Woman* (Harvard University Press, 1981), and Carol B. Stack's *All Our Kin: Strategies for Survival in a Black Community* (Harper and Row, 1974) are all compellingly written life histories.

Mariko Fujita Sano, associate professor, Anthropology Department, Faculty of Integrative Studies, Hiroshima University, is my friend and colleague with whom I have been working on our life histories.

Paul Fussell's *The Great War and Modern Memory* (Oxford University Press, 1975) and Raymond Williams's *Keywords: A Vocabulary of Culture and Society* (Oxford University Press, 1976) report on how the sensibilities and ways of thinking of a generation can shift abruptly.

Marcia Meldrum's "Departures from Design: The Randomized Clinical Trial in Historical Context, 1946–1970," a State University of New York at Stony Brook Ph.D. dissertation from 1994, and Nellie Oudshoorn's *Beyond the Natural Body: An Archeology of Sex Homones* (Routledge, 1994) both explore the birth control pill's clinical trials.

Nancy Henley's *The Politics of Touch* (Know, 1970) taught many of us to powerfully reevaluate all our doctor-patient relations. She argued the point more fully in *Body Politics : Power, Sex, and Nonverbal Communication* (Prentice Hall, 1977). See also the many histories of obstetric and gynecological practices.

Since the early 1970s I have been studying how experimental physicists using very high energy particle accelerators make and revise their ideas about the phenomenal world in their laboratories. I have explored their embodied rationalities and their sentimental education in *Beamtimes and Lifetimes: The World of High Energy Physicists* (Harvard University Press, 1988,

1992, 1995); "Border Crossings: Narrative Strategies in Science Studies and Among High Energy Physicists at Tsukuba Science City, Japan," in *Science as Practice and Culture*, edited by Andy Pickering (University of Chicago Press, 1992, pp. 429–65); "Bodies of Evidence: Law and Order, Sexy Machines, and the Erotics of Fieldwork Among Physicists," in *Choreographing History*, edited by Susan Foster (Indiana University Press, 1995, pp. 211–25).

In several recent articles I have been foregrounding the relationship between my own research practices and my "findings." In addition to the works cited above, see my "Unity, Dyads, Triads, Quads, and Complexity: Cultural Choreographies of Science" in *Science Wars*, edited by Stanley Aronowitz and Andrew Ross (Duke University Press, 1997); "Iconic Devices: An Ethnography of Images in Physics," in *Citadels of Science*, edited by Gary Downey and Joe Dumit [Santa Fe, NM: School of American Research Press, 1997]; "When Eliza Doolittle Studies 'enry 'iggins," in *Technoscience, Power, and Cyberculture: Implications and Strategies*, edited by Stanley Aronowitz (Routledge, 1996); "*Bachigai* [Out of Place] in Ibaraki: Tsukuba Science City, Japan," in *Scientific Imaginaries*, vol. 2 of *Late Editions*, edited by George Marcus (University of Chicago Press, 1995, pp. 355–77).

The Girl in the Cast

RUTH BEHAR

Five persons were killed early yesterday when an auto driven by a newly licensed teen-ager hurtled a dividing barrier on the Belt Parkway at the Pennsylvania Avenue exit and landed on top of an auto going in the opposite direction.

The dead included four neighborhood teen-aged friends, who were riding in the first car, and a 24-year-old Hofstra College senior, who was driving the other vehicle.

The police of the Miller Avenue station house in East New York said that the car in which the four teen-agers were riding was returning from a discotheque dance at Murray the K's World, a restaurant in Roosevelt, Long Island. . . .

The car hurtled the center island divider, a foot-high concrete curb topped by a three-foot metal fence. It landed on top of an auto traveling in the opposite direction operated by Joseph J. Venturino of 46 Radcliff Road, Island Park, Long Island. . . . With him was Miss Betty M. Saltz, a 20-year-old secretary employed by a motion picture firm. . . .

Mr. Venturino, with split-second timing, swung his car to the right to protect Miss Saltz and took the full impact of the blow, killing [him] instantly and trapping his body in the wreckage. Miss Saltz was taken to Brookdale Hospital and held there after treatment for a fractured right leg and left collar bone and multiple lacerations. She was reported in fair condition.

Three other autos, driving behind Mr. Venturino's car, piled into the wreckage. In the first car, Albert Behar, 32, of 141 65 85th Street, Jamaica, Queens, was driving with his wife, Rebecca, 30, a daughter, Ruth, 9, a son, Maurice, 10, and Mrs. Behar's mother, Mrs. Esther Glinski, 60. All were taken to Brookdale Hospital, where only Ruth was detained for a fractured right leg.

This story, with the headline "Five Die in Crash on Belt Parkway," appeared in *The New York Times* on Sunday, May 1, 1966 on page 48, next to an ad for emerald rings and brooches at Bloomingdales department store. What happened to the Behar family is a footnote to the story. What happened to Ruth is a footnote to the footnote.

After the accident my childhood ended.

I was told it was horrible. It was one of the worst car accidents in New York traffic history. *The Daily News* put the story on its front page.

My brother, who was actually six, not ten as the newspaper incorrectly reported, remembers seeing the car flying. It looked like it had wings. My grandmother remembers having to walk over dead bodies. My mother remembers that my grandmother kept screaming and screaming and clutching her heart. My father remembers stretching his arm across my mother's chest to keep her from crashing through the front window.

I didn't see anything. I barely remember anything. I was asleep on my grandmother's lap in the backseat. We were on our way home. When I awoke, I was all alone in the car. Where had everyone gone? I wanted to escape, too, but suddenly I could no longer walk. My right leg had swollen like a watermelon.

I heard my father's voice through layers and layers of distance. He was saying he had to get me out, that maybe the car would catch fire. At that moment, and this I remember vividly, I looked down at my left foot and noticed that my shoe was missing. It had flown out the window. What would I do now with only one shoe? I'd be sad like Cinderella. They were brand-new shoes, black patent leather shoes with little black satin bows.

"Papi, my shoe—"

But my father didn't go and find my shoe. He picked me up and pulled me out of the car. That was when I noticed the pain. That was when I began to cry and cry and cry. At Brookdale Hospital I was wheeled into the emergency room with Betty Saltz. I cried and cried and cried. A doctor there told me to be quiet already, that the woman next to me would be paralyzed for life, and that I should be happy I just had a broken leg.

I was not allowed to feel sorry for myself because it might have been worse, and I was not allowed to be angry with the young men who had caused the accident because they were dead. The adults kept telling me I should be happy.

Happy, happy, happy. It's just a broken leg. A femur bone broken in a few places, that's all. Imagine if the leg had needed to be cut off. Or, worse, what if I had ended up a vegetable? I had to be grateful.

And so the nine-year-old girl stopped crying. It was bad to cry when you were supposed to be happy.

I didn't cry when they wheeled me out of the operating room, reincarnated as a mummy encased in a body cast of thick white plaster. My parents thought the doctor had gone mad. So much plaster for a broken leg? Why hadn't he given me a walking cast? The doctor tried to explain in simple English that with a walking cast there was a risk of one leg growing longer than the other, leaving me with a permanent limp. He wanted to be sure my legs would grow at the same rate, and the only way to do that was to put them both inside plaster. I was going to have to be inside plaster for a long time and he didn't want to take any chances. My parents were not convinced by the doctor's explanations, but they were immigrants making only enough to pay the rent, so what else were they going to do? Two years later, when I was fully healed, they would bless the doctor many times over, but they took home very reluctantly the girl in the cast.

The cast began just below my unformed breasts, took in my waist and hips, and enclosed each leg down to my toes, the tips of which stuck out like little fish coming up for air. A pole linked my legs at the ankles. With that pole, the doctor explained, my mother would be able to turn me on my stomach at night to sleep. My head and shoulders could be propped up with pillows when I ate, or if I wanted to read a book. The rest of the time I was to lie flat on my back.

Just below my belly an opening had been carved out for my private parts. Suddenly, the parts of your body you were supposed to hide, and that as a girl you were supposed to keep tightly locked between your legs, were wide open to view. With the cast, my legs were spread shamefully far apart and fixed in place. Nothing except the bedsheets covered my torso. I learned to pull the sheets up to my shoulders and cling to them tightly when other children were in the room, fearing that in cruel jest they would pull them off and leave me exposed.

I still had a young girl's body, but I already knew that within me there was a woman's body waiting to sprout at any moment, just when you weren't looking. My mother had shown me her box of Kotex napkins and explained to me that in a few years I would become a young lady. I think she must have also tried to explain that once girls became young ladies they could have babies. And she must have hinted at how babies were made.

I remember, though I couldn't have expressed it then, that my attainment of sexual knowledge became connected in my mind to the car accident. The accident happened on our return home from Staten Island, where we had visited my mother's cousin Alma, who had just given birth to her second child, Miriam. At Alma's house I remember I overheard jokes I was not supposed to understand, and they had to do with what women and men did and how when they did it they sometimes had babies. Something about these jokes disturbed me and scared me, but I don't know what exactly. Soon after, we said goodbye, got into the car, and I fell asleep on my grandmother's lap. When I awoke I was a cripple.

For the chubby nine-year-old girl there were two terrible things about being immobile. I was, first of all, put on a strict diet. I cannot forget being denied a second bowl of spaghetti by my mother, who told me that if I got too fat I wouldn't fit in the cast. The cast became a tight chemise I could not take off, not even for a minute to let my hips run loose.

But more terrible yet than the diet was having to relieve myself in a bedpan. That meant that whenever I felt the urge I had to call for my mother. If my brother and my cousins were in the room playing, I had to announce to them to leave the room; otherwise, I wouldn't allow my mother to lift up the covers and slide the pan under me. Once, when she was busy entertaining friends in the living room, she didn't come fast enough and I had an "accident." I felt miserable knowing that everyone knew.

Perhaps because I was told that it was important to keep my body from bursting out of the cast, I became severely constipated. Or, maybe, being an invalid, my bowels seemed to be the only part of my body I could willfully control. My mother would bring in the bedpan and urge me to go, which was impossible so long as she stood waiting and watching. On one occasion, a week passed without my making a bowel movement. Keeping a secret has never been one of my mother's virtues. She spread the word to the entire family that Rutie was not making caca. Zayde, my maternal grandfather, whom I adored, appeared one day with a bottle of prune juice. When he poured out the juice it looked so dark and foul that it reminded me of excrement. My grandfather drank some to show me it was good, but when I tried to sip a little bit with a straw, I gagged and spit up into a tissue.

With his prune juice, my grandfather had tried to spare me the worse fate that my mother intended for me. Walking into the room with a determined look on her face, my mother meant to do something awful to get my bowels to obey. I pushed my mother away with all my strength, but with a quick turn of the ankle pole she had me flat on my stomach. Then she stuck in an enema. This was profoundly humiliating, profoundly violating, and my only comfort was to think of the excrement oozing into the bedpan as coming from someone else's body, not my own.

The public school sent a tutor to teach me and for a year I had private lessons in a wide range of subjects. My mother would serve us toasted English muffins at the start of the lesson and the tutor and I would work without interruption until midday. I came to enjoy those classroom sessions held around my bed as I enjoyed nothing else during my long convalescence. The days became bearable. It was wonderful to be the only student, to have a teacher all to myself, and I made tremendous progress in reading and math.

The accident took place just four years after we arrived in the United States as immigrants fleeing communist rule in Cuba. My father had brought into his exile a couple of pamphlets of Fidel Castro's speeches out of a bizarre sense of nostalgia, but we had no children's books or stories in English. Books were a luxury. The first goal had been to acquire a television. The second goal, a used car. During my year at home, the tutor filled my bed with English storybooks and I read voraciously. When I returned to school I was no longer a Spanish-speaking child struggling with English, but among the more gifted kids who would be steered toward "special progress"—SP—classes in junior high school. The accident spurred my assimilation.

I also discovered, about a year after I returned to school, that I could no longer see the biggest letter on the eye chart. During my year in bed, in which I always faced the same direction, always looked out upon a world that was no bigger than the bedroom I shared with my brother, my field of vision shrank. My eyes, not needing to take in the wider world, contracted until I could only see what was closest to me, the little world of my bed and my immobile body lying there, squeezed tight into its corset.

While writing this essay, I asked my mother if, indeed, she never thought to change my position, so I wouldn't always be facing in the same direction. She immediately became defensive, even annoyed, about my question. How was I going to change your position? You think the room was that big? How was I going to take you outside, when the doctor said you should not be moved? There was an edge to her voice. I was making her feel guilty. I decided I'd show her how grown-up I was. I'm not accusing you, I said to her in an even voice, I'm just trying to remember. But I was lying. Of course I was accusing her.

Our first summer in the United States, in 1962, we lived with my grandparents, crammed into their apartment in Brooklyn. They were both working in a fabric store, my grandmother earning five dollars less than my grandfather. My grandfather knew the owner from the days when he bought lace from him for his store in Havana. He got a job for my father and by the end of the summer we moved to our own apartment in Briarwood, a neighborhood of faded red brick buildings in Queens.

My mother was told Briarwood was one of the better neighborhoods in Queens, even though it was on the outskirts of Jamaica, a black working-class neighborhood where the overhead train used to roar above stores and houses like an angry thundergod. To my mother, the street in Briarwood that would now be her home seemed extremely ugly, but she figured she just didn't know what counted as pretty and what counted as ugly in America. My Aunt Silvia, my mother's older sister, was the one who knew. Not only was she already living in Briarwood, but she had married an American, my Uncle Bill. They had met by chance just before the Revolution, when he was visiting Cuba and seeking to date a nice Jewish girl. Bill knew New York like the back of his hand and he knew Briarwood was a step up from the Bronx. So, during our first years in America, the family reconstituted itself in one brick building at 141–65 85th Road. Silvia and Bill and my cousins Danny and Linda lived on the fourth floor, my grandparents lived on the third floor with my Uncle Micky, a teenager soon to be married, and my parents, my brother, and I lived on the sixth floor.

At the time of the accident we lived in a one-bedroom apartment. My parents slept on a sofabed in the living room and my brother and I shared the bedroom. The world became so reduced for me that I can only begin to imagine how the accident devastated my parents emotionally and economically. I know that my father worked two and three jobs, delivering rental cars and even fumigating apartments, to pay hospital bills and the costly trips to Brooklyn by ambulance for the X rays that were periodically done of my leg.

It later seemed to me that my parents might have been able to request more compensation. But I suspect they were insecure about their status as "aliens" in the United States, not yet having attained the necessary residency period to apply for citizenship. They were just grateful, I think, that they were innocent.

I was immobile for close to a year. The body cast, changed once, stayed on for nine months. Then for one month I had a trimmer cast on my right leg alone, but I was still confined to my bed. When I was released from the cast, a visiting nurse taught me to use crutches, first two, then one. The left leg had emerged from the cast looking like a hairy monster but it felt strong to me and, most important, it felt like *my* leg. Trusting my good leg, I mastered the crutches and could go anywhere with them.

But when I was told it was time to walk again with both feet planted on the ground, I simply refused to believe that my right leg could sustain me. It didn't feel like my leg; it hung there limp, thick as molasses, unbending and foreign. How was I supposed to tell it to walk? No, it would never work. Never! And so I took my bed again, to the despair of everyone around me.

There are some things my mother said to me when I was a child that got branded into my soul as though they were hot iron. During the period when my fear of walking was at its peak, she flung some of these hot iron words at me. I imagine that by that time, after cleaning out my bedpan for a year, she had endured about all she could manage. As my mother busied herself changing the sheets of my bed, she began to talk about how soon I would be *una mujercita* and going to parties and dances. The boys, she blurted out, were going to see that from the waist up I was a pretty girl, but, wow, were they going to be disappointed when they saw what I was like from the waist down. She then went on to say that at the rate I was going I would grow up to be just like Abuela, my father's mother, who was very fat and sat in her chair all day and seesawed when she walked and what a shame, with her face so pretty. . .

The first nurse quit and said I'd never walk. Then they sent another nurse. She told my parents to let her handle me. What I needed was to be treated mean and hard. If they kept on pitying me, I'd be an invalid for life.

It wasn't just that I feared I would fall flat on my face and break my leg again. There was something I found even more unsettling: I simply could not, for the life of me, remember how to walk. Every shred of memory of how people did it— how they stood, moved one foot forward, then another, and got somewhere— had been erased. I begged the tough nurse not to force me to walk. I told her I wasn't ready, to please understand how afraid I was, to please wait just a little longer. And maybe, as my great-uncle recently said to me, I did need a strong push to get me walking. But how I wish I had been urged to stand on my own two feet again with just a touch more gentleness, a touch more loving kindness.

After I relearned how to walk I had a heavy limp that gradually went away with a long routine of physical therapy. It was at the Continental Avenue bus stop, as we walked together to the physical therapist's office, that my mother announced that my Uncle Micky and Aunt Rebeca were expecting a baby. By then I was certain that the knowledge I had intuitively grasped before the accident was resoundingly true. And do you know how people have babies, my mother asked me. Yes, I said, hoping she wouldn't ask me to explain it aloud. But she wanted to be sure I understood, and she started saying, *"La cosa del hombre y la cosa de la mujer . . ."* (The man's thing and the woman's thing . . .)

Yes, I know, I know, I said. And we kept walking.

I kept a diary during sixth grade that ran for about eight months in 1968. All I remembered of the diary was that it locked with a little key and that my mother had managed to pry it open once and find the boy's picture I had stashed inside. Recently, I asked my mother to look for the diary, and it turned up in a box in her attic. My mother reported that the diary was still locked, but that it had apparently been torn open at some point; it was sealed with thick black tape, and the key was lost. Should she open it, she asked. No, I said.

The diary is bound in a red fake leather, the pages have gilded edges, and it is small. I hold it in my hands for a few moments before I tear it open. I wonder whether the eleven-year-old girl will have much to say about what happened to her two years before. I only find two entries that refer to the accident. On January 21, 1968, I write to "Cheryl," the name I have given to the diary: "Today we went to Manhattan and then to this place where older people meet where my grandparents gave me a little party in my honor because I am well now. I'll tell you about my car accident one of these days!" Then on February 1, I report: "Now that I have time I'll tell you about my terrible car accident on April 30, 1966 where I broke the femur bone on my leg. Everybody else had practically nothing. Morrie had stitches on his head and so did Pappy. BYE FOR NOW." Not another word of the accident in those pages. The only intimation that the healing process has been thorny is an entry from July 26: "Mommy, me and Morrie went to Manhattan. Going down the stairs [of the subway] I sprained my foot. It was terrible. I even cried in front of Pappy's secretaries. Now I feel terrible."

And yet, while the accident is notably absent from the day-to-day recording of events, the lack of self-assurance of the eleven-year-old girl is so stark that it becomes the major theme of the diary. On February 11, I write, "Today the Perkals came over. We had delicious Cuban sandwiches, tempting doughnuts, and what is called in Spanish *'panetela borracha,'* a drunk cake. We played Monopoly and bingo. Morris got my guitar out of tune. Pappy always blames everything on me. I bet he doesn't like me." On February 22, I note, "Mommy doesn't like me so much. She thinks I'm so mean." Again, on March 18: "Pappy gets mad at everything now. I really don't know what's happening to this family. He wants me to be Miss Perfection and compares me with everybody. Boy, can't he take me the way I am?"

It soon becomes clear that the tension in the family—which I, at age eleven, am interpreting personally as a withdrawal of affection from me—stems from my parents' plans to move out of Briarwood as soon as I finish sixth grade. On April 30, the anniversary of the accident, I write, "Mommy and Pappy are now American citizens," which suggests that their status in the United States is finally secure. At the same time, it seems clear that they are apprehensive about whether they have attained the means to relocate themselves more firmly within the white middle class. The May 17 entry notes: "There is a plan that we, the 5th and 6th graders, in September will have to go to IS-8 in South Jamaica." Our public school in Briarwood was primarily white, with black students being bused in from Jamaica. Now white children were going to be the ones bused into black schools. And my parents, aware that by age eleven I am already a menstruating *mujercita* about to start junior high school, begin to dream of moving to Forest Hills, where the influences will be better, more white and more Jewish.

My mother explains that we need to move *porque se está echando a perder el barrio,* because the neighborhood is getting bad (literally, as in referring to over-ripe fruit, "beginning to rot"), code language for saying blacks are moving in. I wonder now: Where do my parents learn their racism? In Cuba, a black woman cared for me, shared a bed with me, took me out to lunch with her to eat Chinese food. But in the United States I grow up with a raceless image of Cuban culture, a bleached-out version of the culture, listening to Beny Moré, Pérez Prado, and Celia Cruz, but not knowing they are black. That in the United States my parents, with their thick accents, are often taken for Latinos, and therefore suffer many of the same humiliations as other people "of color" (like getting bad service at restaurants and being stared at in elevators because they are speaking Spanish), somehow becomes irrelevant. We are determined to become white, at least as white as other Jews.

But the apartment hunting seems to have been very stressful. I note on May 5: "Hebrew school was okay. Mom and Pop went looking for apartments and left me and Morris at the movie the Double Man with Yul Brenner. It was great. Pappy was in a pretty bad mood." On May 28, I note, "About the apartment, Mommy and Pappy have been arguing about it. Now Pappy gets angry at anything. I don't know how he can be so mean." On May 29: "Mommy and Pappy are still angry. Pappy is really being mean to Mommy." And again on June 1: "Pappy was in a bad mood just because I didn't give him a kiss!" And then on July 1: "Well, here we are at our new apartment. Mommy looked so nervous. I hope she gets better quickly. I helped a lot with the cleaning."

The new apartment was much nicer than our old one in Briarwood. It had a huge picture window that looked out at the remains of the 1964 World's Fair in Flushing Meadow Park. My parents furnished it in the most modern style of the day, with lots of glass and chrome and mirrors. But I knew that it was not quite the apartment my mother had longed for. She had her heart set on one of the bigger apartments that were like houses, with two floors, and three bedrooms upstairs. My father said they couldn't afford that kind of apartment; it was already going to break his back just to pay for the two-bedroom apartment.

In the new apartment I entered into my adolescence. There, the migraines began, but I didn't yet know my condition had a name. What I knew was that a few times a month a dark shadow fell over my life.

The body doesn't forget.

I learned to walk again, but that old fear never quite went away. It was years before I could run. It was years before I took possession of my legs. I would see people with a leg missing, or in a wheelchair, or hobbling along with one big-heeled shoe and one little-heeled shoe, and I would see myself in them. I would think: That's you, that's you, except you they forced to walk, you they pushed out of bed. Not until after I had given birth to my own child did I begin to regain confidence in my legs. In my early thirties I began to exercise. I enrolled in an aerobics class. After a few years, I found, to my surprise, that I could move grace-fully, that my legs worked just fine. Soon I was in the aerobics class with the most challenging teacher, the one who used a lot of difficult dance routines. I had got-ten so good that I no longer hid in a corner in the back of the room, but staked out a spot for myself at the front of the class with the other accomplished women.

And then, in 1991, the day after I turned thirty-five, while I was at the front of the room doing an especially jumpy dance number, I turned my eyes to the mirror to catch a glance at my feet. That was all I did. The next minute I felt dizzy, strangely out of it. I stopped immediately and in a daze went and sat down on the wicker chair with the tropical print cushion, next to the table with all the magazines about how to achieve the right body. The odor of sweat struggling with deodorant filled my nostrils. I became so nervous I felt certain I would never be able to get home alone. I called David, and he and Gabriel came to pick me up.

After that, things went downhill. When I went back to aerobics a few days later, just lifting my arms brought on the feelings of dizziness and doom. I felt I had to get out quick—as though an alarm were going off inside me. I ran to the locker room and frantically pulled off my exercise clothes. Come on! Quicker! Everything was racing inside me. This time, I told myself, I would get home alone, no matter what it took. I got into the car and drove off. Faster! Faster! All the familiar streets spun around me. I refused to pay attention. Optical illusions. Just keep driving. Don't look. Keep your eyes straight ahead.

If only my heart hadn't started to tear like a sheet of paper, I wouldn't have had to stop. I might have made it. I slammed on the brakes just as I felt myself passing out.

I was only five blocks from my house. I wanted to scream, but I needed all my energy just to be able to breathe. "Someone save me!" I wanted to yell, but I couldn't get the words out.

A young man in a black leather jacket and tall boots was coming out of the house in front of which I had parked. I waved him over. "Could you drive me home?" I asked in a small voice. He gave me a funny look, but he got into the car. I had already moved over to the passenger seat. "Just turn and go straight five blocks," I said, letting my head fall into my hands. Maybe this man is a rapist, I thought, but I've got to get home somehow. He drove me to my house, the Wedgwood blue Victorian house filled with antiques and Mexican pottery bought with my own money, and he said it had been no problem and that he'd walk the five blocks back.

In a matter of days my body shut down. I began to feel terribly, terribly tired and terribly, terribly agitated. I had no idea what was wrong with me. Neither did the doctor. But when I told him I planned to go to a big anthropology conference two days later, where I had three speaking engagements, he said he thought it would be much wiser for me to stay home and rest. Without my asking, he filled out a disability form. I'll go anyway, I thought, I can't be that sick. But when the day came, I could barely get out of bed. And that same day David and Gabriel were leaving for Texas. They planned to visit David's parents, frighteningly nice white retired schoolteachers with a heavy southern drawl, from whom I have studiously kept my distance to protect myself—as I see it—from being swallowed up by their Americanness. It had seemed like a perfect plan: I'd spend a weekend at my anthropology conference in Chicago and they'd spend a weekend in Dallas. We'd go to the airport together, take separate planes, and then meet up again a few days later. Instead, I ended up staying home in my bed. I was fortunate that three women friends checked in on me during that hellish weekend when fear, deep and unspeakable, became my most constant companion.

At the time, I felt myself racing against the clock to finish my book, *Translated Woman*, about the life story of a Mexican street peddler. It was already late November and I had set a final deadline for myself to have the book completely done and in my editor's hands before I left on a two-week trip to Cuba at the end of December. The trip to Cuba had me extremely worried, and though I desperately wanted to go, another part of me wanted to just pull the covers over my head and forget the whole idea. I would be traveling with David and leaving Gabriel behind with my parents, who had heightened the worry level by saying that I'd be lucky if Fidel Castro let me return home. My parents even demanded that I write out a will and leave them custody papers for Gabriel. Nothing scared me more than the thought of never again seeing my son, who was almost five, the same age I was when we left Cuba.

Like other children taken into exile in the United States after the Cuban Revolution, I had grown up internalizing the cold war between the United States and Cuba. I had absorbed both the Cuban immigrant paranoia about Cuba as a dangerous place, best left behind forever, and United States ideology about Cuba as an enemy and a threat. There was also another issue for me, as a Cuban Jew. I kept asking myself what exactly I hoped to find in Cuba. After all, the members of my family were immigrants in Cuba, too. My grandparents, Jews from Byelorussia, Poland, and Turkey, had immigrated to Cuba in the 1920s, after the United States set sharp limits on Jewish immigration. All of my homelands, it seemed, were lost.

To calm these worries, I got into bed with my book manuscript, spreading the various versions of the text all around me. I decided that either I would finish the book or the book would finish me. But I soon discovered that I felt uncomfortable in any other part of the house except for my bedroom. I took to bringing up a tray in the morning with water, rice, and ginger cookies, the only things I seemed to have an appetite for, which I nibbled on in the course of the day. I couldn't stand on my feet for long without getting dizzy, and I would return to my bed out of breath just from going up and down the stairs. I cursed myself for having wanted such a big old house with two floors—the very kind of house my parents had been unable to achieve when I was growing up. The only room I could bear to be in, my bedroom, was the smallest room in the house. I retreated to that room as though I were the littlest woman in a nest of Russian dolls.

After David and Gabriel returned from Texas, I saw the doctor once more. This time, just sitting in the backseat as David drove to the clinic precipitated a flood of heart palpitations. As soon as I entered the clinic, my legs began to feel like Jell-O and I asked for a wheelchair. And this time, the doctor came up with a diagnosis: My body was physically depressed and I needed an anti-depressant to snap out of it. The medication would cause drowsiness and blurry vision, he said, but it would help in the long run. Dizzy as I was, I asked a million questions. Isn't it silly to take a drug that will make me tired when I'm already tired? Won't I get better just with rest and a good diet? Do I really need a drug? Casting hard blue eyes on me, the doctor replied that he knew from clinical experience that people like me took years to recover without a drug.

He turned his back and began filling out more disability forms. I had told him I was planning a trip to the Caribbean the following month. I didn't tell him it was Cuba I planned to visit. He'd think I was a communist. And then who knows what he'd prescribe? He said I would not be strong enough to undertake any travel for a long time. I paid my bill and David wheeled me to the outer office. Gabriel, who had been hyperactive during my visit to the doctor, running up and down the hallways like a wild boy, refused to put on his coat. As David would approach him, he would run away and laugh. Tired of having two children to care for, David suddenly fell apart, crying and scolding Gabriel at the same time. Soon Gabriel was crying and screaming at the top of his lungs. Everyone in the waiting room watched in horror. I sank into the wheelchair. Still crying, Gabriel finally wriggled into his coat and climbed onto my lap. David wheeled us both to the car. My legs hung down from my body like marionette legs. I had no strength left in them anymore.

During the weeks before I came to an understanding of what I was experiencing, I lived in a space of terror. A phone call to a psychiatric emergency number finally provided a ray of light: I had gotten caught in a spiral of anxiety and had developed agoraphobia as a result of confining myself to my bed. Once I understood my condition, I could begin to get well. I read various books on anxiety and learned how common panic attacks and agoraphobia are in women, especially contemporary women, who, as Carol Becker has written, "live in . . . a state of expectation, fearful about 'struggling for autonomy,' waiting anxiously for the ax to fall. . . . They expect to pay some price for the upheaval they have caused, yet are uncertain what the cost might be or what form of punishment they might be subjected to. Often the punishment is nothing more nor less than extreme, amorphous, and unrelenting anxiety. . . . Anxiety is an emotion of conflict—mind and body, internal and external reality, child self, adult self. . . . Anxiety will always accompany the unknown. It is an unwanted but unavoidable catalyst to change."[1]

Empowered by this knowledge, I finished my book. And I was able to push the terror back and go to Cuba, despite the doctor's advice and my parents' paranoia, and return, safe and sound and inspired. I dropped the doctor with the hard blue eyes, though not without writing a letter of complaint to the head of the clinic.

Exposure therapy, my self-help books claimed, was the best method for getting over panic attacks and the phobias they tend to set off. To conquer fear, return to the very sites that scare you, engage in the very things that chill you to the quick. For me, this meant going back to my aerobics class, where it had all begun.

At first, I was afraid to go alone, so David came with me. I found I could still do all the routines perfectly, but the room seemed to be spinning around me. I looked at myself in the mirror and felt a strange dissociation from the woman who was swinging her arms and legs about to the tune of the music. Exposure therapy, I kept saying to myself. Hang in there. I got through that class okay. Confident, a few days later I returned with David for another class.

Everything was going well and my inner voice was saying all the positive things it was supposed to say. You're doing fine, you're doing fine, you're not that nine-year-old girl anymore, your legs are healed, you can dance, you can do anything you want, you're doing beautifully. The room spun around me, but I kept moving. And then suddenly I had the sense I was in the ocean and being knocked down by the waves. They were pushing me down, deep into the water. I was nine again and crying, doing the aerobics and crying. I was seeing the darkness and the car flying over the divider. I was hearing the crash of broken glass and the moans of young men dying. And I was saying to my parents that I forgave them, that I wished they could have saved me, but I understood they had done what they could. Then I had to stop. The teacher told me to keep walking, not to sit, and I went off to the locker room, with David following, and paced back and forth, back and forth, until my heart settled itself. Then I cried and cried and cried for the nine-year-old girl who didn't get out all her tears and for the thirty-five-year-old woman who desperately needed her husband's shoulder because she'd grown afraid of her own life.

It was unbelievable to me that I could have a perfect intellectual understanding of my illness and still find it so difficult to physically carry out the tasks I set for myself. I was astonished at how difficult it was for me to get into a car again. I would become so breathless I had to roll down the car windows all the way in the height of winter to feel I had enough air. Weeks passed before I would get behind the wheel. Finally, I did it, and from then on I forced myself to be the one to drive to wherever David, Gabriel, and I needed to go. Being able to drive by myself was more of a struggle, but that, too, eventually became possible for me again.

Through all of this, I thought of my mother. For years and years after the car accident, she would clutch the sides of the car whenever my father slammed on the brakes or hit the accelerator to pass another car. He would become furious at her for her nervous reactions, saying they made it impossible for him to drive calmly. How sorry I felt for her at those times.

My mother's deepest desire, now that she and my father live in a tree-lined neighborhood of small brick houses, is to get her driver's license and be able to drive. She has taken some driving lessons, but she can't quite muster the courage to get behind the wheel. Every time I see her, she tells me that this year she's going to drive. She's promised it to herself. *Sin falta,* she says, no matter what it takes, and she looks at me with the saddest eyes.

I had always known that one day I would tell the story of the car accident. And yet I kept censoring it, wanting to remain loyal to the adult injunction not to make too much of the whole thing, to insist that it could have been much worse. I would tell friends about the accident and my broken leg, and found that I'd get irritated if they showed too much sympathy for the girl in the cast. I certainly had no sympathy for her. She had been a crybaby and a coward and I was ashamed of her. Not until my unconscious restaged, so many years later, the memory of my confinement to my bed and the dread of having to stand on my own two feet, did I begin to feel empathy for the young girl I had been.

A fuller empathy came afterward, from the stories and interpretations I read to try to understand why the girl in the cast had resurfaced. If, as Alice Miller argues, coming to terms with one's childhood is a process of mourning, of "giving up the illusion of the 'happy' childhood," I needed to find others with whom to share my grief (Miller 1990).

One text that spoke to me immediately was an essay published in 1959 by the psychologist Marjorie Leonard, which explored the case of a two-and-a-half-year-old girl named Nancy, who had developed an intense fear of walking after recovering from a leg fracture caused by her fall from a kitchen counter. The cast stayed on Nancy's leg for only three weeks, but when it was removed she refused even to stand up and would cry bitterly if coaxed, urged, or scolded to try walking. Nancy's parents said she had been "a gay little girl before the accident," but afterward, "she appeared continuously unhappy, whined and cried."

Marjorie Leonard, working with Nancy as a Freudian psychoanalyst, came to the conclusion that the girl's fear stemmed from inner conflicts about her hostile feelings toward a younger brother who had just been born at the time of her accident. After play therapy, in which Nancy was able to act out her aggression on a set of dolls, including castrating the male doll, Nancy started to walk again, although cautiously and with a limp. As Marjorie Leonard astutely notes, "With the magical thinking common to children at that age, Nancy must have believed that her 'bad' impulses were perceived by her parents and that they had let the accident happen in order to punish her. . . . To resume walking meant being faced with the possibility of committing an aggressive act" (Leonard 1959).

No one thought to call in a psychoanalyst to figure out why I was afraid to walk. I suppose such behavior would have been structurally impossible for people of our class and immigrant status. But I can't help thinking that maybe at two and a half they would have taken pity on me and not pushed so hard to get me to walk before I was ready. But the young girl, soon to become a *mujercita*, inspired only impatience.

Of course, I recognize that, in the end, I was lucky. Lucky because I healed well. Lucky because the doctor took not only my broken leg seriously, but my future seriously.

I suspect things would have turned out differently had my skin not been white. Henry Louis Gates Jr., the African-American literary critic, was not so lucky. At the age of fourteen, he incurred a hairline fracture of his leg while playing touch football. Unaware of the fracture, Gates continued to use the leg until the ball-and-socket joint of his hip finally tore. The white doctor who attended to him, in the Appalachia of 1964, mistakenly diagnosed his injury as a torn ligament in the knee and decided to put Gates in a walking cast. While plastering his leg, the doctor engaged the young Gates in a conversation about his future. Gates wanted to be a doctor when he grew up. So the white doctor thought he'd throw him a couple of tough questions. But Gates knew all the answers; he knew who discovered sterilization, who discovered penicillin, and who discovered DNA. Gates recalls that he thought his answers "might get me a pat on the head. Actually, they just confirmed the diagnosis he'd come to." And Gates goes on to describe how racism had everything to do with what happened to him and his leg:

"He stood me on my feet and insisted that I walk. When I tried, the joint ripped apart and I fell on the floor. It hurt like nothing I'd ever known.

The doctor shook his head. 'Pauline,' he said to my mother, his voice kindly but amused, 'there's not a thing wrong with that child. The problem's psychosomatic. Your son's an overachiever."

Although Gates' mother immediately transfered her son to the University Medical Center, the damage had already been done. In years to come, Gates would limp through college while suffering from severe pain as the joint calcified, shortening his leg. Only at the age of forty, as a prominent man of letters, did he have hip-joint surgery to lengthen his leg. At last he was able to throw away his bricklike orthopedic shoes. But because a white doctor had presumed that "a colored kid who thought he could be a doctor was headed for a breakdown," Gates spent twenty-five years wondering how it feels to wear real shoes (Gates 1990).

Oliver Sacks' book *A Leg to Stand On*, an account of his recovery from severe damage to his leg during a solitary mountain climb in Norway, sat unread on my bookshelf for years. After reencountering the girl in the cast during aerobics, I knew the moment was ripe to read Sacks. As I expected, the book shed light on my experience. Both as a patient himself, and as a doctor questioning other patients, Sacks learned that almost anyone who injured a limb, "and whose limb had then been casted, out of sight, out of action, had experienced at least some degree of alienation: I heard of hands and feet which felt 'queer,' 'wrong,' 'strange,' 'unreal,' 'uncanny,' 'detached,' and 'cut off'—and, again and again, the phrase 'like nothing on earth.'" Sacks writes eloquently of the difficulty of repossessing alienated limbs, especially in a medical context where healing is supposed to occur as soon as the injured limbs have mended. And yet healing calls for more than a physiological mending; it calls for a full restoration of one's sense of being in one's body and in the world. Immobilized and bedridden, the patient succumbs to prisoner syndrome, in which visual space contracts, together with the whole of one's existence. Getting better involves not just being able to use the injured limbs again, but regaining the freedom to emerge "from self-absorption, sickness, patienthood, and confinement, to the spaciousness of health, of full being, of the real world." To stand confidently on one's own two feet, the posture of humanity for millennia, becomes for Sacks the symbol of full recovery: "the motions of uprightness, that physical-and-moral posture which means standing-up, standing-up-for-oneself, walking, and walking-away—walking away from one's physicians and parents, walking away from those upon whom one depended and hung, walking freely, and boldly, and adventurously, wherever one wishes" (Sacks 1984:161–62, 156–57, 134–35).

I cried reading these passages. And I really do mean cried. Like *la llorona*, the Weeping Woman of Mexican lore, who is said to weep for the children she abandoned, I wept with fury, wanting to retrieve the child I once was and give her the understanding, the words, the knowledge, I now had. Reading about the terror Sacks experienced after only three weeks as a patient, I imagined the terror of being nine and immobile for almost an entire year. Here was Sacks the neurologist, a man with credentials, bravado, an array of psychological, physiological, and perceptual concepts, and there was I, a child, disempowered, disembodied, lacking the language to clarify my pain.

But it wasn't just for the child that I cried; I wondered, too, about the grown-up woman reading Sacks. I wondered whether the world was as wide open and boundless for her as Sacks seemed to think it was for himself. It would never have occurred to me to go off alone to climb a 6,000-foot mountain in Norway without telling a soul about my whereabouts.[2] I would never want to be that alone in the world. And as a woman, I can't walk freely, boldly, and adventurously, wherever I wish. I just don't feel that safe. The girl in the cast grows up to be a woman in a cast.

"Perhaps women have forgotten girls," writes Carol Gilligan in an essay about her work fostering "healthy resistance and courage" in girls on the edge of adolescence. Her conversations with girls just beyond the sixth grade suggest to Gilligan that the threshold between girlhood and womanhood is a time when girls are pressured to become disconnected from their bodies, their anger, and their knowledge. "On a daily basis," Gilligan asserts, "girls receive lessons on what they can let out and what they must keep in, if they do not want to be spoken about by others as mad or bad or simply told they are wrong" (Gilligan 1990). And so, at this age, girls lose confidence in themselves and begin to delegitimize their voices and perceptions. They fear that if they speak what they know they will be excluded from relationships, left unbearably alone. Under these circumstances, girls choose to not know what they know, beginning already the process of silencing the self that is so emblematic of women's depression (Jack 1991). For Gilligan, the only hope of breaking this cycle in women's development is for women to enter into relationships with girls, not as perfect role-models who keep girls from feeling their sadness and their anger, but as women "harboring within themselves a girl who lives in her body, who is insistent on speaking, who intensely desires relationships and knowledge, and who, perhaps at the time of adolescence, went underground or was overwhelmed" (Gilligan 1990:531).

Gilligan's desire to see the boundaries between girls and women dissolve stems from a feminist vision that can imagine how, one day, the underground knowledge women have stored inside themselves since girlhood will cease to be merely psychologically corrosive and become, instead, a public resistance that will remake the world. Certainly, this vision is utopian and not attuned enough to multiple paths of resistance (Stacey 1990). But its redeeming quality is the challenge it poses to the girl/woman dichotomy, suggesting a need to overcome the classical self/other dichotomy that structures most autobiographies of childhood. If the woman is, in some ways, already harbored in the girl, and the girl in the woman, then Richard Coe's definition of "the childhood"—as a literary structure which is "complete exactly at the point at which the immature self of childhood is conscious of its transformation into the mature self of the adult who is the narrator of the earlier experiences" (Coe 1984:9)—will need to be changed to make room for the more elusive border positionings of girls and women.

The House on Mango Street, a coming-of-age story by the Chicana writer Sandra Cisneros, is a model of how to construct a narrative that respects the fluidity of the border between the girl and the woman. The story exemplifies how the underground knowledge of girls can become the basis for a new social order. Yet Cisneros is always aware, unlike Gilligan, of how ethnicity and class intersect with what girls know. In *The House on Mango Street*, written in a genre between poetry and prose, thirteen-year-old Esperanza, growing up in Chicago, reflects on the possibilities open to her as a Chicana from the barrio. Esperanza is given the space to tell her own story, but in a form that challenges autobiographic isolation. Her story is embedded within the web of stories that emerge from the destinies being chosen by the various girls who live on Mango Street, each of them in various stages of becoming women.

Almost all the girls have bought into a romanticism learned from storybooks and movies, which makes them want to grow up fast and get married, in hopes that this will be their ticket out of the barrio, their path to freedom and autonomy, to owning their houses, pillowcases, and dinner plates. But the shared experience of all these girls is that they end up confined to their houses, where they become virtual prisoners, like Rafaela, who "gets locked indoors because her husband is afraid Rafaela will run away since she is too beautiful to look at." Only on Tuesday nights, when her husband plays dominoes, can Rafaela lean out the window and allow herself to dream of a freer life, drinking the coconut or papaya juice she has asked the younger kids to bring her and wishing "there were sweeter drinks, not bitter like an empty room."

Esperanza is helped in her decision to maintain the young girl's questioning of romanticism by the fact that she is "an ugly daughter . . . the one nobody comes for." She chooses to model herself on the kind of woman she's seen in the movies "with red red lips . . . who drives the men crazy and laughs them all away." She wants a power that is her own. And so, as she crosses the threshold into womanhood, Esperanza begins to wage a "quiet war. Simple. Sure. I am one who leaves the table like a man, without putting back the chair or picking up the plate." By starting to wage her quiet war against sexism before leaving her father's house, Esperanza can envision a house that will be totally her own, with "nobody's garbage to pick up after." Hers will be the power of the writer, the one who will tell the stories of the girl-women of Mango Street (Cisneros 1991:80, 88–89, 108).

Sandra Cisneros told me that it was precisely when she finished writing the vignette entitled "Beautiful and Cruel" that she stood up and said of her protagonist Esperanza, "This girl is a feminist." As she explained, *The House on Mango Street* is supposed to be told from a young girl's perspective, but it was written by her when she was a woman in her mid-twenties. In those years, as a counselor to Latina college students, Sandra Cisneros heard the stories of other barrio women struggling against poverty and sexism to get an education; and it was these stories, meshed with recollections of her own girlhood, that became the basis of her book.

Esperanza's voice is a young girl's voice inflected with the feminism and the politics of the woman Sandra Cisneros hoped she would one day become. For, indeed, Esperanza is a touch overly courageous and resistant for a girl her age. If one looks at how Sandra Cisneros wrote about herself in her diary at age thirteen, it is clear that she was not yet the Esperanza of her fiction. Her entry for August 23, 1967, announces: "I've made out some rules so when I get back to school: 1. I'll try to be more friendly and not so shy. 2. I'll try not to be so timid and answer more questions. 3. And I will try to be dressed prim and nice."[3]

So it seems clear to me now: The woman has to throw an anchor back to the girl she left behind, the girl who's just barely treading water, the girl who's still worrying about why she's so shy and timid and not dressed nice enough. The woman who forgets the girl she harbors inside herself runs the risk of meeting her again as I did in the lonely space of a house that is her own in name only.

As the Indian-English novelist Salman Rushdie has written, it is impossible for emigrants to recover the homelands they left behind. The best they can do is "to create fictions, not actual cities or villages, but invisible ones, imaginary homelands" (Rushdie 1991:9–10). It seems to me that the notion of an imaginary homeland is very helpful for thinking about childhood. Aren't all of our childhoods imaginary homelands? Aren't they fictions about places left behind? Homelands from which we have become exiled in the process of growing up and becoming adults? In becoming adults we are encouraged to put the child behind us, to disbelieve our own stories and our own childhoods.

Here I have asserted that the body is a homeland—a place where knowledge, memory, and pain is stored by the child. Later, the woman that the child has become will search and search and search in her adult language for that child but find that, like Hansel and Gretel trying to return home, the place markers have vanished. She finds that the path back leads to an imaginary homeland that space on the frontier of consciousness where, as James Olney put it, words fail, but meanings still exist; where meanings—unspoken, inchoate, raw, and throbbing with life—wait to be found, to be given voice.[4]

Inevitably, living a childhood and writing about it as an adult are fundamentally different experiences, but the value of autobiography is that it creates forms of embodied knowledge in which the (adult) self and the (child) other can rediscover and reaffirm their connectedness.[5]

The girl in the cast lives within the woman who won't move, can't move, the woman who has been stopped in her tracks, the woman who will not make up her mind as to how to place herself in relation to the lost homeland, the Cuba that is part memory, part forgetting, part longing. It is a homeland she doesn't know if she even has the right to claim as her own. It is a homeland so imaginary that she will only accept as evidence that it exists when her body forces her to stop, listen, and look.

For several weeks after my return from Cuba, I have a distinct fear, when I set foot in the street, that I will not be able to find my way back to the Wedgewood blue Victorian house. I worry that a sudden oblivion will strike. The fear is so acute that I want to pin a piece of paper on my blouse with my address, just in case anybody finds me wandering around, lost. Slowly the fear subsides. I calm down. I talk to myself in the supportive voice psychologists advise you to cultivate. I say, You went to Cuba and you came back. You see? It is possible. Don't be afraid anymore, little girl.

And during those weeks, when I seem to be driving in circles around Ann Arbor, I call to mind the teenagers who were returning from a discotheque dance at Murray the K's World in Roosevelt, Long Island, in 1966, when their car took off and flew, like a bird gone mad. And finally I stop hating them. Finally I mourn for them. Finally I pray that they are blessed among the dead.

Notes

1. My warm thanks to Nereida Garcia-Ferraz for sharing Becker's (1992) important book with me; see pp. 14–17.
2. There is more than a little of masculine heroics in Oliver Sacks's story. The women in his story are primarily nurses and assistants.
3. Phone conversation with Sandra Cisneros, March 3, 1992. In addition to talking at length with me about her work, Sandra Cisneros kindly gave me permission to read the diaries she kept from the ages of thirteen to fifteen, which I hope to write about in more detail on another occasion.
4. James Olney, remarks at a workshop entitled "The Construction of Childhood," held in Trondheim, Norway, 1992. See the proceedings of the workshop in Gullestad 1996.
5. Recently, there have been pleas for a more autobiographical anthropology, rooted in embodied knowledge, in which the distinction between self and other become blurred. For example, see Okely and Callway 1992.

References

Becker, Carol. 1982. *The Invisible Drama: Women and the Anxiety of Change*. New York: Macmillan.

Cisneros, Sandra. 1989. *The House on Mango Street*. New York: Random House.

Coe, Richard N. 1984. *When the Grass Was Taller: Autobiography and the Experience of Childhood*. New Haven: Yale University Press.

Gates, Henry Louis Jr. 1990. A Giant Step. *New York Times Magazine* December 9:34–35.

Gilligan, Carol. 1990. Joining the Resistance: Psychology, Politics, Girl and Women. *Michigan Quarterly Review* 29(4):512.

Gullestad, Marianne (ed.). 1996. *Imagined Childhoods*. Stockholm: Scandinavian University Press.

Jack, Dana Crowley. 1991. *Silencing the Self: Women and Depression*. Cambridge, Mass.: Harvard University Press.

Leonard, Marjorie. 1959. Fear of Walking in a Two-and-a-Half-Year-Old Girl. *Psychoanalytic Quarterly* 28:29–39.

Miller, Alice. 1990. *The Drama of the Gifted Child*. New York: Basic Books.

Okely, Judith, and Helen Callway (eds.). 1991. *Anthropology and Autobiography*. New York: Routledge.

Rushdie, Salman. 1991. Imaginary Homelands, in *Imaginary Homelands: Essays and Criticism 1981–1991*. New York: Viking Penguin.

Sacks, Oliver. 1984. *A Leg to Stand On*. New York: Harper and Row, 1984.

Stacey, Judith. 1990. On Resistance, Ambivalence and Feminist Theory: A Response to Carol Gilligan. *Michigan Quarterly* 29(4):537–46.

(Post)Colonial Psychiatry

The Making of a Colonized Pathology

FRANÇOISE VERGÈS

"To conclude, one may say that the mother in Réunion represses the personality of her child."

In recent years, we have witnessed a pathologization of Creole minorities living in the French Overseas departments.[1] In these former colonies, social difficulties have been explained in psychological terms. Their populations, which demanded political integration in the French Republic in 1946, are said to be responsible for the failure of their integration into a (post)modern, individualistic society. They are responsible because their "psychology," the relations they construct among themselves exhibit a "lack." According to a discourse which blends psychological terms with postmodern notions, the Creole remains caught into the present, the group and magic thinking whereas a postmodern self demands an autonomous individual, capable of projection into the future and abstract thinking. Through a strategic adaptation of psychological and psychoanalytical terms, French psychiatrists have defined a "Creole pathology" which describes the Creole family as a site producing neurotic behavior. Creoles tend to be petty criminal, incestuous, unable to express their feelings, and to exhibit a compulsion to repetitive behavior. Among the groups which constitute the Creole societies, the descendants of slaves are said to be more prone to this pathology than any other group. Psychiatrists describe a family in which the father lacks authority and is often indifferent to his children. But it is foremost the Creole woman who is responsible for the supposed lack of maturity of Creole minorities. As a mother, she is said to hinder the development of her children; as a companion, as a wife, she is said to symbolically castrate her men. She has been constructed as the source of pathological symptoms, and her "unhealthy" relations to her children and men threaten the health of the community.

Psychiatrists and psychologists have lent their expertise to a project of disciplining the poor, and their discourse is a blend of colonial assumptions and postcolonial critique. It is this discourse I wish to examine here. Confronted with a different culture, a different language, different ways of talking about pain and suffering, doctors and psychiatrists have interpreted the paroles of their patients according to assumptions they have usually left unquestionned. Already in 1952, Frantz Fanon denounced the "pre-existing framework" of the French medical personnel meeting with North African workers.[2] The former were often convinced of the "imaginary nature" of the latter's ailments, denying the immigrants access to their parole. Minorities in metropolitan and overseas France still live within this framework.

As Octave Mannoni has written, psychiatry has "*collaborated in the enterprise of isolating and excluding from society those who cannot obey the historically defined norms of propriety.*" Its goal has been to define a "*utilitarian policy,* whose intent is to protect the tranquillity of the majority, but also to inculcate in this majority a certain way of being reasonable." The role of the psychiatrist has been to authenticate and certify the "illness" of the soul and to inculcate a "certain way of being reasonable" (Mannoni 1993). Michel Foucault has proposed a history of psychiatry and discipline that echoes Mannoni's remarks. Their true aim is not to eliminate asocial behavior but to produce ways that reinforce discipline. In the colony, psychiatry's goals and aims have been informed by colonial racism and Eurocentric assumptions. Understanding postcolonial psychiatric discourse implies thus examining the assumptions of colonial medicine and psychiatry.

At the beginning of the twentieth century, a school of "colonial psychiatry" emerged in the French colonial empire. Natives suffered psychological breakdowns, and it was necessary to discover their sources. Was non-European madness different from European symptoms? To begin with, colonial psychiatry assumed that traditional societies protected natives from madness. This approach was congruent with the idea that industrialized societies, with the breakdown of traditions, led to degeneration. But then, colonial psychiatry indicted non-European cultures, their traditions, and their social organization for the mental disorders their population experienced. Revolts, criminality, and resistance to work were explained in psychological terms. Colonization became a psychological adventure. Understanding the native psyche would help the colonial project because colonial administrators would know how to present decisions, how to implement colonial policy. They could either show "respect" to traditions (using local leaders, showing tolerance toward certain traditional customs) or insist on the benefits of a "modern" psyche (more autonomous, more secular, more open to women's needs).

The psychology of colonization asked the vexed question about the relationship between culture and the psyche. Did culture determine the psyche, or were there universal human psychological mechanisms? It appeared respectful of native customs and beliefs as it tried to understand them as parts of a psychological making. Yet it remained faithful to colonial discourse and its hierarchical construction of the colonial world. On the one hand, it presented a modern, adventurous individual, open to scientific speculations, trusting technological progress and medicine. On the other hand, it proposed a series of features said to characterize the colonized: a poor language and consequently an inability to conceptualize, a faith in magic, a belief in spirits, fatalism, credulity, mimicry, and no access to feelings of guilt.

The majority of French colonial psychiatrists were committed republicans, secular and progressive people. Their discourse was not alien to a republicanism that believed in its destiny: progress through colonization. It was French republicanism's responsibility to help backward groups and peoples to escape the world of supernatural and magic thinking. It was consonant with the crusade for laicization launched first in metropolitan France, then in the empire. After World War II, a radical critique of the assumptions of colonial psychiatry emerged. It came from the colonized. It was colonialism that produced madness, the Martinican Frantz Fanon and the Tunisian Jew Albert Memmi said, and not the social and cultural organization of a society (Fanon 1967; Memmi 1965). The colonized's nervous condition was inevitable, considering the violence, racism, and ethnocentrism of colonialism. Yet even to these critics, who often were committed anticolonialists, native ways of healing were rejected, for they kept the population "under the power of superstition." They defended a modern social medicine, attentive to the parole and needs of the patients but inscribed into a progressive and modernizing project.

Today, the concerns and goals of contemporary psychiatric practices, like transcultural psychiatry or ethnopsychiatry, are still trying to answer to the questions raised by colonial psychiatry: What is the relation between culture and the psyche? What is the nature of madness? Is it part of the human condition or a temporary loss of consciousness? What is the place of culture in madness? In this essay, my purpose is to uncover the role and function of the native woman in the (post)colonial psychiatric discourse. Though there was a contest around masculinity—native masculinity being constructed as a "lack" (lack of a post-Oedipal masculinity) against a mature European masculinity—the figure of the native woman haunts the psychiatric narrative. Her sexuality, her relations with her children and her men are reconstructed to reinforce a discourse that opposes a European "decolonized," "free" psyche against an alienated, dependent non-European one.

Returning to the notion of "Creole pathology," I now present the ways in which psychiatric discourse has affected social policy in the Creole society of Reunion Island. Reunion Island is a French overseas territory, located in the Indian Ocean. Populated with the descendants of Malagasy and African slaves, of Indian and Malaysian indentured workers, of Chinese, Muslim, and Vietnamese immigrants and European colonists, Reunion Creole society is multiethnic, multireligious, and multicultural. It created a Creole language and culture and offered syncretic beliefs. Yet the French colonial administration long denied its complex character and history, imposing the French language and Catholicism, and proposing a total identification with French culture. Resistance to French hegemony took multiple forms, from developing underground a music inherited from slavery (the *maloya*) and keeping alive traditional ways of healing and oral culture to anticolonial political and social movements. Today, Reunion Island is still dependent on France. There is a high unemployment rate, and despite a rapid modernization of a rural society in the last thirty years, there has been no economic development. It is an industrialized society without industrialization. Paradoxically, there are more French metropolitans there today than thirty years ago. They constitute the majority of civil servants, working in education, health services, and the administration. As civil servants, they enjoy, like all civil servants in French overseas departments, bonuses inherited from the colonial period: They earn up to 53 percent more, and pay 30 percent less taxes, than their counterparts working in the metropole. Psychiatrists are members of this caste. It is an attractive situation with substantial financial and narcissistic benefits. Mannoni's remark about the colonial personality can still be applied to French metropolitans of the postcolony. The (post)colonial European finds refuge in a world in which he or she does not have to confront competition and the world of others.

The movement of decolonization, new research, and new developments in psychiatry has transformed postcolonial psychiatry. It claimed to explain the violent or self-destructive acts of the (post)colonials by presenting those people as "victims" of a brutal history. Apparently opposed to a racially determined history, psychology argued that colonized people experienced mental disorders because of slavery and colonialism, which had wounded their psyche, shattered their world, and subjected them to physical harm and mental anguish. Yet the way this history has been acknowledged has paradoxically perpetuated its denial. It has tried to transform popular memory (ghosts of slaves, memories of victimization) into a neurotic symptom. Slavery and colonialism have produced specific psychological symptoms: persecutory hallucinations, a backward conception of honor, inhibition of emotions, incest, violence in interpersonal relations. The discovery of a postcolonial pathology legitimates the psychiatrists' presence and their expertise. As Foucault has remarked, the "power that the asylum gives to the psychiatrist will be justified (as well as being masked as a primordial power) through the production of phenomena which can be integrated into medical science."[3]

Though it is perfectly clear that slavery and colonialism have affected social and interpersonal relations in specific ways, I want to argue that when European psychiatrists (and their local allies) are those who present a psychological explanation of their consequences, there is a dehistoricization of colonial crimes. Careers are made explaining the crimes and mental disorders of women and men of color in a French (post)colony. Moreover, as the majority of mental patients are poor men (and this connection—masculinity-colonization-modernization-madness—has yet to be fully investigated), the psychiatric encounter is fraught with ambivalence. Two men occupy the scene of psychological interpretation: the native man and the European psychiatrist. A poor man of color and a European(ized) man. Two masculinities, two different positions in the social world. Two languages, two worlds: The Creole language, a (post)colonized society and its oral culture, and a world in which the written word, the word of the law and of the administration, is the word of French men. And between these two men is the Creole woman, whom the European man will either indict as the source of pathological behavior or protect against a violent native man. The colonial contest is replayed on the psychological scene.

The reasons for the specificity of the Creole psyche can be found, psychiatric experts say, in two interrelated phenomena: the *métis* origin of the population and the specific family organization, the matrifocal family. The former creates confusion about the individual's origins, a confusion leading to a lack of psychological foundations and a weakness of the sense of "self." The latter hinders, psychiatrists contend, individuation, or the possibility for the individual to separate from its first object of love, the mother. Together, *métissage* and matrifocality, psychiatrists claim, block the access of the individual to language and the law.

What really is the assumed source of pathology is the Creole mother. The mother frustrates the child's access to the Oedipal stage, or access to the law, that is, submission to a series of taboos that make culture and society possible. Adapting a psychoanalytical reading of the phallic mother, French psychiatrists examine its consequences in Reunion. Though psychotic behavior could be expected from men unable to escape their mother, it remains a rare diagnosis because, even if male patients exhibit "psychotic attitudes, like alcoholism and violence, they do not exhibit defiant attitudes; they are passive." They act out, rape, and fight against each other, forever caught under the power of their mother hindering their access to adulthood.

A 1993 official document sent to schoolteachers and school psychologists says: "The maternal function has been perverted. The power in the family, which should be patriarchal, is therefore matriarchal.... The father expresses himself either through violence or alcoholism. There is a nostalgia about the past and the past (slavery) weighs on society. It is necessary to forget the past. Creole culture is poor."[4] Normative ideas about the family intersect with a narrative about the culture of poverty, the pathology of dependency. The narrative of French psychiatrists echoes the narrative of the Moynihan Report in the United States, which has defined in the last thirty years federal and state policy toward African-American communities. These discourses are the expression of a "ideological war by narrative means," as Wahneema Lubiano puts it.[5]

The narrative about the welfare single mother has become a "truth," a text whose assumptions and methodology are not even questioned. It based its conclusions upon the theory about matrifocality. The French psychiatric narrative has blamed slavery for the role and function of the mother. "Despite the incentives to create a patriarchal family unit, the descendants of slaves became vagabonds.... The temptation to have an enslaved workforce, an immoral and dishonest but human reflex, favored debauchery. It is important to grasp this historical element, because it has marked the behavior of the group and the individual as well as the collective unconscious, and has been perpetuated under the name of sexual freedom and loose morals."[6] Through the campaign about the normalization of the family, what emerges is, as Foucault said, the "imperative of a new relationship between parents and children, a new economy of intra-familial relations: a strengthening and intensification of the relations father-mother-children (at the expense of the multiple relations that characterized the extended family)."[7]

A demonized female figure, the single mother is said to retard the development of the child because "she denies the existence of the child's personality. She ignores the importance of prime infancy and of the role she has to play at that moment."[8] She debases the father and instills in her children an indifference, if not a contempt, for masculine power.[9] Psychiatry borrows the vocabulary of child psychology to indict the native mother. Moreover, it reorganizes Reunion's society along ethnic lines in order to give the French (called *zoreys* in Creole) the best position on the social and cultural scale. The *zorey*, Jean-Michel Porte has written, "who brings with him hope and civilization, is both admired and rejected." He is the "Other, who, because of his radical alterity, represents the principle of heterogeneity with which the native has an ambiguous relation of identification and rivalry." Living in a culture with "fixed, stagnant cultural references, in which old habits are confused with identity," in a society which is not "open to the outside world," the Creole man takes refuge in a maternal world which keeps him in infancy.

To the narrative trope of the welfare-phallic mother, experts have added the victimized Creole woman. Though women's organizations in Reunion have denounced rape and other forms of violence against women, it has been the discourse of male French legal and psychiatric experts that has shaped the structures of legal and medical discourse. French experts have used rape as a framework to capture both the way Creole women experience sexual harassment and the way the French law protects them. In the narrative about rape, the poor Creole man, whose masculinity is essentially bestial, is *the* rapist. Rapes of maids and of saleswomen by their bosses, the sexual harassment of women that is prevalent in the workplace, do not appear in the studies about violence that focus on poor Creole men, who are easier to catch and indict.[10]

But again, behind the rapist, behind Creole male bestiality, French psychiatrists and legal experts contend, is the Creole woman's behavior. According to Nicole Hamann, a police inspector at Saint-Denis, the passivity of the Creole woman, her resentment, her repressed sexuality lead the Creole man to violence. Women are thus the source of the male pathological violence or mental disorder. The Creole female, herself pathologically passive, produces a pathological violent son, to whom she teaches respect neither for the father nor for other women. The son, in turn, will attack the Creole woman because of his mother, who has not encouraged in him autonomy and access to symbolization. The psychoanalyst

Jacques André, who did a psychoanalytical and ethnological study of blood crimes in the French Antilles, has argued that there is in these Creole societies, a "focal incest," that is, a matrifocal structure that fosters a psychotic attachment to the mother.[11] "Nothing prepares the boy to confront the law," André writes, his destiny is to become the "hero of his mother."[12] The Antillean man "will never cease to be a son," and his "encounter with castration will be avoided, deferred— which explains his weak relation to the rule, the law. He will be assured of an infallible, faultless maternal support that will shield him from the 'affronts' which reality will certainly inflict."[13]

The discourse about pathological matrifocality has a great seductive power. It posits characters that are easy to identify: the powerful mother, the powerless father, the protected son, and the subjugated daughter, and its stories sound familiar. It has created a rhetorical field and a vocabulary in which anyone can become fluent. Proverbs, tales, daily events are used to support its hypotheses, for misogyny and celebration of the son are connected phenomena. The mother, who exercises power through the control over her daughters' sexuality and through her son, is a mythological figure, whose existence is verified daily. Reunion's society is certainly not different from other societies constructed on the celebration of the reformed mother and at the expense of the woman. The Antillean psychiatrist Christian Lesne has asked why out of "complex social phenomena, whose pathological effect should be seen as extremely limited (so much so that single mother headed-families are a minority), only one model is retained about the Creole family, a family without a father which is said to be the source of psychological abnormalities."[14] To Lesne, the separation of this discourse from anthropological studies is possible because the "particular thesis, that this discourse develops and argues, rests on the selection of the data, among a multiplicity of cultural data, that are complex, interactive, even contradictory, and which often vary from one group to another, that would sustain the thesis."[15]

"Creole pathology" appears as a device to maintain a minority under a patronizing tutelage. Psychology and psychiatry no longer refer to a knowledge with their history, ideology, and limits as well as possibilities. They emerge as the accomplices of the French state in its project of disciplining Creole women and men. They remain truthful to the colonial project of defining the native psyche. Their goal is still to integrate a minority through force and violence into a society that keeps it in dependency.

Notes

1. The French Overseas Departments are Martinique, Guadeloupe, Reunion, and Guyana. These territories belongs to the prerevolutionary French colonial empire. Slaves from Africa and Madagascar, indentured workers from Asia, and colonists from Europe were brought together and created a Creole culture and language. In 1946 the territories became departments.
2. Fanon 1967:3–16.
3. Foucault 1989:59.

4. "Comité Académique des programmes. 1993. Commission Transversale Conditions Psycho-Sociales et Contenus d'Enseignement." 1993.
5. See Lubiano 1992:350.
6. Hamann1990.
7. Foucault 1989:78.
8. Xiberras 1979.
9. More studies must be done to define the paternal function in Reunion in its complexity and historicity. Réunionnais children have an image of the "father." According to the child psychologist Olivier Douville, who designed a series of questions for children between 6 and 12, the representation of the father is not as censored as psychiatric reports claim.
10. See the study by the Union des Femmes de La Réunion, "Viols et Violences Domestiques" 1994.
11. André 1987
12. André 1987:69.
13. André 1987:70.
14. Lesne 1990:143.
15. Lesne 1990:144. Similar criticisms have been made about the Moynihan Report.

References

André, Jacques. 1987. *L'inceste focale dans la famille noire antillaise.* Paris: PUF.
Comité Académique des programmes, Commission Transversale. 1993. Conditions Psycho-Sociales et Contenus d'Enseignement.
Couchard, Françoise. 1991. *Emprise et violence maternelle.* Paris: Dunod.
———. 1993. "On bat une fille." *Revue Française de Psychanalyse* 3:773–50.
Fanon, Frantz. 1967. The North African Syndrome. In *Toward the African Revolution.* New York: Grove.
Foucault, Michel. 1989. *Résumé des cours, 1970–1982.* Paris: Juilliard.
Hamann, Nicole. 1990. *Report de la Commission traitant des violence intra-familiale.* Saint-Denis, Réunion: n.p.
Lesne, Christian. 1990. *Cinq essais d'ethnopsychiatrie antillaise.* Paris: L'Harmattan.
Lubiano, Wahneema. 1992 Black Ladies, Welfare Queens, and State Minstrels: Ideological War by Narrative Means. Pp.323–64 in Toni Morrison (ed.), *Race-ing, Justice, En-gendering Power: Essays on Anita Hill, Clarence Thomas, and the Construction of Social Reality.* New York: Pantheon Books.
Mannoni, Octave. 1980. Administration de la folie, folie de l'administration. Pp 137–57 in *Un Commencement qui n'en finit pas.* Paris: Seuil.
———. 1993. *Prospero and Caliban: Psychology of Colonization.* Ann Arbor: University of Michigan Press.
Memmi, Albert. 1965. *The Colonizer and the Colonized.* New York: Orion Press.
Rubin, Gabrielle. 1977. *Les sources inconscientes de la misogynie.* Paris: Robert Laffont.
Xiberras, Georges. 1979. La mère et l'enfant. In *L'enfant réunionnais et son milieu.* Saint-Denis, Réunion: CDDP-CREAI.

Challenging New World
Reproductive Orders

Public Pregnancies
and Cultural Narratives
of Surveillance

ANNE BALSAMO

Pregnant women, as the material sign of the reproductive woman, cannot easily avoid the scrutiny of a fascinated gaze. A recent article in *Self* magazine unselfconsciously gushes that "in the office, on the street, it's everybody's baby":

> A woman who is pregnant immediately knows that her body is no longer her own. She has a tenant with a nine-month lease; and should he spend every night kicking or hiccuping ... there is nothing she can do. Sharing one's body with a small being is so thoroughly wondrous, though, that one can generally overlook the disadvantages. The real problem is sharing one's pregnant body with the rest of the world (Kaplan 1989:156).

Here we can read the three key features of our culturally determined "magical thinking" about reproduction: (1) a pregnant woman is divested of ownership of her body, as if to reassert in some primitive way her functional service to the species—she ceases to be an individual, defined through recourse to rights of privacy, and becomes a biological spectacle—and in many cases she also becomes an eroticized spectacle, the visual emblem of the sexual woman; (2) the entity growing in her, off of her, through her, (referred to variously as a pre-embryo, embryo, fetus, baby, or child) (e.g., Spallone 1989) has some sort of ascendant right (to produce pain, to be nourished properly, to be born) that the maternal body is beholden to; (3) that the state of being pregnant is so "wondrous" or, variously, thrilling, fulfilling, and soulfully satisfying for a woman that she would endure any discomfort, humiliation, or hardship to experience this "blessed event."[1]

This passage also demonstrates how easily the female body is deconstructed into its culturally significant parts and pieces; here the womb serves as a metonym for the entire female body. Not only does this fragmentation culturally reduce a woman to an objectified pregnant body, it also supports the naturalization of the scientific management of fertilization, implantation, and pregnancy more broadly.

To establish a context for a more detailed discussion of public pregnancies, I want to pose a *question* that will be familiar to those informed by the history of cultural studies: What is the relationship between cultural narratives and the social conditions of women? During the course of doing the research for this chapter, it became clear that the question of the relationship between literature and society, one of the abiding questions for scholars and students of cultural studies from the mid-1960s, has transformed into a much different concern about the relationship between mass-mediated cultural narratives, medical discourse, and material bodies. Although it is beyond the scope of this essay to rehearse the specific intellectual genealogy of this transformation, that is, the movement from a concern with literature and society to one of language and materialism, to one of the material effects of cultural representations, I want to suggest that such questions are at the heart of what it means to me to do "cultural studies of science and technology." In this sense, the polemic of this chapter concerns the tensions and contradictions that emerge from a specific intellectual practice. Studying women and the deployment of new reproductive technologies involves asking questions that are theoretically interesting and intellectually gratifying to investigate, but which also illuminate cultural conditions that require immediate, critical political intervention. Is this not also the case for many other cultural studies of science and technology, whether or not they are framed by an explicit commitment to feminist politics? The question that grounds this chapter concerns the relationship between discourse and material bodies that preoccupies both feminist theory and feminist politics.

I begin with a discussion of Margaret Atwood's (1986) novel *The Handmaid's Tale*, which narrativizes current anxieties about reproduction in a technological age. When the Handmaid Offred describes her public encounter with the pregnant Handmaid Ofwarren, we hear the echoes of *Self* magazine: "She's a magic presence to us, an object of envy and desire, we covet her. She's a flag on a hilltop, showing us what can still be done: we too can be saved" (Atwood 1986:35). This reverence is also evident in medical discussions about new reproductive technologies. E. Peter Volpe, an expert in reproductive medicine, subtitles his 1987 book *Test-Tube Conception: A Blend of Love and Science.* He too refers to the passage in Genesis (with Rachel, Jacob, and the maid) as the Ur-narrative of surrogate motherhood (p. 63). The difference, though, between the surrogate story in Genesis and the ones we read about in Volpe's (1987:63–64) book and in our newspapers is that in late capitalism, "the surrogate performs the unusual service for a substantial fee." Conceptualizing the relationship between a woman and her body as one between an individual and personal property offers some measure of liberty and economic freedom for women. "Be thankful," as Offred reminds us, "for small mercies" (Atwood 1986:127).

Reproductive technologies provide the means for exercising power relations on the flesh of the female body. These power relations are in turn institutionalized in several ways, not only through the development of medical centers that offer reproductive services, but also through the establishment of reconstructed legal rights and responsibilities of parents, donors, fetuses, and resulting children. Specific technological practices further augment such institutionalization; for example, the application of new visualization technologies—such as laparoscopy—literally bring new social "agents" into technological existence. In this way, the material applications of new technologies are implicated in, and in part productive of, a new discourse on maternal identity, parental responsibilities, and the authority of science.[2] At the heart of this discursive formation of reproduction are evocative cultural narratives about motherhood, the family, the role of technoscience, and the medicalized citizen. This chapter discusses this articulation among medical instruments, professional histories, and mediated cultural narratives that serves as the cultural context within which new reproductive technologies are used to discipline material, female bodies as if they were all potentially maternal bodies, and maternal bodies as if they were all potentially criminal.[3] The issue under consideration in this chapter is the relationship between fictional narratives, medical discourse, and the construction of public health policy that determines the material conditions of women's lives.

The Handmaid's Tale:
A Speculative Ethnography of the Present

Published in 1985, Margaret Atwood's novel *The Handmaid's Tale* has been, from early on, identified as a dystopian projection of some future society in the tradition of Orwell's *1984* and Huxley's *Brave New World*. As will be familiar to most readers, the novel is set in the fascist Republic of Gilead, which succeeds contemporary United States society some time in the late 1980s or early 1990s. The Gilead regime assigns every female to one of several classes of women: *wives* are married to men with military rank, which allows them a measure of privilege, including the right to employ a *handmaid* or *martha*; *econowives* are coupled with the younger men who form the rank and file of the military regime and who do not have enough status to obtain a handmaid or a martha; *aunts* function as religious teachers and trainers of handmaids; marthas are a class of serving women—housekeepers, cooks, and nannies. Handmaids serve as surrogate wombs for infertile heterosexual (in identity but not necessarily in practice), privileged couples (wives and military leaders).

Handmaids are socialized to perform their reproductive service for the state through an intense religious program of indoctrination that is more widely supported by a system of social rituals. The central preoccupation of the Gileadean society is human reproduction, because most members are sterile or infertile due to the build-up of toxic wastes and nuclear fallout. All potentially fertile young women are forcefully drafted into service as handmaids or banished to the toxic waste "colonies" if they refuse. Thus, the central symbolic figure of the society is the potentially reproductive woman, the handmaid.

The point of Gileadean rituals is always the same for women—the complete destruction of individual identity and the social reproduction of collective identity. The most central ritual, called simply "The Ceremony," invokes a biblical passage in which Rachel offers to her husband Jacob her maid Bilhah to bear him the children that Rachel cannot. In a symbolic repetition of this offering of a fertile, surrogate womb from one woman to her husband, the handmaid lies between the legs of the wife as the commander penetrates the handmaid's exposed sex in an attempt to impregnate her. Any child born of a handmaid is given over to the wife as if it were her own.

Organized in two parts, the first and longest part forms the bulk of the book and includes chapters that described the focal rituals of the Gileadean Society. The episodes are related from the point of view of a woman who was abducted by military guards as she, her husband, and daughter were trying to escape the country. Internal subjective dramas are counterposed to more realistic descriptions of the public situation of women in the new regime: women watched, guarded, intimidated, and policed.

The second part, titled "Historical Notes on THE HANDMAID'S TALE," formally stands as an epilogue or retrospective framing device in which the first part of the novel is revealed to be a "text" at the center of a future symposium on Gileadean Studies held as part of the International Historical Association Convention, held at the University of Denay, Nunavit, on June 25, 2195. The "Handmaid's Tale," we discover, is an historian's reconstruction of a collection of primary materials that come in the form of an (audio) taped account of a 33-year-old handmaid, who, we learn eventually, is the narrator of the first part of the book. Ostensibly we know her only as "Offred," the handmaid in the service of a commander whose first name is "Fred."

The narrative we piece together throughout the novel is limited to Offred's severely restricted point-of-view, but as a picture of Gilead is pieced together through her description of various rituals, the reader also witnesses the piece by piece assembly of the subjectivity of a handmaid. In these fragments, Offred offers readers a sense that the demoralization of handmaids is a well orchestrated social phenomenon: accomplished both through *public* rituals, such as the mandatory monthly visit to the gynecologist to determine a handmaid's fertility status, and in more private moments—in Offred's clandestine visits to the Commander to play Scrabble, and even during her subversive act of intercourse with the Commander's chauffeur.

Although Atwood has consistently asserted that every indignity that the handmaids suffer in her novel has actual historical precedent (some during colonial New England, others in Europe during World War II) the importance of the novel lies not (solely) in its relation to those historical precedents, nor in its offering of a dystopic projection of some future version of the U.S., but rather in the fact that as it helps narrate and make manifest the often obscured situation of reproductive-age women in contemporary U.S. culture. For some women, the regime of surveillance described in humiliating detail in the novel is less fiction than biography. In this sense, we could read it as ethnography rather than as science fiction, as the novel focuses critical attention on the cultural rearticulation of the meaning of reproduction and provides a narrative frame through which to read the meaning of the interaction between the female body and new forms of reproductive technologies that are subtly but unmistakably being used as surveillance devices.

The Reign Of Technology

Although there are several interested histories of the profession of obstetrics, most would agree, according to William Ray Arney (1982:153), that the most "recent period of obstetrical history was characterized by exponential advances in technology." Arney suggests that the orientation of obstetrics shifted after World War II from intervention into the process of childbirth to the monitoring and surveillance of the obstetric patient. In his view, in the late 1940s the "organizing concept in obstetrics changed from 'confinement' to 'surveillance.'... The hospital became the center of a system [of] obstetrical surveillance that extended throughout the community" and eventually into women's personal lives. In our contemporary world, he asserts, "every aspect of a woman's life is subject to the obstetrical gaze because every aspect of every individual is potentially important, obstetrically speaking." Protection of the fetus is often offered as a common-sensical, and, hence, ideological rationale for intervention into a woman's pregnancy, either through the actual application of invasive technologies or through the exercise of technologies of social monitoring and surveillance.[4]

Arney goes on to argue that the increase monitoring of childbirth not only has brought the maternal body and fetus into a broader of system of surveillance, but it also functions to control and monitor the obstetricians themselves. Several control "devices" developed over the last forty years are designed to enhance fetal monitoring: intrauterine pressure catheters that measure contractions, a subcutaneous electrode that reads fetal blood pH, and ultrasonic devices that monitor fetal respiratory movement. With the deployment of these new technologies, a dominant, traditional definition of obstetrics as a specialized practice that involves the exercise of professional judgment comes into conflict with the redefinition of obstetrics as scientistic clinical and technological protocol. Obstetricians themselves claim that the scientific studies that describe what to monitor and when to intervene inhibit professional "subjective" judgment. It is important to remember here, as Paula Treichler elaborates, that this earlier definition of the proper, authoritative role of the obstetrician is itself the outcome of an historical struggle.[5] Whereas the obstetrician's scope of authority may be curtailed with the advent of new monitoring technologies, such that technological monitoring becomes a system of obstetric control that promotes, for example, institutional concerns for cost containment over the practice of clinical judgment, it does not fully dislodge the authority of the obstetrician that has been "historically" accomplished. Thus although in one sense, these new monitoring technologies contribute to the feeling that the "sovereignty of the obstetrician is gone" replaced now by the notion of a technologically enhanced clinical practice, in another sense, the range of the obstetrician's authority has been expanded to include responsibility for interpreting the output of various new monitoring devices.

Situated within another historical context, the use of such technologies in the obstetric field is just another stage in the incorporation of technology into all fields of medicine—a process that has been going on for well over four centuries.[6] In light of this history, the introduction of new monitoring technologies has the consequence of bringing *both* the obstetrician and the pregnant woman into a system of normative surveillance—although, as noted above, the range of agency of the obstetrician remains culturally and institutionally broader.

An equally significant consequence is that these monitoring devices also construct new bodies to watch. The most obvious is the body of the fetus, which is visualized through new imaging technologies.[7] This leads some obstetricians to claim that the fetus is actually the *primary* obstetrics patient. Less obvious is the creation of new identities for the female body. As a *potentially* "maternal body" even when not pregnant, the female body is also evaluated in terms of its physiological and moral status as a potential container for the embryo or fetus.[8] As Barbara Duden convincingly argues: "The public image of the fetus shapes the emotional and the bodily perception of the pregnant woman."[9] In this sense, the newly visible fetal body now determines the moral status of the maternal body, which is subtly redefined as a womb with a view.

The technological isolation of the womb from the rest of the female body promotes the rationalization of reproduction, such that the process of reproduction itself can be isolated into discrete stages: egg production, fertilization, implantation, feeding, and birthing. In this way, the new reproductive technologies include several biotechniques that literally enact the objectification and fragmentation of the female body by isolating and intervening in the physical processes of human reproduction that normally occur within the female body.

Several of these procedures actually allow researchers and physicians to view the internal physiological state of the female body and the developing embryo/fetus. Patrick Steptoe and Robert G. Edwards, the two British scientists responsible for Louise Joy Brown's "test-tube" conception (1978), modified a surgical technique called laparoscopy to obtain ripe eggs from a woman's ovary. E. Peter Volpe describes the procedure of egg retrieval in which a laparoscopy is used as a visualization instrument:

> A clear view of the ovary is obtained with a slender illuminated telescope-like instrument, or laparoscope, which is inserted through a small incision made in the navel. The viewing device illuminates the ovary, enabling the surgeon to examine the surface of the organ. The rounded follicle (containing the ripe egg) is readily detectable on the surface of the ovary as a thin-walled pink swelling. A specially designed hypodermic needle is then passed through a second incision in the abdomen, and the contents of the bulging follicle are aspirated.[10]

As the abdomen is pierced to insert the laparoscope, the technological gaze literally penetrates the female body to scrutinize the biological functioning of its reproductive organs. In the process the female "potentially maternal" body is objectified as a visual medium to look through.

After implantation of an IVF embryo is achieved using these sophisticated techniques, "the pregnancy" is carefully monitored. Given all the work, money, and physical discomfort involved in such conception, promoting a healthy developing embryo/fetus is of great concern:

> ... the pregnancy is monitored using all resources of the present state of the arts. The elaborate protocol includes continual office visits, hormonal analysis, ultrasound scans, serum alpha-fetoprotein testing (for spina bifida), amniocentesis (for prenatal biochemical and chromosomal analyses), routine obstetric laboratory tests, and two-hour postprandial glucose test for signs of maternal diabetes (Volpe 1987:33).

Some experts unabashedly agree that part of the new concern for the fetus is due to advances in visualization technologies and the promise of fetal medicine as a new medical specialty; a recent newspaper article quoted one physician as saying: "We can now view the fetus; we can determine its size and its sex. If it is ill, we can give it blood transfusions; nutrients can be offered in utero. And we now know that nutrition and lifestyle can harm the unborn" (Rich 1988:1,7). Thus, the same technological advances that foster the objectification of the female body through the visualization of internal functioning also encourages the "personification" of the fetus.

Fetal Legal Rights, Public Health, and Maternal Surveillance

New reproductive technologies do not, in a singularly deterministic sense, construct new social tensions. But they are implicated in the production of a new set of possibilities, wherein the rights of a pregnant woman are set against the "rights" of other people either to intervene in her pregnancy or to act on behalf of the unborn fetus.[11]

Of all the legal cases in the late 1980s that sought to establish a precedent for fetal legal rights, none received more media attention than the spectacle that came to be identified as the problem of Cocaine Mothers and Crack Babies. In May 1989, a 24-year-old woman from Rockford, Illinois, Melaine Green, was charged with involuntary manslaughter and the delivery of a controlled substance to a minor for allegedly taking cocaine shortly before her daughter was born.[12] The infant, Bianca Green, died two days after birth from fatal brain swelling due to oxygen deprivation before and during birth. Paul Logli, the Illinois state's attorney who filed the charges against Green, held a press conference to publicize his request for the development of tougher laws that would make it a crime to take illegal drugs while pregnant. As he explained, the voluntary ingestion of drugs by a mother results in the involuntary ingestion of substances by the fetus. From the very beginning, he framed the issue in terms of the rights of the fetus to state's protection (Reardon 1989a, b, c). It is not surprising then that Melanie Green's picture accompanying her newspaper story looked like a police line-up photograph. She's black, pregnant and addicted to cocaine. The Law, in the person of a State District Attorney, intervenes to save her child from her, and failing that, to save society from her. In effect, Logli was mounting a "politics of surrogacy" that would grant rights to fetuses at the expense of maternal rights; as it happened with the Green case, these politics are often enacted by anonymously appointed bureaucrats who function as public health guardians. The Green case has the trapping of what Anna Lowenhaupt Tsing calls, in her study of women charged with perinatal endangerment, a "Monster Story" (Tsing 1990). In terms similar to the ones elaborated by Valerie Hartouni in her analysis of the mass-mediated narrative context of a black woman who served as a surrogate mother for a white couple, Green is "a densely scripted figure, positioned in and by a crude, if commonplace, set of racial caricatures and cultural narratives about 'the way black women are'" (Hartouni 1994:85). The color of her skin activates certain cultural narratives about her questionable moral character. Her story was, in many respects, already written before she ever delivered her baby; the "welfare mother" is a mass-mediated controlling image, to use Patricia Hill Collins' term, of black mothers that elevates racist beliefs about black women and motherhood into an ideological narrative of mythic proportions (Collins 1990). Indeed, in the words of Cynthia Daniels (1993:7), a feminist scholar who studies the emergence of fetal rights:

> The very attempt to prosecute pregnant women for addiction has created a powerful social mythology about women. The power of this mythology may at time eclipse the power of law. Although women's rights may ultimately be upheld in the courts, a broader public culture may continue to endorse resentment toward women and more subtle forms of social coercion against those who transgress the boundaries of traditional motherhood. Social anxiety and resentment are most easily projected onto those women who are perceived as most distant from white, middle-class norms. Political power may ultimately rest not on the technical precedent of legal rights, but on the symbols, images, and narratives used to represent women in this larger public culture.

Here Daniels suggests the importance of representational techniques—"symbols, images and narratives"—in positioning women as objects of discriminatory legal actions. As Daniels rightly asserts, such representational and ultimately discursive techniques may have more effectiveness, and consequently more power than the technical precedent of legal rights. What was evident in the Green case is a warning about the scope of the campaign to establish the connection between maternal liability and fetal health—a campaign that is being waged not only in the courtroom but also in the dissemination of "official" statements about the dangers of maternal excesses. These official statements, which come in the form of throwaway health education pamphlets, public health handouts, and public health media campaigns, often make ample use of the symbols, images, and narratives that circulate in contemporary culture about the identity and meaning of the maternal body and its excesses.

Consider the following example: A governmental booklet published in 1990 by the U.S. Department of Health and Human Services lists the well-known hazards for "the unborn": "alcohol, tobacco, marijuana, cocaine, heroine and other opioids or synthetic narcotics, phencyclidine, tranquilizers and barbiturates." It also lists those licit drugs known to have adverse effects on prenatal infants: antibiotics, anticonvulsants, hormones, and "salicylates including Bufferin, Anacin, Empirin, and other aspirin-containing medication" (Cook, Petersen, and Moore 1990:45). In short, the point of the pamphlet is to educate public health officials and pregnant women about the dangers of maternal behavior. In the introduction to the booklet, the authors outline the "extent of the problem" of maternal influences on fetal health, which they see as a multidimensional problem related to the unreliability of information acquisition. The authors inform us that pregnant women are unreliable in reporting drug use, in remembering the extent of drug use, and in truthfully admitting to illicit drug use. Although they point out that "urine testing is a more reliable" method, they note that it is not sufficient to track changing drug patterns throughout the pregnancy" (Cook, Petersen, and Moore 1990:14), suggesting perhaps that if they could perform multiple urine tests throughout a woman's pregnancy that they could circumvent her duplicity. This conceptual as well as technological separation of the woman from her body is certainly consistent with other cases of "urinal politics," where the material body is used against the "person," who is now understood to be an unreliable source of the truth. In the absence of reliable information about actual drug use in actually pregnant women, these authors suggest that "surveys of current drug-using behavior among women of childbearing age" are useful indicators of the "scope of the problem" of prenatal drug exposure. In a subtle move, the behavior of women of childbearing age is transformed into a sign of a "potential problem," and the female body of childbearing age is redefined as the "potentially pregnant" body. In a similar way, the pregnant woman is constructed as unreliable and duplicitous, while the pregnant female *body* is invoked as a guarantee of drug-use truth.

Historically this increasing interest in teratology, the study of causes of birth defects, is due in part to the high incidence of birth defects in babies born to women who had taken the drug thalidomide—a drug prescribed (routinely before 1960) to soothe the nausea of pregnant women. This lead to an increase in research efforts to determine the safety of fetal exposure to "prescription medications, over-the-counter drugs, industrial chemicals, and pesticides" (Cook, Petersen, and Moore 1990:5). One of the other consequences of the public's growing concern with "thalidomide babies" was its interest in the impact of "social" drugs on developing fetuses. In the intervening twenty years, the scope of teratology was expanded to include research into "more subtle behavioral and developmental abnormalities in offspring that only become apparent later in an infant's life" (Cook, Petersen, and Moore 1990:6). Thus not only was the range of potentially dangerous substances targeted for research expanded, but so too was the range of time when the behavior of the female body could be scrutinized for its influence on a developing fetus or eventual child.

In a telling absence, the behavior of fathers is rarely mentioned. Other than a reference to a study in which the "male-to-female sex-ratio of offspring increased if either parent was a heavy marijuana smoker" (Cook, Petersen, and Moore 1990:25–26), the influence of drug use among fathers on resulting fetuses or children was not discussed in any detail. There is some evidence to suggest that interest is growing in the possibility that paternal health conditions might have an impact on developing fetuses and resulting children. Recent research in male-mediated teratogenesis are finding strong associations between childhood cancer rates and paternal drinking and paternal occupation, especially when fathers work in the petroleum and chemical industries.[13]

This new interest in paternal biological influences notwithstanding, it remains the case that the maternal body is overscrutinized in its relationship to the developing fetus. Having said that, though, it is important to remember that the issue of maternal health care has many sides. Many women who would like to get pregnant don't because of limited access or lack of access to prenatal care. Other women who do get pregnant and do not have access to prenatal care run the greatly increased risk of bearing low birth-weight infants (less than 5.5 lbs). Low birth weight is the single most predictive characteristic of infant mortality. As has been noted in the media many times, the U.S. ranks 19th among industrialized nations in terms of its infant mortality rate—9.7 deaths per 1,000. Black women in the U.S. have a higher incident of bearing low-birth-weight babies than do white women; the infant mortality rate for black babies is almost double the national rate—18.0 deaths per 1,000.[14] Prenatal care is the single most important factor in preventing low-birth-weight babies, but while more than 82 percent of white women receive early pregnancy care, only 61 percent of Hispanic women and 60 percent of black women do.[15] These treatment rates are consistent with the history of maternal and child health programs of the Public Health Service which traditionally were designed to serve the needs of minority populations who are understood to be "medically underserved." Indeed, as the range of minority populations has expanded in the U.S. to include groups from Asia and Central America, new grant programs target the health needs of these new underserved populations.

Whereas the development of public health programs designed for the special needs of certain populations, especially minority women who are or would like to be pregnant, seem entirely beneficial and moral, there are unintended consequences of course. We are led to wonder about the consequences of the articulations among (1) medical research that establishes a broader list of substances and behaviors that endanger a fetus, (2) an expanded argument about the relationship between maternal behavior and fetal development, (3) new public health programs that seek to increase minority patient/client participation and institutional/clinic surveillance, and (4) the criminalization of certain forms of drug consumption in the invigorated "war on drugs." This articulation identifies and structures the set of possibilities for the technological management of the potentially pregnant female body.

In her article that elaborates the political significance of "medical surveillance" practices for women of childbearing age, Jennifer Terry (1989) points out that the dual emergencies of AIDS and drugs use "allow for the emergence of discourses and practices that place women of childbearing age in particular jeopardy." Terry reminds feminists of the racial politics enacted in the articulation I described above, where medical research, public health initiatives, and surveillance practices have differential effects on women of color of a lower economic class than on white women more broadly. In Terry's (1989:21) words:

> the surveillance and punishment that potentially endangers all women is applied selectively to poor women and women of color. These women constitute the majority of patients in public clinics and are among the most likely to be brought into the criminal justice system of social welfare systems on grounds unrelated to their pregnancy.... In such instances it is impossible to distinguish the suspicion of certain women from the criminalization of poverty operating in the U.S. in the past decade.

The real issue in the Melanie Green case, following Terry's analysis, is the "hidden" damage of drug abuse and the inadequate national resources for developing treatment programs, especially for pregnant women. Terry's note about the "suspicion of certain women" is evident in discussions about the racial disparity in the type of prenatal care advice women receive from health care providers. Although, as noted above, Black women have a higher risk of bearing low-birthweight infants, they are less likely to receive the same level of prenatal advice about their risk status as white women. Moreover, according to one study, they are less likely to receive specific advice about drinking and smoking (Dogan et al. 1994:86). Other factors confound the issue of the adequacy of prenatal care advice. For example:

> Advice about two risk behaviors, smoking and drug use, was skewed towards
> poorer women, whereas advice about alcohol use and breast-feeding was
> skewed toward wealthier women. [In this case,] health care providers may be
> giving advice based on their stereotypes of who is involved in what type of
> behaviors and not on a principal of equity.

The sample population for this study showed significant differences between
black women and white women: "Black women were more frequently single, less
likely to be educated beyond high school, and had lower incomes." But the study
indicates a set of complex findings. One the one hand, black women report
receiving less advice overall about the dangers of smoking, alcohol, and illegal
drug use, unless they had a lower income, in which case they received more
advice about illegal drug use. A lack of advice is ill-treatment; but when the
advice is delivered about a specific risk behavior, it is likely to be based on suspicion and the stereotype of poor black women as illegal drug users. In any event,
the study supports what feminists have long suspected, that black women do not
receive the same level of prenatal care advice from public health providers as do
white women. In this sense, more programs do not necessarily ensure better care
for all women.

It is well documented that there are several barriers that prevent women
from seeking prenatal care, especially if they are using illegal drugs. As Norma
Finkelstein points out, although there are undoubtedly psychological issues at
work—such as denial of the problem of substance abuse—it is also likely that the
social stigma attached to drug use as well as the lack of gender-specific treatment
services are equally prohibitive.[16] But if we look at the issue of cocaine use among
pregnant women and at the documented effects of cocaine ingestion on the
developing fetus, we find that the medical and scientific findings do not warrant
the kind of surveillance that interferes with a pregnant woman's search for treatment. For example, several articles in a special issue of the journal *Neurotoxicology and Teratology* (1993)) outline the difficulties in obtaining reliable
information about the specific *toxicity* of cocaine on the developing fetus.
Problems include the determination of toxic dosage, the unreliability of self-
reported drug use, the wide lack of confirmation of catastrophic effects, and the
methodological design of research studies. Noteworthy are several observations
offered by medical researcher Donald E. Hutchings on the cultural context (not
his words, though) in which studies of cocaine "abuse" were conducted. To wit,
in a discussion of recent research on humans and cocaine use, he reports on a
study of the acceptance rate of medical research abstracts to the Society for
Pediatric Research that discussed the effects of prenatal exposure to cocaine. As
Hutchings summarizes: "of the studies that reported adverse effects associated
with cocaine, 58% were accepted whereas only 11% of those that found no effects
enjoyed a similar fate" (Hutchings 1993:283). He argues that this indicates a
selection bias on the part of medical journals that reflects and suggests that this

selection bias is influenced by the wider media and political attention paid to the scandalous new drug menace. Throughout his detailed assessment of the methodological design logics and review of the findings, Hutchings is careful to assert that the toxicity of cocaine is a complex issue that is confounded by the fact that many users actually ingest a number of potentially toxic substances including alcohol, tobacco and marijuana. He cautiously suggests that dosage level may be the more clearly determining factor of toxicity; at the same time he points out that in most studies, especially those that sample subjects from outpatient drug treatment programs, it is difficult to measure dosage level precisely.[17] It is far less possible, based on the current research, to formulate conclusions about the interactive effects of cocaine with other substances. Researchers simply have not made such studies.

Given this debate in the medical literature about the scientific facticity of cocaine toxicity, how are we to make sense of a study conducted in 1991 that tested for the presence of cocaine in the blood system of every infant born in Georgia's public hospitals? As reported by Adam Gelb in the *Atlanta Journal-Constitution* on page 1 (Mar 12, 1991): "Every baby born in Georgia over a one-year period will be tested for cocaine in the most extensive study in the nation of the drug problem among pregnant women."[18] The article goes on to assert:

> The epidemic of "crack babies," the underdeveloped, quivering infants who have become a tragic symbol of addiction is well known. But estimates of its scope range widely from 100,000 born annually, the federal government's figure, to 375,000, the number cites by independent medical experts. "The bottom line is nobody really knows how common this is," said Dr. Paul M. Fernhoff, an Emory University pediatrics professor, who is director of the study.

This is an encapsulated version of the dominant narrative of maternal excess and fetal victimization. When Gelb cites the director of the study, Dr. Fernhoff, he commits a grave error of leading the reader to make an erroneous inference about the gravity of the "problem." It is true, at some level, that no one knows the dimensions of the "problem," but it is also true, given the discussion among medical researchers summarized above that there is a great deal that researchers don't know about cocaine and its impact on fetal development. Although they have no official relationship to the study, researchers from the Centers for Disease Control and the Georgia Department of Human Resources say that they plan to use "the findings to develop education, intervention and treatment programs and boost prenatal care." It is this combination of journalistic sensationalism and public health rhetoric that makes the media treatment of "crack babies" so pernicious.[19] As Nancy L. Daly and Gale A. Richardson (1993:180) ask in their essay on "Cocaine Use and Crack Babies: Science, Media, and Miscommunication"—an essay that also appeared in that special issue of *Neurotoxicology and Teratology* discussed earlier—"how did it happen that an epidemic of such proportions was declared so quickly?" They go on to raise several other issues about the spectacular increase in the concern about cocaine dangers, namely, "What were the other forces within science and our society that propelled the early reports of cocaine effects to such prominence, and that still in large part continue to propagate the belief that cocaine is a terrible scourge visited on the unborn?" They rightly point out, as do others in that special issue, that cocaine has enjoyed a special place in the history of American culture, from its alleged use in Coca-Cola (which remains a great unspoken secret in the official history of the company), to its use as an entertainment chemical by rich yuppies in the Reagan era, to its current demonized status as the drug of addicted welfare mothers. They beseech scientists and medical researchers to "correct the damage that has been done . . . damage that has been done to women and to the 'crack babies' who have been given a label for which there is no cure and little hope" (Day and Richardson 1993:293). They implore medical researchers to assume the responsibility to educate other professionals about the complexity of the issue of determining causality and to remember that "behaviors do not exist in isolation, but are part of and determined by the fabric of a woman's life." But such an admonishment is likely to fall on deaf ears in the sense that it really requires medical practitioners and researchers to rethink and retool their relationships to various social entities such as the press and other media that seize upon "first case" examples as signs of a crisis, and to journalists who are not equipped to discuss the subtle nuances of published medical findings. More importantly, this would also require medical professionals to reconsider women as a social class who are differently and complexly positioned at the nexus of broader social forces such as poverty, violence, and demoralization.

Among the other precipitating conditions for the wide-scale enactment of an apparatus of surveillance is the historical evolution of medicine as an agent of social control. In one of the few explicit discussions of this topic in the professional literature on public health policy, Stephenson and Wagner (1993:176) summarize the situation of reproductive rights and medical control:

> Since 1987 there have been approximately 60 criminal cases in the U.S. (many involving physicians) against women who have either taken illegal drugs during pregnancy or have failed to obey doctor's orders. The charges have ranged from prenatal child abuse to manslaughter. Several women have been convicted. Others have been forced against their will into drug treatment programs or have been "detained" (a euphemism for imprisonment). . . . Advocates for fetal rights have proposed a reporting system where pregnant women would be identified and monitored by state officials. Women would be forced to attend their prenatal visits and obey doctor's orders; and women could be prosecuted and punished for smoking or using drugs and alcohol during pregnancy. While this does not reflect predominant medical opinion, one survey did indicate that 46% of the heads of obstetrical and perinatal training programs through that women who refused medical advice and thereby endangered the life of the fetus should be taken into custody.[20]

Although they are not concerned to discuss specific physician culpability, the authors point out that physician coercion of pregnant women is of a piece with the differential denial of reproductive health care to certain social groups—in their view, these cases demand a return to the consideration of basic medical ethics. The coercion of pregnant women to undergo certain procedures on behalf of the fetus is unethical in the same way as would be forcing a father to undergo a bone marrow transplant to save a son; and they remind us that the international code of medical ethics expressly forbids such coercion of a patient. But they also argue that there is "little reason to believe that medicine, on its own accord, will relinquish its privilege to determine (ad hoc) reproductive policy." When one considers that such ad hoc policy is being established by those in the position to make decisions at the scene—where the agents who establish this policy are predominantly white, middle-class and male—it is likely that the policy will reflect the "dominant culture's beliefs about morality and motherhood." They call for the intervention of courts and legislatures to "begin the difficult but essential task of formulating explicit reproductive health policies"; to assist this project they suggest the guidance of several international human rights treaties.

In an article in *Trial* that discusses the criminal law implications of prosecuting pregnant women for fetal abuse, Dorothy Roberts (1990:58) itemizes how such action violates the rights of women; not only does it

> infringe on fundamental guarantees of reproductive choice and bodily autonomy ... [but] applying drug-trafficking and child-abuse laws to conduct during pregnancy also violates the defendants' due-process right to fair notice. Criminal penalties may not be imposed for conduct that is outside the plain contemplation of the penal code.

Most broadly, such prosecution establishes unequal treatment of women in that there is no corresponding scrutiny of men and male body behavior. In legally restricting women's agency while pregnant, a discriminatory system of surveillance is established. One California woman was charged with criminal neglect of her fetus because she engaged in sexual intercourse while pregnant (against her doctor's instructions); her husband, who also knew about the doctor's orders, was not named as a collaborator in the criminal act.[21] Prosecuting pregnant women for fetal negligence compromises their fundamental reproductive choice and establishes the precedent for the state to determine who has the right to bear children.

These events and discussions establish the fact that a foundation has been set in place to deindividualize the notion of pregnancy and to make women's reproductive health a matter of *public* health policy. Mass-mediated narratives establish the pregnant woman as the agent of a new public health crisis. As the guilty culprit, she requires additional surveillance in order to protect her babies and society from her criminal excesses. So that when one professor of obstetrics and gynecology writes, "The active management of labor attempts to address a problem that is of great public health relevance in North America," we witness the process whereby women are interpolated into a very convoluted narrative that defines wombs as unruly, childbirth as inherently pathological, and women of childbearing age as unreliably duplicitous and possibly dangerous.[22] This narrative foregoes the possibility that drug use by pregnant women may be a consequence of other social forces. This situation requires a careful analysis—one that does not inadvertently delimit women's agency by reifying their identity as victims, and also doesn't bestow upon them exaggerated powers of contamination and infection. Seeing this issue through a "maternalist" logic would suggest the investigation of the social forces that influence women's drug use, the conditions under which drug use becomes abusive to self and other, and the institutional arrangements that support women's stigmatized identity as public health offenders. This reflects a deeper philosophy that seeks to establish a partnership between women and their health care providers in which the objective is to increase the information women have about their choices for self-care, fetal care, and birth, and where the care provider is treated as a consultant for the mother, not an executive of the birth process and of public health morality.

Writing History/Telling Tales

In the process of constructing an analysis of the "official" public health discourse of the surveillance of pregnant women, I learned to read between the lines by reading those statements through an interpretive framework provided by fictional accounts of the treatment of reproductive body. This is one of the contributions that science fiction literature in general makes to our understanding of contemporary situations. As works of fictions that generically extrapolate from the current moment to fictional futures (or pasts), these narratives offer readers a framework for understanding the preoccupations that infuse contemporary culture. In this sense, Atwood's novel provided a sharply focused lens through which to view the emerging situation of women of reproductive age in the U.S. Interspersed within *The Handmaid's Tale* are fragments of yet another discourse, one that articulates Offred's self-reflexive thoughts on the act of storytelling, in which the reader is addressed directly. At one point Offred tells the reader that it is a pretense to believe that she is telling a story because that would imply that she has some measure of control over the ending. At another moment we are told that "this is a reconstruction. All of it is a reconstruction." And indeed at different points in her tale, readers get different versions of the same events: a narrative technique that foregrounds the reconstructive act of narrative itself. Near the end of the novel, she wishes "this story were different. I wish it were more civilized." And she apologizes to us, the readers:

> I'm sorry there is so much pain in this story. I'm sorry it's in fragments, like a body caught in crossfire or pulled apart by force. But there is nothing I can do to change it. . . . But I keep on going with this sad and hungry and sordid, this

limping and mutilated story, because after all I want you to hear it, as I will hear yours too if I ever get the chance, if I meet you or if you escape, in the future or in heaven or in prison or underground, some other place. What they have in common is that they're not here. By telling you anything at all I'm at least believing in you. I believe you're there, I believe you into being. Because I'm telling you this story I will your existence. I tell, therefore you are. (Atwood 1986:267–68)

This passage must be juxtaposed with the concluding section titled "Historical Notes," because both of them foreground the impossibility of the narrative situation that we have just read. Here Offred's telling poses a similar narrative dilemma to the one of the narrator in Charlotte Perkins Gilman's short story "The Yellow Wallpaper." How is it that we come to get the story of a woman forbidden to read or write? The explanation offered in the "Historical Notes" section solves some of the mystery; "The Handmaid's Tale" is a historian's reconstruction based on narrative material discovered on audio tapes. What we are never told, though, is how the tapes came to be made, that is, the relationship between the historical account of the discovery of the tapes and the historical reconstruction of the ending of "The Handmaid's Tale." Are these tapes of Offred or someone else? Whose voice tells whose story? In the final analysis, I want to suggest that the "Historical Notes" section offers the most interesting statement about the contemporary situation of reproductive-age women. Some readers have interpreted this section as a splendid send-up of an academic conference or, as one reviewer describes it, "a desperately needed and hilarious spoof of an academic convention in the year 2195, at which time Gilead is a defunct society, regarded by all as a trivial aberration in cultural history" (Kendall 1986). Ironic as it clearly is, it is also the most utopian part of the entire novel. Set against the more didactic warnings against feminist techno-criticism, on the one hand, and patriarchal technological lust, on the other, this ending offers a false promise of hope and transcendence. It enacts a belief we hear in Offred's recollection of her mother's feminism: "History will absolve me." What it suggests is that something fundamental will change about people's willful acts of ignorance. Offred herself describes the fog we live within now, surrounded as we are by such seemingly isolated instances of technologically enhanced reproductive surveillance:

But we lived as usual. Everyone does, most of the time. Whatever is going on is as usual. Even this is as usual, now. We lived, as usual, by ignoring. Ignoring isn't the same as ignorance, you have to work at it. Nothing changes instantaneously: in a gradually heating bathtub you'd be boiled to death before you knew it. There were stories in the newspapers, of course. . . . The newspaper stories were like dreams to us, bad dreams dreamt by others. How awful, we would say, and they were, but they were awful without being believable. They were too melodramatic, they had a dimension that was not the dimension of our lives. We were the people who were not in the papers. We lived in the blank white spaces at the edges of the print. It gave us more freedom. We lived in the gaps between the stories. (Atwood 1986:74)

There are two messages in this passage. The first concerns our contemporary relationship to technology and the danger of an uncritical belief in technological progress. This we can understand as a act of "ignoring," rather than a quality of ignorance. Contemporary U.S. culture is completely saturated with technology; we must actively work to disregard the long-term consequences of such a saturation. In this case, Atwood's novel provides the perspective we need to understand the relation between seemingly isolated instances of technological surveillance. "Perspective is necessary," Offred tells us, "otherwise you live with your face squashed against a wall."

The second message addresses the place of women in cultural history. People who live on the margins, "in the gaps between the stories"—women whose entire lives never make the news—are not remembered. Their stories, the everydayness of their lives, are not the stuff of history. In this sense, the story we read in *The Handmaid's Tale* is a utopian vision of the development of a historical practice that would promote the importance of recording women's histories. This is not generally the trend within contemporary historical practice. It is, though, the project of feminist cultural studies. As I have argued elsewhere, ethnography can be reclaimed as a feminist practice in which we work to intervene in the production of the history of the present by writing the narratives of women's everyday lives (Balsamo 1990). In this light, I propose that we reconsider Atwood's novel as something generically different from a science-fictional dystopia. I want to read it "against the grain" perhaps as a speculative ethnographic account of our collective life in a technological era; where transcoded from one generic framework to another, it offers us a critical framework of analysis that will counteract our propensity to ignore the probable consequences for the female body of the application of the new technologies of reproductive surveillance. Such a reading requires that we forgo our willful acts of ignoring those "disturbing" newspaper stories as if they were inconsequential for our real work as scholars and critics.

My aim has been to investigate the narrative construction of reality accomplished through the articulation among cultural practices and cultural narratives. "Articulation" describes the process whereby meaning is constructed and assigned to a particular configuration of practices; it is a complex process in the sense that meaning is both an effect of practices and a determining condition of those practices. In this chapter I have described a select set of cultural stories about the maternal body that include scientific discourse about pregnancy and the development and application of medical protocols, as well as a fictional narrative of maternal surveillance. Throughout the analysis of these discursive sources, I have tried to elucidate the connection between these narratives and other social structures and institutional practices. I have also tried to examine the process of cultural analysis itself, whereby literary narratives are "interpreted" in the service of illuminating the meaning of other cultural discourses, which in turn are used to describe and critique the organization of social practices and material effects. As a map of the relationship between a particular configuration of discursive moments and a set of cultural practices, this chapter suggests not only the critical issues that I believe should be attended to by feminist cultural scholars, but also a critical framework for the analysis and intervention into such politically charged situations.

Notes

1. Although I am walking dangerous ground here, my iconoclastic rhetoric about the "romance of motherhood" is offered as an attempt to assert the reality that for some women, motherhood holds no magical promise or wonderment. Survivors of childhood violence, for example, know the haunting shame of growing up in a family where children were not treated as "blessings" of any sort. For a discussion of different models of the mother-fetus relationship, see Rothman 1991.

2. For a related study of the role of ultrasound as a technology of the gendered body see Cartwright 1995, Stabile 1992, and Stone 1991.

3. For a discussion of the way in which legal decisions and policy statements fail to differentiate between the female body, and the mother's body see Eisenstein 1988.

4. This is the argument at the heart of Emily Martin's (1990) work on ideologies of reproduction—namely that reproduction is an area of social life saturated with ideological forms of thought about the naturalness of certain predispositions. She especially challenges feminists to scrutinize our thinking about reproduction for class-biased ideological beliefs.

5. Paula Treichler (1990) illuminates how the earlier definition of obstetrics that I refer to here, as a specialized practice that involves the exercise of professional judgment, is itself a consequence of a power struggle between midwives and early physicians that established the institutionalized authority of those newly professionalized obstetricians over the pregnant female body.

6. Stanley Joel Reiser (1978) traces the historical development of technological advances in the art and practice of medicine during the past four centuries. Although his study concludes before the wide-scale use of new reproductive technologies, he claimed that even in the 1970s modern medicine has now evolved to a point where diagnostic judgments based on "subjective" evidence—the patient's sensations and the physician's own observations of the patient—are being supplanted by judgments based on "objective" evidence provided by laboratory procedures and by mechanical and electronic devices (p. ix).

7. For a discussion of the politics of fetal imagining see: Petchesky 1987; for a discussion of the dimensions of a fetal teleology see Franklin 1991. Faye Ginsburg (1990) discusses the role of the public fetus in the abortion debate; see also the special issue of *Science as Culture,* vol. 3, part 4, no. 17 (1993) on procreation stories, especially the related essays by Franklin (1993), Duden (1993), and Taylor (1993).

8. Jana Sawicki (1991) offers an insightful appraisal of the consequence of new monitoring devices when she writes that "new reproductive technologies . . . facilitate the creation of new objects and subjects of medical as well as legal and state intervention. . . . Infertile, surrogate and genetically impaired mothers, mothers whose bodies are not fit for pregnancy . . . mothers whose wombs are hostile environments for fetuses" (p. 84).

9. For an elaboration of the historical antecedents of the construction of the public body and the public fetus, see Duden (1993a:52).

10. In other cases, ultrasound scans are used to visualize mature eggs in the ovary; the process of retrieval is similar to that using a laparoscopy, but only one abdominal incision is required. Instead of using an optical device for viewing the ovaries, the ultrasound scanner provides a visual guide for inserting the hypodermic needle that is used to aspirate the egg. See Volpe 1987:4.

11. One Chicago obstetrician/gynecologist described the impossible situation that results when a woman refuses to allow surgery on her fetus: If you perform a surgical procedure despite the explicit refusal of a competent adult, you could be liable for battery or assault on the woman. If, on the other hand, you respect the women's refusal and do not intervene and some harm happens to the baby, you might be sued by the woman's husband or family for neglect of the fetus. The only way to get out from under that double liability is to give it to somebody else to decide. So the incentive to go to court is very big in these cases. See Rich 1988:1, 7–8. The moral status of the embryo is also discussed in Volpe 1987.

12. Green was the first woman charged with manslaughter due to delivery of a controlled substance to an infant in the womb. People of the State of Illinois v. Green, 88-CM-8256, Cir. Ct., filed May 8, 1989. (Citation from Daniels 1993).

13. See Little and Sing 1987, Savitz and Chen 1990, Davis 1991, Colie 1993, and Olshan and Faustman 1993.

14. When people discuss the distressing factor of low-birthweight babies, it is not so much in the context of concerns about the baby's or the mother's quality of life, but related to the fact that these are very expensive babies to keep alive. As the authors of one report state: Not only has concern been generated because the United States has a much higher rate of low-birthweight babies than other developed countries . . . but because these are "expensive babies," in monetary, familial, and societal terms. The initial cost of hospitalization for a low-birthweight baby is estimated to be over $13,000. See Brooks-Gunn, McCormick, and Heagarty 1988:288.

15. Statistical information from Mason (1989). Other sources for information on infant mortality rates of different races: Stockwell, Swanson, and Wicks 1988, Brown 1990, Randall 1990, and Painton 1991.

16. See Finkelstein 1994. Finkelstein is the director of the Coalition on Addiction, Pregnancy and Parenting in Cambridge, MA.

17. Ira Chasnoff (1993), whose work has reported the most adverse effects of cocaine use among pregnant women patients at a drug treatment center, is the author of one of the main studies that Hutchings discusses in great detail. His commentary immediately follows the Hutchings article in the same issue of *Neurotoxicology and Teratology,* volume 15, number 5. Both agree that cocaine dangers to fetal health are a media-amplified phenomenon, and that there are many missing pieces of the puzzle due in part to the vicissitudes of drug culture that guides different cities' (and hence populations') availability of drugs, use patterns, polydrug use patterns, and the role women are allowed to play within the culture. As researchers, Chasnoff (1993:287) claims, we have no idea what impact these issues can have on pregnancy and neonatal outcome.

18. To date there have been no follow-up reports. Funding for the study came largely from the March of Dimes.

19. This corresponds with Robyn Rowland's (1992) assertion that language, specifically reprospeak, powerfully shapes the attitudes of a society. See her chapter "'Reprospeak': The Language of the New Reproductive Technologies," pp. 230–45.

20. Stephenson and Wagner cite Field 1989 in their summary of the position of fetal rights advocates.

21. This case is reported in Roberts's 1990 article. The case reference is: People v. Stewart,

NO. M508097 California, San Diego Mun. Ct. Feb 23, 1987.

22. The quotation is from William Fraser (1993), associate professor of obstetrics and gynecology, Laval University and Hospital St-François d'Assise, Quebec.

References

Arney, William Ray. 1982. *Power and the Profession of Obstetrics.* Chicago: The University of Chicago Press, 1982.

Atwood, Margaret. 1986. *The Handmaid's Tale.* Boston:Houghton Mifflin.

Balsamo, Anne. 1990. Rethinking Ethnography: A Work of the Feminist Imagination. *Studies in Symbolic Interactionism* 11:75–86.

Brooks-Gunn, J., Marie C. McCormick, and Margaret C. Heagarty. 1988. Preventing Infant Mortality and Morbidity: Developmental Perspectives. *American Journal of Orthopsychiatry* 58(2):288–96.

Brown, Frank Dexter. 1990. Expanding Health Care for Mothers and Their Children. *Black Enterprise* May:25–26.

Cartwright, Lisa. 1995. *Screening the Body: Tracing Medicine Visual Culture.* Minneapolis: University of Minnesota Press.

Chasnoff, Ira J. 1993. Commentary: Missing Pieces of the Puzzle. *Neurotoxicology and Teratology* 15(5):287–88.

Colie, Christine F. 1993. Male mediated Teratogenesis. *Reproductive Toxicology* 7:3–9.

Collins, Patricia Hill. 1990. Mammies, Matriarchs and Other Controlling Images. Pp. 67–90 in *Black Feminist Thought: Knowledge, Consciousness, and the Politics of Empowerment.* New York: Routledge.

Cook, Paddy Shannon, Robert C. Petersen, and Dorothy Tuell Moore. 1990. *Alcohol, Tobacco, and Other Drugs May Harm the Unborn.* Edited by Tineke Bodde Haase. U.S. Department of Health and Human Services, Office of Substance Abuse Prevention, DHHS Publication # (ADM) 90–1711.

Daly, Nancy L., and Gale A. Richardson. 1993. Cocaine Use and Crack Babies: Science, the Media, and Miscommunication. *Neurotoxicology and Teratology* 15(5): 293–94.

Daniels, Cynthia R. 1993. *At Women's Expense: State Power and the Politics of Fetal Rights.* Cambridge, MA: Harvard University Press.

Davis, Devra Lee. 1991. Fathers and Fetuses. *Lancet* 337:122–23.

Dogan, Michael D., Milton Kotelchuck, Greg R. Alexander, and Wayne E. Johnson. 1994. Racial Disparities in Reported Prenatal Care Advice from Health Care Providers. *American Journal of Public Health* 84(1):82–88.

Duden, Barbara. 1993a. *Disembodying Women: Perspectives on Pregnancy and the Unborn.* Cambridge, MA: Harvard University Press.

———. 1993b. Visualizing "Life." *Science as Culture* 3(4)17:562–600.

Eisenstein, Zillah R. 1988. *The Female Body and the Law.* Berkeley: University of California Press.

Field, M.A. 1989. Controlling the Woman to Protect the Fetus. *Law, Medicine and Health Care* 17:114–29.

Finkelstein, Norma. 1994. Treatment Issues for Alcohol-and Drug-Dependent Pregnant and Parenting Women. *Health and Social Work* 19(1):7–15.

Franklin, Sarah. 1991. Fetal Fascinations: New Dimensions to the Medical-Scientific Construction of Fetal Personhood. In Sarah Franklin, Celia Lury, and Jackie Stacey (eds.), *Off-Centre: Feminism and Cultural Studies.* London: Harper Collins Academic.

———. 1993. Postmodern Procreation: Representing Reproductive Practice. *Science as Culture* 3(4)17:522–61.

Fraser, William. 1993. Methodological Issues in Assessing the Active Management of Labor. *Birth* 20(3):155–56.

Gelb, Adam. 1991. State's Newborns to Get Cocaine Tests. *Atlanta Journal-Constitution* March 12:A1.

Ginsburg, Faye. 1990. The "Word-Made" Flesh: The Disembodiment of Gender in the Abortion Debate. Pp. 59–75 in Faye Ginsberg and Anna Lowenhaupt Tsing (eds.), *Uncertain Terms: Negotiating Gender in American Culture.* Boston: Beacon Press.

Hartouni, Valerie. 1994. Breached Birth: Reflections on Race, Gender, and Reproductive Discourse in the 1980s. *Configurations* 1:73–88.

Hutchings, Donald E. 1993. The Puzzle of Cocaine's Effects Following Maternal Use During Pregnancy: Are There Reconcilable Differences? *Neurotoxicology and Teratology* 15.5:281–86.

Kaplan, Janice. 1989. Public Pregnancy. *Self* April:155–57.

Kendall, Elaine. 1986. [Review of Atwood, *The Handmaid's Tale.*] *Los Angeles Times Book Review,* February 9:15.

Little, Ruth E., and Charles F. Sing. 1987. Father's Drinking and Infant Birth Weight: Report of an Association. *Teratology* 36:59–65.

Martin, Emily. 1990. The Ideology of Reproduction: the Reproduction of Ideology. Pp. 300–14 in Faye Ginsburg and Anna Lowenhaupt Tsing (eds.), *Uncertain Terms: Negotiating Gender in American Culture.* Boston: Beacon Press.

Mason, James O. 1989. The Report from the Assistant Secretary for Health. *Journal of the American Medical Association* 262(16):2202.

Painton, Pricilla. 1991. $25,000,000: Mere Millions for Kids. *Time* April 8:29–30.

Petchesky, Rosalind Pollack. 1987. Fetal Images: The Power of Visual Culture in the Politics of Reproduction. *Feminist Studies* 13(2):263–92.

Randall, Teri. 1990. Infant Mortality Receiving Increasing Attention. *Journal of the American Medical Association* 263(19):2604–6.

Reardon, Patrick. 1989a. "I Loved Her," Mother Says: "Shocked" over Arrest in Baby's Drug Death. *Chicago Tribune,* May 11:1:1, 8.

———. 1989b. When Rights Begin: Baby's Cocaine Death Adds to Debate on Protection of the Unborn. *Chicago Tribune,* May 14:5:8–9.

———. 1989c. Drug and Pregnancy Debate Far from Resolved. *Chicago Tribune,* May 28:1:1, 5.

Reiser, Stanley Joel. 1991. *Medicine and the Reign of Technology.* Cambridge: Cambridge University Press.

Rich, Marney. 1988. A Question of Rights, *Chicago Tribune,* September 18:6:1, 7.

Roberts, Dorothy E. 1990. Drug-Addicted Women Who Have Babies. *Trial,* April:56–61.

Olshan, Andrew F., and Elaine M. Faustman. 1993. Male-mediated Developmental Toxicity. *Reproductive Toxicology* 7: 191–202.

Rothman, Barbara Katz. 1991. *In Labor: Women and Power in the Birthplace.* London: Norton.

Rowland, Robyn. 1992. *Living Laboratories: Women and Reproductive Technologies.* Bloomington: Indiana University Press.

Savitz, David A., and Jianhua Chen. 1990. Parental Occupation and Childhood Cancer: Review of Epidemiological Studies. *Environmental Health Perspectives* 88:325–37.

Sawicki, Jana. 1991. *Disciplining Foucault: Feminism, Power and the Body.* New York: Routledge.

Spallone, Patricia. 1989. Introducing the Pre-embryo, or What's in a Name. Pp. 50–55 in *Beyond Conception: The New Politics of Reproduction.* Granby, MA: Bergin and Garvey.

Stabile, Carole. 1992. Shooting the Mother: Fetal Photography and the Politics of Disappearance. *Camera Obscura* 28:179–205.

Stephenson, P. A., and M. G. Wagner. 1993. Reproductive Rights and the Medical Care System: A Plea for Rational Health Policy. *Journal of Public Health Policy,* Summer:174–82.

Stockwell, Edward G., David A. Swanson, and Jerry W. Wicks.1988. Economic Status Differences in Infant Mortality by Cause of Death. *Public Health Reports* 103(2):135–42.

Stone, Jennifer L. 1991. Contextualizing Biogenetic and Reproductive Technologies. *Critical Studies in Mass Communication* 8:309–32.

Taylor,Janelle Sue. 1993. The Public Foetus and the Family Car: From Abortion Politics to a Volvo Advertisement. *Science as Culture* 3(4)17:601–18.

Terry, Jennifer. 1989. The Body Invaded: Medical Surveillance of Women as Reproducers. *Socialist Review* 19(3):13–43.

Treichler, Paula. 1990. Feminism, Medicine and the Meaning of Childbirth. Pp. 113–38 in Mary Jacobus, Evelyn Fox Keller, and Sally Shuttleworth (eds.), *Body/Politics: Women and the Discourses of Science.* New York: Routledge.

Tsing, Anna Lowenhaupt. 1990. Monster Stories: Women Charged with Perinatal Endangerment. Pp. 282–99 in Faye Ginsberg and Anna Lowenhaupt Tsing (eds.), *Uncertain Terms: Negotiating Gender in American Culture.* Boston: Beacon Press.

Volpe, E. Peter. 1987. *Test-Tube Conception: A Blend of Love and Science.* Macon, GA: Mercer University Press, 1987.

A Study in Reproductive Technologies

VALERIE HARTOUNI

In this essay, I want to consider three cultural artifacts: an ad campaign that ran in 1993 for Evian spring water; a 1993 Supreme Court ruling, *Bray v. Alexandria Health Clinic*; and a 1994 CD-ROM produced by A.D.A.M. Software, Inc., titled *Nine-Month Miracle*. At first glance, this grouping of artifacts may seem contrived, and in some respects, of course, it is. Beyond a shared cultural and historical frame, these artifacts circulate within distinct discursive arenas and could be said to both reflect and enact a diverse set of agendas with quite different effects. What nevertheless interests me about these three texts is the unmistakable resonance that sounds between them: the modes of seeing and literacy that each presumes, requires, and produces along with the shared fantasies and anxieties that organize and are organized by their ostensibly different purposes and visions. Although meaning production in social life is neither orchestrated nor necessarily cohesive, in juxtaposition these texts tell a riveting, at times humorous, and often disturbing collection of stories about the organization of gender in late-twentieth-century North America. Situated in a reproductive landscape that has gradually been transformed over the course of the last decade through a proliferation of new forms and practices of life, these texts are also constitutive components of that landscape and, in the end, this is what makes them both interesting and significant. More interesting than the commentary they may provide on contemporary cultures of reproduction are the ways in which they operate as technologies of reproduction—technologies "that turn bodies into stories and stories into bodies" (Haraway 1997:179) in ongoing cultural contests over how (and which) reproductive bodies will signify.

I want to begin this discussion by first considering the ad for Evian water—or, more previously, by considering a version of the ad that I have altered slightly, for reasons that will become clear as we proceed. In this edited version in which the narrative accompanying the image has been removed, we first encounter a woman in quiet repose at the beach. The lighting is soft, the texture of the portrait grainy. She reclines with eyes closed and clasps her belly in what is a classic maternal pose. She is also smiling; indeed, she appears to be dreaming about something, although about what exactly this might be we can only speculate. The story we tell, of course, will colonize the image or make it make a particular kind of sense. For example, we might speculate that this is an academic who has just gone on leave. The books on her lap and straw satchel by the lounge suggest as much, and there are few of us who would be unable to identify with the kind of pleasure this woman seems to be enjoying at the prospect of being away from the demands of her institution. On the other hand, perhaps she is reading books on child rearing and pauses to imagine the many blissful years that lie ahead (this would be her first child). Perhaps she has just come from a productive therapy session; is quietly anticipating the arrival of her lover, husband, or friend; or is enjoying the moments following a rendezvous with her partner or, for that matter, someone other than her partner. It *is* possible.[1]

Whatever the stories we might be inspired to tell, the point to be made about this image is both simple and obvious: In and of itself, it has no explanatory power or significance—and certainly no social significance—beyond what we might attach to it. Although I introduced the image as part of a campaign Evian launched in the early 1990s to sell bottled spring water, the picture could be in my photo album or yours and lends itself to a range of stories, all of which are entirely circumstantial. But let us now consider the ad as it actually appeared in the *New Yorker*. In this version, the written text—"Mommy, can I have a drink of water?"—contains the array and eruption of possible readings, interrupts the serenity of the image and recasts the composition, and in particular the romanticism that suffuses it, in rather dramatic ways. In this version of the ad, the woman is apparently not alone. Although the obvious first question we could ask might be "Who is speaking?"—there is, after all, no other person depicted in the photograph sharing her small strip of beach—such a question is entirely unnecessary. It is a pregnant woman, already a "mother," already in relationship with a separate speaking subject whose identity is self-evident, indeed, a subject who knows its needs and is, moreover, able to articulate them clearly. A question perhaps more to the point, therefore, than "Who is the speaking subject?" would be "How is the subject speaking?" What are the constellation of assumptions and practices that render the figure that speaks more than a figure of speech? What makes this speech both plausible and possible? And what are its effects?

If the caption enlists us in refiguring who counts as the primary subject in this portrait, the sidebar both presumes and produces our shift in vision. Stimulating anxiety and a sense of inadequacy at the same time that it must also incite desire, the ad positions pregnant women as both support systems for and potential (if inadvertent) adversaries of the fetuses they carry. Keeping the gestating body operational entails more than simply eating, the text advises; there is blood pressure to maintain, body temperature to regulate, systems to cleanse, joints to lubricate, and food to process and be made. And not surprisingly, in order to perform these functions in an efficient fashion, the body requires water, preferably pure, minerally balanced spring water. The fetus apparently knows this and, of course, so does the pregnant woman who, as the saying goes, "listens to her body."

If the Evian ad depicts the good mother, one who is in touch with nature and, for that matter, with what experts have to say about maintaining an optimal gestational environment, it also invokes and requires the specter of the bad. Outside the frame but nevertheless essential to its meaning are the contests of the last decade that have recast the relationship of public and private with respect to the bodily integrity of pregnant women. Pregnant women, typically nonwhite and working-class women, have increasingly been subject to legal scrutiny and criminal prosecution for engaging in activities deemed reckless or detrimental to fetal life. These activities include smoking, drinking, having sex, ingesting both illicit and prescribed drugs, refusing surgery, refusing to follow the advice of their physicians, forgoing prenatal care, and working or living in proximity to teratogenic substances (Hartouni 1997; Daniels 1993). In view of how utterly essential water appears to be for regulating, lubricating, and cleansing the procreative body as well as for generating breast milk, could a woman's failure to drink enough of it be considered reckless maternal behavior? detrimental to fetal life? a failure to deliver support and thus a form of negligence? And if most tap water in the United States is polluted and undrinkable, could a woman's failure to drink Evian or any one of the many competing brands of spring water be regarded as criminal? To underscore the obvious, class standing and lifestyle are clearly not the only things at stake in the liquid one ingests.

Ads like the one for Evian circulate in popular culture and, of course, change from year to year. They do have a lasting effect, however, and this lies in their ability to school a public in particular reading practices and scopic regimes while also normalizing and reinforcing these practices and regimes. In the case of the Evian ad, what is being marketed along with water is a particular version of maternal nature, shaped by a particular vision of fetal life that has assumed its most recent form and authority in the context of popular debates over abortion.[2] The ad produces this vision as part of the fabric of fact and involves its audience in that production; it requires that they not only conjure the fetus as a tiny and autonomous, preformed individual, but render it a child for whom they might have fetched water the previous night. Like that child—indeed, like any child—it has claims as well as needs and demands care, nurturance, and protection. It has a presence that is both insistent and all-consuming—so all-consuming, in fact, that it need not even appear in the frame to engulf and control its meaning.

Although we may be inclined to regard the scopic practices, the particular logic, or the multiple operations of seeing that are enacted in the Evian ad as both fleeting and politically inconsequential, a curiously similar set of practices can be found at play in a very different kind of text, a 1993 Supreme Court ruling, *Bray v. Alexandria Health Clinic* (Hartouni 1997). In this case, the Court was asked to determine whether the "rescue" demonstrations engaged in by anti-abortion activists at abortion clinics for the purpose of disrupting clinic operations deliberately deprived women seeking abortion (and related medical and counseling services) of their constitutionally protected right to interstate travel by making the destination of that travel inaccessible.[3] Although the Court ruled that such demonstrations *did not* infringe upon women's constitutional rights, what is striking about this case is not its outcome. What is striking is the reasoning that produced the Court's ruling, the notion, in other words, that antiabortion demonstrations do not deprive women of having or exercising any constitutionally secured right or privilege because such demonstrations are conducted for the sole purpose of protecting the abortion's "innocent victims" and *thus have nothing to do with women.*

Centrally at issue in *Bray* were the meaning and scope of the Civil Rights Act of 1871, and in particular the first clause of this Reconstruction-era statute. Through a series of decisions handed down by the Court in the intervening century or so, this clause had come to be interpreted as prohibiting activities among two or more persons (conspiracies) motivated by "some racial or perhaps otherwise class-based invidious discriminatory animus" and intended, either directly or indirectly, to deprive others of having and exercising their constitutionally protected rights and privileges. The question in *Bray* was whether this clause could be said to provide a federal cause of action against demonstrators who obstruct clinic access and operations. Or, re-posing and sharpening the question to bring more clearly into focus its stakes as the Court assessed them, does opposition to abortion constitute a basic discriminatory attitude toward women in general? Are antiabortion demonstrations motivated by a discriminatory animus directed specifically at women and conducted for the purpose of impeding their protected right to interstate travel, affecting their conduct, or forcibly preventing them from exercising a right still guaranteed by *Roe v. Wade*?

Writing for the majority, Supreme Court Justice Antonin Scalia *dismissed as absurd* the notion that opposition to abortion—blockading clinic entrances, damaging clinic property, threatening and intimidating clinic cliental, and overwhelming local law enforcement—could "possibly be considered an irrational surrogate for opposition to (or paternalism towards) women (*Bray v. Alexandria Women's Health Clinic,* 113 S. Ct. 753, 1993:13). As Scalia figured the matter, "the characteristic that formed the basis of the targeting . . . , was not womanhood, but the seeking of abortion" (*Bray v. Alexandria:*15). Motivated by the desire to stop abortion and reverse its legalization, rescue operations, he argued, were simply that: "physical interventions between abortionists and the innocent victims of abortion" with the clear and ultimate goal of "rescuing" innocent human lives (*Bray v. Alexandria:*12). As such, they were not aimed at or defined with reference to women, nor could they be said to reflect a derogatory view of women, an overtly hostile attitude toward them, or a conscious, discriminatory intent with respect to them. "Whatever one thinks of abortion," Scalia argued, "there are common and respectable reasons for opposing it other than hatred of or condescension toward (or indeed any view at all concerning) women as a class" (*Bray v. Alexandria*:13).

Any view at all? While recognizing that opposition to abortion is not, as Justice Stevens put it in his dissenting opinion, "ipso facto to discriminate invidiously against women," we might nevertheless be inclined, as was Stevens, to reconsider the obvious: Only women have the capacity to become pregnant and thus to need or have an abortion (*Bray v. Alexandria*:51–53). In this respect, abortion is and has always been a "uniquely female practice," a practice in which only women engage.[4] It is, moreover, a right that only women possess and have the capacity to exercise, and one might argue that it is precisely this capacity that is constrained or thwarted when violence is used to intimidate women entering clinics.[5] Finally—and this Stevens noted only furtively in his dissent—abortion is an issue that has shaped and been shaped by a dense constellation of questions and an equally dense set of cultural contests, in this century as well as the last, despite its shifting meanings, having to do with the control and containment of women's fertility and sexuality, the terms and conditions of childbearing and rearing, the meanings of motherhood and manhood, and the structure, meaning, and organization of the family as well as of gender, marriage, reproduction, and heterosexuality (see, e.g., Siegel 1992). If Operation Rescue claims—as it did in a 1990 editorial—that it is the rightful heir of the women's movement and has become "the true defender of women in this generation . . . [by] allowing women to be what God intended them to be," both childbearers and rearers (Phelen 1993:143), how is it possible that they could, as Scalia maintains they do, oppose abortion and not have "any view at all concerning women"?[6]

What is the view that Scalia contends, and the majority of the Supreme Court apparently agrees, is no view at all? If law functions, among other ways, to keep intact existing social relations, what are the social relations that Scalia's reading produce as given, as part of the fabric of fact, as part of the natural order of things? What are the effects of this view-that-is-no-view, this particular formation of the visual and thus social field? And how does it shape who comes to be seen as a legal subject and what comes to count as a legitimate moral question,a plausible set of claims, or a possible constellation of representations in ongoing struggles over the meaning and organization of reproductive bodies and labor?

Although these questions are not entirely rhetorical, they are nevertheless driven by an argument that there can be no "innocent seeing" or passive vision, as the majority opinion in *Bray* and as much of the reproductive discourse of the 1980s and 1990s seems to inscribe as a matter of fact. Pure vision, a vision that is unsituated, unmediated, and thus uncontaminated by imagination, purpose, and desire, is not possible; indeed, putting the matter more simply still, "the innocent eye is blind" (Mitchell 1986:38). A compelling, if somewhat literal, illustration of this point and one worth pausing over is a story that Oliver Sacks recounts of a man he calls Virgil (Sacks 1993:59). Virtually sightless for forty-five of his fifty years as a result of a series of childhood illnesses, Virgil underwent surgery that successfully restored function to his retina and optic nerve. However, quite to the surprise of those who gathered to watch as his bandages were removed following surgery, nothing actually happened. In Sacks' words, "the dramatic moment stayed vacant."

> No cry ("I can see") burst from Virgil's lips. He seemed to be staring blankly, bewildered, without focusing, at the surgeon, who stood before him, still holding the bandages. Only when the surgeon spoke—saying "Well?"—did a look of recognition cross Virgil's face. (Sacks 1993:61).

What awaited Virgil once his bandages were removed was not a world of independent, obvious, or self-evident meaning, but a confusing collage of undifferentiated, largely unidentifiable lines, objects, and colors. Although Virgil could "see" in a literal or physiological sense, what he "saw" upon his first visual contact with the world after forty-five years was simply incomprehensible.

> Virgil told me later that in this first moment he had no idea what he was seeing. There was light, there was movement, there was color, all mixed up, all meaningless, a blur. Then out of the blur came a voice that said, "Well?" Then, and only then, he said, did he finally realize that this light and shadow was a face—and, indeed, the face of his surgeon. (Sacks 1993:61).

Unable to decipher and organize into coherent and recognizable patterns of meaning what he was seeing, and lacking visual memories that would allow him to infer these patterns, Virgil emerged from surgery no longer visually blind, but in a state of mental blindness. The surgery had restored his capacity for sight, but it did not and could not simultaneously restore his capacity to see. Contrary to our working assumptions and everyday experience as sighted creatures, seeing is not only or even primarily a physiological event, an automatic, spontaneous, or mechanical process—something that happens in either a natural or unmediated fashion when we open our eyes to the world. Seeing is rather an act of immense construction, loosely governed by templates that are laid down in the first years of life and performed "seamlessly, effortlessly, and, for the most part, unconsciously, thousands of times a day at a glance" (Sacks 1993:65). Seeing is a set of learned practices and processes that allows us to organize the visual field and that engages us in producing the world we seem only to passively greet and take in. Indeed, to be able to "see" the world at all, as Sacks's account forcefully illustrates, is already to be making sense of it, or making it make the sense it seems a priori to possess. There are not things as they "really" are and things as we come to see or interpret them, truth and opinion, reality and representation. Point of view, perspective, and interpretation, while typically considered practices that corrupt, prevent, or occlude sight, are, on the contrary, practices that enable it or, putting the matter more strongly still, constitute its very condition of possibility.

What renders Virgil's first moment of visual contact with the world disruptive and thus particularly instructive is that is disables any easy embrace of the idea of passive vision and, along with this idea, dominant epistemological and ontological assumptions that sustain and are themselves sustained by it. As Donna Haraway, among others, has argued, ways of seeing—of decoding, deciphering, classifying, translating, and interpreting—are not something with which we are simply born, but constitute and are constituted by particular ways of life (Haraway 1991:190). They contain and are themselves contained by particular ways of organizing a world (and humans within it) that otherwise seems self-evidently what it is and objectively knowable as such.[7] That Scalia and the Court's majority in *Bray* fail to see the paternalism and the belief in women's innate maternalism that lie at the heart of the interventions of antiabortion demonstrators is disturbing, particularly since both systems have worked historically in invidiously discriminatory or exclusionary ways. Their failure, however, is not surprising given that the system of representation reinscribed by the Court in *Bray* and the social relations of gender it both presumes and produces—the view, in other words, that Scalia contends is no view at all—is at play in Evian's oddly romanticized depiction of "maternal-nature-as-support-system" and, more generally of course, within the culture at large: Clearly, the court's rendering of antiabortion activities would not otherwise be plausible nor would this view work as an effective marketing device for bottled water. In both the ruling and the ad, the maternal body is stage to a host of cultural dramas. And although the drama of fetal life and death may be among the most obvious and publicly captivating, as we will see with *Nine Month Miracle,* a software package that purports to reveal the "ultimate inside story" on reproduction, it is hardly the only drama for which this body is considered a natural medium.

Nine Month Miracle is a CD-ROM that A.D.A.M. Software, Inc., began distributing in 1994 as an animated learning tool primarily for use by a computer-literate, nonmedical, lay public. Although consumers can easily navigate through an assorted collection of files that map an aspect or function of the reproductive body, the software basically provides three high-tech excursions. These include (1) a trip through the anatomy of males and females (with settings to alter the color and ethnicity of the images—the default setting being "white"—and "modesty" options that permit anyone who loads the program initially to permanently cover or, as the case may be, uncover, parts of the body otherwise considered "sensitive" (or not); (2) a look at pregnancy that is for children and ostensibly from "a child's point of view"; and (3) a tour through what is referred to as "the family album," ten files that in effect operate as a not-so-sophisticated apparatus for the production of the nuclear family—the family, as it turns out, of a couple named Adam and Eve. Once the software is booted up, the first image that opens the program and greets viewers is of a fig leaf gracefully floating down and across an otherwise dark and empty computer screen: clearly, there will be no innocent seeing here, for the story that is about to unfold concerns the production of life after the fall.

Each chapter (or file) in the family album of this original family provides a detailed month-by-month account of pregnancy, from an initial preconceptive moment of heterosexual desire through birth. For example, following an explanation of the hormonal changes that precede conception and the dramatic cellular activity that results from it, Chapter 2 details Eve's first month of pregnancy. Included in this chapter is an account of Eve's initial prenatal visit in which her pregnancy is confirmed, a description of her developing embryo, and a list of foods, drugs, exercises, and behaviors that she is advised primarily to avoid, but also to consume as in the case of particular vegetables especially rich in vitamins and minerals. Chapter 3 provides a description of Eve's second month of pregnancy: the embryo becomes a fetus, a heartbeat develops, and Eve is advised by her obstetrician, Dr. Richards, to consider genetic screening and to modify her exercise routine in order to maintain a stable uterine environment. Month four finds Eve wrestling with body-image issues and coming to terms with the fact that she is now obviously supporting two "individuals"; month five identifies this second "individual"—the individual occupying her uterus—as a boy, and with this information Adam is able to resolve the feelings of anxiety and ambivalence about pregnancy and parenthood that overtook him with the onset of the second trimester. Month six takes viewers to a labor class while also celebrating the fetus' growing awareness of and engagement with the outside world; month seven finds Adam and Eve inviting their next-door neighbor, seven-year-old Emily, to explore her fears and hopes about the arrival of a new sibling in her own household; month eight details potential problems that could precipitate a Cesarean section; and month nine follows Eve through labor and a vaginal delivery.

Although this month-by-month account of pregnancy merely brings together a range of information that one could find perusing the parenting section of any bookstore, what distinguishes A.D.A.M.'s commodity, in addition to the convenience it may provide some consumers, is the way in which it packages this "information"—in particular, the real-time video side trips that convey viewers to women's groups, genetic counseling sessions, pregnancy-related surgeries, and exercise and labor classes, as well as doctor-patient meetings. Perhaps the most interesting, and certainly the most spectacular, of these trips, however, is the monthly excursion into "Eve's Virtual Uterus." With a click of the mouse on what is supposed to be a prosthetic imaging device, the "EVU 3000," one is transported "into" Eve's uterus where a much-shrunken version of Eve's obstetrician, Dr. Richards, greets Adam and Eve along with viewers, and briefly describes the changing gestational environment while also answering the couple's questions regarding the growth and appearance of their embryo/fetus.

The images of fetal life—or, more accurately, of what is supposed to be Adam and Eve's "baby"—that occupy the screen during these monthly excursions are colorful, stunningly beautiful compositions and clearly the work of

Lennart Nilsson. In fact, Eve's fetus is the same fetus that has starred in numerous PBS specials, graced the cover of *Life* magazine, and circulated on the posters of pro-life activists for the last decade and a half in the context of the contemporary debate over abortion. Autonomous and very much in control of its own miraculous development,[8] this fetus, unlike its maternally embodied, less public kin, resides in a securely locked file/uterus that cannot be tampered with, cloned or, perhaps more to the point, deleted.[9]

Although it is the "EVU 3000" that ostensibly makes this seeing (indeed, this knowledge production) possible, what actually gives viewers—science, medicine, and popular culture—access to Eve's uterus and permits them/us not only to witness the production of life but to interact with it in the latter months of pregnancy is Eve's disembodied condition. As she cheerfully explains it while introducing the "EVU 3000," "I'm only an illustration"—a computer-generated graphic, or virtual human. Although she shelters what she claims is—and what is clearly meant to be perceived as—an "actual human life" or life "in its natural state," Eve herself is only a technical effect. To be sure, the fetus is likewise merely a technical effect, a representation, illustration, or artificial life form, like Eve. But this apparently obvious little detail is not so very apparent or obvious in the context of the narrative that *Nine Month Miracle* develops, and in any event it seems irrelevant: Eve may be an illustration, but the fetus clearly is not. The ostensibly passive gaze of the camera—Nilsson's camera, A.D.A.M. Software's "EVU 3000"—seem only to capture and convey what has been awaiting discovery. With mouse in hand, viewers too can "strip the veil of mystery from the dark inner sanctum" and encounter the "true" nature of what resides there—not quite the prenatal three-year-olds at nursery school described by fetologist Frederick Frigoletto, but a close resemblance and, in any event, unmistakably human, unlike Eve.[10]

If A.D.A.M. Software is marketing *Nine Month Miracle* as a "learning tool," it is not especially difficult to discern the forms of knowledge this tool produces and inscribes as both possible and plausible. While the software may indeed reveal the "ultimate inside story" about life in the making, in the end that story, like the one contained in the Evian ad and authorized by the majority of the Court in *Bray,* is about the making of particular forms and practices of life—the making of particular kinds of families, parents, pregnancies, bodies, and (gendered) persons; the making, in other words, of a particular kind of world in which highly contingent and otherwise contested social arrangements, relations, institutions, and identities are installed as simple matters of fact.

In the world figured by Evian, A.D.A.M. Software, and the Court's ruling in *Bray,* women are natural if also disembodied mothers (which retires at least one confused and persistently troubled arena of legal contest);[11] uteruses are accessible, well-trafficked public space, a site for production, learning, high-tech intervention, entertainment, professional work, and manly combat; fetuses are autonomous, preformed, speaking subjects. To be sure, this vision and version of life is clearly both partial and skewed, but that is in part the point. Sentimentalized by Evian, romanticized and biologized by A.D.A.M. Software and sanctioned in *Bray*, this curious vision of life circulates and competes with others in ongoing cultural contests over the making of subjects and social realities. If there is an ultimate inside story to be told, that story, in all its many versions, is about such making, indeed, is about reproduction and reproductive bodies, but bodies that are, in the end, always already social.

Notes

1. But not likely. Adultery is probably not a practice that Evian or its many competitors would sanction or use to compel consumers to buy bottled water—particularly not, for obvious reasons, the adulterous practices of a pregnant woman.
2. For a more detailed analysis of contemporary renderings of the fetal form, see Newman 1996; Casper 1994; Franklin 1995; Stabile 1992; Balsamo 1996.
3. In areas where abortion services are unavailable, women seeking abortions are typically forced to travel across state lines for health services. At the particular clinic in question, 20 to 30 percent of the clientele were from out of state.
4. There is a subtle shift worth noting with respect to how abortion is being read/configured in this dissent. In *Roe v. Wade*, abortion was defined as first and foremost a medical matter and the purview of medical professionals. In *Bray*, Stevens characterizes abortion—and apparently Blackmun accepts the characterization—as a distinctly female practice or practice in which only women engage. Clearly, the public discourse on fetal life has forced at least some members of the Court to reframe the issue in a manner that foregrounds women.
5. What is at issue here is what kind of right abortion is. See pp. 54–55 of Stevens's dissent.
6. Cited in Phelen 1993:143. "What has happened to the women's movement?" the organization's newsletter, *Rescue Report*, asked in a 1990 editorial.

> We have picked it up; we have become the true defenders of women in this generation by allowing women to be what God intended them to be. We are the ones who are intervening for women in the courts. We are the ones helping single women raise their families.

In this passage, the discursive terrain occupied by feminists is appropriated and reinflected to produce a world not unlike the one to which the women's movement of the mid-1960s arose in response. It is a world in which women are regarded as helpless (in need of defense), vulnerable (in need of protection), powerless (in need of refuge), and "allowed" or expected to subordinate all aspects of their lives to their primary, divinely ordained purpose or natural function, the bearing and rearing of children. What Operation Rescue represents as its "feminist turn," in other words, is an innate maternalism, paternalistically rendered, or a not-so-new variation on an old and tired tune. It recasts women who seek abortions as helpless victims in need of protection and support and incapable of making such decisions for themselves, while valorizing the deeds of the "born-again male hero" or "man-father-Father figure." He acts on their behalf, for their sake, in their best interest and, one could presume given the logic of paternalism, to check their (mistaken) convictions when necessary in order to "save [them] as well as [their] babies from the capacious maw of death" (Harding 1991:81).

A benevolent paternalism might be preferred to and certainly has greater popular appeal than a more punishing variety that condemns women who seek abortions as selfish, sinful, murderous, and dangerously unnatural—this was the view of women

Operation Rescue espoused prior to its "feminist" conversion. Paternalism may also seem neither aberrant nor irrational, but perfectly consistent within still prevalent social and dominant legal understandings that see who and what women are and are for as physiologically rooted and determined. As legal scholar Reva Siegel observes, "Facts about women's bodies [or what Siegel refers to as physiological naturalism] have long served to justify regulation enforcing judgements about women's roles [alleged needs, assumed wants, and supposed desires]." (Siegel 1992:277) In either case, however, whether benevolent or punitive, respectable or aberrant, Operation Rescue's paternalism and the innate maternalism for which its "feminism" functions as a cover story, would seem nevertheless to betray and perpetuate precisely what the majority opinion in Bray dismissed as erroneous: a basic attitude or animus toward women, indeed, a derogatory view of women which the record clearly shows could work and has worked, historically, in invidiously discriminatory or exclusionary ways.

7. Haraway 1991:190. For a fuller discussion of these and related issues see Mitchell 1986; Crary 1995; and Daston and Galison 1992.

8. This is Sarah Franklin's characterization which she develops quite brilliantly and in greater detail in Franklin 1991.

9. Throughout, the software clearly bears the imprint of the contemporary politics of abortion—the locked fetal-image file is just one site among many where a conservative, prenatal politics registers.

10. As quoted in Hubbard 1984:348–49.

11. As Sarah Franklin observes, "The very term 'individual,' meaning *one who can not be divided*, can only mean the male, as it is precisely the process of one individual becoming two which occurs through a woman's pregnancy. Pregnancy is precisely about one body becoming two bodies, two bodies becoming one, the exact antithesis of individuality. This is, claims Donna Haraway, "why women have had so much trouble counting as individuals in modern western discourses. Their personal, bounded individuality is compromised by their bodies' troubling talent for making other bodies, whose individuality can take precedence over their own" (Franklin 1991:203). Franklin's quote from Haraway is found in Haraway 1988:39.

References

Balsamo, Ann. 1996. *Technologies of the Gendered Body: Reading Cyborg Women.* Durham: Duke University Press.

Casper, Monica. 1994. Reframing and Grounding Nonhuman Agency: What Makes a Fetus an Agent? *American Behavioral Scientist* 37(6):839–56.

Crary, Jonathan. 1995. *Techniques of the Observer.* Cambridge, MA: MIT Press.

Daniels, Cynthia. 1993. *At Women's Expense: State Power and the Politics of Fetal Rights.* Cambridge, MA: Harvard University Press.

Daston, Lorraine, and Peter Galison. 1992. The Image of Objectivity. *Representations* 40: 81–128.

Franklin, Sarah. 1991. Fetal Fascinations: New Dimensions to the Medical-scientific Construction of Fetal Personhood. Pp. 190–205 in Sarah Franklin, Celia Lury, and Jackie Stacey (eds.), *Off-Centre: Feminism and Cultural Studies.* London: Harper Collins Academic.

———. 1995. Postmodern Procreation: A Cultural Account of Assisted Reproduction. Pp. 323–45 in Faye D. Ginsburg and Rayna Rapp (eds.), *Conceiving the New World Order: The Global Stratification of Reproduction.* Berkeley: University of California Press.

Haraway, Donna. 1988. The Biopolitics of Postmodern Bodies: Determinations of Self in Immune System Discourse. *Differences* 1:3–43.

———. 1991. "Situated Knowledges: The Science Question in Feminism and the Privilege of Partial Perspective." Pp. 183–201 in *Simians, Cyborgs, and Women: The Reinvention of Nature*. New York: Routledge.

———. 1997. *Modest_Witness@Second_Millennium.FemaleMan©_Meets_OncoMouse™*. New York: Routledge.

Harding, Susan. 1991. If I Die Before I Wake: Jerry Falwell's Pro-life Gospel. In Faye Ginsberg and Anna Lowenhaupt Tsing (eds.), *Uncertain Terms: Negotiating Gender in American Culture*. Boston: Beacon Press.

Hartouni, Valerie. 1997. *Cultural Conceptions: On Reproductive Technologies and the Remaking of Life*. Minneapolis: University of Minnesota Press.

Hubbard, Ruth. 1984. "Personal Courage Is Not Enough": Some Hazards of Childbearing in the 1980s. Pp. 331–55 in Rita Arditti, Renate Duelli Klein, and Shelly Minden (eds.), *Test-Tube Women*. Boston: Pandora Books.

Mitchell, W. J. T. 1986. *Iconology: Image, Text, Ideology*. Chicago: University of Chicago Press.

Newman, Karen. 1996. *Fetal Positions: Individualism, Science, Visuality*. Stanford, CA: Stanford University Press.

Phelen, Peggy. 1993. *Unmarked: The Politics of Performance*. New York: Routledge.

Sacks, Oliver. 1993. To See and Not See. *New Yorker*, May 10.

Seigel, Riva. 1992. Reasoning from the Body: A Historical Perspective on Abortion Regulation and Questions of Equal Protection. *Stanford Law Review* 44:261–381.

Stabile, Carol. 1992. Shooting the Mother: Fetal Photography and the Politics of Disappearance. *Camera Obscura* 28:179–206.

Will the "Real" Mother Please Stand Up?

The Logic of Eugenics and American National Family Planning

PATRICIA HILL COLLINS

In the United States, motherhood as a constellation of social practices, a social institution, and an American cultural icon remains central to multiple systems of oppression. Just as mothers are viewed as important to family well-being, the status of motherhood as an institution remains essential to American health and prosperity. But in a nation-state like the United States, where social class, race, ethnicity, gender, sexuality, and nationality comprise intersecting dimensions of oppression, not all mothers are created equal.

In this politicized climate, the issue of which women are "real" mothers best suited for the tasks of reproducing both the American population and seemingly American family values takes on added importance. "Real" has many meanings, such as authentic, genuine, indisputable, and true. "Real" also has physical connotations, meaning concrete, tangible, and material. Another constellation of meanings of "real" references sincerity—earnest, honest, truthful, trustworthy, and reliable. Within these intersecting meanings of "real," dichotomies emerge that construct certain groups of women of the right social class, race, and citizenship status as "real" mothers worthy and fit for the job. Affluent, white and holding American citizenship, "real" mothers are those whose authenticity lies in their biological and natural reproduction versus their social mothering; whose physicality operates via their willingness to participate in every facet of their children's lives; whose sincerity lies in beliefs about mother love; and whose surety lies in their indisputable ties to their biological offspring. Against these idealized "real" mothers, other categories of women of the wrong social class, race, and citizenship status are judged to be less fit, less worthy to be mothers. Within this intellectual framework, women deemed fit to be "real" mothers encounter population policies supporting their contributions as mothers to national well-being. In contrast, those deemed unfit to be "real" mothers experience population policies that are markedly different.

In this paper, I explore this relationship between motherhood, American national identity, and population policies. First, I examine how the traditional family ideal functions to structure notions of "real" motherhood and how this family ideal in turn frames American national identity. I suggest that not only does the metaphor of the biological, nuclear family operate to shape notions of an American nation whose health is assessed using family rhetoric, but that this American national family draws upon race for much of its meaning.

Second, I investigate how a logic of eugenics provides an intellectual context for assessing contemporary population policies by which the nation-state aims to attend to its health. Societies that embrace eugenic philosophies typically aim to transform social problems such as unemployment, increasing crime rates, childbearing by unmarried adolescents, and poverty into technical problems amenable to biological solutions. Via social engineering, societies shaped by eugenic thinking see "race and heredity—the birth rates of the fit and the unfit—as the forces that shape . . . political and social developments" (Haller 1984:78). Moreover, eugenics movements that seek biological solutions to what are fundamentally social problems often arise when other mechanisms of controlling subordinate populations seem no longer adequate. The United States may be experiencing such a period, and American understandings of population policies aimed at regulating the mothering experiences of women from diverse racial, social class, and citizenship groups might benefit by viewing such policies within the context of a logic of eugenics.

Finally, in order to highlight the centrality of motherhood in these relations, I survey population policies targeted toward middle-class white women, working-class white women, and working-class African-American women. These three groups of women each occupy different social locations in their ability to be "real" mothers of the nation. As a result, population policies applied to each group demonstrate how the American nation-state seeks to regulate experiences with motherhood of women from different racial, ethnic, social class, and citizenship groups in defense of nation-state interests.

"Real" Mothers in Family, Race, and Nation

As sociologist Paul Gilroy observes, "race" differences are displayed in culture that is reproduced in educational institutions and, above all, in family life. Not only are families the nation in microcosm, its key components, but they act as the means to turn social processes into natural, instinctive ones (Gilroy 1987:43). In the United States, families constitute primary sites of belonging: the family as an assumed biological entity, the racial family or community reinforced via geographically identifiable and racially segregated neighborhoods, and the national family symbolized via images of Mom, Dad, baseball, and apple pie.

The particular model of family is germane here, for a specific family ideal frames family rhetoric in the United States. According to the American traditional family ideal, a normative and ideal family consists of a heterosexual couple that produces its own biological children. A state-sanctioned marriage confers legitimacy not only on the family structure itself but on children born in this family (Andersen 1991). This metaphor functions as a deep taproot in American social policy. Just as individuals acquire varying degrees of authority, rights, and wealth based on their mode of entry into their biological families, a nation-state's population reflects similar power relations. The nation gains meaning via family metaphors. Moreover, this family metaphor articulates both with structures of institutionalized racism and with the labor needs of capitalism, such that the American national family is defined in race- and class-specific terms in the United States.

Several features characterize the links between the biological, nuclear family and the American national family. First, presumptions of blood ties underlie both constructs. Just as women's bodies produce children that are part of a socially constructed family grounded in notions of biological kinship, women's bodies produce the population for the national family or nation-state, conceptualized as having some sort of biological oneness. In nuclear families, the legitimate sons and daughters of a heterosexual marriage, related by blood to biological parents, are contrasted to illegitimate children who, while they may also be related by blood, stand outside state-sanctioned marital relationships. In a similar fashion, those lacking the appropriate blood ties to the American nation-state are seen as outsiders, non-family-members, and are treated accordingly. "Real" mothers remain central to reproducing these genuine blood ties

Second, family metaphors and those of nation both rely on distinctive notions of place, space, and territory. This dimension of the link can be seen through multiple meanings that people attach to the concept of home, meanings that range through levels of family household, neighborhood as family, home as the place of one's birth, and one's country as home. For example, the theme of the home as a sanctuary from outsiders and the turmoil of the public sphere creates boundaries for the biological family along lines of privacy and security. Similarly, the notion of homeland or national territory that must be defended against marauding aliens or foreigners operates in a similar fashion. Both spaces are seen as needing protection from outsiders. "Real" mothers are those who take care of the home, who provide that sanctuary that must be protected (Coontz 1992).

Third, in the same way that those born into a biologically defined family acquire certain lifelong rights and obligations to other family members, those born into the American national family as so-called natural or real citizens acquire certain rights attached to that citizenship. Citizens are also expected to fulfill certain obligations to one another. For example, people within family units routinely help members of their own families by baby-sitting, lending money, assisting relatives in locating employment and housing, or caring for economically unproductive family members such as the very young or the elderly. Family members are entitled to these benefits merely by belonging. In contrast, those who lie outside the family orbit are not entitled to such benefits—but individuals may earn them by being redefined as fictive kin or by being particularly worthy. Since citizenship is often conferred through both birth or attachment to the mother, determining the "real" mother of a child can serve as a test of citizenship and belonging (Anthias and Yuval-Davis 1992).

Fourth, within biological families a pecking order or naturalized hierarchy emerges with, for example, good sons and daughters compared to their less ambitious or less fortunate siblings. This internal hierarchy parallels notions of first-class and second-class citizenship in the national family. Hierarchy may be determined by order of arrival: either birth order or immigration order. Claims that White Anglo-Saxon Protestants who migrated to the United States earlier are entitled to more benefits than more recent immigrants reflect this notion. Or hierarchy accompanies gender. In many families, girls and boys are treated differently regarding economic autonomy and freedom to move in public space. This differential treatment serves as a foundation for sex-typing of occupations in the paid labor market and male domination of public arenas such as politics and professional sports. As is the case with all situations of hierarchy, actual or implicit use of force, sanctions, and violence may be needed to maintain unequal power relations.

Finally, families contain policies or rules regulating their own reproduction. Family planning comprises a constellation of reproductive options ranging from coercion to choice, from permanence to reversibility. Within individual families, decision-making lies with family members—technically, it is they who decide whether to have children, how many children to have, and how those children will be spaced. But can this analogy from family to nation be extended to public policies on the national level? In what ways do social policies designed to foster the health of the American nation-state, especially those concerning motherhood, follow a similar family planning logic?

Planning for the National Family: The Logic of Eugenics Thinking

Eugenics movements or movements for "racial hygiene" of the early twentieth century compellingly illustrate the thinking underlying population policies designed to control the motherhood of different groups of women for reasons of nationality and/or race. Eugenics philosophies and the population policies they support emerge within political economies with distinctive needs and within societies with particular social class relations.

Common to eugenics movements throughout the world has been the view that biology is central to solving social problems. Societies that embrace eugenic philosophies typically attempt to transform social problems into technical problems amenable to biological solutions effected via social engineering. Eugenic approaches thus combine a "philosophy of biological determinism with a belief that science might provide a technical fix for social problems" (Proctor 1988:286). Two sides typically exist to eugenic thinking. So-called positive eugenics consists of efforts to increase reproduction among the "aristogenic" or "fit," who allegedly carry the outstanding qualities of their group in their genes. So-called negative eugenics aims to prevent reproduction by the "cacogenic" or "unfit," those likely to have undesirable or defective offspring (Haller 1984).

The case of population policies enforced by the Nazi nation-state offers an unsettling example of a nation-state that was able to follow the logic of eugenics thinking grounded in national family planning rhetoric to its rational conclusion. Because German scientists borrowed from eugenics philosophies developed elsewhere in Europe and in the United States, German nation-state policies during the Nazi era of 1933–1945 provide a particularly compelling case for understanding the connections among the logic of eugenics, institutionalized racism, institutionalized sexism, and social policy. The intellectual climate characterizing the Nazi German nation-state was *not* unique. Rather, it emerged from a common intellectual heritage framing Western industrialized countries, including the contemporary United States (see, e.g., Haller 1984). Unlike other countries that held similar beliefs about eugenics or "racial hygiene" but were unable to implement them as fully, the Nazi German nation-state actually enforced eugenics philosophies.

Under the Nazis, eugenics thinking followed three main paths. First, the German population was racialized, with Jews and Aryans, among others, constructed as categories of immutable difference (Gilman 1985). Second, these putative racial differences were linked to issues of national identity and prosperity. Jews were blamed for failed economic and political policies and characterized as outsiders in the homeland of the German national family who hindered the nation-state's prosperity (Bridenthal, Grossmann, and Kaplan 1984). Finally, specific population policies were designed for the worthy and unworthy segments of the general population (Bock 1984; Proctor 1988). For example, the Jewish population encountered a continuum of policies designed to control their numbers. Stripping Jewish citizens of their property rights, legal protections, and employment opportunities; relegating the Jewish population to ghettos; deploying specific reproductive policies such as sterilization; and the so-called final solution of genocide targeted against the already born population collectively constitute eugenics as public policy.

All three elements of eugenics thinking characterize the history of American social institutions. First, because the United States has operated as a racialized state since its inception, race operates as a core concept in constructing American national identity. Despite promises of political and religious freedom for all American citizens in the Constitution, by excluding sizable segments of the population from citizenship, this same Constitution simultaneously codified race, gender, and class into the founding laws of the country (Berry 1994). Enslaving African-Americans to exploit their labor and reproductive capacities and conducting military actions against Native Americans in order to acquire their land constituted population policies targeted explicitly for these racialized groups. Moreover, race remains important in framing the basic institutions that comprise political, economic and social institutions in the United States (see, e.g., Massey and Denton 1993; Omi and Winant 1994). While the categories of race may shift in response to changing political and economic conditions, the fundamental belief in race as a guiding principle for viewing segments of the American population remains remarkably hardy.[1]

The second element of eugenics-inspired population policies consists of associating diverse racial groups with perceived national interests. This element also has a long history in the United States. At various times, this has taken the form of restrictive immigration legislation targeted toward non-European racial and ethnic groups, a response to what was seen as the non-white threat from outside national boundaries. Slavery, de facto segregation, and other repressive policies applied to African-Americans, Latinos and other nonwhite populations within American borders also operated in response to perceived threats from nonwhite populations. While recent interconnections of racism and national policy may be more covert than in the past, operating, as sociologists Michael Omi and Howard Winant suggest, in a "hegemonic" fashion, such ties continue. Racialized discourses exist around themes that serve as proxies for race, themes such as poverty, crime, immigration, affirmative action and urban policy. While none of these terms directly refers to people of color, all have been used as codes to indicate how the presence of people of color is problematic for national unity or national aspirations (Omi and Winant 1994).[2]

The third feature of eugenics-inspired population policies, the direct control of different segments of the population through different population control measures, also characterizes American politics (Davis 1991:202–44).[3] Ironically, the United States pioneered the eugenics thinking actually implemented in Nazi nation-state policies. Nazi science looked to England and the United States for inspiration in crafting its eugenics policies. Francis Galton, the founder of the eugenics movement in England, claimed that "Anglo-Saxons far outranked the Negroes of Africa, who in turn outranked the Australian aborigines, who outranked nobody. Because he believed that large innate differences between races existed, Galton felt that a program to raise the inherent abilities of mankind involved the replacement of inferior races by the superior" (Haller 1984:11).

Galton's ideas proved popular in racially segregated United States. Preceding the sterilization laws of other countries by twenty years, American eugenics laws were seen as pioneering ventures by eugenicists of other countries. The U.S. Supreme Court's 1927 *Buck vs. Bell* decision held that sterilization fell within the police power of the state. Reflecting the majority opinion, Oliver Wendell Holmes contended,

> It would be strange if it could not call upon those who already sap the strength of the state for these lesser sacrifices, often not felt to be such by those concerned, in order to prevent our being swamped by incompetence. It is better for all the world, if instead of waiting for their imbecility, society can prevent those who are manifestly unfit from continuing their kind. The principle that sustains compulsory vaccination is broad enough to cover cutting the Fallopian tubes.... Three generations of imbeciles is enough. (Haller 1984:139)

Given this intellectual context, it seems reasonable to conclude that differential population policies developed for different segments of the American population, especially those identifiable by race, citizenship status, and social class, have long existed in direct relation to any group's perceived value within the United States. Rather than the more familiar definition of population policies emphasizing reproductive policies, I define population policies more broadly. Population policies comprise the constellation of social policies, institutional arrangements, and ideological constructions that shape reproductive histories of different groups of women within different racial/ethnic groups, social class formations, and citizenship statuses. Examining population policies through this lens reveals the fallacy of viewing race-based policies and gender-based policies as basically regulating different forms of social relations. Current assumptions view African-Americans as having race, white women as having gender, and African-American women as experiencing both race and gender, with white men lacking both race and gender. Such assumptions dissipate when confronted with actual population policies aimed at regulating the mothering experiences of different groups of women. Since the 1970s, major changes in the American political economy, stimulated by four recessions and a declining standard of living, provided a social context fostering differential population policies for different groups of women in the United States. Given this context, how does the logic of eugenics thinking frame the population policies targeted to different groups of women?

Policies for "Fit" Mothers: Middle-Class White Women

According to the logic of eugenics, falling birth rates of the dominant group constitute "race suicide." In this situation, women of the dominant group are routinely encouraged to increase their reproductive capacities. In the United States, white women's reproduction remains central to American national aspirations. Currently, efforts to encourage white women to produce more white babies, a so-called positive eugenics goal, occur for several reasons. First, only white women possess the genetic material necessary for creating white babies. Thus, white women hold the key to notions of racial purity central to systems of white supremacy. Second, white women remain central in socializing young white people into a system of institutionalized racism. Their activities as mothers receive praise in light of this goal. Finally, white women allegedly fulfill the symbolic function of mothers of the national family. White women have been central as symbols of the nation that must be protected and defended and as the group responsible for transmitting national culture to the young.

Overall, access to new reproductive technologies, dominant ideologies about motherhood promulgated in the media, and social institutions work to keep middle-class white women firmly entrenched in popular culture and scholarship as the essence of desirable motherhood that is worth protecting. Health care policies in particular reflect a fascination with increasing middle-class white women's fertility, often to the detriment of other pressing maternal and child health needs. Specifically, the construction of infertility as a national tragedy and the huge amounts of media attention paid to this condition reflect this preoccupation with increasing reproduction among women of the dominant group. Infertility is typically presented either as a human tragedy, the case of the unfortunate woman who cannot bear the child she so desperately wants, or, increasingly, as a personal failing—women who pursued careers, waited too long to have babies, and now find themselves childless because they turned their backs on their rightful roles as women (Ikemoto 1996). Middle-class women found to be infertile are assisted with a dazzling array of medical advances to cure this socially constructed tragedy. Usually insured by private insurance carriers, these women are able to defray part of the enormous costs of infertility procedures. New reproductive technologies such as in vitro fertilization, sex predetermination, and surrogate embryo transfer are routinely differentially distributed depending on the race, class and sexual orientation of women (Rowland 1987; Nsiah-Jefferson 1989).

Popular culture and media representations play a part in both identifying middle-class white motherhood as ideal and in creating a climate where acquiring and raising a healthy white baby takes on such importance. For example, films of the 1980s and 1990s such as *The Hand That Rocks the Cradle,* whose plot centers around an affluent white woman who innocently hires a crazed nanny who tries to steal her baby, trumpet social messages that children belong at home with their "real" mothers. The mothering capacities of working mothers came under particular scrutiny. Films such as *Baby Boom,* a portrait of a successful career woman who suddenly discovers how unfulfilled her life had been when she inherits a baby, seem designed to portray the message that working mothers are acceptable just as long as motherhood comes first.

Social institutions also reflect efforts to assist middle-class white women in attaining this curiously idealized "real" mothering experience. Despite the increase in the numbers of working mothers, school day schedules that can begin as early as 7:30 A.M. and dismiss children as early as 1:30 P.M. continue to privilege stay-at-home mothers. Modest reforms designed to make the workplace accommodate the family needs of women remain more a reaction to the stated needs of middle-class white women professionals to juggle both family and career than they do any sustained national commitment to child care. While working-class mothers do benefit from corporate day care, because so many working-class women do not work for large corporations, the children of white middle-class women remain the primary beneficiaries of this upper-tier child care.

Racial segregation, and to a lesser extent social class segmentation, in American housing, education, and public services also support middle-class white mothering. The growth of gated communities and planned suburban developments designed to keep out unwelcome others speaks to the need to protect white children and their mothers. Privatizing educational and recreational experiences of white middle-class children reflects efforts to insulate this group from the perceived harm of attending school with working-class whites and working-class children of color. While the signs of racial segregation have been taken down, the results that these signs were designed to produce have not changed as rapidly. Middle-class white children still receive markedly better treatment than all other children in areas such as education, health care, housing, recreational facilities, nutrition, and public facilities such as libraries and police protection. Through public policy, ideological mechanisms, and institutional policies, their mothers receive strong messages to reproduce.

Policies for "Less Fit" Mothers: Working-Class White Women

The position of working-class white women, especially those living in poverty, differs dramatically from that of middle-class white women. On the one hand, working-class white women's ability to produce white babies renders this group "fit" to produce the biological or population base of the nation. But on the other hand, when it comes to passing on national culture, raising academically and economically productive citizens, and being symbols of the nation, working-class white women remain less "fit" for motherhood. Public policies, popular ideology, and the structure of social institutions all work to encourage white middle-class women to fulfill their expected place as mothers of the nation by encouraging them both to have children and to raise children. In contrast, working-class white women are encouraged to have children but receive much less support for their ability to raise them.

Social policies reflect this basic contradiction. With the passage of *Roe v. Wade* in 1973, working-class and poor white women gained legal access to safe abortions. As a result, many young white women chose not to carry their babies to term. The decreasing stigma attached to single motherhood, coupled with changes in eligibility for social welfare benefits, lessened the social and economic barriers confronting single mothers of any racial background. Many white women who formerly would have given their children up for adoption chose to raise their children themselves, often alone. Together, these factors, among others, resulted in a sharp decrease in healthy white babies who formerly would have been available for adoption into white middle-class families.

Recent efforts to decrease social welfare benefits, to weaken antidiscrimination legislation against women in the workplace, and to limit access to abortion and other selected family planning services for working-class and poor women have meant that working-class white women's reproductive "choices" have changed. If working-class white women carry babies to term, the result will be an increase in the number of healthy white babies. This changing political climate suggests that young white mothers will find it more difficult to raise their children in poverty and, denied access to the choice of whether to choose to carry a child to term, will be increasingly pushed toward adoption as the best "choice."

Ideological portrayals of working-class white women as mothers must be careful to validate motherhood as a biological function yet support the notion that working-class White women do not make particularly fit mothers. In some cases, working-class white women become fit mothers by giving up their children. In her study comparing unmarried white and African-American mothers in the 1950s, Rickie Solinger (1992) reveals how working-class African-American women were actively discouraged from placing their babies up for adoption, while working-class white women encountered serious pressure to become fit mothers by releasing their children for adoption. They were told that they became good women by doing what was best for the child. Through these policies, working-class white women could gain respectability. Recent ideological representations of working-class white women must also walk this fine line between constructing them as simultaneously fit for some dimensions of motherhood, and unfit for others. Take, for example, *Roseanne* and *Grace Under Fire,* two popular American television shows of the 1990s portraying working-class white mothers. While Roseanne clearly violates many of the rules of fit motherhood, she remains married and thus gains legitimacy. In contrast, Grace, a single mother with three children, is portrayed with dignity, yet her checkered past of illicit sexuality, wife battering, and alcoholism speaks to her past transgressions. As the series continued, Grace also was revealed to have had an illegitimate child that she relinquished for adoption. Both Roseanne and Grace gain respectability within the parameters set for working-class white women.

Social institutions such as housing, schools, employment, and health care also collectively frame the mothering experiences of working-class white women. Many working-class white women are in the labor market, often in part-time work or in service jobs that offer less desirable salaries and benefits, especially health care benefits. Working-class white women thus encounter a specific constellation of population policies, ideological constructions, and social institutions. They are denied abortion services. They are denied opportunities to support their children financially. They encounter increased exposure to cultural messages that encourage them to have their biologically white babies but to give them up for adoption to "good" homes. Because they receive insufficient economic support in raising their children from the disadvantaged position of working-class white males, from their own position in the labor market, and from the insufficient government supports affecting poor people, working-class white women are increasingly encouraged to give up their babies to infertile middle-class white women.

Policies for "Unfit" Mothers: Working-Class African-American Women

Working-class African-American women, especially those who live in poverty, encounter markedly different treatment. In this section, I emphasize working-class African-American women's experiences not because I see these experiences as reflecting some sort of essential blackness, but because this group's experiences are constructed as normative for African-Americans as a collectivity by dominant groups. Whereas working-class white women's fitness for motherhood is measured against the assumed norms of middle-class white women, African-American women experience a reversal of this process. Specifically, working-class African-American women's experiences are stereotyped and labelled as deviant from those of middle-class white women and are simultaneously considered normative for African-American women as a collectivity. In policy discussions of reproduction, middle-class African-American women are compared not to middle-class white women, but to working-class African-American women, when they are rendered visible at all.[4]

Controlling both the biological reproduction and mothering experiences of working-class African-American women has long been essential to maintaining a racialized American nationalism. In prior eras, a combination of a need for cheap, unskilled labor and the political powerlessness of black populations worked to produce population policies that encouraged African-American women to have many children. Because they did not require costly training and could be easily fired, such children cost employers little. In Southern states, for example, school years for African-American children were often shorter and adjusted to allow them to work in agriculture. Because they were denied education and social welfare benefits routinely extended to other groups, they cost the state little. Black children were viewed as expendable.

The post–World War II political economy changed all this. The mechanization of agriculture, industrial relocation out of inner-city areas, and other economic trends fostered a decreasing demand for low-skilled labor (Squires 1994). Instead, the so-called postindustrial economy required higher skilled labor requiring expensive investments in schooling and health care . During this same period, African-Americans gained political rights unavailable prior to the passage of the Civil Rights Act and Voting Rights Act in the early 1960s (see, e.g., Amott's 1990 discussion of African-American women and Aid to Families with Dependent Children) that allowed them to benefit from entitlement programs long enjoyed by whites. From the perspective of employers, a large African-American population with political rights of full citizenship became both economically unfeasible and politically dangerous. Since fewer African-Americans were needed, population policies, ideological constructions of African-American women, and the structure of social institutions combined to discourage working-class and poor African-American women from having children.

Providing lavish services to combat infertility for white middle-class women while withholding family planning services except sterilization from poor

African-American women reflects contemporary population policies emerging within the logic of eugenics thinking. Currently, poor women and women of color are often *discouraged* from having children and are rewarded by government policy if they do so. In the context of lack of abortion services, government-funded permanent sterilization often becomes one of the few viable methods of birth control. The introduction of Norplant and Depo-Provera as reversible quasi-sterilization methods illustrates how population policies directed at African-American women reflect notions of their seeming unfitness to be mothers. Ideological constructions of African-American women also foster a climate in which it is claimed that they make bad mothers and thus are irresponsible if they reproduce. Long-standing images of African-American women as matriarchs or "unfit" mothers are now joined by newly emerging images that portray them as sexually irresponsible, as abusive mothers, and/or as welfare queens (Lubiano 1992). Building on stereotypes of people of African descent and women as being less intellectual, more impulsive, and more emotional than whites, the image of the welfare queen in particular provides a context for quasi-coercive population policies such as Norplant and Depo-Provera. Ironically, images designed for middle-class African-American women, especially high-achieving professionals, also perpetuate views of African-American women as unfit mothers. By choosing to remain childless, such women are seen as being selfish, hoarding resources, being overly aggressive and unfeminine, and thinking only of themselves. Moreover, these new "black lady" overachievers, as Wahneema Lubiano (1992) describes them, are simultaneously constructed as affirmative-action hires, the middle-class unworthy recipients of government favors that parallel their less affluent welfare queen sisters. Within this nexus of images, while both middle-class and working-class African-American women can be constructed as the enemy within, whose reproduction or lack of it threatens American national interests, working-class and poor African-American women remain most vulnerable to attacks that result from this logic.

In this climate, where African-American women are constructed as unfit mothers, social institutions that they encounter take on a particularly punitive cast. Black working-class and poor mothers are often employed, yet are severely disadvantaged—child care remains hard to find, health benefits are limited for those in part-time or seasonal employment, and lack of job security makes it difficult to plan. A history of racial segregation mean that working-class African-American women encounter limited opportunities in their own education, housing, employment, access to health care, access to quality schools and recreational facilities for their children (Omolade 1994).

New Realities

If the nation-state is conceptualized as a national family, with the traditional family ideal structuring normative family values, then standards used to assess the contributions of family members in heterosexual, married-couple households with children become foundational for assessing group contributions to national well-being overall. The United States may be in an important historical moment where the logic of eugenics is being appropriated by interest groups who aim to reconstruct the American national family to its former glory. In understanding these new realities, several themes are of special significance.

First, the range of reproductive choices available to white women could not have occurred without the exploitation of the labor of African-American women and of other women of color. As women of the desirable group, middle-class white women have long depended on the labor of poor women and women of color in order to fulfill their responsibilities as mothers. Historically, for example, African-American women served as child care workers and performed the domestic labor that allowed middle-class white women to maintain their social position as fit mothers. These traditional functions are more recently being taken over by new "employable mothers," namely, undocumented immigrant women of color. In her analysis of undocumented Latinas, Grace Chang (1994) notes that in the past, analyses of immigration retained a focus on male migrant laborers who allegedly stole jobs from "native" American workers. Since the mid-1980s, this concern has shifted to an emphasis on how immigrants impose a heavy welfare burden on American "natives." As Chang observes, "Men as job stealers are no longer seen as the immigrant problem. Instead, immigrant women as idle, welfare-dependent mothers and inordinate breeders of dependents are seen as the great menace" (Chang 1994:263). In this context, the treatment of undocumented Latina mothers and other women who lack the benefits of American citizenship closely resembles historical patterns of regulation of African-American mothers. In these cases, the notion of nonwhite mothers as employable exists alongside prevailing views that maternal employment harms children's development.

Second, the connection between welfare-state capitalism and perceived national interests remains significant, especially regarding women of varying race, social class, and citizenship groups. The welfare state mediates the conflicting demands placed on all women. On the one hand, social norms encourage women to remain in the home in order to care for their children and thus reproduce and maintain the labor force. But on the other hand, these same norms encourage women across social classes to perform traditionally female low-wage work in the paid labor force, such as teaching, secretarial work, and domestic work. By encouraging and subsidizing some women to remain at home in order to nurture the current and future workforce while forcing others into low-wage work, the welfare state uses race, social class and citizenship differences among women to resolve this conflict. Working-class women of color of varying citizenship statuses bear the brunt of capitalist development. Such women are simultaneously engaged in low-wage work as paid employees doing the reproductive labor for families other than their own (Dill 1988; Glenn 1992; Chang 1994).

Third, new reproductive technologies are emerging as central to reorganizing the experiences of all women with motherhood. Working with longstanding patterns of race and social class in the United States, these technological advances fragment the meaning of motherhood. The proliferation of reproductive technologies in the post–World War II era has allowed the splitting of motherhood into three categories: genetic, gestational, and social motherhood (Rowland 1987; Raymond 1993). Genetic mothers are those who contribute the genetic material to another human being. Gestational mothers are those who carry the developing fetus in utero until birth. Social mothers care for children actually born. Traditional views of motherhood forwarded by the traditional family ideal present one middle-class white women as fulfilling all three functions, assisted by domestic servants. But new reproductive technologies have made it possible for women to specialize in one of these mothering categories. With the growing technological ability to make distinctions among genetic motherhood, gestational motherhood, and social motherhood, African-Americans, Latinas and other women of color become candidates for gestational motherhood, supplementing and perhaps even supplanting white working-class women's participation as genetic and gestational mothers.

Fourth, the mother glorification targeted toward middle-class white women coexists with a heterogeneous collection of social policies designed to retain the *image* of motherhood as vitally important for all women while simultaneously discouraging selected groups of women from becoming mothers because they fail to attain the standards of "real" mothers. For example, mid-1990s phenomena such as the assault on affirmative action policies in higher education and the workplace, the passage of the 1996 Personal Responsibility and Work Opportunity and Reconciliation Act, which effectively abolished AFDC by placing it under the supervision of fifty individual states, the emergence of increasingly strident anti-immigration rhetoric in public discourse, and the increasing privatization of schools, health care, and selected public services can all be seen as part of an overarching framework designed to maintain differences between fit and unfit mothers. But the rhetoric of mother glorification must be tempered with a long look at how children are actually treated in the United States. Children were disproportionately hurt by social policies of the 1980s and have become the most impoverished age group in the United States. In 1974, 15 percent of American children lived below the poverty line. By 1986, 21 percent did so—a 40 percent increase in just twelve years. Approximately 40 percent of African-American and Latino children live in poverty (Katz 1989:127). Yet despite these startling statistics, infertility continues to be presented as a major public health issue affecting large numbers of Americans.

Finally, the emergence of new family forms in the United States has the potential of either supporting or challenging the traditional family ideal and the entire edifice of population policies that it sanctions. For example, growing support for the categories of "biracial" and "multiracial" in the U.S. Census speaks to newly emerging family forms that defy boundaries of race. Of particular interest are the white mothers raising biracial or multiracial children, through either adoption or biological reproduction. How are we to interpret current efforts to include multiracial categories as part of government data? Are the efforts at reclassification an effort to make such children honorary whites with all the benefits that accrue to white middle-class children? Or are the efforts designed to deconstruct a system of racial classification that routinely distributes privileges based on such classification? In a similar fashion, the emergence of families organized around gay and lesbian couples with children raises similar challenges to the traditional family ideal and the complex social structures it simultaneously shapes and sanctions. The very existence of these emerging family forms and their increasing legitimacy within state agencies mean that the bedrock of family as defined by the traditional family ideal can no longer serve as in the same way as the glue linking systems of race, gender, class, nationality, and heterosexist oppression. What comes of these challenges remains to be seen.

Notes

1. Racial formations in the United States demonstrate a shift from theories of race based on the racist biology that characterized nineteenth-century science, and toward a cultural racism more useful in defending current racial practices. But this means neither that racism based in biology has atrophied nor that it may not take on new forms. Troy Duster (1990) offers an unsettling argument concerning the reracialization of genetic arguments in contemporary American scholarship. Duster argues that advances in genetic research show that genetic disorders are distributed differently through different racial/ethnic groups. Duster queries, "The importance of race and ethnicity in cultural history has refueled the old logic to give rise to a new question: If genetic disorders are differentially distributed by race and ethnicity, why aren't other human traits and characteristics?" (p. 3).

2. Scholarship on the welfare state reveals how state policies reflect race-, class-, and gender-specific concerns. For analyses of how social policies have had differential impact on different groups, see Mink 1990, Nelson 1990, and Gordon 1994. Gilkes 1983 and Brewer 1994 provide analyses of how race frames state policy.

3. This process is neither historical nor confined to the United States. For discussions of similar population policies, see Heng and Devan's (1992) analysis of Singapore and Kuumba's (1993) discussion of South Africa.

4. Middle-class African-American women occupy a peculiar place in the nexus of population policies targeted toward African-American women as a group. On one hand, these women clearly have the economic resources to care for their children. In this sense, African-American middle-class children will not be drains on nation-state resources. But at the same time, these children are not of the "right" genetic stock to become symbolic of the nation. They compete with the "rightful heirs" of the nation—its white children—for resources. The analogy between the king's rightful heir and the king's bastard son seems apt here—both are seen as being part of the royal family, but their status is not the same. As mothers, African-American professional women who excel in their careers and who are mothers may be cast as "bad" mothers because they do not stay at home with their children.

References

Amott, Teresa L. 1990. Black Women and AFDC: Making Entitlement Out of Necessity. Pp. 280–300 in Linda Gordon (ed.), *Women, the State, and Welfare*. Madison: University of

Wisconsin Press.

Andersen, Margaret L. 1991. Feminism and the American Family Ideal. *Journal of Comparative Family Studies* 22(2):235–46.

Anthias, Floya, and Nira Yuval-Davis. 1992. *Racialized Boundaries: Race, Nation, Gender, Colour and Class in the Anti-Racist Struggle.* New York: Routledge.

Berry, Mary Frances. 1994 [1971]. *Black Resistance, White Law: A History of Constitutional Racism in America.* New York: Penguin Books.

Bock, Gisela. 1984. Racism and Sexism in Nazi Germany: Motherhood, Compulsory Sterilization, and the State. Pp. 27–96 in Renate Bridenthal, Atina Grossmann, and Marion Kaplan (eds.), *When Biology Became Destiny: Women in Weimar and Nazi Germany.* New York: Monthly Review Press.

Brewer, Rose. 1994. Race, Gender and U.S. State Welfare Policy: The Nexus of Inequality for African American Families. Pp. 115–28 in Gay Young and Bette Dickerson (eds.), *Color, Class and Country: Experiences of Gender.* London: Zed Books.

Bridenthal, Renate, Atina Grossmann, and Marion Kaplan (eds.). 1984. *When Biology Became Destiny: Women in Weimar and Nazi Germany.* New York: Monthly Review Press.

Chang, Grace. 1994. Undocumented Latinas: The New "Employable Mothers." Pp. 259–86 in Evelyn Nakano Glenn, Grace Chang, and Linda Rennie Forcey (eds.), *Mothering: Ideology, Experience, and Agency.* New York: Routledge.

Coontz, Stephanie. 1992. *The Way We Never Were: American Families and the Nostalgia Trap.* New York: Basic Books.

Davis, Angela Y. 1981. *Women, Race, and Class.* New York: Random House.

Dill, Bonnie Thornton. 1988. Our Mothers' Grief: Racial-Ethnic Women and the Maintenance of Families. *Journal of Family History* 13(4):415–31.

Duster, Troy. 1990. *Backdoor to Eugenics.* New York: Routledge, Chapman and Hall.

Gilkes, Cheryl Townsend. 1983. From Slavery to Social Welfare: Racism and the Control of Black Women. Pp. 288–300 in Amy Swerdlow and Hanna Lessinger (eds.), *Class Race, and Sex: The Dynamics of Control.* Boston: G.K. Hall.

Gilman, Sander L. 1985. *Difference and Pathology: Stereotypes of Sexuality, Race, and Madness.* Ithaca, NY: Cornell University Press.

Gilroy, Paul. 1993. It's a Family Affair: Black Culture and the Trope of Kinship. Pp. 192–207 in his *Small Acts: Thoughts on the Politics of Black Cultures.* New York: Serpent's Tail.

Glenn, Evelyn Nakano. 1992. From Servitude to Service Work: Historical Continuities in the Racial Devision of Paid Reproductive Labor. *Signs* 18(1):1–43.

Gordon, Linda. 1994. *Pitied but Not Entitled: Single Mothers and the History of Welfare.* Cambridge: Harvard University Press.

Haller, Mark H. 1984 [1963]. *Eugenics: Hereditarian Attitudes in American Thought.* New Brunswick: Rutgers University.

Heng, Geraldine, and Janadas Devan. 1992. State Fatherhood: The Politics of Nationalism, Sexuality and Race in Singapore. Pp. 343–64 in Andrea Parker, Mary Russo, Doris Sommer, and Patricia Yaeger (eds.), *Nationalisms and Sexualities.* New York: Routledge.

Ikemoto, Lisa C. 1996. The In/Fertile, the Too Fertile, and the Dysfertile. *Hastings Law Journal* 47(4):1007–61.

Katz, Michael B. 1989. *The Undeserving Poor: From the War on Poverty to the War on Welfare.* New York: Pantheon.

Kuumba, Monica Bahati. 1993. Perpetuating Neo-Colonialism through Population Control: South Africa and the United States. *Africa Today* 40(3):79–85.

Lubiano, Wahneemah. 1992. Black Ladies, Welfare Queens, and State Minstrels: Ideological War by Narrative Means. Pp. 323–63 in Toni Morrison (ed.), *Race-ing Justice, En-gendering Power: Essays on Anita Hill, Clarence Thomas, and the Construction of Social Reality.*

New York: Pantheon.

Massey, Douglas S., and Nancy A. Denton. 1993. *American Apartheid: Segregation and the Making of the Underclass.* Cambridge, MA: Harvard University Press.

Mink, Gwendolyn. 1990. The Lady and the Tramp: Gender, Race, and the Origins of the American Welfare State. Pp. 92–122 in Linda Gordon (ed.), *Women, the State, and Welfare.* Madison: University of Wisconsin Press.

Nelson, Barbara. 1990. The Origins of the Two-Channel Welfare State: Workmen's Compensation and Mothers' Aid. Pp. 123–51 in Linda Gordon (ed.), *Women, the State, and Welfare.* Madison: University of Wisconsin Press.

Nsiah-Jefferson, Laurie. 1989. Reproductive Laws, Women of Color, and Low-Income Women. Pp. 23–67 in Sherrill Cohen and Nadine Taub (eds.), *Reproductive Laws for the 1990s.* Clifton, NJ: Humana Press.

Omi, Michael, and Howard Winant. 1994. *Racial Formation in the United States: From the 1960s to the 1990s.* Second Edition. New York: Routledge.

Omolade, Barbara. 1994. *The Rising Song of African American Women.* New York: Routledge.

Proctor, Robert N. 1988. *Racial Hygiene: Medicine Under the Nazis.* Cambridge, MA: Harvard University Press.

Raymond, Janice. 1993. *Women as Wombs: Reproductive Technologies and the Battle over Women's Freedom.* San Francisco: HarperSanFrancisco.

Rowland, Robyn. 1987. Technology and Motherhood: Reproductive Choice Reconsidered. *Signs* 12(3):512–28.

Solinger, Rickie. 1992. *Wake Up Little Susie: Single Pregnancy and Race Before Roe vs. Wade.* New York: Routledge.

Squires, Gregory D. 1994. *Capital and Communities in Black and White: The Intersections of Race, Class, and Uneven Development.* Albany: State University of New York Press.

The Social Construction of the "Immoral" Black Mother

Social Policy, Community Policing, and Effects on Youth Violence

BETH E. RICHIE

In this paper, I set out to explore the impact of social policy on the micro processes of mothering. In particular, I am concerned with how deteriorating structural conditions in low-income black communities serve as a significant backdrop to the interactions among these micro processes and social policies, and how the results are stigmatization, marginalization, and a particular construction of social problems, especially youth violence.

Few areas of social life have been as contested in social policy debates as the concept of the family. Highly charged rhetoric about gender and generational relationships surrounds most recent proposals for reform. From nostalgic calls for conservative approaches by religious right-wing forces to seemingly progressive legislative initiatives advocating gay/lesbian marriages, debates about family life are played out on various ideological templates. Even in progressive contexts, such as the recent reconsiderations of adolescent pregnancy, the problem has been constructed as the need to "strengthen fragile families" (National Center on Fathers and Families 1997). Similarly, in the field of public health, we see an emphasis on the family as the cornerstone of emotional and social well-being, examined via resiliency factors that emerge from particular forms of household arrangements (Edari, McManus, and McKissic 1995). In these and other examples, current social policy reform is increasingly attached to the organization and meaning of the role of the family in contemporary society, and overall the constructs have a distinctively conservative tendency.

Motherhood, as a subcategory of the family debates, is constituted through a similar vast range of intellectual, political, and popular rhetoric, and with similar conservative undertones. While characterized by mixed conceptual frames (ranging from the best practice of motherhood to the healthiest type of relationships between mothers and children), still at the center of the ideological debate are universalistic assumptions that revolve around "desirable" family forms, "appropriate" gender roles, and the maintenance of a separation between public and the private spheres. For example, policy makers continue to interrogate researchers about the effects on children when women work outside the home, and legislators argue about what single form family leave should take. Questions concerning the control of reproduction and how assisted reproductive technology will be used continue to be deeply embedded in religious and scientific discourses, and whole movements have emerged in the past few years to defend the rights of other kinds of parents, be they noncustodial fathers or lesbian partners. At times the intensity of the debates has been reminiscent of the early days of the modern feminist quest for gender equity in the public and domestic spheres (Hochschild 1990; Chodorow 1978; Glenn, Chang, and Forcey 1994; Jones 1985).

Despite renewed intensity, for the most part the overall tenor of these debates is not new. What is somewhat surprising about them, however, is the particular ways in which the debate has narrowed. For while some feminist scholars and other progressive critics have attempted to broaden the scope of gender concerns (Glenn, Chang, and Forcey 1994), the issues under consideration are quite narrowly bound by hegemonically circumscribed parameters, as if only *some* women's mothering is even worth contesting in current debates. Indeed, the social policy debates between progressive and conservative forces that surround mothering in this country concern women from much more privileged positions than those interviewed for this paper. In some instances the dominant issues in the mainstream debate may even be understood to be in opposition to poor women's interests, such as the need for in-home child care or housekeeping services for middle-class families clashing with the need for fair labor practices and decent working conditions for poor women and women of color (Nelson 1994). Notably absent from these debates, for example, are discussions about who is raising the children of nannies, what the quality of *their* child-care arrangements is, and how *their* family life is affected by their working without insurance or occupational protection; we don't even have data to accurately understand their conditions.

Far from the mommy track and the landscape where soccer moms negotiate their identities, where much of the current debate is centered, are the low-income communities where black women and other women of color are trying to raise their children against increasing odds. Here we see how even multicultural feminism and progressive antiracist scholarship have failed to make visible the concerns of poor black women within the context of the new motherhood debates (Johnson 1997).

Instead of being featured in the debates, most black women in low-income communities fall far outside the normative, hegemonic parameters of such discussions. With noted exceptions (Dickerson 1995), most considerations of the mothering that poor black women do is introduced into the political, social, and empirical debates from a very different social location. At best, their mothering is studied as a culturally distinct add-on to the dominant inquiries. In its worst and far more common form, low-income black women's mothering is used as a not-so-coded metaphor for much of what is wrong with contemporary society (Hill 1997). Black women are portrayed as creating pathological forms of families as "single heads of households," as draining public resources, or as breeding too many children who pose physical, social and economic risks to others (Hemmons 1995). Their mothering is viewed as something quite different from the mothering efforts of other groups—as a category of activities enacted in such dissimilar ways from the dominant model that they are constructed as confusing, atypical, and dysfunctional. Ultimately, I will argue here, this outside position renders black women's mothering immoral, if not criminal, in the perspective of those who formulate and enforce social policies.

My argument here is that, worse than simply ignoring the role that mothering assumes in poor black women's lives, the current analytical and ideological framework does great harm to these women, their children, and their communities. Rather than seeking to understand and then address the social needs of black women and their families within the contexts in which we actually live, current conceptualizations ignore the specificity of the micro processes of mothering and misinterpret key behaviors and actions of mothers. The social policies that ensue reinforce such conceptualizations pathologizing and stigmatizing effects. The overall result is increased marginalization, structural disenfranchisement, hypersurveillance and overregulation of poor black women's mothering in new and profound ways. The particular case that I will use to argue this point concerns the consequences that social policy on youth violence has on black women's mothering.

I frame this discussion with findings from a study of twenty-four adult women who are female caretakers of adolescent children in a low-income community in a major urban area where, like many other cities, youth violence is a devastating social and public health problem. The broader research project of which this is a part examines how youth violence is distinctively and decidedly gendered in nature, and how the interventions designed to address these problems ignore this important dimension. Hence the problem of youth violence, typically constructed as a problem that affects young men of color, is neither linked to the issue of gender violence nor understood to have any effects on girls and women when, in actuality, it certainly does.

Race/ethnicity, cultural patterns, and social position are distinguishing factors in gender identity and relationships. Further, identity and the organization of gender relationships are linked to violence in public as well as private spheres of life (Richie 1996). In order to understand (and prevent) youth and gender violence in communities of color, a particular look at the distinctive features of gender relationships, dynamics and social circumstances in those communities is required (Crenshaw 1991). Yet the youth violence prevention movement—consisting of community-based initiatives, organizing efforts, public policy reform, and research projects—is significantly limited by its inattention to the issue of gender violence (Richie 1995). Similarly, the feminist-based antiviolence movement, while cognizant of the issues of gender inequality and oppression of women, does not deal very effectively with the issues of race/ethnicity (Kanuha 1996).

Defined broadly, the concept of gender violence that I am using includes the particular forms of violence that women and girls experience (rape, sexual harassment, battering in intimate relationships) *as well as* the ways that male-to-male violence includes a gender component (the use of degrading images of women within the context of a fight). The invisibility and lack of attention to the unique experiences of young women and girls of color from low-income communities in both of these advocacy areas is politically and intellectually problematic and constitutes a major gap in research and public policy (National Research Council 1996).

These gaps reflect more than passive disinterest and failed social policy in low-income communities. The consequence of avoiding a gender analysis symbolizes the generalized disregard for poor girls and women in caretaking roles in their own families and for how they are affected by devastating social and public health problems in their own communities. While debates rage about contemporary motherhood and the acute pressures on family life, the paucity of concern for the issues of mothering in the face of youth violence is startling. Its absence seriously impacts our understanding of the problem and reflects essential and persistent bias in the research. Moreover, its absence is evidence of how low-income black women's mothering is seen as a problem separate and apart from other, more privileged women's/mothers lives. This leads to the severe marginalization of the process of mothering and even the criminalization of poor black women and their children.

Theoretical Background

A critical review of the dominant literature provides further evidence of this premise. Four theoretical arguments are used to explain the increase in youth violence, all of which have built-in biases against women, particularly in their roles as mothers. These models offer limited analytic power and provide few opportunities for creative solutions that do not, in effect, reinscribe traditional gender roles and reproduce gender inequalities as they strive to provide safer options for young people and their families. Prior to reviewing the arguments, it should be reemphasized that the problem of violence in the lives of young people has been cast as a particular problem of young men of color—African-American or other (Cook and Hudson 1993). Consequently, the theoretical arguments and the interventions upon which they are based *do* have particular salience for scholars, practitioners, and activists who are interested in a racialized analysis of social conditions. What remains missing is an interpretation and critique of these theoretical arguments from the perspective of their gender bias, and attention to the gendered consequences for adults in the community, particularly for women who are mothers.

Family-Based Arguments

A considerable body of literature attributes the increase in youth violence to a decline in the quality of family life (Zinsmeister 1992). This work, which harkens back to the epistemological assumptions that influenced social science research in the early 1970s, discusses issues such as the lack of male role models, the predominance of households headed by women, and the general disorganization of the family unit as key factors in the moral decline of young people, which leads to violence. These arguments, which locate the traditional heterosexual nuclear family at the center of its "normative" family dynamics, ignore the role of material influences, the impact of historical adaptations of family structures, and the effects of community conditions on the organization of the family in contemporary society. In this way, they appear to blame family structure for the violence in young people's lives (Austin 1992; Free 1991).

A closer examination of this theoretical argument reveals that not only are families blamed in a general sense, but women as mothers of such families are viewed as particularly damaging. The lack-of-a-male-role-model argument, for example, assumes that women as role models are somehow inherently inadequate for the appropriate socialization of young women and men. It also does not take into account the risks to women and children inherent in the heterosexual nuclear family form. The nuclear family and other intimate relationships have long been the most dangerous place for women and children in terms of violence against them (Grisso et al. 1996; Bachman 1994). Moreover, this argument reinscribes the rigid separation of public and private spheres. For example, those taking this approach do not advocate for more male teachers, only husbands/fathers. And it reinforces negative stereotypes of single motherhood, particularly black single motherhood.

Psychologically Based Theories

Numerous scientific and popular arguments have emerged that depend on psychological theories to explain increased violence among young people. The most popular of these look at the poor self-esteem and nihilism that (supposedly) characterize contemporary life in the urban "ghetto." Proponents of this theoretical approach focus on how lack of opportunity for development of a sense of self-efficacy and limited outlets for positive self-expression affect the development of a strong ego and a strong moral code. While the best of this work attributes such psychological decay to structural and situational issues to some degree, the argument remains essentially individualistic in nature (Sampson and Laub 1993). It focuses attention on the need to resocialize young people and inject a more principled, honorable code of ethics (based on the dominant culture's sense), into the psyches of young people. The not-so-subtle subtext provides a quite critical reading of mothering as it relates to impulse control, anger, self-hatred, and morality.

Certainly hopelessness, a sense of failure, and the lack of a sense of future create emotional distress for social actors. However, these explanations for violence do not look at the *different* effects of these factors on the moral development of young women and men, or their impact on adults. Nor do such explanations address the range of responses that in some instances may be adaptive rather than pathological, given the facts of the lived situation.

Additionally, feminist scholars and practitioners have raised the questions of the formation of a gendered identity and of the ways gender shapes self-esteem (Goldberger 1996). Without a gendered evaluation of the impacts that moral socialization and self-esteem have on the uses and experiences of violence, analysis and intervention strategies are incomplete.

The Structural Inequality Theory

The proliferation of academic and public policy attention to the questions of structural inequality, persistent poverty and the permanent underclass has deeply influenced the analysis of youth violence (Wilson 1996). This approach has typically focused on the lack of employment opportunities for young men, the alarming rate at which they drop out of school, and the development of an extensive underground/illegal political economy (Williams 1989). This assessment ignores gender as a particular factor in structural inequalities, ironically positioning women/girls as having some sense of privilege over men. In the case of school dropout, for example, proponents point to the rate of male dropout without attention to what happens to girls *even though girls may be more likely to stay in school* (McLoyd and Jozefowicz 1996). This completely ignores the evidence that would suggest that initiatives that focus only on male retention, educational initiatives for boys, and so on are narrow and ultimately discriminatory. Such strategies, based on lack of careful attention to gender differences in response to structural inequality, potentially reproduce the gender inequality in educational attainment between boys and girls.

Another illustration of how the structural inequality paradigm fails to adequately address the ways that violence is a gendered experience—and differentially affects adult women—concerns the effects that unemployment has on crime in general and on the incarceration of young black men. This position, like the family-based theoretical argument, is favored by black as well as white conservative intellectuals. It posits that unemployment renders black men "unmarriable" and leads to overall community decay, increased economic dependency of women, and the creation of a subculture that depends on alternative sources of material resources—notably violence and crime (Wilson 1996). Like other theoretical orientations, this argument ignores the question of how structural inequality affects women in a particular way, and how solutions need to address gender inequality as well as other forms of exclusion and domination.

The Afrocentric Theoretical Argument

Under the rubric of Afrocentric approaches to community development, violence as a social problem has recently been given considerable attention. From this perspective, violence is seen as a manifestation of cultural invisibility, ethnocentrism, compulsive masculinity, and the effects of the diaspora on African-American people (Oliver 1994). While there is little argument that such conditions have had detrimental effects on individuals and communities of color in this country, the solutions offered have potentially dangerous implications for women.

For example, paternalistic attitudes are reflected in those violence-prevention strategies that promote "protecting the black woman," the creation of a male-dominated community "court" to hear local grievances such as turf battles, and other male-centric, heterosexist approaches. On the one hand, Afrocentric principles reflect the need for community-level accountability. However, in their worst form, the misapplication of theories of Afrocentric thought advocate a family form that (1) reinscribes patriarchal privilege to men, (2) is historically inaccurate, and (3) takes advantage of women's consciousness/loyalty about race/ethnicity to serve the needs and desired of male power structures (Ali 1990). Here again, the absence of gender-specific consideration of a theoretical approach leads not only to ineffective solutions, but also to strategies that may ultimately create *more* violence in the lives of women in an attempt to decrease violence in the lives of young men.

Theories of Black Women's Mothering

There has been considerable historical work that examines how the domestic lives of Black women are shaped by social circumstances. The roles of black women during slavery, the absence of a gendered division of labor in the public sphere, and yet highly gendered experiences such as sexual abuse, high rates of forced pregnancy, and so on are well documented. Black feminist theorists and others have challenged and reconsidered questions of matriarchy, the issues facing households headed by women, and the consequences of poverty for women.

Specific theoretical arguments about black mothering are offered by numerous contemporary black feminist scholars who have focused on the dialectic of controlling imagery, on one hand (which leads to oppression), and motherhood as a site of power, resistance, and activism, on the other. Patricia Hill Collins (1990), for example, introduces the concept of blood mothers, other mothers, and community other mothers as an alternative way to think about black women's roles. Gloria Wade-Nobles (1978) talks about how black mothers are blamed for the ills of contemporary society, and she and Angela Davis (1981) offer compelling critiques of this literature. Bonnie Thornton Dill (1988) looks at work, values, and the raising of black children, and Barbara Omolade (1994) has broken new ground in her thinking about black single mothers. Toni Morrison (1988) and Alice Walker (1982) are leaders in the literary field in their work on black motherhood, and surely there are others.

This literature, taken with the other, more problematic theoretical approaches, offers a starting point, but is not completely satisfactory as a theoretical basis, for understanding how black women who are mothers are affected by the current surge in youth violence.

Methodology

My study was designed to explore the impact of youth violence on mothers and mothering, using the life-history interview technique to elicit data on the ways that black women thought and felt about their experiences. The life-history method was selected because it is particularly useful in gathering information about stigmatized, uncomfortable, or difficult circumstances in the subject's lives (Marshall and Rossman 1989). Compared to other, more structured qualitative methods, conducting life-history interviews offers a more open and intense opportunity to learn about the subjects' backgrounds, opinions, and feelings, as well as the meanings they give to both the mundane and exceptional experiences in their lives (Mishler 1986; Watson and Watson-Franke 1985). Mothering is obviously in this realm.

Selection of Sample

The people to be interviewed were drawn from populations of black women whose children are involved in or at serious risk of experiencing or witnessing violence in the private or public spheres of their lives. Twenty-four women agreed to participate, ranging in age from nineteen to sixty-nine years old. Included in the sample were (1) mothers or guardians of pregnant or parenting adolescents; (2) mothers who resided in public housing, subsidized housing or public shelters; and (3) primary caretakers of children detained in institutional settings for juveniles. The women interviewed were recruited from a number of sites, but all were raising children who were currently or had been involved in some form of violence-prevention initiative. By the end of the study, word of mouth was the major source of new informants.

Four basic areas were covered by the interviews, beginning with an open-ended question: "Tell me the things about yourself that are important to you." Next the women were asked about factors they felt influenced their role as mothers: "What is it like raising children in your household and neighborhood?" Third, I sought to capture their experiences and perceptions of gender and youth violence and how it affected their lives: "In what ways does violence or the threat of violence affect you and your family or neighborhood?" Last, I asked how their life might be different in the future, what they wanted, dreamed, hoped for, and expected for themselves and their children.

The overall empirical goal was to understand the landscape of mothering in this context. I also was interested in hearing the particular perspectives of each woman. Since the project was designed to explore the relationship between lived micro processes and structural conditions, the women's stories were recorded in their own words and then coded by theme.

The Five Themes

Five themes emerged as significant, and most are highly gendered. First, these women were increasingly limited in their ability to parent because of diminished economic resources and social supports in their community. A related issue was that they feared losing their children to public agencies, such as child protective services. The third theme was the threat posed by the presence of weapons and the risk of physical injury from violent and dangerous young people. Increasingly they felt afraid of children they lived near or with. Fourth, the women described a complicated, culturally constructed loyalty to their families and a protectiveness of their community that positioned them as vulnerable black women in very particular ways. Last, they described how women who engage proactively in prevention strategies can and do feel even more isolated, marginalized, and at greater physical risk. This counterintuitive finding—that becoming involved in community-based initiatives to respond to the problem of youth violence ultimately left women with a diminished capacity to parent their children—was an important and startling conclusion to this study.

Before reviewing these themes in more detail, it is important to note the limitations of this small sample of women's opinions and experiences. First, the themes are obviously not discrete, nor do the findings fit into a neatly ordered sequence. Rather, relationships among them were noted, and a discernable pattern emerged that warrants further attention. It is also important to acknowledge that the sample was not representative of the wider universe of opinion. While the extent to which the findings would hold as generalizable is an important question, it is beyond the scope of this study. Again, my interest here was in exploring and understanding theoretically issues of concern to Black mothers in violent situations.

Theme 1: The diminished ability to parent due to limited economic and social supports within the context of urban decay
The context within which the women lived was marked by their economic marginalization. They described the following characteristics of their world. First, observation and experience had led them to conclude that "doing the right thing for your children" would not necessarily work for them as members of a marginalized ethnic group. They described feeling that, as low-income women

whose attempts to mother had repeatedly failed, they somehow fell outside of society's parameters of goodness or fairness. This sense translated into feelings of powerlessness, frustration, and discontent with their own mothering abilities. They were typically self-blaming even when, paradoxically, they articulated an insightful analysis of the social conditions that led to their marginalized position as women and as mothers.

A second dimension of this theme was the degree to which their household fabric has been limited by changes in their efficacy as adults in the social world. Their household composition changes frequently, usually in response to economic shifts, and this often limits important intergenerational contact. They and other adults lose jobs or are only marginally employed. Their families double up in inadequate housing. They simply do not have the resources to perform their parenting roles as well as they desire. Successful role models for both their children and themselves were limited, and extended family networks were quite tenuous.

While many of the women interviewed grew up in poor families, the effects of persistent multigenerational poverty are taking a toll on them. For while poverty may not be new, the level and the nature of hostile public sentiment, the prolonged feelings of despair, and the extent of the violence in their communities are new. They did not grow up watching and knowing of their friends being killed the way their children do, and this huge experiential gap has left most of them unprepared to help their children make sense of these tragic events or offer much support.

The women interviewed for this study also described how public socializing systems are failing them and their children. Schools are considered dangerous, rigid places where the mothers described feeling as alienated as the young people do. One woman said, "They look much like prisons, and I feel like they are holding my child captive there for some crime of going to school. I have no rights as a visitor, and definitely no input into what happens there."

A broader exploration of structural conditions reveals that community institutions and most public spaces are decaying. Businesses, movie theaters, libraries, and parks are closing, and services at hospitals and mental health facilities are being cut back. One informant complained: "They are even closing those nasty community rooms in the projects where we used to send the kids to play." The women reported that a decline in availability of public transportation (buses have changed their routes and cabs won't stop to transport them) has left them isolated within their communities. In those same communities, at the same time public services are being eroded, jails and prisons are being built, and walls are constructed to surround and isolate their neighborhoods.

The women understand these isolating and confining strategies as symbolic of the larger community's fear of them and their children. Many schools have metal detectors through which children must pass. Surprisingly, so do laundromats, video arcades, and the music stores young people frequent. Gated retail establishments favor merchandizing large bottles of beer and candy packaged like liquor over fresh produce. In these and other obvious ways, raising children is limited by perverse environmental conditions, lack of social support, symbolic fear, and persistent economic decay.

Such structural factors are complicated by the fast pace of life for young people. From these women's point of view, very few of the essential everyday activities take much time anymore: "Fast food, fast money, fast highs . . . things change quickly here and are only temporary." The women described the problematic ways in which their children are influenced by what they called the "just do it" lifestyle. Very few mundane events require contemplation, analysis, or delaying of gratification. Subjectively, this robbed their children of opportunities to develop critical life skills, which resulted in the women feeling "rushed" in the raising of their children, as if they are "not able to catch up," and as if they are "running out of time." Again, the objective conditions have an interactive relationship with the subjective feelings that women have about their roles as mothers which, in turn, impact how they perform in this role.

Theme 2: The constant fear of losing children to public agencies

This second theme can best be characterized by the words of one of the women, who said, "The state is actually raising our children, and as far as I can see they are not doing a very good job. Our job as mothers has therefore become to keep running from child protection, from truant and probation officers, from social workers and the like who are trying to take our kids from us. Family values, not! It's like the slave days . . . they want to take our kids." This was one of many moving testimonies to how women are struggling to escape the intervention of authorities and maintain their custodial rights.

The phenomenon of women being surveilled and monitored in their domestic activities as mothers has an important relationship to the problem of youth violence, which is obviously also a problem of policing. The impact of feeling monitored as a mother while your children are being policed is profound. One informant described it as a "land mine, where you are constantly chasing your kid through dangerous streets hoping you will catch him before the police do. In the meantime, though, you have to watch out for yourself too."

This impression of mothers being scrutinized while they themselves are at risk takes several forms. One form is related to the increasing public anxiety related to the safety of children whose mothers are being battered. On the one hand, this attention is important and long overdue. Yet in a more problematic sense, we see how concern for women has been placed in conflict with the needs of their children, thus positioning advocates for battered women at odds with child protective service workers in some communities.

A second manifestation of the policing of women's mothering is the rigid monitoring of women whose children have been identified as at risk of abuse because of a series of early juvenile offenses. Against the backdrop of the national trend to hold parents accountable, women whose children are in more trouble face increased jeopardy themselves. Paradoxically, the women in this study described feeling that when the "authorities are watching," their children feel even *more* inclined to act out, especially when custody issues are pending. The children then can manipulate their mothers, knowing that they are likely to get away with undercutting her parental authority. One woman said, "It's like the kids *know* what they are doing. And I find myself begging my kids to behave rather than rearing them in any strong way. I don't have any dignity left when the kids know that my ability to mother them has been called into question by outsiders."

Without a doubt, many cases—including highly publicized tragic scenarios—require rapid, rigorous investigation and monitoring by an external authority. I would argue, however, that the extreme cases have skewed both public perceptions and policy initiatives. When child protective services so seriously fail to protect children (as they have recently done in cities such as Chicago and New York), the policing of those mothers who need support rather than punishment increases. Indeed, the rise in bureaucratic institutions and the random, ineffective involvement of child protective services that are operated like law enforcement agencies have not protected children very well. On the contrary, when poor mothers are generally stigmatized by extreme cases and stripped of their symbolic and legal rights, their children are even less supervised and subsequently are in more danger.

The relationships of mothers with other (non-child-specific) public institutions are also important. Most of the women interviewed considered law enforcement agencies dangerous, public assistance programs adversarial, and human services typically unhelpful. These women don't feel there is much of a safety net that they can trust or depend on to support their families. Most described profound despair and were disheartened. Yet they persist in trying to raise their children with very limited resources and in dangerous isolation.

Theme 3: The fear of abuse and injury

One of the consequences of women's in low-income communities continued attempts to enhance the safety of their children is the considerable risk of violence the women themselves face. This finding had specific gendered dimensions. The women were at risk because they were women and mothers. The responses demonstrated keen awareness that their neighborhood or "the block" is dangerous for all community members. However, they accepted and espoused the rhetoric that considered boys and men at particular risk, and therefore they themselves took particular risks for their male children as an extension of their mothering role.

For example, the women described trying to intervene with other young people when their children were in trouble. The combined mistrust of outside agencies, the sense of community loyalty (which emerged as the fourth theme), and the subjective desire to enact some degree of agency in their family and community life compelled some of the women I interviewed to try to resolve conflicts on their children's behalf. This left them extremely vulnerable. In almost half of the reported cases the women were injured by young men when they tried to protect their children. These assaults usually involved a weapon.

The mothering of girls posed a different set of dilemmas, pointing to an interesting and troubling pattern. Typically, girl children were kept inside, stifling the children's natural desire and need to explore the social environment. They described this as a "naive way to fool myself into thinking I could keep the girl-child safe." In most cases it did not work. In those instances where girls were involved in gangs, for example, the women's vulnerability to violence was compounded by this strategic response. First, when a violent incident occurred inside, there were fewer witnesses or escapes. Secondly when the mothers were perceived as *protecting* a girl (as opposed to attempting to *settle a dispute* for her male child), the affront to a perpetrator was more serious. Protecting a girl was seen as less justifiable, understood to be challenging the perpetrator and therefore the consequence to the mother was potentially more dangerous. Third, the women themselves often became the primary object of the abuse—indicating a blending of the daughter's vulnerability and the mother's, and a merging of their identities around female victimization. The women describe how this undermined their roles as mothers. The extent to which parental authority in the domestic sphere is constrained by the presence of weapons that parents do not and cannot control remains a relatively unexplored topic.

Theme 4: Generalized, culturally-constructed, loyalty to black young men

As one informant said, "The puddle is muddied by the position of black men in society, especially the 'endangered species' [meaning young black men]. But as a community we are as sick as our secrets." This powerful statement suggests that given the well-known effects that violence, poverty, racism, and lack of opportunity have had on black boys, it can be very difficult and problematic to raise the issue of the condition of black girls and the compromised positions of their mothers. More broadly, the frequently expressed sentiments of the women in this study suggest that the nature of gender relationships in the black community are complicated by cultural loyalties. The rhetoric sounds like this: "Men are vulnerable to societal abuse and women have had more opportunity than they." "Boys are the endangered species, and girls need to be more responsible." "It's black mothers who are raising these sons but no one pays attention to us."

These sentiments represent the opinion of a considerable segment of black communities in this country, and the extent to which this culturally constructed loyalty interacts with and is influenced by mothering warrants further investigation. In this study, it suggested a skewed set of community priorities bolstered by a simplistic public policy agenda that not only ignores the vulnerability of women and girls but also particularly punishes mothers for attempting to protect their daughters.

Theme 5: Involvement in prevention initiatives and community activism

The fifth theme concerns the problematic nature and outcomes of women's community activism to prevent youth violence. There is a long history of documentation and analysis of black women's activism that emerged, in part, from the unique position we've assumed vis-à-vis the labor force, constitutional rights, social justice initiatives, and reform movements. This literature has generally concluded that black women's community work has been an important source of empowerment and expression of agency. Historically, it has been considered a way for women to reclaim motherhood and to engage productively with social forces. I was therefore interested in and troubled to note how, in this instance, the women's experiences were quite different—mixed at best.

To understand this finding, it is important to characterize the initiatives around the country to get mothers involved in responding to youth violence. They range from groups of "mothers against gangs" to women's involvement in tenant patrols. Programmatically and conceptually, they are often linked to community policing efforts, and have a bias toward external law enforcement rather than community control. At first glance, these initiatives promise a subjective and objective re-framing of women as problem-solvers rather than being the cause of the problem for youth violence. They encourage women to take responsibility for their own children and others'; they reward cooperative collaborations between governmental agencies and individuals; they fill critical voids in communication and articulation of common agendas; and they provide a much-needed outlet for women's frustration at the problems in their communities. Theoretically, it is solid community organizing.

The interviews revealed a different picture. The women accounts of their actual experiences were full of powerlessness, a sense of failure, increased risk of injury and fear for their safety, and renewed pessimism regarding their ability to accomplish the role of mothering in ways they desired. In a troubling sense, what has historically been a source of liberation for black women has become, in the face of these contemporary problems, actually a way to further marginalize women and stigmatize their inability to protect and nurture their children. Now this is in the public sphere as well as at home. The combination of structural conditions and hostile relationships between outside agencies and community groups contaminates these initiatives and causes them to fail. Most regrettably, women are set up as scapegoats here as well.

This conclusion emerged from several accounts of women who had been convinced to report their children's criminal activities in exchange for some help or leniency. They quickly learned that with current enhanced prosecution practices, their children are facing very significant prison terms. Others described how their initial enthusiasm for working with the violence-prevention program associated with a law enforcement agency were tempered when they felt compelled to "set kids up." Many reported feeling alienated from their families and neighbors and afraid of retaliation because of their assumed cooperation with police. Three who testified about their role as community liaisons and mentors found themselves quoted in a legislative report supporting repressive welfare reforms. A simple case of tokenism? Perhaps. Certainly these stories indicate the clash between the women's subjective need to feel competent and recognized in their roles as mothers and the objective limitations of their power in the social worlds within which they live. These findings suggest that when forces in the public sphere—the conditions of social life in low-income black communities—are regulated through co-opting members of the community, these community members become easy targets to blame for programmatic and policy failure. These finding describe more than the failure of programs to successfully engage low-income black women in violence prevention initiatives. Such programs set women up as local targets even more than they were in the first place.

Conclusion

In this chapter, I have attempted to explore how the micro process of black women's mothering is constrained by stigmatization, persistent social problems, and misguided social policy. First, the findings show how, despite claims of multicultural feminist scholarship, even the progressive motherhood debate is too narrow because it fails to consider black women's mothering at home or in the streets of their own communities. Not only has theory failed but, through the combined effects of deteriorating conditions and rhetoric from the community itself, the negative impacts are multiplied. Uninformed social policy, which ignores such structural conditions, has profound and unchallenged effects on black women's efforts at the micro processes of mothering. Intervention programs are misguided, pathologically oriented, and dangerous for black women. In the case of youth violence, they have further stigmatized women and punished black mothers.

The problematic social policy is something we might have predicted, based on past policy failures. The self-blame, the keeping of secrets, and the lack of accountability in low-income black communities are counter to our expectations are difficult. Herein lies the need for more research, more theoretical reconsiderations, better public policy, and, ultimately, more and different activism, such that activism should not merely shift sites, but fundamentally reorder and reconfigure the intimate family, community, and larger institutional arrangements. Attempts at *prevention* of youth violence—if they incorporate an analysis of gender—offer promise. This promise will remain unrealized until debates on reform are based on research far beyond the current boundaries, until conceptual frames extend to the margins of society and until intervention and activism in the black community are untangled from gender and other conservatisms.

It is these deeply entrenched gender, race, and class conservatisms that concern me as an African-American feminist scholar, and they have shaped my intellectual interests in portraying fairly the communities I care deeply about. In attempting to unveil how social policy has constructed black women's mothering as immoral, my hope is that the findings will be interpreted in ways that expand options for all black women—mothers and non-mothers—and that subsequently social policy will have a liberatory rather than damaging effect on life in our community.

References

Ali, S. 1990. *The Black Man's Guide to Understanding the Black Woman.* Philadelphia: Civilized Publications.

Austin, R. 1992. Race, Female Headship, and Delinquency: A Longitudinal Analysis. *Justice Quarterly* 9:585–607.

Bachman, R. 1994. *Violence Against Women: A National Crime Victimization Survey Report.* Washington, DC: U.S. Department of Justice.

Chodorow, N. 1978. *The Reproduction of Mothering: Psychoanalysis and the Sociology of Gender.* Berkeley: University of California Press.

Collins, P. 1990. *Black Feminist Thought: Knowledge, Consciousness, and the Politics of Empowerment.* New York: Routledge.

Cook, D., and B. Hudson (eds.). 1993. *Racism and Criminology.* London: Sage Publications.

Crenshaw, K. 1991. Mapping the Margins: Intersectionality, Identity Politics, and Violence Against Women of Color. *Stanford Law Review* 43(6):1241–99.

Davis, A. 1981. Reflections on the Black Woman's Role in the Community of Slaves. *The Black Scholar: Journal of Black Studies and Research* 12(6):2–16.

Dickerson, B. (ed.). 1995. *African American Single Mothers: Understanding Their Lives and Families.* Thousand Oaks: Sage Publications.

Dill, B. 1988. Our Mothers' Grief: Racial Ethnic Women and the Maintenance of Families. *Journal of Family History* 12:415–31.

Edari, R., P. McManus, and D. McKissic. 1995. *Resiliency in the African American Family: A Protective Factor Against Interpersonal Violence.* Madison: Black Health Coalition of Wisconsin.

Free, M. Jr. 1991. Clarifying the Relationship Between the Broken Home and Juvenile Delinquency: A Critique of the Current Literature. *Deviant Behavior* 12:109–67.

Glenn, E., G. Chang, and L. Forcey (eds.). 1994. *Mothering: Ideology, Experience, and Agency.* New York: Routledge.

Grisso, J., D. Schwartz, C. Miles, and J. Holmes. 1996. Injuries Among Inner-city Minority Women: A Population-based Longitudinal Study. *American Journal of Public Health* 86(1):65–70.

Goldberger, N. (ed.). 1996. *Knowledge, Difference and Power: Essays Inspired by Women's Ways of Knowing.* New York: Basic Books.

Hemmons, W. 1995. The Impact of the Law on Single Mothers and the Innocent. Pp. 94–116 in Bette Dickerson (ed.), *African American Single Mothers: Understanding Their Lives and Families.* Thousand Oaks: Sage Publications.

Hill, R. 1997. Social Welfare Policies and African American Families. Pp. 349–63 in Harriette McAdoo (ed.), *Black Families.* Thousand Oaks: Sage Publications.

Hochschild, A. 1990. *The Second Shift.* New York: Basic Books.

Johnson, L. 1997. Three Decades of Black Family Empirical Research: Challenges for the 21st Century. Pp. 94–113 in Harriette McAdoo (ed.), *Black Families.* Thousand Oaks: Sage Publications.

Jones, J. 1985. *Labor of Love, Labor of Sorrow: Black Women, Work and the Family, from Slavery to the Present.* New York: Vintage Books.

Kanuha, V. 1996. Domestic Violence, Racism and the Battered Women's Movement in the U.S. Pp. 34–50 in J. L. Edleson and Z. Eisikovits (eds.), *Future Interventions with Black Women and Their Families.* Thousand Oaks: Sage Publications.

Marshall, C., and G. Rossman. 1989. *Designing Qualitative Research.* Newbury Park, CA: Sage.

McLoyd, C. and D. Jozefowicz. 1996. Sizing up the Future: Predictors of African American Adolescent Females' Expectancies about Their Economic Fortunes and Family Life Courses. Pp. 355–79 in Bonnie J. Ross Leadbeater and Niobe Way (eds.), *Urban Girls: Resisting Stereotypes, Creating Identities.* New York: New York University Press.

Mishler, G. 1986. *Research Interviewing: Context and Narrative.* Cambridge: Harvard University Press.

Morrison, T. 1988. *Beloved.* New York: Plume.

National Center on Fathers and Families. 1997. *Fathers and Families Roundtable: Discussions on the Seven Core Learning.* Philadelphia: University of Pennsylvania Graduate School of Education.

National Research Council. 1996. *Understanding Violence Against Women.* Washington, DC: National Academy Press.

Nelson, M. 1994. Family Day Care Providers: Dilemmas of Daily Practice. Pp. 181–209 in E. Glenn, G. Chang, and L. Forcey (eds.), *Mothering: Ideology, Experience, and Agency.* New York: Routledge.

Wade-Nobles, G. 1978. Towards an Empirical and Theoretical Framework for Defining Black Families. *Journal of Marriage and the Family* 40:679–88.

Oliver, W. 1994. *The Violent Social World of Black Men.* New York: Lexington Books.

Omolade, B. 1994. *The Rising Song of African-American Women.* New York: Routledge.

Richie, Beth E. 1996. *Compelled to Crime: The Gender Entrapment of Battered Black Women.* New York. Routledge.

Sampson, R. and J. Laub. 1993. *Crime in the Making: Pathways and Turning Points Through Life.* Cambridge, MA: Harvard University Press.

Walker, A. 1982. *The Color Purple.* New York: Washington Square Press.

Watson, L. and M. Watson-Franke. 1985. *Interpreting Life Histories.* New Brunswick: Rutgers University Press.

Williams, T. 1989. *The Cocaine Kids: The Inside Story of a Teenage Drug Ring.* Reading, MA: Addison-Wesley.

Wilson, W. 1996. *When Work Disappears: The World of the New Urban Poor.* New York: Vintage Books.

Zinsmeister, K. 1992. A Lack of Traditional Family Structure Causes Youth Violence. Pp. 65–69 in Michael Biskup and Charles Cozic (eds.), *Youth Violence.* San Diego, CA: Greenhaven Press.

Revised and Disruptive Agendas for Women's Health

Rethinking Feminist Ideologies and Actions

Thoughts on the Past and Future of Health Reform

SHERYL BURT RUZEK

As public anxieties over medical care rise, majorities of voters continue to oppose cuts in government spending on medical care, particularly for the poor, the elderly, and children. Yet candid discussion of how to control costs, assure quality and widen access remains stalemated, mired in partisan politics and ideological quicksand. We have not yet had the civic conversation that should have taken place during Clinton's 1993–94 health reform effort about how to revitalize and reshape health care (Skocpol 1996:183–87).

The path that failed to achieve universal access to medical care was much like Alice's experience at the Mad Hatter's tea party. As the Red and White Queens extravagantly promised the American public that health reform would simultaneously cut costs, increase access, and maintain quality—all without "rationing care"—party-goers wavered between skepticism and confusion. By the time interest groups poisoned the teapots and politicos canceled the tea party, national disappointment seemed tempered by relief that the country had been spared a health system that might have been worse than what at least some people had. But the tea party wasn't really over—it just moved.

We need to know what went wrong—and formulate careful analyses of the conditions that would enable the only Western democracy without national health coverage to extend universal access to medical care. If this is indeed a feminist priority, a basic issue that profoundly affects all women, we need to rethink some fundamental assumptions about the role of choice and individualistic ideologies as adequate principles on which to shape a national health plan. I believe that some feminist ideas and ideologies are incompatible with achieving universal access to medical care; either we reformulate these ideologies or abandon empty rhetoric about feminism's relevance to women who are less privileged in American society.

Finding long-term solutions to problems of access may well require rethinking, possibly even giving up, attachments to ideologies that elevate individual choice to the level of an ultimate good. We may also need to rethink the usefulness of consumer models of health that omit a key component of other forms of consumption—the right and responsibility of the individual to weigh the value of goods and services relative to other forms of consumption. Individualism and choice are deeply ingrained concepts in Western feminism. They have been critical precepts for extending reproductive rights, widening options for maternity care, and giving patients a say in decision making, in requiring informed consent for medical care. But as useful as individual choice is in these arenas, can choice be taken as the first principle on which to base a national medical care system? Are there other competing and conflicting principles that warrant equal or greater consideration? Will a market-driven consumer model of health address pressing issues of access and equity? To what extent do individualism and choice conflict with the need of society to ensure a single, affordable standard of care for all?

The failure of Clinton's health reform effort precipitated an ideological crisis for liberals who were forced to struggle to find alternatives to big-government solutions to social needs. If liberals can rethink big government, can feminists rethink unrestrained choice as the first principle around which medical care systems might be structured? In this chapter, it is argued that feminist commitments to widening access and increasing quality are not achievable until recognition of the urgency of cost containment, some degree of rationing, and some restriction of individual choice is integrated into feminist agendas for health reform.

The medical care system that evolved rapidly in the wake of the failure of national health reform is so inadequate and so costly that reform efforts are certain to reappear, particularly given fiscal pressures that will increase with the aging of the population. Consumer dissatisfaction is mounting, along with demoralization among medical professionals, and efforts to regulate and unionize are likely to grow. Some analysts doubt that significant reform is possible, because American political institutions pit factions against factions (Steinmo and Watts 1995). Yet no one doubts that national efforts will have to be made to change Medicare and Medicaid and address the growing ranks of the uninsured and underinsured. To prepare for the next round of reform, feminist health advocates need to develop a framework for reshaping medical care, a framework grounded in understanding what went wrong not only in the Clinton health reform plan, but in ideologies that may in fact be incompatible with achieving universal access.

Containing Costs and Promoting Access: A Nation at Odds

Skocpol (1996) argues that Clinton's effort to extend coverage to all Americans boomeranged, triggering an electoral and ideological backlash against the legacy of the New Deal. But beneath this partisan political rift lies a sea of uncertainty over the extent to which health activists, not just politicians, are willing to examine cherished beliefs about the value of medical care relative to other social goods. The health reform debate was indeed about the wisdom of further extending the hand of government into medical care. It also revealed structural limitations to reform in a system in which interest groups play key roles (Steinmo and Watts 1995).

The Clinton-era reform debates also generated two distinct dialogues—one on *cost containment,* the other on *access.* Quality of care, that shadow issue, remained shrouded in gender and class divides.[1] The question of what went wrong in national health reform reveals not only antigovernment backlash and the excessive influence of interest groups, but blind spots of both those advocating cost containment and those promoting access. These ideal typifications of players are oversimplifications, but provide a useful basis for understanding where we have been.

For years, advocates of cost containment—mostly male economists and health systems analysts—had warned Congress, doctors, and anyone else who would listen that health care inflation was no longer sustainable. Politicians by and large understood this, and took up this past round of reform under pressure from the electorate to "fix health care." Promoters of access, mostly women, feminists, and consumer and public health advocates, seized the moment and lobbied not only to ensure access for all, but extend access to an ever-widening array of services that even the most generous health plans rarely include. Cost containment and advocates and access promoters both skirted a contradictory but critical matter: How would costs, quality, and access be reconciled?

Policy makers understood all too well that unless effective cost containment mechanisms were in place, covering more people would increase, not decrease, total costs—a situation that was socially as well as politically suicidal. Feminist health activists, along with other interest groups, expanded expectations with no regard for how to pay for the growing package of services deemed desirable. Both health activists and the general public seem unwilling to confront the social consequences of overinvestment in medical goods and services at the expense of public investment in education, job training, housing, transportation, and economic development—the material basis of living and working conditions that actually *produce* health. Cost is as unpopular a topic for feminists as it is for those apologists who cling to the costly, inefficient fee-for-service medical care system that fuels greed and profiteering. During the Clinton health reform era, some feminists resisted discussing the need to reduce cost by arguing that defense spending could, and should, be reduced to pay for medical care. This argument essentially cuts off discussion of what we are currently paying for medical care relative to other industrialized nations.

Posing the problem largely as a choice of defense spending versus medical care spending also diverts attention from critical issues that plague the health care sector. It is time for feminists to confront the necessarily dreary details of cost containment.

Why Medical Care Costs Must Be Contained

Over the past three decades, the proportion of the Gross Domestic Product (GDP) spent on medical care rose dramatically. The United States now spends far more per person on medical care than any other country, but fails to provide all women with medical care coverage. In 1993, the per capita health expenditure in the United States, $3,331, was over twice that of most other industrialized countries.[2] Paul Starr argues that slow economic growth, resistance to higher taxes, failure to effectively challenge the level of profits enjoyed by the medical care industry, and increases in medical care costs have steadily reduced resources available for other public investments such as roads, bridges, and economic development projects. Between 1945 and 1952, nearly 7 percent of public spending was in such investment. By the 1980s, public investment dropped to slightly over 1 percent of public spending (Starr 1994:12). At the rate we are going, it will soon be zero, just at a time when the proportion of the working population will shrink relative to the dependent population under eighteen and over sixty-five. In 1950, there were 16.6 workers for every person receiving Social Security benefits. By 1990 this had dropped to 3.4 workers, and projections indicate that by 2010 there will be only 2.9 workers for every Social Security beneficiary. Both the Social Security and Medicare trust funds will be depleted early in the next century, and with so few workers in the labor force for every retiree, how will the public safety net survive (Bronfenbrenner et al. 199:251–53)? How will economic growth be sustained through this demographic transition?

Economists widely regard reductions in public and private investment as critical impediments to economic growth, because such investment creates jobs that in turn provide the material resources for producing health—food, shelter, schools, communities. Spending patterns have shifted significantly since 1965, when the United States spent about 6 percent of GDP on education, 6 percent on health care, and 7.5 percent on defense. By 1994, military spending had fallen below 6 percent, education edged up to a bit to over 7 percent, but health care's share more than doubled, to over 14 percent, and it is projected to consume 18 percent or more of GDP by the year 2000. This dramatic shift in national expenditures is occurring without public discussion of the long-term adverse repercussions for society (Starr 1994:14).

Ignoring the looming crisis in safety-net services will only delay changes that, if made now, could avert massive cutbacks in services within ten years. It is time for feminist scholars to do more than critique the system. We must find solutions to the social, ethical and economic issues that all industrialized nations face in reshaping medical care systems to serve increasingly aging populations. Because aging populations in industrialized countries are disproportionately female, and because women have many distinct medical care needs over the life-cycle, feminist perspectives on how to restructure medical care systems are urgently needed.[3] Reformulating feminist commitments to individualism, choice, cost containment, and rationing may be essential steps toward effective shaping of public policy. This critical review of pressing issues in health reform, and of some feminist blind spots in addressing reform, is intended to spur feminist rethinking of core values that could contribute to public discussion in the next round of health reform.

Public-Private Issues in Cost-Escalation

We render invisible the hidden costs of medical cost escalation because, I suspect, we find it problematic to look closely at how our own individual choices and decisions have cumulative consequences for society as a whole. It is all too easy to occupy ourselves with conundrums over this and then that new biotechnology or analyze how virtually any limits on reimbursement, choice of health provider, or reimbursement policies will result in social inequities. What we need to do is look closely at the consequences of acting largely in accordance with our own perceived self-interest, ideologically elevated to the status of individual rights and freedom of choice. A challenge to contemporary feminism is to rethink the balance between the desires and needs of some women and the desires and needs of all women, finding some common ground for extending access to medical care to all.

This tension, this delicate balance of rights and responsibilities, is not exclusively a feminist problem, but because many branches of feminism have sought social justice and equity, feminists' ability, to address critical issues in health reform provide an opportunity to challenge theory and ideology with praxis. At the close of this century, American society seems caught in a form of insular individualism that avoids acrimonious public discussion by relegating many moral issues to the status of individual choice (Dougherty 1996:28–29).

If feminists are to be on the cutting edge of social change, we must ask hard questions about what women need, both as individuals and as participants in society. Feminist ideologies of inclusiveness, and commitments to extending health and medical care benefits to all women across class and race lines are credible only if they are conceivably attainable. Professing commitment to universal access without looking at the fiscal issues involved in enacting such coverage or being willing to give up some measure of convenience or choice as a condition of widening access creates dissonance between ideology and action.

Feminists who are employees are, like other employees, generally unaware of how much employers pay for their health coverage—on average, about $3,600 in larger companies. Between 1991 and 1994, the annual cost of health insurance per employee-hour worked increased on average 7.4 percent. Many small businesses (in which most women and people of color work), opposed the Clinton health reform plans because they could not afford such benefits without significant subsidies. Disparities in employer-provided medical coverage are enormous in both the public and private sectors. In 1994, in the private sector, the cost of medical benefits ranged from $ .90 per employee-hour worked for nonunionized workers ($156/month) to $2.09 per employee-hour for unionized workers ($362/month). The cost of medical benefits for state and local government employees was $1.95 per employee-hour worked ($340/month) (National Center for Health Statistics 1996:247).

These dramatic differences in the cost of medical benefits provide incentives for employers to move out of unionized regions, privatize government services, and hire part-time or temporary workers. Thus to avoid medical benefit costs, employers put people out of work, which in turn increases the cost of public insurance and unreimbursed care. Until medical benefits are separated from employment through some form of single-payer system, we will continue to lose jobs, particularly jobs for less-skilled workers. Without jobs, we can not sustain communities; without decent-paying jobs, workers cannot sustain their families. Thus feminist analysis must move beyond detailing how women are disadvantaged, and address how families and communities, of which women are part, are ill-served by long-term reliance on employer-paid medical benefits.

Employer-paid medical insurance is also regressive in that it provides higher-income workers (both female and male) an invisible tax advantage. Economic insulation gives beneficiaries of the best employee health coverage reason to demand the best of everything in medical care; they pay little directly for care, and see no reason for frugality. As employers fight against medical cost escalation, employees lose plans, providers, and treatment choices, while employers, insurers, and physicians pocket the savings (Morreim 1995). Thus, disparities in benefits institutionalize social inequities that will only be remedied when medical insurance is independent of individual employers. Some form of national medical coverage will have to be crafted in the decades to come.

Rising Medicare and Medicaid Costs

Over the past decade, the proportion of women and men who were dependent on public insurance—particularly Medicaid—increased. Between 1984 and 1994, the proportion of the population covered by Medicaid increased from 5 percent to 8.6 percent of all men under age sixty-five and from 7.1 percent to 11.7 percent of all women under age sixty-five (National Center for Health Statistics 1996:260). Overall, there were 35.1 million Medicaid recipients and 36.9 million Medicare enrollees in 1994 (National Center for Health Statistics 1996:263–65). Unlike employees, who are at the mercy of individual employers, Medicare and Medicaid beneficiaries are constituents of politicians—as are key players in the medical care industry. Expenditures in both programs are widely regarded as out of control.[4]

Government already pays about one third of all medical care costs, and

Congress is becoming more forthright in asserting that unless dramatic modifications are made in both systems, neither will be able to meet the growing need for services into the next century. Even low-income workers are taxed 1.45 percent of wages for Medicare, which provides benefits to many elders who have substantial incomes, while workers cannot afford coverage for themselves or their own families.

In 1993 Medicare expenditures reached $146 billion—8 percent of the entire federal budget—and is projected to continue rising (U.S. Office of Management and Budget 1996:9).[5] As the population ages, both Medicare and Medicaid face enormous financial pressures. In just five years, from 1988 to 1993, the cost of Medicaid services almost doubled—from $51 billion to $101 billion—primarily because of increases in enrollment, medical price inflation, and increases in expenditures per beneficiary through expansion of federally mandated coverage.

The elderly and disabled actually account for two thirds of all Medicaid spending (including an estimated 40 percent of all care for persons with AIDS). Medicaid is now the single largest item in state budgets, and states have reduced spending on education and welfare to pay for it.[6] The Medicaid situation is particularly complex because middle-class families have found ways to transfer assets to relatives to "spend down" assets so that they are eligible for Medicaid-funded nursing home care. This practice results in government payment of billions of dollars for persons who could pay substantial parts of their own nursing home care (Ginzburg 1994:132). The Kaiser Commission on the Future of Medicaid concluded that "efforts to resolve a 'Medicaid crisis,' viewed in isolation, are a mistake. Rather, the real crisis is the growing need for health insurance among the poor and disabled, unrestrained health care costs, and fiscal constraints on state and federal governments" (1993:37).

Medicare and Medicaid, both programs that serve disproportionately female populations, will be restructured dramatically over the next two decades. Income disparities make younger, low-wage workers particularly disadvantaged in access to medical care; regressive taxation of low and moderate-income families leaves workers unable to purchase medical care for themselves while being taxed to pay for services for others. How will feminists contribute to the reshaping of these massive social programs and tax structures? Will values beyond individual choice emerge in public dialogue about the inevitable restructuring of the social safety net?

Cost Containment Strategies

Despite widespread agreement that medical care costs must be curbed, there is considerable disagreement over various contributing factors. The experts themselves disagree on how much malpractice litigation, the aging of the population, consumer demand, the growth of insurance coverage, physician fees, administrative overhead, and technological developments contribute to medical cost inflation. Research has shown that as much as a fourth of all medical care is questionable or of dubious benefit to patients (Davis 1993:289). Many advocates of cost containment, having failed to control costs through regulation, see market competition and systemwide reordering of financial incentives as the only way to control costs.

In theory, shifting financial incentives, so that doctors and hospitals are rewarded financially for doing *less* rather than *more* (as in the past), cost inflation can be controlled. But what patients care about is getting well cared for. While traditional fee-for-service (FFS), or indemnity plans, indeed put women at risk of being overtreated, the risk in managed care is undertreatment.[7] The extent to which denial of services is appropriate or not is not easy to assess.

Well-run managed care systems have provided many women with quality medical care. In fact, health maintenance organizations have been shown to provide more frequent preventive screening, earlier diagnosis of breast and cervical cancer, and reductions in unnecessary surgery, including hysterectomy and C-sections—excesses of medicine long denounced by feminists and others.[8] In the rapidly shifting world of managed care, women also report considerable dissatisfaction with their doctors and health plans (Bernstein 1996; Collins 1996).

Doctors, insurers, and other interest groups as well as the media have vilified managed care without distinguishing between high-quality operations and those that deserve their ill-repute. For women, gaining access to responsible, quality care requires being able to tell the difference between what Clancy and Brody (1995) call "Jekyll" and "Hyde" plans, regardless of what their owners call them—health maintenance organizations (HMOs), independent practice organizations (IPOs), or provider networks. The "Jekyll" plan encourages long-term relationships between patients and primary care providers and creates a culture of practice that supports cost-effective care. In contrast, "Hyde" plans consist of nominal networks of medical providers who feel pitted against one another to reduce costs and return profits to stockholders. These essentially discounted fee-for-service plans restrict access to a panel of doctors who agree to accept network patients for lower-than-usual fees.

Proponents of market reforms argue that patients need to regain some control over their own choice of plans based on price relative to quality and coverage. Bringing patients into the system of financial incentives is seen as crucial, because until insured patients assume some financial consequences for medical decisions, they will not be motivated to question the necessity and appropriateness of medical care (Morreim 1994).

At a practical level, several options have been proposed. Medical savings accounts, or MSAs, where patients control their own lifetime allocations in some way, would in theory make patients prudent consumers by paying directly for all but catastrophic or major medical expenses. This is likened by advocates of cost containment as similar to automobile insurance that carries a high deductible and eliminates costly small claims.[9] For people who are unable or unwilling to absorb such costs, managed care plans, particularly HMOs, are expected to continue to be attractive. Yet it is especially within these plans that there might be a need to find some way of aligning consumer interests with strategies for cost containment.

Discussion about how to align consumer interests with cost containment warrants serious attention. Some proposals include reimbursements or "points" that could be saved for future use. Some form of financial incentive could increase, rather than decrease, the use of preventive or follow-up care by awarding credits or bonuses for doing so. Patients who wanted services that exceeded plan guidelines (for example, utilization defined as "overuse" of costly procedures for routine conditions) could "purchase" these with saved bonus points. What is sought is some system that would reward prudence but not be a cash barrier to getting medical care. Unlike plans with copayments and deductibles, people would not be forced to choose between medical care and food or other necessities at the time of seeking care. Theoretically, patients who were seriously ill would benefit by having easier access to services if healthier patients didn't use up resources on unnecessary care (Morreim 1995:5–11).

The most frequently expressed concern is that such plans would stratify medical care into systems for haves and have nots. What this stance ignores is the extent to which we are already there. While it is easy to quibble about the relative merits of one reimbursement system versus another, the issue of what is "necessary" remains elusive. Access promoters continue to have what Morreim (1995) describes as an unrealistic image of medicine as an "Artesian well of money" that will never run dry. Doctors and patients share problematic values and beliefs that warrant examining. These include beliefs that potentially beneficial care should never be denied because of money; individual ability to pay is irrelevant to the kind and level of care that should be received; physicians should never compromise care to save money except if the patient is paying; and it is generally better to intervene too much than too little (Morreim 1995). From a market perspective, if people believe that health care is "free" (at least to them personally) and that they have an unlimited right to the best medical care, it fosters the view that systems should spare no expense (Havighurst 1992; Reinhardt 1992). If asked what a plan should offer, health care consumers may well say "everything" (Azavedo 1994).

Consumer Visions of Health Services

In the scramble for health care reform, consumer advocacy groups, including feminist organizations, pressed to include virtually everything in a national health plan. Is an Artesian well mind-set deeply embedded in feminist ideology?

The Campaign for Women's Health provides a clear view of consumers' deeply felt desires—and their limited understanding of how critical cost containment is to expanding coverage to everyone. The campaign was sponsored by the Older Women's League, a well-respected organization that was founded during the 1960s wave of feminism. Led by Anne Kasper, a feminist health advocate and policy analyst, the campaign enlisted participation from a hundred organizations representing over eight million women. Groups that joined the campaign represented women from all walks of life—liberal, conservative, professional, activist, and of many different faiths. In joining, these diverse groups affirmed their commitment to the principles of universal coverage, equal access, mandated comprehensive benefits, accountability and civil rights protections, a wide range of providers and settings, and commitment to a national women's health research agenda.[10] That the campaign was able to involve such diverse constituencies underscores the depth of women's dissatisfaction with American medical care—and the perceived need for change. The campaign also demonstrated that certain women's health issues are so pressing that women from a wide spectrum of society can move beyond their particular differences to articulate and pursue a shared vision of how health care could better meet all women's needs. But this broad-based action was achieved largely by glossing over disparities in women's incomes and access to medical care and sustaining the myth that the "Artesian well" would not go dry.

The campaign's model benefits package called for comprehensive "services which are necessary or appropriate to the maintenance and promotion of women's health," including "a full range of drug therapies proven safe and effective" appropriate to women's care. Specifically, the proposal called for comprehensive screening; health status evaluations; and counseling services for a wide array of conditions, such as domestic violence, HIV, health practices, and reproductive health; maternity care; and long-term care for chronic illnesses and disabilities.

A striking feature of the model benefits package was the call for coverage of the services of a much wider range of health providers than is covered by most health plans, including nurse practitioners, midwives, social workers, chiropractors, home health care workers and specialized therapists, practicing in a broad variety of settings, ranging from private offices to school-based clinics, birthing centers, and long-term care facilities (Campaign for Women's Health 1993).Such a benefit package, if adopted, would require a massive infusion of resources for primary and preventive services, particularly mental health and alternative and ancillary services that currently are not reimbursed by most medical care plans.[11] The question of how to pay for expanded coverage was left largely unexplored by the campaign[12].

Generating open discussion of how to reduce cost is difficult because women are both health care consumers and providers, and there are conflicting interests at stake. Drawing attention to disparities in wages and salaries of health care workers might well have disturbed the fragile alliance among women physicians, nurses, and ancillary health care workers. Nonetheless, the emphasis on a wider range of providers might have been developed into a vision of how women would benefit from being able to get care from less over-priced professionals.

To the degree that advocacy groups continue to see medical care as flowing from an "artesian well," they will resist directly addressing cost or the need to establish any limits on coverage. Policy makers, who need to cut costs, may understandably wish to avoid contact with advocacy groups out of fear that these groups will "cause" some increased demand that they will then have to "manage." Ironically, some feminist groups might see themselves aligned with established, responsible managed care organizations, given their long commitment to treatment based on scientific evidence, an approach that holds potential for reducing cost in meaningful ways.

National Health Reform Deferred

Neither politicians nor the Campaign for Women's Health found socially and politically acceptable ways to determine coverage or regulate costs, described by the League of Women Voters (1994) as "among the most divisive issues in the health care debate." But the death of national health reform only deferred the hard choices that will have to be made— choices that may require giving up an "artesian well" worldview. While policy makers sought to control costs and consumers demanded an ever-expanding array of services, the insurance and medical care industries sidestepped the stalemate and pursued their own agendas.

Costs clearly had to be contained, and the insurance industry, hospitals, and doctors committed themselves to showing that they could do it on their own, without the heavy hand of government. How would they do it? By aggressively pursuing mergers and acquisitions—buying up hospitals and doctors' practices, negotiating contracts to corner markets, staking out territories, and forging alliances and partnerships to achieve virtual integration. Thus managed competition, rejected by the public and policy-makers, evolved into unmanaged competition—leaving just about everyone uneasy.

Consumerism and Consumer Advocacy

In the many months of struggle for national health reform, systems planners failed to address how at odds proposed changes were with cultural values, how changes were perceived as threatening individual choice. Yet the bitter and divisive debates that centered around choice entirely ignored how choice differs depending on one's life circumstances, raising uncomfortable questions about where we are heading. Is medical care really a consumer product, or is it something that constitutes a larger social good? If it is a social good, not just a product, how will some social consensus about it be formed? Is it possible to reconcile the contradiction between decrying the extent to which medical care is a business and demanding the right to pick and choose among all competing products and providers? To what extent was a consumer model of health care itself a factor in the failure of health reform and an impediment to extending access to medical care to all women and their families?

If the "artesian well" consumer model is hopelessly flawed, alternative models need to emerge to ensure universal access to a reasonable amount of medical care for everyone. Interest groups will need to envision very different types of health care delivery systems than we now imagine. Can or will feminists who were at the forefront of demanding consumer rights in medical care reconceptualize what is needed to ensure access to medical care for all into the next century? Can the consumer model be revised and revisited to reflect emerging fiscal and social realities?

The highly individualistic consumer conceptualization of health care, coupled with fragmentation and segmentation of subgroups by both social class and ethnicity, impedes the development of a vision of a common good, because the very notion of a common good implies sharing a common sense of humanity, which is a precondition for sharing resources.[13] In contrast, when we adopt a narrow consumer model of health care, we adopt a market frame of mind. To find a good doctor, we shop around, arm ourselves with information, seek out the best— whatever that may mean to us. The search becomes a lot like finding a plumber or a building contractor to entrust with the diagnosis and maintenance of our hidden systems—organs and wiring that we don't understand very well. Even as we "shop around," we complain about the commodification of medical care. Under fee-for-service, we tacitly accepted the highest price (as long as we assumed that somebody else was paying). Managed care organizations, to survive the marketplace, seek the lowest price. It may be impossible to reconcile being consumers with making medical care anything but a business. If we maintain the consumer model, then we will have to accept financial responsibility for how we spend medical care dollars—and figure out how to ensure that everyone has some reasonable amount to spend.

Feminist perspectives need to inform debate over what a reasonable level of medical care is. A consumer model appeals to people who are affluent because an unspoken assumption is that those who have more will get "the best." This assumption elevates choice to an ultimate value, an entitlement, something to be protected against erosion.[14] Health insurance that maximizes options and minimizes roadblocks fits the feminist consumer model of medical care and increases one's belief in the likelihood of finding the ideal doctor-patient relationship— an elusive but powerful image. For some patients, finding the best doctor entails "gaming"—getting a provider who will "work the system" to maximize individual benefit (Morreim 1991). Although the capacity of people to act on this varies by their means, even poorer patients engage in doctor switching and try to maximize what they can get from the system (O'Connor 1995:168).[15] What is conveniently ignored is how individual gains from "working the system" inevitably come at the expense of others—at the very least in the form of increased premiums, at worst in the form of medical care costs that are so prohibitive that jobs disappear.

As a society, we have yet to confront the fact that to meet the challenges of the demographic transition less than a decade ahead of us, the costs of health services will have to be contained. To do so will require spreading a fixed budget around in some "reasonable and rational" way—not just to widen access, but to maintain access as the ratio of workers to retirees and children widens. This will require accepting some degree of inconvenience or restriction on choice if we want everyone to have access to medical care.

Stepping back from current skirmishes over Medicare, Medicaid, and private insurance, it is time to explore how a consumer conceptualization of health care might undermine our willingness to share resources. Within it are myths and myopic expectations that put access to medical care for all out of reach. We need to explore how to move beyond an unrealistic "artesian well" image of medicine (Morreim 1995). A dilemma may be how to generate public discussion of the matter without feeding into public fears, fears that are exploited by insurers, physicians, hospitals, and others who profit by maintaining the inequitable but previously highly profitable system of private insurance and acute-care medicine.

Temporary solutions such as demanding universal, comprehensive health care without limitations—which many advocacy groups promote—are short-sighted solutions that may have the unintended consequence of increasing the ranks of both the uninsured and unemployed. Commitment to an unattainable ideal feeds the ideology that by not enacting partial national health coverage, we avoid setting-up a two-tier system of medical care. America already *has* at least three or four tiers of medical inequities. Universal access, which progressive reformers seek, will only be achieved by accepting responsibility for making hard choices about who gets what.

Many observers believe that some form of single-payer system is essential (Schiff et al. 1994). Such systems collect tax dollars nationally, but distribute services through a variety of approved medical care systems. Single-payer systems do not require government facilities as opponents charge. Skocpol (1996) points out that universal coverage could be achieved in a variety of ways. Partisan politics limit the development of social consensus on how to do this. Big-government solutions are unacceptable to conservatives, while vouchers (not only for medical care but for education and social services) are routinely opposed by liberals. Thus while universal access could be largely achieved through tax reform measures, partisan politics and interest group lobbying impede significant change. Feminist discussion of tax policies as well as social programs might yield particularly important policy insights and directions.

A feminist analysis of medical insurance might also move the debate in other new directions as well. Given women's disadvantaged benefit status, linked partly to movement in and out of the labor force (Muller 1990:96–99), it would seem important to separate medical benefits from employment. For women, who are disproportionately represented among low-wage workers, employer-provided coverage will never provide a real safety net. Policies that ensure at least some choices between health plans are also needed to ensure that people who have diverse needs will have real opportunities to meet those needs. Leaving a growing proportion of the population uninsured or underinsured, ostensibly to avoid creating a two-tiered system, is a recipe for maintaining the illusion of social justice while protecting one's own privileged access to tax-exempt employer-provided coverage.

In the next wave of health reform, the medical care organizations now evolving, with a variety of financing incentives, will be entrenched interests and as such wield enormous power in making the hard choices about "where next."[16] Choices are inevitable. No society can put an unlimited proportion of resources into medical care. Any woman who has struggled to balance a family budget understands this. In a highly stratified consumer society, the next round of reform will have to address the extent to which certain medical goods and services are social rights or necessities and others are consumer goods to be chosen, like other consumables, in relation to other possible expenditures.

Making "Hard Choices"

Without guiding principles to help determine what will be reimbursed under what circumstances, insurance plans are likely to become ever more adversarial, bureaucratic, and destructive of healing relationships. The big issues need to be answered within a moral framework, not a technocratic one. As Dougherty (1996) argues persuasively, increased reliance on market reforms is inconsistent with human dignity, caring, and protecting the least well-off. But to move to a more acceptable system, we will have to address cost containment and create a belief in a common good that is served by extending universal coverage.

If feminists are committed to achieving universal coverage, we will need dialogue about matters such as appropriate or acceptable limits on intensive care, and the number of cycles of infertility treatment that will, or will not, be reimbursed. As medical research hurtles forward with inevitable errors as well as breakthroughs, will experimental treatments be made available without scientific evidence of their efficacy? How will the needs of women who have chronic, long-term health needs be met? How will quality be balanced against cost?

Science cannot answer the moral and ethical issues that are embedded in complex fiscal matters. Nor can a society tax the many to support the development of biotechnologies that will benefit only the few who can afford them without risking social alienation and political upheaval. Questions need to be raised today about taxing low-wage workers (who are likely to be uninsured or underinsured) to subsidize medical benefits for high-income workers and affluent elderly persons as well as the most vulnerable—the disabled and the most economically disadvantaged. As the large baby-boom generation become Medicare-eligible, the proportionately smaller "baby-bust" generation will be left to pick up the tab. The next generation of workers (currently entering the labor force) are economically disadvantaged relative to previous birth cohorts (Bureau of the Census 1992: Table B-10). Their contributions will not support rising Medicare costs, which Jones and Estes (1997) point out are particularly threatening to women's ability to obtain care in old age. These pressing issues must be addressed in the broader context of how to care for everyone, or else we risk setting generations against each other and losing the will to create a sense of common destiny, of community.

No system of medical care can afford to provide "everything." Involving consumers in what to provide will work only if providers, insurers, health service delivery organizations, and consumer advocates cocreate new values, roles, and rules that take into account, simultaneously, social-psychological as well as scientific and economic realities. What we will really have to rethink is what matters in medical care, because reimbursement decisions are really value judgements about "what matters." To the degree that Western medicine has largely devalued and ignored the social-psychological and spiritual dimensions of health and healing, disregarded traditional healing practices, and overstated allopathic medicine's actual use of scientific evidence to shape clinical practice, discontent is inevitable. If we want providers to communicate and attend to the social-psychological dimensions of health and healing, who should those providers be, and how should they be educated and reimbursed? If we value choice, what structural arrangements would best allow patients to choose one type of care over another, or even forgo some medical care in order to be able to purchase social goods such as better education or housing? How can choice be structured in new ways? If feminists view health care as a consumer good, what choices should be considered essential and what considered discretionary?

Into the Future: What Values, What Directions?

It is naive to believe that even with more efficient organization of health resources, choices will not have to be made about what should be paid for universally. All societies ration medical care, although until recently Americans largely denied that "we have come to this yet." In other Western industrialized societies, the citizenry views the state as responsible for providing at least some basic level of care.[17] It seems highly unlikely that universal access can be achieved through market mechanisms, given the growing proportion of the population that is uninsured or underinsured.

Although the Campaign for Women's Health and the League of Women Voters did not adequately address cost, they laid critical groundwork for bringing women into national, state, and local arenas in which health care decisions are made. The campaign, and its member organizations, established the link between women's health and health care reform in the minds of women, policy makers, and others. Feminist analysis of the policy implications of various dimensions of the model benefits package might stimulate debate over new ways to organize medical benefits and medical services.

As we approach a new millennium, women and advocates of cost containment continue to inhabit separate intellectual and political spheres. Health care finance analysts and consumers remain poorly informed about each others' concerns and quandaries. Economists, whose concerns about costs are well founded, seem ill prepared to address how cost containment strategies will affect quality of care in human terms. Women's health advocacy groups, who do grasp the human side of quality, too often fail to confront hard questions about how to finance services or how to temper entitlements. No social consensus has emerged over principles that should guide a wealthy, industrialized nation provide a floor of equity of medical care.

The economics of health care and health care financing have received scant attention in national feminist women's health conferences, publications or discussions. In these arenas, women have focused largely on gaps and limitations in health services and on "what women want." Questions about how to pay for or make hard decisions about medical care are often ignored or resisted.[18]

We can ill afford an intellectual and political gender gap. Outside of a few policy corridors in Washington, where cost issues are well understood, women themselves may be continuing to create a division of policy labor along gender lines. The content and experience of health care continues to be disproportionately "women's work" in the social sciences, while health care financing, particularly cost containment, is largely men's work at the research and policy levels. Men need to understand women's perspectives on quality of care, particularly the interpersonal aspects of caring and healing; women need to grasp the social consequences of rising medical care costs.

The health care crisis is really one of confusion and disagreement over values, not just how much money can be spent.[19] Medical care is too complex a social and cultural creation to be "fixed" simply by changing financial incentives, even as critical as these incentives are for reducing inappropriate levels of care. Entrenched interests in the health care industry continue to find ways to keep medical care coverage focused on costly capital-intensive curative medicine, even while giving lip service to the ideology of managed care and prevention (Shortell et al. 1993). Preventive and primary care services, such as those rendered by lower-cost providers, are labor-intensive and thus produce fewer profits than capital-intensive medical machinery and drugs. As the medical care system becomes increasingly privatized and controlled by overtly for-profit corporations whose mission is to provide a return on capital to investors, insuring quality relative to cost will be imperative.

Quality assurance itself needs to be rethought, because what must be addressed are tacit assumptions about the value of "curing," which lead to excess use of unproven technologies, technologies that remain profit centers for vertically aligned health care systems. Capital-intensive high-tech medicine can produce surplus value for investors; labor-intensive primary care and direct bedside caring produce labor costs. Failure to confront profiteering, particularly when disguised as "generosity" in insurance coverage, will simply drain resources away from caring and creating communities that actually produce health.

National commitment to universal access remains segmented, tenuous, and hampered by lack of clarity of just what it might entail. Supporters of universal access appear willing to extend access to others only on the condition that their own benefits do not decline. Although it has been argued that American women view universal access as a priority for government, and women may in fact be willing to pay higher taxes to achieve it (Kasper 1994), the lack of clarity about what various groups of women want makes generalizing highly problematic. We need to turn attention to questions about the proportion of societal and personal resources that we believe should be spent on medical services, or what proportion of one's income it might be reasonable to pay (Brodie and Blendon 1995). Lack of social consensus on these issues, coupled with unrealistic expectations about the role of medicine in promoting health, makes public policy making inherently problematic.

Most Americans seem loath to give up the notion of unending medical progress and appear unwilling to make trade-offs—even between broader coverage but longer waits for elective procedures. The medical care crisis that we approach will force Americans to rethink the view that medical care should be unlimited, that access can be widened without imposing some forms of restrictions on reimbursement, and that rationing is not yet with us. Reversing financial incentives to overtreat can benefit women and society if cultural change and political will join forces to reduce overuse of costly, ineffective technologies and overpaid, excessively specialized providers for routine medical care. Reversing financial incentives will fail to benefit women if clarity and conscience lose out to vested interests that ignore what matters—and devalue communication, caring, and continuity of care.

Failure to reach a consensus on how to allocate care, other than on the basis of ability to pay, reflects systemic issues and moral values that must be addressed. Mechanisms to eliminate health services that contribute nothing to women's actual health and well-being simply must be developed, or the price of cost containment will be borne by doctors and patients who will find themselves locked into increasingly adversarial relationships. To be effective as a force for social change, academics will have to move beyond critique to praxis, and return to closer contact with ordinary people whose lives are directly affected by both products and paradigms.

The profound inequities in the current patchwork of services will be righted only through social conflict and cultural transformation. Maximizing individual choice is not an adequate framework for shaping a national health care system. Nor is extending coverage to one group and then another, in piecemeal fashion, age group by age group or disease by disease. What needs to emerge is a new sense of "we-consciousness," a concept that health is part of a common good that requires society to provide at least some universal care not just to older citizens, or to young children, but to all members of families, to all residents. To do otherwise inevitably pits the young and old against each another in a society already deeply divided by social class and race. Feminist perspectives need to emerge to address the urgency of providing all citizens primary and preventive care, even though this may require rethinking how much we should support costly tertiary care, and a massive biomedical research enterprise that institutionalizes inequalities, unless equal access to the benefits of medical innovations are widely distributed. As the population ages, and as fewer and fewer employed persons are called on to care for old and young alike, feminists must be prepared to propose realistic alternatives to rationing medical care based on ability to pay. To move in this direction we must be willing to engage in serious dialogue about the limits of individual choice as a first principle for social action. It is only when we let go of uncritical attachment to precepts that might have served women well in the past that new visions will emerge to shape our futures.

Notes

1. Following the failure of health reform, increased attention was directed to quality of care, particularly patient satisfaction. For discussions of quality issues in health reform and managed care, see Bartman 1996; Bernstein 1996; Emanuel and Dubler 1995; Ruzek 1997.

2. The comparative per capita health expenditure data for other countries are adjusted to U.S. dollars using gross domestic product purchasing power parities: Australia, $1,493; Canada, $1,971; France, $1,835; Japan, $1,495; Netherlands, $1,591; Sweden, $1,266; United Kingdom, $1,213 (National Center for Health Statistics 1996:240).

3. For discussions of women's social as well as biomedical health and medical care needs, see Costello and Stone 1995; Friedman 1994; Horton 1995; Ruzek, Olesen, and Clarke 1997.

4. For a fuller description of access issues and discussion of public and private insurance issues for women, see Costello and Stone 1995; Muller 1990; Ruzek 1997.

5. The cost of Medicare varies by age, sex, race and region. In 1993, average payments per enrollee were $3,412 for women and $3,678 for men (National Center for Health Statistics 1996:264).

6. In 1994, Medicaid costs averaged $5,964 per enrollee in the three highest level-of-benefit states and under $2,100 in the three states with the lowest level of benefits (National Center for Health Statistics 1996:272). Although recent Medicaid expansion of coverage to pregnant women and children raised the number of enrollees substantially, these programs account for only a small proportion of cost growth (10.8 percent). However, if all states covered all pregnant women with incomes of 185 percent of the poverty level, the level recommended but not required by the federal government, about half of all U.S. births would be Medicaid-funded (Kaiser Commission 1993:9).

7. For a discussion of the shift from systems that encouraged overtreatment to those that may undertreat, and the implications for women's health, see Collins 1996; Weisman 1996; Ruzek 1997.

8. See Bernstein 1996; Bernstein, Thompson and Harlan 1991; Miller and Luft 1994; Makuc, Freid and Parsons 1994; Riley et al. 1994; Weisman 1996.

9. There are controversies over the soundness of this approach as a basic form of insurance coverage. Most proposals involve large deductibles and in the view of managed care organizations would overturn the systems of accountability and review that lead to more appropriate use of services. Oberman (1995) argues that this would essentially return medicine to an FFS basis and lose the advantages of managed care.

10. These groups, brought together through the leadership of a feminist organization, might not normally be expected to join together to pursue political action—such as the Black Women's Agenda, B'nai B'rith Women, Boston Women's Health Book Collective, Catholics for a Free Choice, Mennonite Central Committee, National Abortion Rights Action League, National Association of Commissions for Women, National Black Women's Health Project, National Council of Jewish Women, National Council of Negro Women, National Displaced Homemakers Network, National Institute for Women of Color, National Organization for Women (NOW), Organization of Pan-Asian Women, Religious Coalition for Abortion Rights, Women's International Public Health Network, and the YWCA of the USA. Because the campaign quickly mobilized such diverse groups to take an official position on what had been promised would be comprehensive universal coverage, it is not surprising that the campaign's proposed model benefits package was all-inclusive. The structure of the political process encourages interest groups to demand more than they hope to get.

11. For more detailed discussion of the proposed benefit packages, see especially Campaign for Women's Health 1993; Kasper 1994; and Norsigian 1994.

12. This lack of attention to cost was not unique to the campaign. Virtually all interest groups who sought to make national health coverage available to everyone either ignored or denied the potential cost explosion implied in their expectations for expansive benefits.

13. For a particularly insightful discussion of the need to believe in a common good to extend health care as a right, see Dougherty 1996.

14. The concept of choice raises complex issues given the discrepancies in the choices available to women in different life-circumstances. Some conflicts and contradictions over the meaning of choice are addressed in Ruzek, Clarke, and Olesen 1997.

15. For example, in focus groups of Medicaid managed-care clients (conducted in 1993 for the Maternity Care Coalition of Philadelphia), women reported frequent switching of plans to get specific services covered by one provider but not another.

16. For prognostications about difficult issues that will have to be addressed, see especially Callahan 1987; Conrad and Brown 1993; Dougherty 1996; Duncan 1994; Mechanic 1989; Schroeder 1994; and Skocpol 1996.

17. Norsigian (1994) is one of the few feminist health advocates who has publicly addressed the extent to which we have, and will inevitably have, some form of rationing.

18. This observation grows out of my participation in numerous women's health conferences over the past two decades. Although there are a small number of women social scientists who research the economics of health care, and a growing number of women in health care finance and administration, they have been noticeably absent at feminist health conferences. For example, at the Reframing Women's Health Summer Institute, held in 1994 at the University of Illinois, Chicago, some participants raised questions about why such speakers were not on the program. My own efforts to raise issues of cost containment and discuss the role managed care might play in reducing unnecessary medical care largely have been met with hostility. Some women with long-standing involvement in feminist health advocacy who work for managed care organizations have privately noted their discouragement over the resistance of some feminists to recognize the appropriateness and necessity of containing costs.

19. The lack of attention to values has been raised particularly well in Duncan 1994; Dougherty 1996; Emanuel and Dubler 1995; and Morreim 1995. Skocpol's insightful analysis of how values and ideologies of political parties limit policy solutions that can be envisioned clarifies the structural resistance that must be overcome to bring about universal access (1996).

References

Azavedo, D. 1994. Why Can't Other HMOs Work as Well as this One? *Medical Economics* 71:102–10.

Bartman, Barbara A. 1996. Women's Access to Appropriate Providers Within Managed Care: Implications for the Quality of Primary Care. *Women's Health* Issues 6:45–50.

Bernstein, Amy B. 1996. Women's Health in HMOs: What We Know and What We Need to Find Out. *Women's Health Issues* 6:51–59.

Bernstein, A. B., G. B. Thompson, and L.C. Harlan. 1991. Differences in Rates of Cancer Screening by Usual Source of Medical Care: Data from the 1987 National Health Interview Survey. *Medical Care* 29:196–209.

Brodie, Mollyann, and Robert J. Blendon. 1995. The Public's Contribution to Congressional Gridlock on Health Care Reform. *Journal of Health Politics, Policy and Law* 20:403–10.

Bronfenbrenner, Urie, Peter McClelland, Elaine Wethington, Phyllis Moen, and Stephen J. Ceci. 1996. *The State of Americans: This Generation and the Next.* New York: Free Press.

Bureau of the Census. 1992. *Money Income of Households, Families and Persons in the United States: 1991.* Washington, DC: Government Printing Office.

Callahan, Daniel. 1987. *Setting Limits: Medical Goals in an Aging Society.* New York: Simon and Schuster.

Campaign for Women's Health. 1993. *A Model Benefits Package for Women in Health Care Reform.* Washington, D.C.: Older Women's League.

Clancy, Carolyn M., and Howard Brody. 1995. Managed Care: Jekyll or Hyde? *Journal of the American Medical Association* 273:338–39.

Collins, Karen Scott. 1996. Women's Health and Managed Care: Promises and Challenges. *Women's Health Issues* 6:39–44.

Conrad, Peter, and Phil Brown. 1993. On Rationing Medical Care: A Sociological Reflection. *Research in the Sociology of Health Care* 10:3–22.

Costello, Cynthia, and Anne J. Stone (eds.) for the Women's Research and Education Institute. 1995. *The American Woman, 1994–95: Where We Stand: Women and Health.* New York: W. W. Norton.

Davis, Karen. 1993. Health Care Reform in the United States. The Contribution of Health Services Research to the Debate. *Annals of the New York Academy of Sciences* 703:287–90.

Dougherty, Charles J. 1996. *Back to Reform: Values, Markets, and the Health Care System.* New York: Oxford University Press.

Duncan, Karen A. 1994. *Health Information and Health Reform. Understanding the Need for a National Health Information System.* San Francisco: Jossey-Bass.

Emanuel, Ezekiel J., and Nancy Neveloff Dubler. 1995. Preserving the Physician-Patient Relationship in the Era of Managed Care. *Journal of the American Medical Association* 273:323–29.

Friedman, Emily (ed.). 1994. *An Unfinished Revolution: Women and Health Care in America.* New York: United Hospital Fund.

Ginzburg, Eli, with Miriam Ostow. 1994. *The Road to Reform: The Future of Health Care in America.* New York: Free Press.

Havighurst, C. 1992. Prospective Self-denial: Can Consumers Contract Today to Accept Health Care Rationing Tomorrow? *University of Pennsylvania Law Review* 140:1755–85.

Horton, Jacqueline A. (ed.). 1995. *The Women's Health Data Book: A Profile of Women's Health in the United States,* Second edition. Washington, DC: Jacobs Institute of Women's Health, Elsevier.

Jones, Vida Yvonne, and Carroll L. Estes. 1997. Older Women: Income, Retirement, and Health. Pp. 425–45 in Sheryl Burt Ruzek, Virginia L. Olesen, and Adele E. Clarke (eds.), *Women's Health: Complexities and Differences.* Columbus: Ohio State University Press.

Kaiser Commission on the Future of Medicaid, 1993. *The Medicaid Cost Explosion: Causes and Consequences.* Baltimore: Kaiser Commission on the Future of Medicaid.

Kasper, Anne. 1994. The Making of Women's Health Policy: Health Care Reform. Paper presented at the Chicago Intensive Summer Institute: "Reframing Women's Health," Univesrity of Illinois, July.

League of Women Voters. 1994. Critical Choices in Health Reform. League of Women Voters Education Fund and the Henry J. Kaiser Family Foundation, Washington, DC.

Makuc, Diane M., Virginia M. Freid, and P. Ellen Parsons. 1994. Health Insurance and Cancer Screening among Women. Advance Data No. 254 (Aug. 3), National Center for Health Statistics, Hyattsville, MD.

Mechanic, David. 1989. *Painful Choices: Research and Essays on Health Care.* New Brunswick, NJ: Transaction Publishers.

Miller, Robert H., and Harold S. Luft. 1994. Managed Care Plan Performance Since 1980: A Literature Analysis. *Journal of the American Medical Association* 271:1512–19.

Morreim, E. Haavi. 1991. Gaming the System: Dodging the Rules, Ruling the Dodgers. *Archives of Internal Medicine* 151:443–47.

———. 1992. Access Without Excess. *The Journal of Medicine and Philosophy* 17:1–6.

———. 1995. The Ethics of Incentives in Managed Care. *Trends in Health Care, Law and Ethics* 10:56–62.

Muller, Charlotte F. 1990. *Health Care and Gender.* New York: Russell Sage Foundation.

National Center for Health Statistics. 1996. *Health United States, 1995.* Hyattsville, MD: Public Health Service.

Norsigian, Judy. 1994. Women and National Health Care Reform: A Progressive Feminist Agenda. Pp. 111–17 in Alice Dan (ed.), *Reframing Women's Health.* Thousand Oaks, CA: Sage Publications.

Oberman, Debra. 1995. Medical Savings Accounts: In the Spotlight on Capitol Hill. *HMO* 36:81–88.

O'Connor, Bonnie Blair. 1995. *Healing Traditions: Alternative Medicine and the Health Professions.* Philadelphia: University of Pennsylvania Press.

Reinhardt, Uwe. 1992. American Values: Are They Blocking Health-System Reform? *Medical Economics* 69:126–41.

Riley, Gerald F., Arnold L. Potosky, James D. Lubitz, and Martin L. Brown. 1994. Stage of Cancer at Diagnosis for Medicare HMO and Fee-For-Service Enrollees. *American Journal of Public Health* 84 (10):1598–1604.

Ruzek, Sheryl Burt. 1997. Access, Cost and Quality of Care. Pp. 183–240 in Sheryl Burt Ruzek, Virginia L. Olesen, and Adele E. Clarke (eds.), *Women's Health: Complexities and Differences.* Columbus: Ohio State University Press.

Ruzek, Sheryl Burt, Adele E. Clarke, and Virginia L. Olesen. 1997. What Are the Dynamics of Differences? Pp. 51–95 in Sheryl Burt Ruzek, Virginia L. Olesen, and Adele E. Clarke (eds.), *Women's Health: Complexities and Differences.* Columbus: Ohio State University Press.

Schiff, Gordon D., Andrew B. Bindman, and Troyen A. Brennan, for the Physicians for a National Health Program Quality of Care Working Group. 1994. A Better-Quality Alternative: Single-payer National Health System Reform. *Journal of the American Medical Association* 272:803–8.

Schroeder, Stephen. 1994. Rationing Medical Care—A Comparative Perspective. *New England Journal of Medicine* 331:1063–67.

Shortell, Stephen, Robin R. Gillies, David A. Anderson, John B. Mitchell, and Karen L. Morgan. 1993. Creating Organized Delivery Systems: The Barriers and Facilitator. *Hospital and Health Services Administration* 38:447–66.

Skocpol, Theda. 1996. *Boomerang: Clinton's Health Security Effort and the Turn Against Government in U.S. Politics.* New York: W. W. Norton and Company.

Starr, Paul. 1994. *The Logic of Health Care Reform: Why and How the President's Plan Will Work.* Revised and expanded edition. New York: Whittle/Penguin.

Steinmo, Sven, and Jon Watts. 1995. It's the Institutions, Stupid! Why Comprehensive National Health Insurance Always Fails in America. *Journal of Health Politics, Policy and Law* 20:329–72.

U.S. Office of Management and Budget. 1996. *A Citizen's Guide to the Federal Budget, FY 1996.* Washington, DC: Government Printing Office.

Weisman, Carol S. 1996. Proceedings of "Women's Health and Managed Care: Balancing Cost, Access, and Quality." Introduction to the Proceedings. *Women's Health Issues* 6:1–4.

Agendas for Lesbian Health

Countering the Ills of Homophobia

JENNIFER TERRY

Researching and analyzing the matter of lesbian health is an emotionally taxing process. In my historical studies, I have felt compelled to scrutinize how and why it is that lesbians have stimulated such intense anxiety and hostility among physicians.[1] If one reads medical cases and scientific studies involving lesbians carefully and against the grain, it is possible to locate strategies of resistance deployed by lesbians who participated in studies about them and who engaged in their own processes of self-inquiry about what made them distinct. Since at least the beginning of this century, many lesbians, though often under duress, have told their stories to experts and allowed doctors to examine their bodies in the interrogative spirit of asking the questions of how and why they/we are different. But what often began as a question of difference for these women quickly blurred into the assumption of pathology in the view of scrutinizing experts, whether the participating subjects of studies intended it to be so or not.

Lesbians have been prompted—and often compelled—to try to understand themselves to a very great degree in relation to a discourse, medicine, that construes their difference as primarily pathological. The relationship, then, of lesbian identity to categories of difference-as-pathology has a long and rich history that cannot be simply summed up as delusion, collusion, or complicity between lesbians and physicians. Nor can it be reduced to mere co-optation by doctors.[2] The value of analyzing specific studies of lesbians in their social and historical contexts is that it allows the reader to witness complex engagements of lesbians with medical discourse that do not result simply in cruel subjection or thoroughgoing domination. Lesbians often talk back, and not always in ways that doctors can understand or appreciate. To an overwhelming degree, we have been deemed abnormal, degenerate, and sick through the declarations of physicians whose cultural prestige has allowed their declarations to pass as truth in the larger society and to thus become taken-for-granteds in mainstream American culture over the past century or so. This has made talking back a risky but often necessary undertaking.

When affectionate and sexual relations between women became the grounds for constructing a type of sick person—known variously as the "female invert," the "degenerate tribade," the "mannish woman," and the "neurotic lesbian"—a historical process ensued by which something we might now call modern lesbian subjectivity emerged. One important effect of this process was the generation of constraints and possibilities occasioned by the label of pathology, in relation to which women identified with this label forged identities and subcultures. A century or so later, there is no easy way to disentangle the association of modern Western lesbian subjectivity with pathology. Indeed, while it is laudable to locate or create a lesbian space outside of this specter of pathology, to study this history and to note its very present manifestations can be useful for staking claims in the powerful domains of science, medicine, and health care politics. Lesbian subjectivity cannot be summarized nor wholly refashioned through a discourse that remains exclusively within the field of medicine. But the very practical matters of dealing with the normative concepts of disease and health in a homophobic society animate much of the history and recent expressions of lesbian identity and political activity.

My aim in this chapter is to examine several developments spanning the last couple of decades that reveal a relationship between lesbian subjectivity, primarily in the United States, and struggles to overcome the label of pathology as they manifest in attempts to define lesbian agendas for health. From lesbian-feminist self-help politics of the 1970s through lesbian health care activism in the context of the late 1980s and 1990s, it is possible to identify certain continuities as well as significant shifts in rhetoric, strategy, and goals. These emanate from particular and changing social contexts that shape the persistent questions of what counts as lesbian health, what strategies are most effective for ensuring the health of lesbians, and what ought to be the relationship of lesbian health care activism to authoritative experts.

I approach these questions by sketching out several key moments and texts. Specifically, I do so by looking at how these questions have been approached by lesbians from the 1970s through today. Admittedly, this is a cursory sketch of a much larger project, so I run the risk of simplifying complex matters. Furthermore, in this preliminary and provisional staking out of the territory, I will further confess that my data are largely textual rather than more fully ethnographic.

Lesbian/Feminists Helping Themselves

In 1972 Phyllis Lyon and Del Martin published *Lesbian/Woman*, a text about lesbian life that explicitly valorized the subjective views of lesbians themselves, countering the many previous volumes by "experts" whose careers were built on speculating, often in pejorative terms, about "twilight women," "female sex inverts," and "lesbians" (Lyon and Martin 1971). *Lesbian/Woman* was an important lesbian-feminist text that spoke back against not only the content but also the presumptuous methods deployed to pathologize lesbianism in existing medical and popular discourse. While Lyon and Martin viewed "objective" science of the sort Kinsey conducted more favorably because of its refusal to assume lesbianism was, by definition (Kinsey et al. 1953), a malady, the authors were also intent upon allowing lesbians to speak for themselves in the pages of the volume. This, they believed, would be a crucial antidote to being represented by scientific experts in the form of detached and abstract statistics, data that had been used to support the view that lesbians were at the very least anomalous, if not wholly diseased. Lyon and Martin, in the spirit of second-wave feminism, deployed the subjective experiences of lesbians as—among other things—a means for criticizing a kind of credentialed expertise that had for too long made pronouncements about lesbianism that were at best merely tolerant and more often openly hostile.

Though it may be assessed retrospectively as an assimilationist text that argued for the acceptance of lesbianism on the grounds that "normal" (that is, white, middle-class) women engaged in it, *Lesbian/Woman* advanced a powerful and now foundational argument that the main health problems facing lesbians were those resulting from culturally pervasive homophobia. And deeply implicated in this homophobia was the medical profession itself, particularly psychiatry, which, under the guise of providing care, had administered a kind of poison that kept lesbians from appreciating their own worth, from trusting doctors, and from seeking health care for any number of common medical problems when needed. The Lyon/Martin Health Clinic in San Francisco, one of the few clinics of its kind still in existence, was thus established in the spirit of countering this poison by offering affordable, homophilic health care and information to women in general and lesbians in particular.

While *Lesbian/Woman* had much to say about other aspects of lesbian existence, its focus on countering the assessment of lesbianism as inherently pathological reveals the extent to which the authors believed that the biggest problems facing lesbians were inextricably linked to the deployment of medical thinking to underpin male dominance and homophobia via the excoriation of lesbianism as a form of illness. Thus, the authors turned the tables on the medical profession and pronounced it to be not only a primary cause of lesbian oppression but itself a disease-making enterprise whose success in convincing the general population of lesbians' inadequacy manifested in myriad psychological and physical suffering among lesbians and, moreover, in a resistance among lesbians to seek health care. The solution to this problem trafficked under the sign of self-help, an ethos of care directed at establishing autonomous feminist health care that would empower women to take care of themselves and each other through greater knowledge of their bodies. Moreover, self-help, when taken up by lesbian feminists, had at its core the goal of enhancing lesbians' appreciation of their lives and loves.

Self-help in the domain of health care was one of the many "taking back" strategies championed by the feminist movement. Taking control of medical information via self-help was a tactic aimed at providing women with public spaces free from male domination, violence, and devaluation. The public space of medicine, figured through the making public of women's bodies to women themselves, was, significantly, a key site of contestation and revisioning of medicine as well as of lesbian identity in this frame. Lesbian identity not only became a rallying point for resistance to the crippling effects of homophobia and male dominance, but also figured as a symbol for expressing women's overall value, because lesbians placed women at the center of their affections, sexual desires, and politics.

Following *Lesbian/Woman*, in 1973 the second edition of *Our Bodies, Our Selves* featured a chapter entitled "In Amerika They Call Us Dykes," which introduced issues of concern to lesbians in this other important early text of the feminist self-help health movement (Boston Women's Health Collective 1973).[3] Its dual purpose was to offer support to women who were lesbians or were exploring lesbian identity and to give heterosexual women "a clearer picture of our lives." The chapter foregrounded how gaining dignity and respect for lesbians was crucial not only to their health but to the health of the women's movement in general, where the "lavender menace" of lesbianism, in Betty Friedan's parlance, had been construed as an embarrassment or deleterious virus within the movement for women's equality with men. The themes of coming out and public visibility of lesbianism were emphasized in this important addition to the second edition of *Our Bodies, Our Selves*.

As in the rest of the volume, health, in the chapter on lesbianism, was defined to encompass emotional as well as biological matters and, indeed, was directly linked to politics. Lesbian health was conceptualized as fundamentally holistic, or to put it another way, as shaped by the interrelations between psychological, physiological, societal, and political factors. Physical health, then, could be seen as separate neither from emotional health nor from political struggles for dignity and respect. Thus homophobia, discrimination, shame, and self-hatred were understood to be risks to lesbian health equal to any virus or cancer or addiction. And furthermore, the authors of *Our Bodies, Our Selves* stressed that the latter could be exacerbated and even caused by the former. Homophobia itself was figured as disease, not merely an aggravating cofactor. The chapter was indeed about *self*-help, dedicated to demystifying health care expertise and, importantly, concerned with helping lesbians to imagine themselves free from homophobia. It was hoped that such imaginings would lead to new conceptions, revisionings if you will, of lesbian health not only by positing the novel possibility of healthy lesbians but by shifting the historical onus away from the equation of lesbianism with pathology toward combating the endemic sexism and homophobia in health care provision that made lesbian lives risky.

In 1978 *Our Right to Love: A Lesbian Resource Guide*, a similarly styled volume with multiple authors, featured a chapter on lesbian health (Vida 1978). Several short pieces described the emergence of support groups for lesbians in women's community health collectives in New York and Boston. As in *Our*

Bodies, Our Selves, the authors listed a growing agenda of health care issues faced particularly by lesbians, whom they defined very inclusively as women who are sexually or affectionately drawn to women, including some who might also be celibate (that is, having removed themselves from the heterosexual contract of relations with men). One author noted that lesbians faced the same problems experienced by most women when they needed medical care. These included the lack of availability and high cost of medical care, rudeness of providers, and experts' mystification of medical knowledge. But, the author continued, lesbians had even less control over their health care than heterosexual women. Lesbianism itself, she noted, was often seen by doctors as the *cause* of all other problems of a patient. That is, it was viewed not only as inherently pathological, but also as a willful invitation to further disorders and disease. Significant problems resulted from this basic assumption. For example, lesbians were denied information about sexually transmitted diseases that could be passed from woman to woman; they were denied rights to visit with or accompany lovers in the hospital, the doctor's office, the emergency room, and the intensive care unit; and they were often subjected by providers to inquisitions about their personal lives or to monologues about lesbianism and its merits or liabilities.

This homophobic treatment, the author went on to note, inhibited lesbians from seeking health care, which could explain why so many suffered from conditions, ranging from endometriosis to cancer, that might have been prevented or prophylactically treated had they received regular checkups. In this framework of critique, self-help was proposed as an antidote that allowed women to share information in order to make responsible decisions about their health care. It was a first and crucial step toward "regaining control over our total lives."

Reiterating much of what these earlier volumes argued, in 1980 the Santa Cruz Women's Health Collective published a great little book called *Lesbian Health Matters!* (Santa Cruz Women's Health Collective 1980). The book was both a guide to health care for lesbians and a political text about the deep-rooted homophobia and misogyny characteristic of medical practices, and which were themselves disease-causing and disease-aggravating factors affecting lesbians. As a practical guide to health care, *Lesbian Health Matters!* devoted attention to standard medical issues of concern to women, especially regarding gynecological care and self-administered breast examinations. It stressed the importance of achieving emotional happiness as a primary foundation for maintaining health and identified the need to counter internalized and externally generated homophobia as a crucial step toward repairing the ills of the past—in terms of one's own bodily and psychical history and the history of the larger social context, afflicted as it was by homophobia.

What is strikingly absent from all of the texts I've mentioned so far is a sustained analysis that would tie the problem of homophobic health care to adjacent and affiliated problems of racism and class oppression as they function to compromise the health of economically disadvantaged lesbians and lesbians of color in compound ways. We can remember that these connections were rarely made in 1980. Only recently do we have analyses that feature the ways that oppressions based on gender, race, class, and sexuality are produced through interwoven structures and institutions of domination embedded within the medical profession (cf. Comaroff 1993; Gomez and Smith 1990; Hammonds 1992; Mays and Cochran 1986; Trujillo 1993; White 1990).

The basic contours of the early agenda for lesbian health persist today, with some important additions and modifications. In the early years, a primary domain of intervention concerned mental health, where problems such as stress, anxiety, depression, substance abuse, eating disorders, attempted suicide, and recovery from incest and childhood sexual assault were common. Perceived as being suffered in epidemic proportions among lesbians, the prominence given to psychological maladies in most early agendas underscores the argument advanced by the texts I've mentioned: The sexism suffered by girls and women and the opprobrium with which lesbianism is met in U.S. society registers in substantial psychological fallout among lesbians. Again, as the lesbian-feminist argument went, lesbians' psychological suffering was not endemic to their sexual orientation per se, but was an effect of the scorn and prejudice they experienced because they were women and lesbians. In addition to psychologically based problems, early agendas concerning lesbian health focused on forms of chronic illness (notably cancer, heart disease, and diabetes), gynecological care, and disability issues. In each of these areas, lesbian health care activists frequently noted that mainstream medicine, abetted by sexist and homophobic attitudes in the larger society, tended to ignore or misdiagnose particular problems when they appeared in lesbians, or to exhibit open hostility toward lesbians.

During the 1980s and 1990s several new issues have been added to the earlier outlines of lesbian health matters.[4] The so-called lesbian baby boom of the past decade or so corresponded to the addition of reproductive and child-rearing issues to the agenda of lesbian health. Donor insemination, fertility therapies, prenatal genetic screening, postpartum maternal and infant health, and parenting advice now find their place on the agenda. In addition, we find a greater attention to the process of aging as a growing number of lesbians cross the threshold into old age. As a symptom of our times, new agendas for lesbian health also cite the need for changes in hospital and emergency room procedure to treat lesbian victims of traumatizing homophobic assaults, including rape, and to permit their lovers and elected (that is, nonbiological) kin to visit them while hospitalized, just as conventional family members are normally allowed. The recruitment of more lesbians into the health care professions and the demand for protection against homophobic discrimination and harassment in health care work settings are also new additions to the agenda. Last but not least, the presence of HIV and AIDS among lesbians, together with the historically contingent fact that many AIDS activists were and are lesbians, has brought AIDS into prominent focus in recently drafted agendas for lesbian health.

Each of these new issues indexes important historical shifts and developments over the past few decades, including the emergence of the AIDS epidemic, the reality of aging among lesbian-identified women, the expansion and growth of lesbian communities, and the presence of openly lesbian health care providers. In addition, the new agenda items reflect the development of new technologies (especially new reproductive technologies) and the possibilities to which they give rise, as well as new political priorities articulated by national and local gay, lesbian, and transgender organizations that center on what, for lack of a better term, are often referred to as "family issues" (such as childbearing and -rearing concerns as well as legal provisions to ensure lesbian partners' power of attorney over health care decisions).

A glance at the larger context of social relations, economics, and politics that shaped both the earlier agenda and the later, expanded one reveals some interesting contrasts. Besides the relationship of women's health care activism in the 1970s to a vital feminist movement and other progressive movements, the texts I mentioned earlier were written during a time of relative economic expansion of publicly funded health care and a time when there was hope in progressive political struggles at both the national and local levels. It was a time before Reaganomics and the intensified assault on the public sector. It was no picnic then but, compared to events of the 1980s and the 1990s, it was a time of new possibilities and of radical thinking and organizing, a time of widespread social experimentation, especially around matters of gender and sexuality. And it was marked by the emergence of powerful critiques of compulsory heterosexuality.[5] It was also a time when lesbian and gay communities were growing and beginning to have an important presence in the American cultural and political landscape, giving rise, on one hand, to greater support from progressive sectors and, on the other, to a homophobic backlash from conservative and sexually repressive sectors. It was also a time before AIDS.

The general rightward direction of American politics, economics, and culture during the 1980s had an extremely damaging impact on lesbians and gay men, on feminism and women generally (especially poor women), on people of color, and on progressive movements. Homophobic and antifeminist cultural politics of the sort espoused by Christian fundamentalist leaders and ruling-class conservative culture warriors were flanked by Reaganomic policies to deregulate industry, drive wages down and unemployment rates up, and declare war on welfare. The consolidation of economic and political power on the right occurred, not surprisingly, during a decade when such prominent spokespeople as Jesse Helms and Patrick Buchanan referred to AIDS as God's punishment for homosexuality. Enormous energy was expended by lesbians and gay men to care for people with AIDS and to fight ongoing battles against intensified homophobia unleashed by the AIDS epidemic.

But also during the 1980s, in spite of the closure of many grassroots feminist health centers and the collapse of many lesbian feminist organizations, lesbian health care activism did not disappear and, in fact, in some ways gained a kind of vitality and organizational prominence in the face of great adversity. By some accounts, the radical edge of the feminist movement died in the 1980s, owing to its mummification in the academy or its co-optation into mainstream institutions. Whether or not such pronouncements are anything more than cynical acts of discursive murder, it is quite true that by the late 1980s, grassroots feminist publications, bookstores, women's centers, women's health collectives, and political groups had diminished in number due to many pressures, not least of which were a lack of financial support, burnout, dysfunctional squabbles, political splits, and the mainstreaming of some of the more moderate aspects of feminist politics, including women's health clinics.

At the same time, vital critiques of the lack of respect for diversity in the women's movement in terms of race, class, and sexual practice led to a broadening of the base and definitions of feminism. And these debates transformed and multiplied lesbian identity into lesbian identi*ties* to account for important differences in the social positions and cultural affinities, especially of women of color[6] as well as of women who challenged many of the assumptions about sexuality that had come to dominate radical feminism in the late 1970s.[7] In many ways the "sex wars" of the 1980s transformed lesbian identities through a greater emphasis on sexual practices and especially "outlawed" sexual practices. Earlier key figures encompassed in the woman-identified-woman paradigm of lesbian feminism were the "political lesbian" (who may have slept with men but claimed a lesbian identity in opposition to patriarchy) and the celibate woman (whose refusal to participate in sexual relations was also seen as an act of opposition to patriarchy and toward women's autonomy). During the 1980s sexual practices between women were emphasized as the grounds for constituting lesbian identities at a time when women's sexual subjectivity—the nature and multifarious forms of expressing female desire—became the focus of critical theorizing and practice. Lesbian sisterhood had been powerful in the 1970s, but in many ways it was to be explicitly sexual in the 1980s and 1990s.

The Impact of AIDS

The move to consider sexual practices as key to lesbian identities occurred coterminously with a number of other events that influenced and expanded the issues and strategies associated with elaborating a lesbian health agenda. Besides the skyrocketing costs of health care and a trend toward professionalizing and mainstreaming women's health care, an important development of the 1980s that expanded the agenda and strategies of lesbian health was the emergence of the AIDS epidemic, which mobilized many lesbians from the moment it appeared in 1982. Among gay and lesbian health care professionals, the AIDS epidemic has been described as something on the order of a second Stonewall in the sense that large numbers of doctors, nurses, and other caregivers came out of the closet at work and agitated for better preventive education, more humane clinical care, and more effective research and treatment. Lesbians joined gay men in pioneering community-based efforts along these lines, providing emotional and practical support to people with AIDS. Many took leadership in emerging grassroots institutions and later national organizations to fight AIDS. The Women's AIDS Network in San Francisco was formed relatively early in the epidemic, with a strong presence of lesbians working alongside heterosexual- and bisexual-identified women to set an agenda for women in relation to HIV disease.[8] Toward the end of the 1980s, the Women's Caucus of ACT UP New York formed to address the issues concerning women and HIV, using media activism and grassroots organizing to battle governmental neglect and to counter a nationwide backlash against people with AIDS and homosexuality in general (ACT UP/New York Women and AIDS Book Group 1990).[9] A majority of the caucus consisted of lesbians, and many were interested in reforming policies of the Centers for Disease Control (CDC) to track the particular risk patterns of woman-to-woman transmission and lesbian intervenous drug use, and to demand that the federal Food and Drug Administration (FDA) conduct pharmaceutical treatment studies that included women subjects to test the efficacy of drugs in HIV-positive women. The new activist strategies combined earlier self-help emphases with direct action strategies deployed by ACT UP. ACT UP worked to educate HIV-positive people about new medical findings so that they could make informed decisions about treatment. In addition, efforts to develop direct and explicit sex education to prevent HIV transmission were coupled with demands to reform epidemiological, clinical, and pharmaceutical procedures, and to expand Medicare and Medicaid support to serve the needs of people with AIDS.

Debates ensued within lesbian communities about whether lesbians were at high or low risk for HIV infection. Some lesbians saw the emphasis on lesbians being at risk for HIV as a phantom paranoia, backed by little scientific evidence, and having the very undesirable effect of scaring women away from sex and from lesbianism. On the other side of the debate, lesbian activists who emphasized lesbians' risks claimed that a lack of research on woman-to-woman transmission, resulting from homophobic myopia among epidemiologists, obscured the real and possible risks lesbians faced. A corollary outcome of the debate was a shift toward warning against risky behaviors that could permit transmission of HIV among lesbians rather than focusing on at-risk identities, an issue that had come up earlier when the focus of ACT UP was mainly on gay men's risks. Hence, safer sex materials were modified to address "women who have sex with women" in order to work around (and in some ways to counter) predominant notions of lesbian identity that had assumed, sometimes wrongly, that lesbians do not have sex with men, that they do not exchange bodily fluids, and that they do not engage in intervenous drug use. Countering such assumptions that lesbians, by virtue of their identity, were not at risk for HIV was done in a fashion that hailed individuals who might be at risk for HIV infection but would not understand or primarily identify themselves as lesbians. The shift was meant to highlight situationally specific risks that could and did arise in relations between women, while breaking down the homophobic conflation of lesbian identity per se with pathology.

No doubt, within the context of ACT UP, the emphasis on lesbians' risks was partly fueled by women's efforts within the group to get lesbians' issues on the agenda. In the dynamics of ACT UP, there was a way in which political voice and visibility accrued to those perceived to be HIV infected or at risk for HIV; the words and views of those whose lives were on the line had a palpable gravity and urgency in meetings and political demonstrations. It would be wrong to assess the women's group's emphasis on lesbians' risks for HIV transmission as merely a tactical move to gain power, since it is quite true that lesbians could very well engage in risky behavior, including having unprotected sex or sharing needles with HIV-infected people. But, by foregrounding women's and lesbians' risks for HIV transmission, the women's caucus effectively redefined their roles and broadened their influence via the specter of risk. No longer could they be assumed to be sympathetic solidarity workers who were shielded from risk; instead, they too were positioned as at risk for HIV, a move that placed them on more equal rhetorical footing to men whose risk for HIV had been unquestioned.

Concurrent to AIDS activism, several important lesbian AIDS activists began in the early 1990s to emphasize the importance of focusing on cancers that afflicted women at alarmingly high rates. Jackie Winnow, a Bay Area lesbian AIDS activist who was diagnosed with breast cancer in the late 1980s, was a key figure here. Winnow, who helped in the founding of Women's Cancer Resource Center, noted that gynecological and breast cancers directly affected women and lesbians at rates equivalent to or greater than HIV seemed to be, but were ignored in the focused and highly publicized context of AIDS activism. Winnow made a call for women and lesbians to pay attention to the politics of breast cancer and to incorporate activist strategies from AIDS struggles in the fight against cancer. In her words, "Both of these diseases are life-threatening and yet I have seen my community rally around one and overlook the other.... No one takes care of women or lesbians except women or lesbians, and we have a hard enough time taking care of ourselves, of finding ourselves worthy and important enough for attention" (Winnow 1992:68).

AIDS activism invigorated lesbian health activism to move in new directions and adopt new direct-action strategies. But AIDS activists borrowed many of their key strategies from grassroots feminist health care activism from the previous decade, including questioning expertise, championing self-help, and challenging the sexist and homophobic attitudes that pervade the medical establishment. This reliance on feminist strategies, while seldom acknowledged by many male activists, was due in large part to the fact that many lesbian AIDS activists had been involved in feminist health care politics or had been deeply influenced by this earlier history. In the 1980s, Jackie Winnow and scores of other feminists and lesbians saw the urgent need to get involved in the struggle against AIDS. By the early 1990s, many became aware of the importance of keeping women's health issues in perspective and not losing sight of them by focusing narrowly on the epidemic.

Research by Lesbians on Lesbians for Lesbians

The idea of having reliable, authoritative data generated by experts on lesbian health is emphasized more now than it was in the 1970s. Some of this can be attributed to efforts on the part of AIDS activists to urge the medical-scientific establishment to study HIV disease more closely and carefully. In addition to the urgent need for reliable information of this sort upon which to base prevention and treatment campaigns, AIDS activists believed that confronting powerful medical institutions and demanding that AIDS be taken seriously was an important symbolic gesture as well. To get institutions such as the CDC, the FDA, and the National Institutes of Health (NIH) to take AIDS seriously was to put the epidemic on the national agenda, something that President Ronald Reagan and his successor, George Bush, had been more than a little reluctant to do.

But the focus on large-scale medical institutions implied a sense of faith in traditional scientific expertise that had not been present in the grassroots feminist health care activism of the 1970s. As an activist friend of mine put it, when lesbian AIDS activists urged the CDC to do epidemiological reporting of woman-to-woman transmission of HIV, it was the first time in recent history that lesbians abandoned anecdotal information, lived experience, and observed reality among lesbians in favor of a fantastical scientific discovery of which there was little material evidence. Given the historically documented low incidence of sexually transmitted diseases passed between women, it would seem that HIV was difficult to spread through sexual activities most commonly practiced by lesbians. Not to disregard the potential risks faced by lesbians, it seems important to point out that many AIDS activist strategies involved a belief in objective and truthful science. Beseeching the CDC to study lesbians implied a certain kind of faith in the established practice of epidemiology, sometimes at the cost of ignoring or overlooking more local and personal channels of information sharing among lesbians.

Without question, having science on one's side is still a good way to gain prestige and legitimacy in the mainstream, and also to save lives. The current move to advocate scientifically sound health care research on lesbians extends beyond the domain of HIV and AIDS to encompass many other issues. It occurs in the context of a prevailing contemporary belief in the power and objectivity of science and medicine. Such a belief was not so apparent among lesbian-feminists in the 1970s. In the current context of lesbian health care, activists, many of whom are themselves medical professionals, have expanded an earlier focus on autonomous health clinics and self-help to promote soundly designed and responsible research through various community organizations and government-funded institutions, including the CDC, the NIH, the National Institute of Mental Health, and the National Cancer Institute. The goal is to investigate particular risks lesbians face in relation to a gamut of health issues.

During the 1990s, demands for greater research on women's health in general increased as more women gained prominent positions in the medical profession. A similar interest in gathering data about lesbian health is now being advanced by lesbian scientists and physicians, some of whom are concerned, for good reason, that most of the proposed research on women neglects to pay attention to the particular conditions and circumstances of lesbians. Indeed, in two of the more recent volumes published by the Committee on the Ethical and Legal Issues of Including Women in Clinical Studies on Women and Health Research, there are no references in the index for "lesbian," "gay," or "homosexual" (Mastroianni et al. 1994). The only reference to sexual orientation in the text states "that variables such as race, ethnicity, rural and urban background, socioeconomic status, and sexual orientation should be examined in clinical studies," but offers no further suggestions about how or why this would be necessary or desirable (Mastroianni et al. 1994:114). There is ample reason to believe that without ongoing agitation, studies of women's health will disregard lesbians and thus fail to take into account many important problems, not the least of which is the homophobia endemic to sectors of the medical profession that undermines lesbians' health.

Because so few government agencies have been willing to study lesbian health care issues, such efforts have been limited and undertaken mostly by lesbian researchers working under the auspices of lesbian and gay organizations. In 1988, the first nationwide study of lesbian health was published based on data gathered during 1984–85 from 1,925 lesbians throughout the fifty states and and several U.S. territories (Bradford and Ryan 1988; Ryan and Bradford 1988). The National Lesbian Health Care Survey was carried out with limited financial support and included an ethnically diverse subject population who identified themselves as exclusively or primarily lesbians according to a seven-point sexual orientation spectrum.[10] Designed and conducted under the sponsorship of the National Lesbian and Gay Health Foundation (NLGHF) by Caitlin Ryan and Judith Bradford, the study was stimulated by a recognition of the need for accurate normative information about the health and health care needs of lesbians (Bradford and Ryan 1988; Bradford, Ryan, and Rothblum 1994).

Although it was originally opposed by some gay male board members of the NLGHF, the study proceeded to find, on the basis of its snowball sample and a ten-page questionnaire, that across a relatively diverse population, lesbians have significantly high rates of depression, suicide ideation (over half of the sample), and stress. There was also a significant level of risk for suffering chronic illnesses due both to economic constraints that prevent lesbians from going to the doctor and from the experiences of facing homophobia and heterosexism when they do. Thus the study found that early detection of breast and ovarian cancer, as well as testing for HIV, are often delayed among lesbians, possibly causing them to die at greater and accelerated rates due to problems that could possibly have been treated had they been detected earlier.

It would appear that the political claim, articulated many years earlier by Lyon and Martin and the women's health collectives that compiled *Our Bodies, Our Selves* and *Our Right to Love*, still holds today: The greatest health risks faced by lesbians stem from the homophobic hostility with which lesbianism is treated by health care providers and the larger society in which they are situated. "Lesbians risk rejection whenever they disclose their sexual orientation to heterosexuals. To live in a two-world existence requires a great deal of psychic energy and is thereby inherently stressful" (Bradford, Ryan, and Rothblum 1994:229). In addition, African-American lesbians and other lesbian members of ethnic minority groups are likely to suffer the impact of both racism and heterosexism (Mays and Cochran 1986). The National Lesbian Health Care Survey revealed that these factors caused lesbians of color to suffer intense psychological and physical stress and to experience more severe health problems than white lesbians on the whole.

Ryan and Bradford's survey data is available for other researchers to use, and they worked with local lesbian communities to help define their particular needs—enacting what Ruth Hubbard and others have called "a democratic science for the people."[11] For example, in communities where women reported high rates of homophobia among doctors and psychotherapists, the research could be used to confront local medical organizations and clinics to address these problems. In addition, the researchers used their data to lobby for lesbian issues to be included in President Bill Clinton's subsequently thwarted 1994 proposal for national health insurance.

Among many important findings, the study reported that although 69 percent of their subjects had graduated from college, nearly as many (64 percent) earned less than $20,000 per year. These stark economic figures, coupled with the fact that health care costs continue to skyrocket, suggest that in addition to avoiding medical care as a way of avoiding homophobia, lesbians may be doing so because, like many other Americans, they simply cannot afford it.

Good Versus Bad Science

In her book *Women's Health: Missing from U.S. Medicine,* Sue Rosser focuses her attack on existing research protocols that overlook women and makes a very provocative argument about the importance of including and discerning lesbians in research on women's health (1994). Specifically, she argues that studying lesbians in their diversity not only may improve the quality of their care, but will also provide a more accurate picture of the risks heterosexually active women face. To fail to identify and fund separate studies of lesbian health issues, Rosser argues, "usually results in lesbians being lumped together with heterosexual women," thus possibly obscuring not only the true incidence of diseases but also their causes. Rosser continues, "When lesbians are lumped together with heterosexual women in studies of the incidence and/or cause of sexually transmitted diseases or other gynecological problems from which they are exempt or for which they are at low risk because they do not engage in heterosexual intercourse, both lesbians and nonlesbians suffer" (1994:107).

Rosser argues that looking at lesbians or women who have sex with women can sharpen the scientific research on women's health considerably. Otherwise, not only are lesbians deprived of important information about their bodies, but heterosexual women are deprived of accurate information about the significance of the risks they are facing (Rosser 1994:109). Thus, in Rosser's view, it behooves researchers concerned with women's health to discern variables related to sexual orientation and practice, as they might yield more accurate scientific information and benefit both lesbians and heterosexually active women. Her argument confronts the homophobia of mainstream proponents of women's health research initiatives on the grounds that their present practice of ignoring lesbianism amounts to bad science.

Rosser's argument implies that procedurally insufficient or sloppy research that overlooks key variables is bad in strictly procedural terms, but also reflective of ethically and morally bad science. Her argument addresses the constitutive or internal procedures of science as a way of also assailing the contextual or external (that is, societal/homophobic) values that manifest in ignoring lesbians in research on women.[12] Her argument is aimed primarily at experts and has implications for clinical practice. But her focus is not particularly on self-help. Rosser's emphasis on doing scientific research in a procedurally correct manner is rhetorically powerful when it comes to addressing scientists. It is one of several strategies, not unlike lesbian AIDS activists' demand that the CDC report more precise data about HIV infection among women who have sex with women. But it represents a significant shift of emphasis from earlier community-based knowledge building, anecdotal information sharing, and questioning of expertise. It places substantial value on scientific expertise.

I am curious about the implications of this focus on producing expert knowledge, and about the kind of faith upon which it rests. Does this focus transform notions of expertise or colonize them, since lesbians themselves are engaged in doing studies of lesbian health? Can it work alongside self-help, community-based information sharing, and grassroots activist critiques of scientific expertise? Or does it become privileged above them?

Taking the Ryan and Bradford study as an example, it appears that lesbians who research health care policies and practices remain closely attuned to communities of lesbians, and are concerned not only with the practices of science narrowly understood but with countering the attitudes that support homophobia in and out of the clinic and scientific laboratory. In my view, the work of Ryan and Bradford is heartening. But biomedical disciplines—even the more socially attuned and progressive field of epidemiology—tend to privilege particular notions of expert knowledge and are often detached from, if not hostile to, community-based health care activism and critiques of the social and political values that structure the production of scientific knowledge. Avoiding the dangers of a hierarchical divide between experts and lay people, of professionals and the community, and scientific truth and subjective knowledge is a challenge for the coming years. But, it should be added, nothing is more challenging than the basic fact that health care is beyond the economic, to say nothing of the epistemological, reach of more and more people living in the United States.

Conclusions

I want to return to an issue I raised at the outset concerning the relationship between lesbian subjectivity and pathology. As demonstrated briefly here, the matter of health is a crucial site of contestation and struggle for lesbians. And the efforts of lesbians to counter the medical demonization of lesbianism are inspiring. Since at least the 1970s, lesbians have introduced radical approaches to revisioning health care provision in a manner that identifies homophobia as the key disease-causing agent threatening lesbians, and, indeed, the larger society. It is conceivable that a lesbian agenda for health exists only insofar as oppression exists, including not only overt and subtle homophobia but, for many lesbians, racism and economic inequality, as these function as vehicles of cruel oppression that obstruct the health of lesbians in clinics, research studies, and the larger world. Perhaps a specifically *lesbian* agenda for health would disappear if equity and respect were extended to all women, regardless of their class, color, or sexual practices. There is no sound evidence that women who engage in sex with other women are biologically or genetically distinct. Their diverse identities and desires are generated through countless variable factors. What they have in common are experiences of homophobia linked to a longer history of their difference being taken for pathology. Confronting this history, in many ways, fuels efforts to establish a lesbian agenda for health. But the "lesbian" modifier deployed to establish an agenda for health may exist only as long as it takes to rid the the medical establishment, and therefore U.S. culture, of homophobia.

I want to close with the wise insights of novelist and AIDS activist Sarah Schulman, who wrote, "The reality of lesbian victimhood is that gay women are severely punished in every aspect of social life, and yet we have not done anything wrong. So it has been hard for us to get a grasp on the overwhelming injustice of our condition and to convey that to others. So we have to translate our actual pain into a vocabulary recognized by the larger society as legitimate pain—in order to get the kind of recognition we need. But the burden of responsibility here is on the lack of broad cultural agreement that homophobia, sexism, and racism are *social pathologies* and are *anti-social*. . . . The trick here is to find a way to take phenomena that have been relegated to individual pathology and bring them to the surface as cultural pathology" (Schulman 1995). In the spirit of Schulman's wisdom, self-help in a revisioning of women's health for the future need not be directed exclusively inward toward healing one's individual psyche or toward maintaining the health of one's own body as if isolated from the context which either enhances or endangers it. Instead, a revisioning of self-help would revive the terms set forth in the Boston Women's Health Collective's book chapter "In Amerika They Call Us Dykes." It would take aim at the *cultural* pathologies that continue to make the possibility of a happy and healthy lesbian self nearly inconceivable.

Notes

I thank Adele Clarke and Virginia Olesen immensely for their editorial suggestions and inspiration, and Caitlin Ryan and Sarah Schulman for conversations that helped me to formulate this chapter.

1. Terry 1990; 1994; 1995; 1997; forthcoming. See also Stevens and Hall 1994.
2. For similar arguments concerning the participation of homosexual men in early medical and scientific discourse, see Kennedy 1997; Oosterhuis 1997; Steakley 1997.
3. The first edition of *Our Bodies, Our Selves*, published in 1970, included a lengthy section on sexuality that discussed childhood sexual development, sexual feelings, virginity, orgasm, fantasies, monogamy, celibacy, and homosexuality (Boston Women's Health Collective 1970). The brief one-page section on homosexuality used women's first-person statements to reassure readers that lesbianism, while often the source of male fantasies, was okay and should not be the source of self-hatred or anxiety. The section suggested that some women felt greater equality in sexual relations with women than with men and were happy to be with a lover who "could sense what the other needed, just because they were both women" (p. 20). Though the assessment of lesbianism was positive, the portion of the book devoted to dealing with the subject was minimal. The inclusion of an entire chapter on lesbianism in the second edition of *Our Bodies, Our Selves* resulted from efforts by lesbians and bisexual women within the Boston Women's Health Collective who felt the need for a more expanded and politically explicit treatment of the issue of lesbianism. The chapter included sections on coming out, finding community, relationships, and sexual practices, as well as legal issues concerning lesbian marriages, medical rights, parenthood, and artificial insemination.
4. For more detailed information on recent agendas proposed for lesbian health, see Haas 1994; Stevens 1992; Stoller 1989.
5. See, for example, Firestone 1970; Klaich 1974; Koedt, Levine, and Lapone 1973; Morgan 1970.
6. See Bethel and Smith 1979; Combahee River Collective 1979; Hull, Stansell, and Thompson 1982; Moraga 1983; Moraga and Anzaldua 1981.
7. See Duggan and Hunter 1995; Samois 1981; Snitow et al. 1983; Vance 1984.
8. For more on the Women's AIDS Network, see Terry 1989.
9. ACT UP, the acronym for AIDS Coalition to Unleash Power, was founded as a grassroots organization in New York City in 1988 and quickly developed chapters in many cities and towns around the United States, as well as affiliated groups in various other countries. The groups' organization was democratic and had no officially designated leaders, operating instead in a formally nonhierarchical structure of consensus building. ACT UP reached an apex of membership and activism in the early 1990s. Its largest chapter was in New York City. In the second half of the 1990s, the membership and prominence of ACT UP has declined, with several local chapters closing or splitting over various ideological and strategic differences. For more on the history of ACT UP, see Epstein 1996.
10. The scale, similar to that devised by Kinsey, ranged from 1 to 7, the former being exclusively homosexual and the latter exclusively heterosexual (Kinsey et al. 1953). Ninety-four and a half percent of the subjects in the National Lesbian Health Care Survey circled 1, 2, or 3 on this scale, with only two participants identifying themselves as exclusively heterosexual and the remainder selecting 4, 5, or 6 on the scale. Eighty-eight percent were white, 6 percent were African-American, and 4 percent were Latina; the authors noted that "a very small number of Asian and Native Americans were included." Subjects ranged in age from seventeen to eighty years, with 80 percent between the ages of twenty-five and forty-four. Most lived in metropolitan areas on the Pacific Coast or the

Northeast, with few inhabiting the cities where they had been born. Nine respondents were in prison, nineteen were living in shelters, and two lived on Indian reservations (Bradford, Ryan, and Rothblum 1994:229).

11. "Science for the people" represents a move to democratize science along several principal lines: (1) to make the products and findings of science available and useful to larger numbers of people, (2) to encourage greater demographic diversity within the profession in order to allow scientific knowledge to reflect the diversity of the society and thus, hopefully, include perspectives and research priorities of other groups, including women and people of color, who historically have been discouraged from going into science; (3) to include the public in decision making about what scientific projects should be undertaken and to consult the public on how scientific research might be applied in a manner responsive to a community's needs; and (4) to inform the public so that they may be able to participate knowledgeably in assessing moral and ethnic conflicts arising from scientific research. The journal *Science for the People* published by and large by progressively oriented scientists, embodies these principles. For more on democratizing science, see Hubbard 1989 and Dickson 1993.

12. Helen Longino's distinction between *constitutive* and *contextual* standards for discerning good versus bad science is useful here (Longino 1990). Constitutive standards, she notes, are those used by scientists to judge the value of hypotheses, experimental techniques, and findings of particular scientific research projects. In what Longino refers to as the *integrity thesis of science*, contextual values or standards are taken to be those factors external to the scientific experiment itself, including moral, ethical, and social values that pertain to what kind of scientific research is funded and and how it is used rather than how it is actually conducted. In her critique of the integrity thesis of science, Longino decries the distinction between constitutive and contextual values on the grounds that it allows scientists to disregard the influence of contextual values in the very ways that they structure and carry out their research. She argues that the distinction is spurious, noting that what is presumed to be confined to the laboratory—those factors presumed to be *constitutive* of science—are never free from the influence of *contextual* values. If we consider homophobia in this framework and apply Rosser's argument, we can see how, as a contextual value, homophobia inflects the kind of research to be undertaken (that is, research on women but not on lesbians); and, in terms of constitutive standards, homophobia shapes the very ways that the research is conducted (that is, research on women that fails to isolate the variable of sexual orientation is blind to the specific conditions of lesbians' health as well as heterosexual women's health).

References

ACT UP/New York Women and AIDS Book Group. 1990. *Women, AIDS, and Activism.* Boston: South End Press.

Boston Women's Health Collective. 1970. *Our Bodies, Our Selves.* Boston: New England Free Press.

Boston Women's Health Collective. 1973. *Our Bodies, Our Selves.* Second edition. New York: Simon and Schuster.

Bradford, Judith B., and Caitlin Ryan. 1988. *The National Lesbian Health Care Survey: Final Report.* Washington, DC: National Lesbian and Gay Health Foundation.

Bradford, Judith B., Caitlin Ryan, and Esther D. Rothblum. 1994. National Lesbian Health Care Survey: Implications for Mental Health Care. *Journal of Consulting and Clinical Psychology* 62(2):228–42.

Comaroff, Jean. 1993. The Diseased Heart of Africa: Medicine, Colonialism and the Black Body. Pp. 305–29 in Shirley Lindenbaum and Margaret Lock (eds.), *Knowledge, Power, and Practice: The Anthropology of Medicine and Everyday Life*. Berkeley: University of California Press.

Combahee River Collective. 1979. A Black Feminist Statement. Pp. 362–72 in Zillah R. Eisenstein (ed.), *Capitalist Patriarchy and the Case for Socialist Feminism*. New York: Monthly Review Press.

Dickson, David. 1993. Towards a Democratic Science. Pp. 472–83 in Sandra Harding (ed.), *The "Racial" Economy of Science*. Bloomington: Indiana University Press.

Duggan, Lisa, and Nan D. Hunter. 1995. *Sex Wars: Sexual Dissent and Political Culture*. New York: Routledge.

Epstein, Steven. 1996. *Impure Science: AIDS, Activism, and the Politics of Knowledge*. Berkeley: University of California Press.

Firestone, Shulamith. 1970. *The Dialectic of Sex: The Case for Feminist Revolution*. New York: Bantam Books.

Gomez, Jewelle L., and Barabara Smith. 1990. Taking the Home Out of Homophobia: Black Lesbian Health. Pp. 198–213 in Evelyn C. White (ed.), *The Black Women's Health Book*. Seattle: Seal Press.

Haas, Ann Pollinger. 1994. Lesbian Health Issues: An Overview. Pp. 339–56 in Alice J. Dan (ed.), *Reframing Women's Health*. Thousand Oaks, CA: Sage Publications.

Hammonds, Evelynn M. 1992. Missing Persons: African American Women, AIDS and the History of Disease. *Radical America* 24(2):7–24.

Hubbard, Ruth. 1989. Science, Facts, and Feminism. Pp. 113–31 in Nancy Tuana (ed.), *Feminism and Science*. Bloomington: Indiana University Press.

Hull, Gloria T., Patricia Bell Scott, and Barbara Smith (eds.). 1982. *All the Women Are White, All the Men Are Black, but Some of Us Are Brave*. Old Westbury, NY: Feminist Press.

Kennedy, Hubert. 1997. Karl Heinrich Ulrichs, First Theorist of Homosexuality. Pp. 26–45 in Vernon Rosario III (ed.), *Science and Homosexualities*. New York: Routledge.

Kinsey, Alfred, Wardell B. Pomeroy, Clyde E. Martin, and Paul H. Gebhard. 1935. *Sexual Behavior in the Human Female*. Philadelphia: W. B. Saunders Co.

Klaich, D. 1974. *Woman Plus Woman: Attitudes Towards Lesbians*. New York: Simon and Schuster.

Koedt, Anne, Ellen Levine, and Anita Rapone (eds.). 1973. *Radical Feminism*. New York: Quadrangle Books.

Longino, Helen. 1990. *Science as Social Knowledge*. Princeton: Princeton University Press.

Lyon, Phyllis, and Del Martin. 1972. *Lesbian/Woman*. New York: Bantam Books.

Mastroianni, Anna C., Ruth Faden, and Daniel Federman (eds.). 1994. *Women and Health Research: Ethical and Legal Issues of Including Women in Clinical Studies*. 2 volumes. Washington, DC: National Academy Press.

Mays, Vickie, and S. D. Cochran. 1986. Relationship Experiences and the Perception of Discrimination by Black Lesbians. Paper presented at the 94th Annual Convention of the American Psychological Association, Washington, DC.

Moraga, Cherrie. 1983. *Loving in the War Years*. Boston: South End Press.

Moraga, Cherrie, and Gloria Anzaldua (eds.). 1981. *This Bridge Called My Back*. Watertown, MA: Persephone Press.

Morgan, Robin (ed.). 1970. *Sisterhood Is Powerful: An Anthology of Writings from the Women's Liberation Movement*. New York: Vintage Books.

Oosterhuis, Harry. 1997. Richard von Krafft-Ebing's "Step-Children of Nature": Psychiatry and the Making of Homosexuality Identity. Pp. 67–88 in Vernon Rosario III (ed.), *Science and Homosexualities*. New York: Routledge.

Rosser, Sue. 1994. *Women's Health: Missing from U.S. Medicine.* Bloomington: Indiana University Press.

Ryan, Caitlin, and Judith Bradford. 1988. The National Lesbian Health Care Survey: An Overview. Pp. 30–40 in M. Shernoff and W. Scott (eds.), *Sourcebook on Lesbian and Gay Health Care.* Washington, DC: National Lesbian and Gay Health Foundation.

Samois (ed.). 1981. *Coming to Power: Writings and Graphics on Lesbian S/M.* San Francisco: Up Press.

Santa Cruz Women's Health Collective. 1980. *Lesbian Health Matters!* Santa Cruz, CA: Santa Cruz Women's Health Center.

Schulman, Sarah. 1995. Personal correspondence with the author.

Snitow, Ann Barr, Christine Stansell, and Sharon Thompson (eds.). 1983. *Powers of Desire: The Politics of Sexuality.* New York: Monthly Review Press.

Bethel, Lorraine, and Barbara Smith (eds.). 1979. *Conditions: The Black Women's Issue.* Brooklyn, New York: Conditions.

Steakley, James D. 1997. Per Scientiam ad Justitiam: Magnus Hirschfeld and the Sexual Politics of Innate Homosexuality. Pp. 133–54 in Vernon Rosario III (ed.), *Science and Homosexualities.* New York: Routledge.

Stevens, Patricia E. 1992. Lesbian Health Care Research: A Review of the Literature from 1970 to 1990. *Health Care for Women International* 13(2):91–120.

Stevens, Patricia E., and Joanne M. Hall. 1994. A Critical Historical Analysis of the Medical Construction of Lesbianism. Pp. 233–51 in Elizabeth Fee and Nancy Krieger (eds.), *Women's Health, Politics, and Power: Essays on Sex/Gender, Medicine and Public Health.* Amityville, NY: Baywood Publishing.

Stoller, Nancy. 1989. New Research Issues in Lesbian Health. *Women's Studies* 17:125–37.

Terry, Jennifer. 1989. The Body Invaded: Medical Surveillance of Women as Reproducers. *Socialist Review* 89(3):13–44.

———. 1990. Lesbians Under the Medical Gaze: Scientists Search for Remarkable Differences. *Journal of Sex Research* 27(3):317–40.

———. 1994. Theorizing Deviant Historiography. Pp. 276–303 in Ann-Louise Shapiro (ed.), *Feminists Revision History.* New Brunswick, NJ: Rutgers University Press.

———. 1995. Anxious Slippages Between "Us" and "Them": A Brief History of the Scientific Search for Homosexual Bodies. Pp. 129–69 in Jennifer Terry and Jacqueline Urla (eds.), *Deviant Bodies: Critical Perspectives on Difference in Science and Popular Culture.* Bloomington: Indiana University Press.

———. 1997. The Seduction of Science and the Making of Deviant Subjectivity. Pp. 271–95 in Vernon Rosario III (ed.), *Science and Homosexualities.* New York: Routledge.

———. Forthcoming. *An American Obsession: Science, Medicine, and the Place of Homosexuality in Modern Society.* Chicago: University of Chicago Press.

Trujillo, Carla. 1993. Chicana Lesbians: Fear and Loathing in the Chicano Community. Pp. 117–26 in Norma Alarcon et al. (eds.), *Chicana Critical Issues.* Berkeley: Third World Women's Press.

Vance, Carole S. (ed.). 1984. *Pleasure and Danger: Exploring Female Sexuality.* Boston: Routledge and Kegan Paul.

Vida, Ginny. 1978. *Our Right to Love: A Lesbian Resource Guide.* Englewood Cliffs, NJ: Prentice Hall.

White, Evelyn C. (ed.). 1990. *The Black Women's Health Book.* Seattle: Seal Press.

Winnow, Jackie. 1992. Lesbians Evolving Health Care: Cancer and AIDS. *Feminist Review* 41:68–76.

Midlife Women's Health

Conflicting Perspectives of Health Care Providers and Midlife Women and Consequences for Health

NANCY FUGATE WOODS

As the baby boomers arrived at midlife, they have had a profound influence on medical and lay literature focusing on this part of the lifespan. Papers about menopause and health have become increasingly prevalent in the medical and lay literature, including feminist perspectives such as Greer's (1992). Among popular books are dozens of guides to the menopausal experience. Studies have been launched about the menopausal experience and the health of midlife women and men, and in 1993 the National Institute on Aging and the National Institute of Nursing Research held a conference on menopause to develop a research agenda. The cohort of women that experienced the medicalization of the menstrual cycle (for example, the dramatic increase in work on PMS) is now facing redefinition of their menopause as a medical phenomenon. The purpose of this paper will be to examine the current medical discourse about midlife women's health, comparing it to findings from recently published and ongoing works about women's health-related experiences during midlife.

Biomedical Discourse about Midlife and Menopause

In her essay "Rethinking Women's Biology," Ruth Hubbard (1990) points out that the concept of women's biology is one that is socially constructed and that has a powerful influence on us women as we grow and develop. Medical discourse has constructed menopause as both disease and risk factor for disease.

References to menopause as producing "estrogen deficiency diseases" and women as having "outlived their ovaries" have become increasingly common in the biomedical literature. In a recent article in a gynecology journal, the authors proclaim that "there has been increasing recognition that ovarian failure and the resultant postmenopausal syndrome represent an endocrinopathy," citing their own work as the source. They argue that menopause meets the criteria of a documented failure of a discrete endocrine organ and a quantifiable deficiency of specific endocrine hormones, resulting in a series of pathological consequences. Because hormone replacement prevents, delays, or ameliorates these pathologies, the authors reason that its use over an extended period of time is essential (for some thirty years), and women's compliance thus becomes paramount. Pointing out that less than 20 percent of women are using HRT and fewer than 50 percent of women use hormones for more than one year, the authors present suggestions for facilitating compliance with HRT in the face of women's fears of cancer, objection to regular withdrawal bleeding, and problems with irregular or unpredictable bleeding, skin irritation, nausea, breast tenderness, weight gain or bloating, mood swings, irritability, or cyclic depression (Stumpf and Trolice 1994). While these recommendations may be helpful to some clinicians and the women they treat, the article illustrates how the reasoning by analogy to other endocrinopathies has been used to reify menopause as disease and to support new diagnostic and treatment practices as part of women's health care.

Medicalization of menopause has been the object of feminist critique for the past two decades (Bell 1990; Kaufert and McKinlay 1985; MacPherson 1981, 1985, 1992; Worcester and Whatley 1992). Such critique has become increasingly important as women have experienced an increase in the rate of endometrial cancer as a result of using estrogen alone, and more recently a group of side effects usually attributable to the progestogen used to offset the effects of "unopposed" estrogen therapy (Bush 1991).

The consequences of the medicalization of menopause now include a cascade of diagnostic and therapeutic strategies resembling the domino effect of interventions in birth that is initiated when Pitocin is used to induce labor. The use of estrogen or combined hormone therapy (referred to as HRT in the remainder of the discussion) increases the need for surveillance for endometrial and breast cancer; stimulates uterine bleeding or spotting, necessitating the use of menstrual hygiene products; requires purchase of a prescription medication for as long as three or more decades; and necessitates access to a health care provider to refill the prescription and perform the requisite health assessments. Occasionally women will require surgical procedures such as dilatation and curettage or hysterectomy owing to complications of the therapy. Because of uncertainty about HRT's contribution to breast cancer incidence, women and their health care providers are vigilant about development of breast disease. The amount of time a woman requires to manage this regimen (and money) has not yet been calculated. All of this activity is designed to forestall the aging process to prevent osteoporosis and heart disease among a fraction of the population (Grady et al. 1992). Moreover, the health consequences of widespread prescription of hormone replacement therapy include the use of estrogen by women for whom contraindications exist (Whitlock et al. 1995).

Medicalization of menopause puts this period of the lifespan squarely into the province of illness and the illness care system and in the hands of providers who are trained to diagnose and treat disease. In the case of menopause, however, healthy women who have not asked for treatment will be encouraged to adopt HRT with the goal of extending their lifespan by an average of a few years and with the hope of preventing or delaying cardiovascular disease (CVD) or osteoporosis (Writing Group for the PEPI Trial 1995; Grady et al. 1992). The ethical implications of such a policy require close examination given the lack of certainty about the safety of long-term use and the nature of long-term outcomes. Data from a clinical trial to substantiate long-term benefit and risk are currently being derived from the Women's Health Initiative Trial, but the incidence of disease endpoints (heart disease and osteoporotic fractures) will not be available for at least a decade (Rossouw et al. 1995). It remains uncertain whether the risk of breast cancer can be evaluated with the results of the trial, especially if it is ended early due to the beneficial effects of hormones on heart disease (see Institute of Medicine 1993 for a detailed critique of this study).

In the extreme, the patient-provider interchanges influenced by the current biomedical model of menopause persuade some women that the typical discomforts of living, such as hot flashes, suffering a backache, or having a bad day, are diseases that require elaborate tests and treatments. Medicalization of menopause encourages women to view themselves not as naturally healthy women in their prime, but as vulnerable to disease and disability. When used to guide health care, this model has the power to persuade women that they are potentially sick (vulnerable) and at the same time invalidates their complaints regarding everyday events. Just as women with PMS can be discounted when they complain about gender inequities at home or in the workplace, menopausal women can be discounted when they criticize the inequities they see for aging men and women in the society. They are, after all, "menopausal."

Coney, author of the book *The Menopause Industry,* says "medicine depoliticizes the situation of the midlife woman by reducing our socially caused anxieties and complaints to 'symptoms' of bodily processes that can be solved by medication" (1993:22). There is more at stake here for women than an individual choice about whether or not to use HRT. Redefinition of a normal life experience as a medical event is not benign and has profound consequences.

Advertisements for menopause products reinforce the view of menopause as disease and menopausal women as vulnerable to disease. These ads portray women as consequences of failed reproduction, women with deteriorating bodies (remember the ad labeling a woman with gray hair a "loser" and linking her changing estrogen levels to bone loss?), loss of sexual desire and response, and dysfunctional. What is more distressing is that these themes are found not only in advertisements. For many years they have been embedded in medical texts, as illustrated by Martin's inquiry *The Woman Within the Body* (Martin 1987).

Whose interests are served by this model? Coney asserts that the "relationship between midlife women and the health care system is distorted by negative stereotypes of aging women which are exploited by vested interests for their own needs" (Coney 1993:12). The use of HRT, as supported by position papers based on recent metanalyses of epidemiological studies (American College of Physicians 1992; Grady et al. 1992) creates a dependence on the medical care system that may be unhealthy for women. As perennial patients, women can become passive consumers of a variety of products. Marketing goals can be met by establishing menopause clinics that focus practitioners' energies on the reproductive system. Consequently, overtreating menopause as a diagnosable disease may occur at the expense of potential underdiagnosis and undertreatment of other health problems. Focusing disproportionate amounts of attention on menopause distorts its importance with respect to other aspects of a woman's health, such as nutrition. Thus the model of menopause as disease has not only descriptive functions but also prescriptive functions with respect to a viewpoint for women and their health care providers and a course of therapy for women during this part of the lifespan. Some of the less apparent functions of the disease model of menopause include development of new technologies to diagnose its pathology, such as the transvaginal ultrasound and the pipelle method of endometrial aspiration used to monitor the development of uterine hyperplasia related to estrogen therapy; development of therapies to treat the syndrome or disease, such as patches impregnated with a variety of hormones; development of new products to market to menopausal women, such as menstrual hygiene products for the bleeding induced by hormone therapies; and creation and reinforcement of images of vulnerability rather than strength and resilience of old women. These powerful functions overtly serve to control the health of women and covertly work to advance the necessity for medical care and products and services that Coney has termed the menopause industry.

At the same time models of menopause organize an industry, they also function covertly to influence women's images of themselves and their bodies. As such, there is a powerful political force at work to undermine midlife women's conceptions of themselves and their position in the society. Menopausal women begin to doubt their well-being, raising questions about their memory problems (often precipitated by the overload of information necessitated by their multiple roles), physical stamina (perhaps due to their sedentary occupations, with limited opportunity to exercise), and sleep problems (often induced by stressful life experiences as well as hot flashes and night sweats).

What evidence is there that the model of menopause as a deficiency disease is widespread among physicians? We recently asked a group of physicians to respond to a questionnaire regarding their prescribing policies about HRT use. Physicians trained in family medicine, internal medicine, and obstetrics and gynecology rated an item about HRT use on which one end of the continuum (rated 1) read: "I do not treat menopause as a disease. Part of me wonders if it is natural to replace estrogen. If a woman is naturally going to stop producing estrogen, I do no harm by allowing this to happen." On the other end of the continuum (rated 7) was the statement "I treat menopause like any other endocrine deficiency. We don't say that it is 'natural' for the body to quit producing insulin and let it occur. We should treat estrogen loss just as we would a need for insulin." The majority (nearly 80 percent) of physicians rated the statement as a 6 or 7 on the 7-point scale, indicating their opinions were consistent with envisioning menopause as a deficiency disease (Saver et al. 1997). Women who are patients in these physicians' practices were somewhat less enthusiastic than their physicians. On a scale of 1 to 7 where 7 was strongly agree, women agreed a little that menopause was a condition (average of responses: 4.6) and that distressing symptoms should be treated with hormones (average: 4.8) (Woods et al. 1997).

Women's Views of Menopause

Given the contemporary views of physicians who care for midlife women and those of their patients, it is tempting to assume that most women's own conceptions of menopause would be similar. As part of a longitudinal study of midlife women, Ellen Mitchell and I have asked over 500 women from multiethnic neighborhoods in Seattle who had not yet experienced menopause for their definitions of menopause and what they expected their menopause to be like (Woods and Mitchell in preparation). Women defined menopause in several ways, including the cessation of periods, the end of childbearing, an age and an aging process, a changing body, changing emotions, and a "change of life." We also examined women's comments for explicit references to menopause as a hormonal event and a medical event. Of importance is that very few women defined menopause as a medical event. Most definitions incorporated reference to cessation of periods, fertility, and changes in body, feelings, and life.

Most commonly, women defined menopause as the cessation of menstrual periods or cycles, the end of ovulation. They described menopause as a time when the menses changed, becoming lighter or less frequent or heavier. Some added that menopause was a time of freedom from their periods, an end to the nuisance they associated with menstruation. As one woman put it, menopause is the "end of periods which can be good and bad, not having to go through the nuisance and mess of it, which will be very pleasant."

Women also defined menopause in relation to their changing fertility and an end to childbearing. Some commented on the loss of fertility: "It's kind of a sad thing, because it means your body is getting old and won't bear children anymore." Other women commented on their freedom from worry about pregnancy, and one woman compared it to having a tubal ligation.

Another common element of women's definitions of menopause was reference to aging. Many women referred to the age they thought menopause occurred, usually spanning the mid-forties to the mid-fifties. Also, women frequently referred to menopause as a natural process of aging. Some saw menopause as a signal of aging, and a few referred to the negative aspects of aging, or "going downhill," as in the following quote: "It's a downhill run, it's a normal process of life. You're not a youth anymore (but I think young, I do young, I enjoy). I feel like it's a normal thing."

Another dimension of women's definitions was reference to a changing body. Some referred to changing appearance: "A woman's body is changing, irregular menstrual cycles, hot flashes, upset, real upset, heart pounding—I had that at first, but not now—no urge for sex, throbbing in your vagina during sex."

Changing emotions were also included in some women's definitions of menopause. Many women associated depression and irritability with menopause: "I'm thinking of irritability, emotional upheaval and hot flashes." Another woman linked menopause to feelings of loss of usefulness and femininity and difficulty coping with stress: "It's losing your usefulness, makes you less of a woman, physical looks change, ability to cope with stress is affected." One woman reflected on Margaret Mead's concept of postmenopausal zest with some skepticism: "Margaret Mead did talk about postmenopausal zest, though I've never heard anyone else say that."

"Change of life" was another frequently mentioned dimension of menopause. Women described the change of life in both positive and negative terms. For some the change of life represented beginning a new phase, getting better, a time to hurry up and do things one wanted to do, and freedom. For others menopause represented loss of femininity and usefulness, and presented the opportunity for a midlife crisis. One woman commented: "It means you'd better hurry up and do what I have to do before I kick over."

One woman's comments exemplified the confusion some felt about the euphemism of menopause as a "change" and what it means: "Going through the change, but what change? People say menopause is going through the change. What do you do, grow a tail? Your ears get longer? What do they mean? They say you have hot flashes. It starts in your forties, but it doesn't just start, lasts one to two months, then it's gone. You go through changes for years. I'm confused."

Hormone changes were mentioned by only a few women. Most of these descriptions characterized menopause as changing hormone levels; "Knowing that your hormones are going to be lacking causes certain concern, I've got to be aware of that and get attention if it should be a problem."

A final element of a few women's definitions of menopause included a reference to seeking health care. Seeking advice or information to resolve uncertainty was illustrated by one woman who said, "It's a natural part of life but I certainly have some apprehensions about what it might entail, but I would go to my doctor about it." Other women spoke of getting a prescription for hormone therapy: "I analyzed that I suddenly had overwhelming feelings of anger at the same time as hot flashes. This is why I'm taking hormones now, otherwise I would never take anything like that." Another reflected on her perception about having to make a decision about HRT: "You have to make an icky decision about taking hormones, which I understand can help you, but also carries a substantial risk."

Expectations of Menopause

Women's expectations of their own menopause spanned the range of positive, neutral, negative, and uncertain. Positive expectations included a sense of freedom, maturity, and wisdom; being freed from worries about birth control, not needing to have periods and spend money on feminine hygiene products. Some women talked about aging gracefully, and having postmenopausal zest. "I think it may be a positive thing. I associate aging with it and I don't think it will be that part I like. I've heard some women have more energy and I'm looking forward to that." Another commented "I just don't think much about those things. . . I don't think it'll be any problem. I'm looking forward to hot flashes, maybe it'll come in the wintertime, I'm always so cold."

Negative expectations included worries about emotional and physical changes such as depression, mood swings, dry skin, vaginal itching, hot flashes, facial hair, changes in sexual function, aching bones, osteoporosis, weight gain, and wrinkles. "I'm already sweating more. . . . I think it's going to get worse. I'm pretty sure I'll have hot flashes. The only lifestyle change I can think of would be if I gained a lot of weight." Some women mentioned that getting old made them feel sad.

Neutral expectations were also voiced. As one woman said, it is "just something your body is going through," and another commented that you "just stopped your periods."

Uncertainty was most common. Many women commented about not knowing what to expect and were uncertain about when menopause would occur. Some women expressed a need for information, but others said they really weren't thinking about it. Only two women mentioned they expected to use hormones, and only one said she would "depend" on her physician.

Only one in six women described her expectations of menopause as only negative. Most characterized their expectations as a mixture of positive, neutral, and negative dimensions, and many were uncertain.

Two Different Worlds:
The Clinical Encounters Between Women
and their Health Care Providers

How is it that midlife women and their health care providers have come to view menopause so differently? I assert that women and their health care providers live in two different worlds and that these are both assumptive and real worlds.

The assumptive world of the health care provider is socially constructed—largely by other health care providers and by others in the health sciences and in the health-care-related industries, such as hospitals, HMOs, pharmaceutical houses, and so on. The very notion of hormone replacement therapy is not in the popular vocabulary, but it takes on significance as it has been constructed by a convergence of a number of forces, including political and economic ones that shape biomedical science and clinical practice (Coney 1993).

The way we think, which we call diagnostic reasoning, and the words we use to describe phenomena, such as "menopausal syndrome," were constructed in a sociopolitical and historical context. The notion of the menopausal syndrome is relatively new in history, but menopause is not (Leidy in preparation). Motivations for creating and using diagnostic categories have their origins in the disease to treat disease and improve human health, yet we cannot ignore that these professional motivations are also linked to the covert goals of earning an income by providing services to people, commanding market share by selling pharmaceuticals, and conducting studies of problems that will be seen as important by one's peers and that in turn will generate revenue for one's department or university (Coney 1993).

The constructs used to describe menopause are learned in many ways, including through knowledge codified and taught in institutions of higher education and in continuing education seminars sponsored by a variety of concerns—universities, pharmaceutical industries, professional organizations—each with their own agenda. Those of us who have been exposed to higher education represent an elite subset of the population. Until recently those in medicine have been mostly men, mostly white, and mostly those with the economic resources to support their long years of study. Nursing and other health professions may differ somewhat in their representations of both genders, but the nursing profession has been similarly privileged.

Health care professionals' real-world experiences with midlife women are shaped by their more frequent contacts with women who are seeking care because they are experiencing poor health than with women who are healthy and who do not seek health care. When one considers the reasons women seek health care during midlife, one finds that the majority of visits are for preventive care and morbidity-related causes. Menopausal and postmenopausal disorders account for about 1.2 percent of these visits, nearly 1.7 million visits per year (U.S. Vital and Health Statistics 1991). Recent emphasis on prevention of disease has heightened health care providers' attention to risk factors and diagnosis of disease in early stages, a pattern no doubt encouraged by changing health care financing systems. Clinical knowledge is shaped by experiences that distort our visions of midlife women as clinical problems that present to be solved and menopause as a signal event for disease risk. It is not an accident that women who use HRT differ significantly from those who do not, particularly with respect to their privileged social status and interest in prevention (Barrett-Conner 1991; Callahan 1993; Mansfield and Voda 1994; Johannes et al. 1994; Scalley and Henrich 1993).

The worlds of women patients are distinctly different from those of health care providers. Women are overrepresented among the poor and tend to occupy low-status occupations even within the health care industries; women's access to higher education, especially for the professions, has been limited until the past two decades (Collins et al. 1993). Most women have far less purchasing power than their physicians or other health care providers. Many experience a limited access to health-related information, and that places them in positions of having little power to negotiate in the relationship with health care providers, giving rise to the possibility of subtle coercion (Todd 1989; Fisher 1986). It is also no accident that books written to demythologize menopause and HRT are accessible only to a few because of their requirements for literacy skills and expense.

Unlike health care providers, midlife women express concerns about their health that are not focused on disease. Indeed, midlife women's concerns about health relate to everyday life. When asked to describe health, women described health as feelings of well-being, ability to adapt flexibly to the demands of everyday life and to perform their roles, and experiencing few or no distressing symptoms (Woods et al. in preparation). When population-based samples of midlife women are asked to rate their health, the majority report that they are in excellent or good health (Woods and Mitchell in preparation; Kaufert, Gilbert, and Tate 1992; Avis et al. 1993).

Women's resistance to the constructions of menopause as a deficiency disease is evident in their responses to attitudinal surveys. The majority deny that menopause is a disease, and most indicate that menopause is the beginning of newfound freedoms from reproduction and parenting (Avis and McKinlay 1991). Moreover, most women are not anxious to resume their menstrual periods, nor do they tolerate the side effects of HRT without worry about cancer and other negative health consequences (Ferguson, Hoegh, and Johnson 1989; Rothert et al. 1990; Ravnikar 1987; Woods et al. 1997; Wren and Brown 1991). Health professionals wonder about women's reluctance to comply with therapy that would extend their lives for a few years during old age.

Women who are troubled by menopausal symptoms, such as hot flashes, frequently express interest in learning about "natural methods" rather than risking the development of side effects or serious disease such as cancer (Woods et al. 1997). Health care providers have come to regard HRT as the "natural" therapeutic agent, providing healthful, preventive consequences with long-term use. Hubbard points out that what people interpret as "natural" depends on their experience and viewpoints, and is not likely to be agreed on by individuals with different backgrounds or interests (Hubbard 1990:117).

Both the demographic differences between health care providers and women patients and their differences in access to information contribute to a situation in which neither party has a complete perspective on the matter of menopause. The partial perspectives of both health care providers and women patients create a situation in which each party participating in the health care dialogue projects a different worldview in the discussion. Unless and until there is some examination of the differences in perspective, the conversation will go on without mutual understanding. Physicians and nurse-practitioners will continue to give women prescriptions that many women will not fill or will use for a limited time and discard. Women will continue to exert their power as consumers to find alternative sources of support during the menopausal transition and search for health outside of the medical care system. The net effect may be that few women are well served by a system that is driven by the definition of menopause as a risk factor for disease, if not as pathology itself, to be treated by applying technologies for curing disease in the name of prevention. Unless health care providers can expand our perspectives to encompass a broader health promotion and disease prevention agenda for midlife women, it is unlikely that we will contribute much to advancing the health of midlife women.

Note

This paper was supported in part by a grant from the National Institute for Nursing Research, NINR, P50-02323

References

American College of Physicians. 1992. Guidelines for Counseling Postmenopausal Women about Preventive Hormone Therapy. *Annals of Internal Medicine* 117(12):1038–41.

Avis, N., P. Kaufert, M. Lock, S. McKinlay, and K. Vass. 1993 The Evolution of Menopausal Symptoms. *Balliere's Clinical Endocrinology and Metabolism* 7(1):17–31.

Avis, N., and S. McKinlay. 1991. A Longitudinal Analysis of Women's Attitudes Toward the Menopause: Results from the Massachusetts Women's Health Study. *Maturitas* 13:65–79.

Barrett-Connor, E. 1991. Postmenopausal Estrogen and Prevention Bias. *Annals of Internal Medicine* 115:455–56.

Bell, S. 1990. Sociological Perspectives on the Medicalization of Menopause. Pp. 173–78 in M. Flint, F. Kronenberg, and W. Utian, *Multidisciplinary Perspectives on Menopause.* New York: The New York Academy of Sciences.

Bush, T. 1991 Feminine Forever Revisited: Menopausal Hormone Therapy in the 1990s. *Journal of Women's Health* 1:1–4.

Callahan, J. 1993. *Menopause: A Midlife Transition.* Indianapolis: Indiana University Press.

Collins, K., D. Rowland, A. Salganicoff, and E. Chait. 1994. Assessing and Improving Women's Health. Pp. 109–53 in C. Costello and A. Stone (eds), *The American Woman: 1994–1995. Where We Stand.* New York, Norton.

Coney, S. 1993. *The Menopause Industry: How the Medical Establishment Exploits Women.* Alameda, CA: Hunter House.

Ferguson, K., C. Hoegh, and S. Johnson. 1989. Estrogen Replacement Therapy: A Survey of Women's Knowledge and Attitudes. *Archives of Internal Medicine* 149:133–36.

Fisher, S. 1986 *In the Patient's Best Interest: Women and the Politics of Medical Decisions.* New Brunswick, NJ: Rutgers University Press.

Grady, D., S. Rubin, D. Petitti, C. Fox, D. Black, B. Ettinger, V. Ernster, and S. Cummings. 1992. Hormone Therapy to Prevent Disease and Prolong Life in Postmenopausal Women. *Annals of Internal Medicine* 117(12):1016–37.

Greer, G. 1992 *The Change: Women, Aging and the Menopause.* New York: Alfred Knopf.

Henderson, M. M., L. H. Kushi, D. J. Thompson, S. L. Gorbach, C. K. Clifford, W. Insull Jr., M. Moskowitz, and R. S. Thompson. 1990. Feasibility of a Randomized Trial of a Low-Fat Diet for the Prevention of Breast Cancer: Dietary Compliance in the Women's Health Trial Vanguard Study. *Preventive* Medicine 19(2):115–33.

Hubbard, R. 1990. *The Politics of Women's Biology.* New Brunswick, NJ: Rutgers University Press.

Institute of Medicine, Committee to Review the NIH Women's Health Initiative. 1993. An Assessment of the NIHG Women's Health Initiative/Committee to Review the NIH Women' Health Initiative, Food and Nutrition Board and Board on Health Sciences Policy, Institute of Medicine: National Academy Press, Washington DC, 1993.

Johannes, C., S. Crawford, J. Posner, and S. McKinlay. 1994 Longitudinal Patterns and Correlates of Hormone Replacement Therapy Use in Middle-aged Women. *American Journal of Epidemiology* 140:439–52.

Kaufert, P., P. Gilbert, and R. Tate. 1992. The Manitoba Project: A Re-examination of the Link Between Menopause and Depression. *Maturitas* 14:143–55.

Kaufert , P. and S. McKinlay. 1985 Estrogen-replacement Therapy: The Production of Medical Knowledge and the Emergence of Policy. Pp. 113–38 in E. Lewin and V. Olesen (eds.), *Women, Health and Healing: Toward a New Perspective.* New York: Tavistock.

Leidy, L. In preparation. Menopause in Evolutionary Perspective. In W. R. Trevathan, J. J. McKenna and E. O. Smith (eds.). *TK.* Oxford University Press.

Lock, M. 1993. *Encounters with Aging: Mythologies of Menopause in Japan and North America.* Berkeley: University of California Press.

MacPherson, K. 1981. Menopause as Disease: The Social Construction of a Metaphor. *Advances in Nursing Science* 3(2):95–114.

———. 1985. Osteoporosis and Menopause: A Feminist Analysis of the Social Construction of a Syndrome. *Advances in Nursing Science* 7(4):11–22.

———. 1992. Cardiovascular Disease in Women and Noncontraceptive Use of Hormones: A Feminist Analysis. *Advances in Nursing Science* 14(4):34–49.

Mansfield, P., and A. Voda. 1994. Hormone Use Among Middle-aged Women: Results of a Three-year Study. *Menopause: The Journal of the North American Menopause Society* 1:99–108.

Martin, E. 1987. *The Woman in the Body: A Cultural Analysis of Reproduction.* Boston: Beacon Press.

Ravnikar, V. 1987. Compliance with Hormone Therapy. *American Journal of Obstetrics and Gynecology* 156:1332–34.

Rossouw, J., L. Finnegan, W. Harlan, V. Pinn, C. Clifford, and J. McGowan. 1995. Evaluation of the Women's Health Initiative: Perspectives from NIH. *Journal of the American Women's Medical Association* 50:50–55.

Rothert, M., D. Rover, M. Holmen, N. Schmitt, G. Talarczyk, J. Knoll, and J. Gogato. 1990 Women's Use of Information Regarding Hormone Replacement Therapy. *Research in Nursing and Health* 13:355–66.

Saver, B. et al. 1997. Physician Policies on the Use of Preventive Hormone Therapy. *Preventive Medicine* 13(5):358–65.

Scalley, E. and J. Henrich. 1993. An Overview of Estrogen Replacement Therapy in Postmenopausal Women. *Journal of Women's Health* 2(3):289–94.

Stumpf, P. and M. Trolice. 1994. Compliance Problems with Hormone Replacement Therapy. *Obstetrics and Gynecology Clinics of North America* 21:219–29.

Todd, A. 1989. *Intimate Adversaries: Cultural Conflict between Doctors and Women Patients.* Philadelphia: University of Pennsylvania Press.

U.S. Vital and Health Statistics. 1991. *National Ambulatory Medical Care Survey.* U.S. Government Printing Office. Washington, DC.

Whitlock, E., B. Valanis, D. Ernst, and L. Smith. 1995. Prevalence of Contraindications to Hormone Replacement Therapy in Middle-aged Women in a Managed Care Setting. *Journal of Women's Health* 4(3):293–302.

Woods, N. et al. 1997. Deciding about Using Hormone Replacement Therapy for Prevention of Diseases of Advanced Age. *Menopause: The Journal of the North American Menopause Society* 4(2):105–14.

Woods, N. and E. Mitchell. 1997. Women's Images of Midlife: Observations from the Seattle Midlife Women's Health Study. *Health Care for Women International* 18(5):439–53.

———. In preparation. Images and Expectations of Menopause: Observations from the Seattle Midlife Women's Health Study.

Worcester, N. and M. Whatley. 1992. The Selling of HRT: Playing on the Fear Factor. *Feminist Review* 41:1–26.

Wren, B. and L. Brown. 1991. Compliance with Hormonal Replacement Therapy. *Maturitas* 1991(13):17–21.

Writing Group for the PEPI Trial. 1995. Effects of Estrogen or Estrogen/Progestin Regimens on Heart Disease Risk Factors in Postmenopausal Women. The Postmenopausal Estrogen/Progestin Interventions (PEPI) Trial. *Journal of the American Medical Association* 273(3):199–208.

Resisting Closure,
Embracing Uncertainties,
Creating Agendas

VIRGINIA L. OLESEN AND ADELE E. CLARKE

Coming at the end of a rich array of widely diverse essays and approaches, this chapter reiterates the mission of the book to avoid a "fatal unclutteredness" in theorizing, conceptualizing, and acting for and on women, health, and healing (Mukherjee 1994:6). Reaching for "fatal unclutteredness" here would hold out the tempting possibility of creating an interpretation for understanding and action that would unite or at least link these diverse essays into a new grand agenda for women, health, and healing. Such an approach would be fatally flawed. Aside from glossing the multiple complexities of substance, concepts, theories, and women's individual and communal lives which have been explored in these pages, *and* ossifying an unfortunate and inappropriate "othering," such an exercise in closure would stunt or even foreclose the potential for these essays to open out into each other and into new territories.

The work of unsettling, transgressing, transversing, and problematizing banal and profound topics within the area of women, health, and healing (and, indeed, those very terms themselves) slips across some disciplinary boundaries to harvest productive if not provocative ideas in new realms. Feminist thought, science studies concepts, and cultural studies thought provide, as has been seen in this volume, passports to transcend those boundaries and potent solvents to dissolve obdurate taken-for-grantednesses, including those emergent from and framed in biomedicine. In so doing, the thinker, the topic, and the territory shift and alter to produce diffractions that produce new, partial, temporary, and conditional knowledges.

We emphasize *temporary* new knowledges. The stories of feminist concerns for women's health, as our introduction made clear, are ones of shifting bases.

Ideas that were firmly held in the first moment of the women's health movement have given way to much more differentiated conceptualizations. This does not mean that those ideas were wrong or unimportant in their time, but rather that knowledge production is continually dynamic—new frames open, then give way to others, which in turn open again and again. Moreover, knowledges *at best* are only partial. Some may find these views discomfiting and see in them a slippery slope of ceaseless constructions with no sure footing for action of whatever sort. They *are* discomfiting; it *is* much easier and more reassuring to think of firm, settled knowledges that have long shelf lives. However, as we have already emphasized, the ceaseless play of competing knowledges that come to feminist and /or public attention assures that while some knowledges of women's health will have long shelf lives, others will not. There is no closure, only transitory platforms from which to address, explore, and intervene at whatever level. What is important for concerned feminists is that new topics, issues of concern and matters for feminist inquiry are continually produced and demand attention, yielding more nuanced understandings of and action on critical issues.

Not a few of those new topics will be lodged in the seeming obduracy of biomedicine as a key locus for women, health, and healing, a concern that we expressed in our introduction. Yet biomedicine itself is a cultural feature of complex society, hence open to incisive feminist theorizing about production and use of knowledges, as several authors in this volume have done. As an analysis of discourses around breast cancer and its causes shows (Yadlon 1997), biomedical knowledges about avoiding or managing this disease are primarily rooted in profound cultural themes of individual responsibility (following a correct diet) and idealized female behavior (the imperative of motherhood). Far less prominent in the discourses of prevention and management are knowledges that evoke or pursue environmental causes of breast cancer.

Moreover, no knowledges are innocent, irrespective of the producers and their context, locus, or standpoint. Producers and those with whom they create knowledge are always located somewhere, and that somewhere is always imbedded in cultural specifics that shape how knowledges are produced and disseminated. This may also make some uneasy, for it forces recognition of one's own limitations, privileges, possibilities, presence, and participation in knowledge production. Recognizing how this perspective unsettles authority and expertise has consequences for us not only as feminists, but as embodied beings in an increasingly biomedicalized world.

This also constitutes a critical challenge at the heart of this volume: the exploration of how and where knowledges about women, health and healing are produced and utilized or not utilized. That exploration also assumes theorizing those other economic and social vectors that have serious impacts on women's health, namely, the racial, gender, and class stratification formations. These also configure ways in which knowledges are produced and used.

What, then, becomes "the agenda"? It is clear from our introduction, the contributors' chapters, and this final chapter that there are many agendas. In our introduction we acknowledged the importance of "laundry lists" of women's health issues. Here instead our move is to embrace agendas of problematizing, reconceptualizing, retheorizing, and revisioning any and all topics within women, health, and healing, especially those that derive from and are found in distinctively cultural arenas that limit women's potentials and produce inequities and injustices. Here the agendas reach from issues of conceptualization, representation, and presentation to incisive projects that cut to the bone of biomedicine. Following leads in this direction will approximate, if not partially and temporarily reach, what Donna Haraway in an apt, sensible and comforting comment has called "a no nonsense commitment to faithful accounts of a 'real' world, one that can be partially shared and that is friendly to earthwide projects of finite freedom, modest meaning in suffering and limited happiness" (Haraway l988:79).

References

Haraway, D. l988. Situated Knowledges: The Science Question in Feminism and the Privilege of Partial Perspective. *Feminist Studies* l4:75–99.

Mukherjee, Bharati. l994. *The Holder of the World*. London: Virago.

Yadlon, Susan. l997. Skinny Women and Good Mothers: The Rhetoric of Risk, Control, and Culpability in the Production of Knowledge About Breast Cancer. *Feminist Studies* 23:645–77.

About the Contributors

Anne Balsamo teaches in the School of Literature, Communication and Culture at Georgia Institute of Technology, where she is also the director of the graduate program in information design and technology. Courses she teaches include "Science, Technology and Gender" and "Science and Technology and Post-modern Culture." Her first book, *Technologies of the Gendered Body: Reading Cyborg Women* (Duke University Press, 1996), examined the cultural impacts of several new biotechnologies that work to construct gendered bodies, including bodybuilding, cosmetic surgery, and imaging technologies. Her next book will also address contemporary cultural formations of technology.

Ruth Behar is professor of anthropology at the University of Michigan in Ann Arbor. She has traveled to Spain, Mexico, and Cuba and written on a range of cultural and feminist issues as a poet, essayist, editor, and ethnographer. Her books include *The Presence of the Past in a Spanish Village: Santa Maria del Monte* (Princeton University Press, 1986; expanded paperback edition, 1991), *Translated Woman: Crossing the Border with Esperanza's Story* (Beacon Press, 1993), and *The Vulnerable Observer: Anthropology That Breaks Your Heart* (Beacon Press, 1997). Behar is also the editor of *Bridges to Cuba/Puentes a Cuba* (University of Michigan Press, 1995) and coeditor of *Women Writing Culture* (University of California Press, 1995). She is currently writing a memoir about her Jewish-Cuban family and her reencounter with the Afro-Cuban woman, still living on the island, who was her caretaker as a child.

Adele E. Clarke is associate professor of sociology and of history of health sciences at the University of California, San Francisco. Her work centers on social studies of science, technology, and medicine, including common medical technologies such as contraception, the Pap smear, and RU486. Dr. Clarke's major work on the formation of the reproductive sciences in biology, medicine, and agriculture, circa 1910–1963, is *Disciplining Reproduction: Modernity, American*

Life Sciences and the "Problem of Sex" (University of California Press, 1998). With Sheryl Ruzek and Virginia Olesen, she edited *Women's Health: Complexities and Diversities* (Ohio State University Press, 1997). With Lisa Jean Moore, she is studying representations of genitalia in human anatomies from medieval texts to cyberspace. Her current project is a book on qualitative research methods, *Grounded Theorizing After the Postmodern Turn: Mapping and Analyzing Historical Data, Visual Images, and Social Worlds.*

Patricia Hill Collins is a professor in the Departments of African-American Studies and Sociology at the University of Cincinnati. She received her B.A. and Ph.D. degrees from Brandeis University, and an M.A.T. degree from Harvard University. While her specialties in sociology include such diverse areas as sociology of knowledge, organizational theory, social stratification, and work and occupations, her research and scholarship have dealt primarily with issues of gender, race, and social class, specifically relating to African-American women. She has published many articles in professional journals and edited volumes. Her first book, *Black Feminist Thought: Knowledge, Consciousness, and the Politics of Empowerment,* (Unwin Hyman, 1990), has won many awards. Her second book, *Race, Class, and Gender: An Anthology* (edited with Margaret Andersen), originally published in 1992 with a second edition (Wadsworth: Belmont, CA, 1995), is widely used in undergraduate classrooms throughout the United States. She is currently completing her third book, tentatively entitled *Fighting Words: Knowledge, Power, and the Challenge of Black Feminist Thought,* which will be published by the University of Minnesota Press.

Adela de la Torre, an agricultural economist, is the director of the Mexican American Studies and Research Center at the University of Arizona. She was earlier an executive fellow in the Office of the Chancellor of the California State University system. From 1991 to 1995, she was the chairperson of the Chicano and Latino Studies Department as well as a professor of health care administration at California State University, Long Beach. Dr. de la Torre is a nationally syndicated columnist in the *Los Angeles Times,* addressing economic, political, educational, health care, and immigration issues. She is a coeditor of the book *Building With Our Hands: New Directions in Chicana Scholarship* (University of California Press, 1993). De la Torre has published extensively in health and public policy journals and has a paper in *Chicanos: The Contemporary Era* (University of Arizona Press, 1997).

Marjorie L. DeVault is associate professor of sociology and a member of the women's studies program at Syracuse University. She is the author of *Feeding the Family: The Social Organization of Caring as Gendered Work* (University of Chicago Press, 1991), and has also written extensively on feminist and qualitative research methods. A major essay, "Talking Back to Sociology: Distinctive Contributions of Feminist Methodology" appeared in *Annual Review of Sociology* in 1996. Her current projects focus on gender, race, and class dynamics in professional work and constructionist approaches to family studies.

Donna Haraway is a professor in the History of Consciousness Department at the University of California at Santa Cruz, where she teaches feminist theory, science studies, and women's studies. Her work argues that women's health movements are crucial to the history and practice of these fields and to their worldly relevance. Haraway is the author of *Crystals, Fabrics and Fields: Metaphors of Organicism in Twentieth-Century Developmental Biology* (Yale University Press, 1976), *Primate Visions: Gender, Race, and Nature in the World of Modern Science* (Routledge, 1989; Verso, 1992), *Simians, Cyborgs, and Women: The Reinvention of Nature* (Routledge, 1991; Free Association Books, 1991), and *Modest-Witness@Second_Millennium.FemaleMan_Meets_OncoMouse™* (New York and London: Routledge, 1997).

Valerie Hartouni is associate professor of communications and director of the Women's Studies Program at the University of California, San Diego. Her work focuses on discursive representations of women, especially as related to reproduction. Her book *Cultural Conceptions: On Reproductive Technologies and the Remaking of Life* (University of Minnesota Press, 1997) advances this project. Hartouni served as convener of a residential research group at the University of California's Humanities Research Institute, titled "Feminist Epistemologies and Methodologies," and she will edit a book by participants aimed especially at graduate-level women's studies courses.

Patti Lather is a professor in the School of Educational Policy and Leadership at Ohio State University, where she teaches qualitative research in education and feminist pedagogy. Her work includes *Getting Smart: Feminist Research and Pedagogy with/in the Postmodern* (Routledge, 1991) and, with Chris Smithies, *Troubling the Angels: Women Living with HIV/AIDS* (Westview/HarperCollins, 1997). Her favorite academic achievements thus far are a 1989 Fulbright lectureship in New Zealand; a 1995 sabbatical appointment as a Fellow at the Humanities Research Institute, University of Calfornia-Irvine, part of a "think tank" on feminist research methodology; and a 1997 visiting appointment at Göteborg University in Sweden. She is part of a Women, Health and Diversity interdisciplinary program at Ohio State University for 1998.

Emily Martin is a professor of anthropology at Princeton University. Her B.A. is from the University of Michigan (1966) and her Ph.D. in anthropology is from Cornell University (1971). Beginning with *The Woman in the Body: A Cultural Analysis of Reproduction* (Beacon Press, 1987), she started to work on the anthropology of science and reproduction in the United States, in particular on how gender stereotypes have shaped medical language and how they circulate among and are contested by women in different age groups and communities. The next phase of her research focused on the interplay between scientific and popular conceptions of the immune system. In *Flexible Bodies: Tracking Immunity in America from the Days of Polio to the Age of AIDS* (Beacon Press, 1994), she analyzes the manner in which the concept of "flexibility" in immune discourse has been involved in a transformation of contemporary notions of health and business practices. Her present work is on theories of normalization and the evolving constitution of selfhood in contemporary society.

Virginia L. Olesen is professor emerita of sociology, Department of Social and Behavioral Sciences, School of Nursing, University of California, San Francisco. She began the emphasis on women's health there in 1973 and organized the first national research conference in 1975, "Women and Their Health: Research Implications for a New Era" (DHEW-HRA 77-3138). With Ellen Lewin, she coedited *Women, Health and Healing: Toward a New Perspective* (Tavistock, 1985), and with Nancy Fugate Woods, *Culture, Society, and Menstruation* (Hemisphere, 1986). With Sheryl Ruzek and Adele Clarke, she is an editor of *Women's Health: Complexities and Differences* (Ohio State University Press, 1997). She is currently working on issues in feminist theory and qualitative research and questions of skepticism in ethnographic studies.

Rayna Rapp teaches in the Department of Anthropology, New School for Social Research, where she chairs the master's program in gender studies and feminist theory. She is the editor of *Toward an Anthropology of Women* (Monthly Review Press, 1975) and coeditor of *Promissory Notes: Women in the Transition to Socialism* (Monthly Review Press, 1989), *Articulating Hidden Histories: Exploring the Influence of Eric R. Wolf* (University of California Press, 1995), and *Conceiving the New World Order: The Global Politics of Reproduction* (University of California Press, 1996). Her new book, *Moral Pioneers: Fetuses, Families, and Amniocentesis* (Routledge, 1998), analyzes the social impacts and cultural meanings of prenatal diagnosis in the United States. She has worked with *Feminist Studies* for many years.

Beth E. Richie has been an activist and advocate in the movement to end violence against women for the past twenty years. The emphasis of her work has been on the ways that race/ethnicity and social position affect women's experiences of violence, focusing on African-American battered women and sexual assault survivors. She has been a trainer and technical assistant to local and national organizations, and is a frequent lecturer for grassroots as well as academic groups. Dr. Richie is on the faculty at the University of Illinois at Chicago in the Departments of Criminal Justice and Women's Studies and is a senior research consultant with the Institute on Violence, Inc. She is the author of numerous articles, curricula, and books, including *Compelled to Crime: The*

Gender Entrapment of Battered Black Women (Routledge, 1996). Her current work explores the gender dimensions of youth violence and focuses on young women and girls of color in correctional facilities.

Sheryl Burt Ruzek, M.P.H. is professor of health studies and women's studies at Temple University. She coedited *Women's Health: Complexities and Differences* (Ohio State University Press, 1997) with Virginia Olesen and Adele Clarke and is the author of numerous books and articles on women's health issues, particularly in the areas of maternity care and consumer perspectives on medical technologies. Her current research on consumer health movements will be included in a second revised edition of her 1978 book *The Women's Health Movement: Feminist Alternatives to Medical Control.* She has been a consultant to the Food and Drug Administration and other national, state, and regional public health agencies, and chairs the ECRI–World Health Organization Collaborating Center for Technology Transfer Committee on Women's Medical Technologies. A charter member of the National Women's Health Network, she also serves on the Policy and Advocacy Committee of the Maternity Care Coalition of Philadelphia.

Denise A. Segura is associate processor of sociology and director of the Center for Chicano Studies at the University of California, Santa Barbara. She has written numerous articles on Chicana and Mexican immigrant women workers, family life, and Chicana political consciousness, including "Chicana/o Family Structure and Gender Personality" (*Signs,* 1993) with J. Pierce. Currently she is doing research on adaptation strategies and community construction among Mexican immigrants. She is also working on a coauthored book on Chicana feminism.

Jennifer Terry is assistant professor of comparative studies at Ohio State University. She coedited, with Jacqueline Urla, *Deviant Bodies: Critical Perspectives on Difference in Science and Popular Culture* (Indiana University Press, 1995) and, with Melodie Calvert, *Processed Lives: Gender and Technology in Everyday Life* (Routledge 1997), and has authored articles on reproductive politics, the history of sexual science in the United States, and contemporary scientific approaches to the sex lives of animals. Terry's forthcoming book is entitled *An American Obsession: Science, Medicine, and the Place of Homosexuality in Modern Society* (University of Chicago Press).

Sharon Traweek is an associate professor in the History Department and director of the Center for Cultural Studies of Science, Technology, and Medicine at the University of California, Los Angeles. She received her Ph.D. in the history of consciousness in 1982 from the University of California, Santa Cruz. Her first book was *Beamtimes and Lifetimes: The World of High Energy Physicists* (Harvard University Press, 1988, paperback, 1992). She is completing work on a second book on Japanese big science and a third book on crafting cultural studies of science, technology, and medicine. Dr. Traweek also coedited a special issue of *Configurations*, "Located Knowledges at the Intersection of Cultural, Gender, and Social Studies of Science and Technology."

Françoise Vergès is a Lecturer at Sussex University. She has written on colonial and postcolonial psychiatry, the medical discourse about "pathologies" of minorities and the philosophical foundations of emancipatory politics. Her research now focuses on the history of French colonial psychiatry and its constructions of masculinities and femininities. Her book, *Monsters and Revolutionaries: Colonial Family Romance and Metissage* is forthcoming from Duke University Press.

Nancy Fugate Woods's work has focused on women's perimenstrual symptom experiences. With her collaborators at Duke University and the University of Washington, she conducted the first study about the prevalence of perimenstrual symptoms in U.S. women. In collaboration with colleagues at the University of Washington in 1989, Dr. Woods established the Center for Women's Health Research, focusing on women's health across the lifespan. Her books include *Women's Health Care: A Comprehensive Handbook,* edited with Catherine Fogel (Sage, 1995), *Menstruation, Health and Illness* (Hemisphere, 1991), edited with Diana Taylor, *Nursing Research: Theory and Practice* (Mosby, 1988), edited with Marci Catanzaro, and *Culture, Society and Menstruation* (Hemisphere, 1986), edited with Virginia Olesen.

Index

---○---

Abortifacient, RU486 as, 62
abortion
　availibility to poor women, 71, 74, 274
　Christian view of, 85(n10)
　clinics for, 30, 263(n3;n6)
　debate over, 249(n7)
　legalization of, 14, 70
　by menstrual extraction, 67
　use for sex preselection, 18
acculturation
　of Latina and Chicana/Mexicana women, 155
　as predictor of health behaviors, 159
ACT UP (AIDS Coalition to Unleash Power), 332, 333, 339(n9)
Adam
　in *Creation of Adam*, 57–58
　female cartoon figure as, 51, 60, 74
A.D.A.M. Software, 31, 254, 262, 263
adoption, population policies affecting, 275
African Americans
　asthma in, 103
　autoimmune disease in, 113(n3)
　critiques of white feminisms by, 10
　health of, 17
　infant mortality in, 240
　population policies directed at, 271
　poverty of, 73
　racist pseudofacts of, 90(n39)
African-American children, poverty among, 279
African-American girls, mothering of, 295
African-American men, violence among, 286–288
African-American women
　activist careers of, 170
　community-based initiatives of, 291, 296–297
　control of childbearing of, 24
　feminist thought of, 88(n32), 289, 297–298
　health-risk information given to, 242

HIV/AIDS in, 153(n6)
loss of children to public agencies, 291, 293–294
low-birth-weight infants of, 241
loyalty to black men of, 295
maternal mortality in, 73
medical racism toward, 69
middle class of, 277, 280(n4)
as mothers, 31, 32, 275, 276–277, 279, 280(n4), 289–290 "immoral" concept of, 289–299
prenatal testing on, 125, 127
as professional nutritionists, 172, 179
reproductive freedom and health of, 71, 83
sterilization of, 72–73
as surrogate mothers, 63, 238
working-class, population policies for, 275–277
youth violence effects on, 290–298
African-Caribbean women, prenatal testing on, 127, 130
African-Cuban woman, as child nurse, 209
aging, menopause and, 347–348, 349
agoraphobia, in women, 212
AIDS. *See* HIV/AIDS
Aid to Families with Dependent Children (AFDC), 276
alcohol
　father's use of, 225
　effects on fetus, 240
　use by Chicana/Mexicana women, 158, 160
　warnings about use in pregnancy, 241, 242
alternative medicine, 20–21, 35(n44), 317
　for menopause, 33
American Medical Women's Association (AMWA), 14
amniocentesis, 85(n6), 119, 123, 130, 193
　genetic counseling for, 27
　pregnancy loss following, 194

---365---

single mothers
  African-American women as, 285
  demonization of, 226
Sister, the Newspaper of the Los Angeles Women's Center, Wonder Woman cartoon in, 67, 68, 74, 88(n30)
situated activism, 24
smoking, warnings given to pregnant women, 241, 242
social imaginaries, of mind and body, 97
socialist feminists, 6
social mothers, 279
Social Security, 306
social suffering, concept of, 36(n47)
social work, as women's profession, 169
South Africa, population policies in, 280(n3)
speculum
  personal use of, 193
  as symbol of female medicine and feminist politics, 16, 66–67, 70, 85(n11)
sperm, pathogens borne by, 110
standpoint theory, 17, 35(n34), 88(n32)
sterilization
  California regulations on, 88(n33)
  of poor and minority women, 71, 73–74, 276–277
straight/gay binary, 8
straight/gay/bisexual/transgender, 8
stress, psychosomatic manifestation of, 190, 197
structural inequality theory, of youth violence, 288
subject/object binary, 8
surrogate mothers, 63, 232–233, 238, 273
surveillance medicine, 14, 21–23
  definition of, 22
  in obstetrics, 235, 237–246
  of women, 241–245
Sweden, health care expenditure in, 320(n2)

"technofetus" concept, 62
technoscience, 56
  comics in, 50
  feminist studies of, 61–65, 71, 87(n24)
  women's health studies by, 6, 7, 9, 10
technoscientific liberty, 51, 84(n3)
teratogens, 240, 256
Terry, Jennifer, 32, 363
test-tube conception, 236, 273
thalidomide, birth defects from, 240
tobacco use, by Chicana/Mexicana women, 158
toxins
  in women's bodies, 46(n46)
  in workplace, poor women's exposure to, 71, 74, 89(n35)
Traweek, Sharon, 29, 363
Troubling the Angels: Women Living With HIV/AIDS (Lather & Smithies), 136, 140–144, 145, 146, 149, 152

UBS Women's Health Index, on stock market, 21
ultrasonography
  cohort biography of, 193–194
  for female egg visualizastion, 250(n10)
  of fetus, 51, 80, 85(n6;n7), 249(n2)
UN Decade for Women, 15, 121
"unfit" mothers, population policies affecting, 276–277
United States
  family planning in, 266–282
  obstetrics and gynecology in, 29
  women's health movements in, 3–4

vegetarians, women as, menstrual irregularity in, 105
Velázquez, Diego, *The Toilet of Venus* of, 58, 60, 86
Vergès, Françoise, 29, 32, 364
Vesalius, Andreas, 57
"victim art", 153(n7)
Vietnam War, 67
violence
  among men of color, 286
  on Reunion Island, 226
  against women, 4
  against women of color, 286
  of youth. *See* youth violence
Virtual Speculum [cartoon], 51, 52, 57, 60–61, 65–66
virtual speculum theory, 25, 32, 49–96

Washington, D.C., women's health networks in, 14
"wave" metaphor, for immune system, 106, 107
welfare mothers, 24, 90(n40), 238
  racialized caricatures of, 30
welfare reform, analysis of, 11
welfare state
  state policices in, 280(n2)
  women and, 35(n29)
The West, biomedicine in, 20
wet nurses, poor women as, 36(n48)
white women
  middle-class, population policies for, 272–274
  working-class, population policies for, 274–275
Wilson, Pete, 63
women
  autoimmune disease in, 100, 101, 102, 113(n3)
  demonization of, 29, 226
  health care providers for, 349, 352
  medical surveillance of, 241–245
  as nutrition professionals, 166–183
  professions of, 28, 167, 318
Women, Infants, and Children Program (WIC), 91, 177–178, 182(n6)
women of color
  demonization of, 29, 226

1838
786-6262
x5643
Brad Beerson
3.90